Data Mining and Machine Learning Applications

Scrivener Publishing
100 Cummings Center, Suite 541J
Beverly, MA 01915-6106

Publishers at Scrivener
Martin Scrivener (martin@scrivenerpublishing.com)
Phillip Carmical (pcarmical@scrivenerpublishing.com)

Data Mining and Machine Learning Applications

Edited by

Rohit Raja
Kapil Kumar Nagwanshi
Sandeep Kumar

and

K. Ramya Laxmi

Scrivener
Publishing

WILEY

This edition first published 2022 by John Wiley & Sons, Inc., 111 River Street, Hoboken, NJ 07030, USA and Scrivener Publishing LLC, 100 Cummings Center, Suite 541J, Beverly, MA 01915, USA
© 2022 Scrivener Publishing LLC
For more information about Scrivener publications please visit www.scrivenerpublishing.com.

Wiley Global Headquarters
111 River Street, Hoboken, NJ 07030, USA

For details of our global editorial offices, customer services, and more information about Wiley products visit us at www.wiley.com.

Library of Congress Cataloging-in-Publication Data

ISBN 978-1-119-79178-2

Cover image: Pixabay.Com
Cover design by Russell Richardson

Contents

Preface

Data, the latest currency of today's world, is the new gold. In this new form of gold, the most beautiful jewels are data analytics and machine learning. Data mining and machine learning are considered interdisciplinary fields. Data mining is a subset of data analytics and machine learning involves the use of algorithms that automatically improve through experience based on data. However, the term data mining is a misnomer because it means to mine but not extract knowledge. A more apt term would be "knowledge discovery from data," since it is the practice of examining large pre-existing databases to generate information. Data mining algorithms are currently being investigated and applied worldwide.

Massive datasets can be classified and clustered to obtain accurate results. The most common technologies used include classification and clustering methods. Accuracy and error rates are calculated for regression and classification, and clustering to find actual results through algorithms like support vector machines and neural networks with forward and backward propagation. Applications include fraud detection, image processing, medical diagnosis, weather prediction, e-commerce and so forth. Data mining algorithms are even used to analyze data by using sentiment analysis. These applications have been increasing in different areas and fields. Web mining and text mining also paved their way to construct the concrete q2 field in data mining.

This book is intended for industrial and academic researchers, and scientists and engineers in the information technology, data science and machine and deep learning domains. Featured in the book are:

- A review of the state-of-the-art in data mining and machine learning,
- A review and description of the learning methods in human-computer interaction,

- Implementation strategies and future research directions used to meet the design and application requirements of several modern and real-time applications for a long time,
- The scope and implementation of a majority of data mining and machine learning strategies, and
- A discussion of real-time problems.

This book is a better choice than most other books available on the market because they were published a long time ago, and hence seldom elaborate on the current needs of data mining and machine learning. It is our hope that this book will promote mutual understanding among researchers in different disciplines, and facilitate future research development and collaborations.

We want to express our appreciation to all of the contributing authors who helped us tremendously with their contributions, time, critical thoughts, and suggestions to put together this peer-reviewed edited volume. The editors are also thankful to Scrivener Publishing and its team members for the opportunity to publish this volume. Lastly, we thank our family members for their love, support, encouragement, and patience during the entire period of this work.

Rohit Raja
Kapil Kumar Nagwanshi
Sandeep Kumar
K. Ramya Laxmi
November 2021

Introduction to Data Mining

Santosh R. Durugkar[1], Rohit Raja[2], Kapil Kumar Nagwanshi[3]*
and Sandeep Kumar[4]

[1]Amity University Rajasthan, Jaipur, India
[2]IT Department, GGV Bilaspur Central University, Bilaspur, India
[3]ASET, Amity University Rajasthan, Jaipur, India
[4]Computer Science and Engineering Department, Koneru Lakshmaiah Education
Foundation, Vaddeswaram, Andra Pradesh, India

Abstract

Data mining, as its name suggests "mining", is nothing but extracting the desired, meaningful exact information from the datasets. Its methods and algorithms help researchers and students develop the numerous applications to be used by the end-users. Its presence in the healthcare industry, marketing, scientific applications, etc., enables the end-users to extract the meaningful required information from the collection. In the initial section, we discuss KDD—knowledge discovery in the database with its different phases like data cleaning, data integration, data selection and transformation, representation. In this chapter, we give a brief introduction to data mining. Comparative discussion about classification and clustering helps the end-user to distinguish these techniques. We also discuss its applications, algorithms, etc. An introduction to a basic clustering algorithm, K-means clustering, hierarchical clustering, fuzzy clustering, and density-based clustering, will help the end-user to select a specific algorithm as per the application. In the last section of this chapter, we introduce various data mining tools like Python, Rapid Miner, and KNIME, etc., to the user to extract the required information.

Keywords: Data mining, KDD, clustering, classification, Python, KNIME

1.1   Introduction

1.1.1   Data Mining

'Mining'—extracts the meaningful information from the databases. This method helps the researchers, students, and other IT professionals *remove*

---

*Corresponding author: dr.kapil@ieee.org

Rohit Raja, Kapil Kumar Nagwanshi, Sandeep Kumar and K. Ramya Laxmi (eds.) Data Mining
and Machine Learning Applications, (1–20) © 2022 Scrivener Publishing LLC

the exact significant details and develop the desired applications [1, 2]. It is also known as Knowledge Discovery from databases—KDD. The applications of KDD may include medical/hospitals, Marketing, Educational systems, Scientific applications, E-commerce, Retail industries, Biological analysis, Counterterrorism, use in data-warehouse, in the energy sector for decision making, Spatial data mining, and Logistics [4–6].

1.2   Knowledge Discovery in Database (KDD)

It helps detect the new patterns of previously unknown data, i.e., extracting the hidden patterns, data from the massive volume of datasets [3, 6]. Figure 1.1 gives an idea about Knowledge discovery in Database—KDD, which consists of the following phases:

- *Data cleaning:* This step can be defined as removing irrelevant data. Removing irrelevant data is nothing but unwanted data; records can be removed. Data collection may consist of missing values which must be either needs to be removed or should impute the missing information [7].

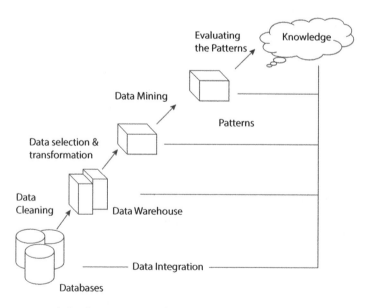

Figure 1.1 Knowledge discovery in Database—KDD.

- *Data integration:* Data is collected from heterogeneous sources and integrated into a common source like data-warehouse (DW). A very common technique, Extract-Transform-Load (ETL), is beneficial in this regard. Integrating the data from multiple sources requires proper synchronization between the systems [2].
- *Data selection & transformation:* Once the required data is selected, the next task is data transformation. As its name suggests transformation, it is nothing but transforming it into the desired mining procedure [8, 9].
- *Pattern evaluation:* Evaluation is based on some measures; once these measures are applied, retrieved results are strictly compared/evaluated based on the stored patterns [9–11].
- *Knowledge representation:* It is nothing but representing the processed data into the required formats such as tables and reports. One can say knowledge representation generates the rules, and using the exact visualization is possible [10].

1.2.1   Importance of Data Mining

- o Useful in predictive analysis.
- o They are storing and managing data in multidimensional systems.
- o They are identifying the hidden patterns.
- o Knowledge representation in desired formats, etc. [11].

1.2.2   Applications of Data Mining

- *Fraud Detection*
  - o Data mining identifies patterns, i.e., user-specific patterns, and builds a model based on valid and invalid states. Using data mining techniques, one can classify records based on fraudulent and non-fraudulent patterns [14].
- *Marketing Analysis*
  - o It is based on Association mining, i.e., identifying user's preferences. With such techniques, one can identify purchasing habits of the users. Using this technique, one can compare different items, pricing of the items, etc. [13].

- *Customer Relationship Management*
  - Every organization is keenly observing and maintains this segment which is popularly known as CRM. In this segment, one can distinguish users/customers based on loyalty towards the organization. User's/Customer's data can be collected and analyzed to get desired results [13].
- *Banking and Finance*
  - The banking and finance sector holds huge data related to clients. Banking and financial software systems help different managers to identify the correct client segment, loyal clients. These software systems process 'n' transactions which a person cannot handle manually. Such software systems stores process a large volume of data and produce desired results less time [13].
- *Healthcare Industries*
  - Everyone concerns about health. Different parameters and values help the health care professionals to diagnose the disease. The number of patients, diseases and symptoms can be processed to get an accurate prediction. Software systems used in the health care industry process a large chunk of observed values and compare them with the stored patterns to draw an accurate conclusion [13].
- *Educational Purpose*
  - Using data mining, one can identify the student's interests in different fields. It also helps in improving teaching methodology with new trends [13].
- *Crime Investigation*
  - Data mining helps in identifying different patterns applied in other crimes. Crimes, criminals, and their crime characteristics are analyzed under this category. A large volume of (stored data) can be processed to identify different relationships with criminals. In this category, face recognition, fingerprint recognition, etc., are considered and used in the investigation [14].

1.2.3   Databases

It is a collection of records. With databases and their structures, records may vary with the applications. Here are the following types of databases that can be used in many applications [15].

- *Transactional Database:* It is a popular type of database that consists of rows and columns, i.e., known as transactions. The transaction has the following parameters.

  - *Transaction id*
  - *Timestamp*
  - *List of items*
  - *Item description*
  - *The transaction id* is a unique identifier generated by the system. Transactional databases are mostly related to financial matters such as banking transactions, booking a movie ticket, booking a flight, etc. [16].

- *Multimedia Database:* The data integration phase from the KDD process integrates data from multiple sources, and that data could be in the form of text, document, video, image, audio, etc. Storing these different data types (multimedia data) requires high dimensional space, which is a characteristic of a multimedia database [17]. Its examples are

  - *Video-on-demand*
  - *Digital libraries*
  - *Animations*
  - *Images.*

- *Spatial Database:* Similar to multimedia and transactional database, there is a spatial database which can store geographical information. This information maps, positioning of the object, etc. Geographic coordinates are handy in determining the topographic data [17].

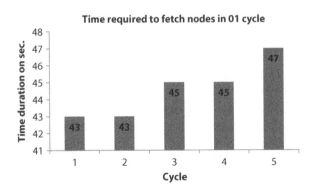

Figure 1.2 Time series database.

- *Time-Series Database:* As its name suggests time-series database—holds information related to a specific item w.r.t. time. E.g., weekly, monthly, yearly, etc. Such patterns help predict the trends and movements of an item in a particular time zone and are represented in Figure 1.2.

1.3   Issues in Data Mining

Data mining consists of tasks like user interfacing, mining, security, performance, and data source. The following is a discussion on various tradeoffs of data mining [3–5, 14].

- o   User interface design
   - ■   As discussed in the KDD process where discovered knowledge needs to be represented using good, accurate visualization. The user interface design issue addresses the interaction required within users and the systems, information rendering. This issue requires analysts, programmers to work on different conceptual levels.
- o   Mining methodologies issues
   This issue addresses the following sub-points:
   - ■   *Algorithms to be used*
   - ■   *Error-free data*
   - ■   *Less time complexity*
   - ■   *Metadata processing.*
- o   Security issues
   - ■   Security is a very important issue in data mining. Data collection, data processing requires maintaining the integrity, confidentiality of the data. Data mining systems deal with the private and sensitive information of the users and hence providing security to this data is a primary objective of this method.
- o   Performance issues
   - ■   There are many data mining applications existing in the market that are used in different sectors. These applications process a large volume of data and hence data mining algorithms; applications must process this data without compromising the performance of the system.

o Data source issues

  ▪ Data is collected from different sources, and it's an incremental process. The number of data mining applications is increasing, which produces a large volume of data. It became a necessary task to store, process and categorized this large volume of data is a necessary task.

1.4 Data Mining Algorithms

Adaboost, KNN, PageRank, Naïve Bayes, Support Vector Machine (SVM), Apriori, and C 4.5 are some data mining algorithms. Data mining algorithms are primarily used for predictive modeling, which includes clustering and classification problems. Let us discuss each of them in detail [1–6].

• Classification
It is a task in data mining where data can be modeled and distinguished into classes. One can say it is a process where given objects are classified/categorized to form a new class. Initially, the training set is identified, and new observations are derived. Hence, this task is classified into two phases, i.e., the learning/training phase and the classification of the given objects. E.g., a bank manager can wish to classify the loans borrowed by customers based on risky category, less risky category and trustworthiness, etc. To execute this classification technique on the given objects, the idea is to use classifier/s—where rules are applied, training is given, and given data is classified into the desired classes. The following are the classification algorithms that can be used in data mining:

  • Logistics regression
  • Naïve Bayes
  • K nearest
  • Decision tree
  • Random forest
  • Support Vector Model.

• Clustering
It is a grouping of objects based on similarity. A threshold is applied, and an object can be added to the specific cluster where the criteria can be satisfied. This technique is helpful in various applications such as—

- Market basket analysis
- Pattern recognition
- Image processing
- Financial analysis.

It is categorized as unsupervised learning, where the given data is used to compare with the threshold (predefined value). The clustering approach can be categorized into intra-cluster and inter-cluster.

- Types of Clustering

Clustering is nothing but a grouping of elements based on similarity and its unsupervised learning technique. One can apply partition clustering, which is also known as non-hierarchical clustering, to classify the data/records/values into 'k' groups/clusters. This is an iterative process and works until the last element is processed. Users can use the *SVM model—support vector machine*, where 'n' features will be identified in the initial phase, and then those features will be processed to identify the relevant results.

- o *K-means clustering* algorithm can be used to train the samples. Using this clustering method, it is possible to identify the nearest cluster by training the samples. Training the samples is nothing but finding the distance between samples and the nearest clusters. Distance is calculated between the samples, and the sample with a larger distance is likely to be selected as a center point. (One can use Euclidean distance metric in this case). K-means stores centroids ('k' points) that it uses to define the clusters to be formed. An object/value is considered to be in a specific cluster if it is closer to that cluster's centroid.
- o *Hierarchical:* It is one of the popular algorithms used in data mining and machine learning. The idea is to find the two clusters which are closer to each other and merge them to form a single cluster. Repeat this process until all the desired clusters are merged. This is categorized into top-down and bottom-up approaches, i.e., known as agglomerative and divisive approaches. We can define this type as the nesting of clusters that can be nested together to form a tree (merged cluster).
- o *Fuzzy:* Clusters are treated as fuzzy sets and allocate the objects to these clusters. It is unsupervised, and as its name suggests,

one can check the probability of each point whether it belongs to multiple clusters instead of belonging to a single cluster. It is also treated as soft clustering. One of its popular applications is *pattern recognition*. Minimization of the objective function is its primary objective, and hence the *number. of iterations* may increase. As for the number of iterations are 'n', it may increase the time complexity of the algorithm.

1.5   Data Warehouse

It is a warehouse which means it collects data from multiple heterogeneous sources. It supports analytical data processing and helps in decision-making. As data is collected from various sources, before storing this data into the

Table 1.1 Comparison in a data warehouse—OLTP.

	Data warehouse	OLTP
Queries	Deals with ad-hoc queries.	Only predefined queries.
Data modification/ updating	Automatically updates	By the end-users
Data storage	Stores data for many months/years	Stores data but less as compared to data warehouse.
Domain	It is subject-oriented.	It is application-oriented.
Data redundancy	Data redundancy may exist.	No data redundancy.

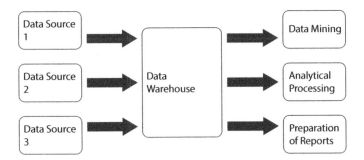

Figure 1.3 Data warehouse.

warehouse (Table 1.1), data cleaning, data integration, and data consolidation, etc., steps must be performed and represented in Figure 1.3 [18]. Data warehouse properties are as follows:

- *Subject-oriented*—designed for a specific subject/s
- *Integrated*—integrates different data from multiple sources.
- *Non-volatile*—data once stored remains stable and does not change over time.
- *Time-variant*—it looks at change over time.

One can compare data warehouse and OLTP as follows:

1.6   Data Mining Techniques

- *Decision trees:* It is a tree-like structure that helps identify the possible outcomes/results/consequences, etc. It is usually used in a decision support system. One can say it can be used in classification and prediction. It resembles a tree-like structure where leaf nodes represent the outcomes/results, etc. as shown in Figure 1.4. As it is a tree-like structure, classification/prediction starts from the root node and traverses through the leaf nodes. Its benefit is there is no need for high computation to find perfect predictions [1–6].

If there are 'n' nodes (root node and leaf nodes) in a sorted manner, then the best option/desired option can be found within less time.

- *Genetic algorithms (GAs):* It helps in finding possible solutions. These algorithms help to optimize the given problem and find

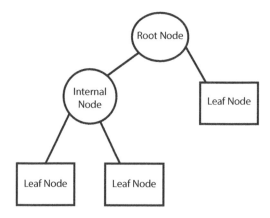

Figure 1.4 Decision Tree.

better solutions. One can categorize the identified solutions into optimal and near-optimal solutions. It may comprise of 'n' computations and hence known as an evolutionary approach to find the perfect solution. In NP-hard problems, it has been proven that usable near-optimal solutions can be found using GAs. This concept is related to biology, i.e., chromosomes, genes, and population. These terms can be described in the computations as follows:

- *Chromosome*—one possible solution
- *Populations*—set and subset of all possible solutions
- *Genes*—one element of the chromosome

GAs could have the following steps involved—

- Population initialization
- Fitness function calculation
- Crossover (finding the probabilities)
- Mutation (a method to get a new solution)
- Survivor selection (selecting the required and removing the unwanted)
- Return the best solution.

- *Nearest neighbor method:* As its name suggests, the nearest neighbor method tries to find the new possible solution, data based on some similarity. It classifies the given data and predicts the possible new data. Proximity among the given objects is calculated and as per the set threshold, objects close to each other are selected. E.g., KNN—'k' nearest neighbor algorithm. One has to decide the value of 'k' for better involvement of the objects. If someone decides the value of k = 1, possible outcomes become unstable, and as the value of 'k' increases, it involves the majority of objects which results in better predictions. Such algorithms can be used in Banking and financial systems and To calculate the credit of the users.

1.7   Data Mining Tools

Various data mining tools are available for researchers and organizations. We will discuss the hands-on process of installing three major tools, namely Python, KNIME, and Rapid Miner [19–25].

1.7.1   Python for Data Mining

We will discuss Python for data mining in this last section with various techniques. Regression is a technique to reduce errors by estimating the relationship that may exist between variables. It is also possible to form clusters in Python. One can implement this regression method using Python as follows:

User can develop a regression model for given variables and helps researchers, students to estimate the relationship exists between them. It also helps in classifying the given objects, analyze the clusters formed, etc., using tools provided in Python [24].

- ❖ **"Panda,"** a library supported by Python, helps to clean and process the input data.
- ❖ **NumPy**—a package supported by Python to perform computations.
- ❖ **Matplotlib**—once the data is processed, there is a need to visualize this data, and it is possible using this package supported by Python.
- ❖ **Scikit-learn**—a library supported by Python to model the data.

Python used in data mining, and machine learning executes the following steps:

1. Import the required libraries
2. Dataset loading (import)
3. If the dataset consists of missing data, then it must handle this missing data
4. Classifying or handling categorical data
5. Dividing the dataset into training and testing dataset
6. Features scaling (actually, it is a transformation of variables).

Installation and Setup of Python

1) Click on the link below and select OS: https://www.ana-conda.com/download/ [24]
2) Download Python 3.7 version (around 500 MB)
3) Once installed, launch the Anaconda Navigator (search by clicking the windows button)
4) Run the required Application (Jupyter, Spyder, etc.)

Make sure you constantly update the entire Anaconda distribution as it takes care of updating all the modules and dependencies inside (For more on installation, go to https://docs.anaconda.com/anaconda/install/windows/ for Windows version).

1.7.2   KNIME

Features of KNIME: KNIME [25] is an open-source analytical platform for data science. It helps to understand and design data science workflows, understanding time-series data analysis, to build machine learning models, and understand the data using visualization tools (charts, plots, etc.). It also helps to export the reports generated. KNIME workbench consists of *KNIME explorer, Workflow bench, Node Repository, Workflow Editor, Description, Outline, and Console.* It supports the data wrangling technique where one can collect and process the data from any source. It comes in two flavors:

- o   KNIME analytical platform
- o   KNIME server.
- • Both these platforms are available in Microsoft Azure and Amazon AWS

KNIME TOOL Installation
You can download the installer from the KNIME website. Once you successfully download it start the installation as specified in the next diagrams (Figure 1.5). Every installation requires you must accept the agreement,

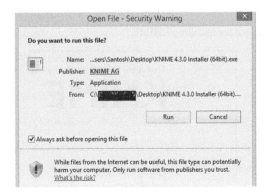

Figure 1.5 Installation of KNIME.

click on the button and accept the agreement (Figure 1.6). Installation requires specifying the path for installing the software, and as shown in the above diagram, it is a default path. If you wish, you can change the path by clicking on the "Browse" (Figures 1.7 and 1.8).

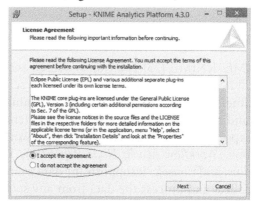

Figure 1.6 Installation of KNIME (2).

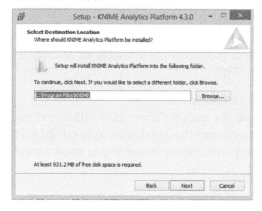

Figure 1.7 Setting path for installing KNIME.

Figure 1.8 Starting installation of KNIME.

Figures 1.9–1.16 show the complete workflow for selecting a Workspace path, and if you want to change the way, you can change it by clicking on the "Browse." Finally, Figure 1.16 gives you the home screen for mining purpose.

Figure 1.9 Selecting directory as a workspace.

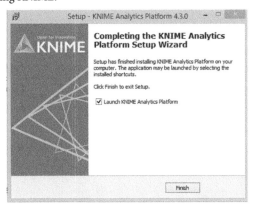

Figure 1.10 Starting KNIME.

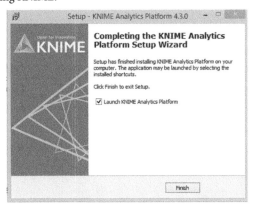

Figure 1.11 Completing setup wizard.

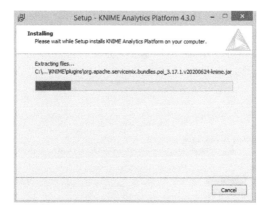

Figure 1.12 Installing Workspace in KNIME.

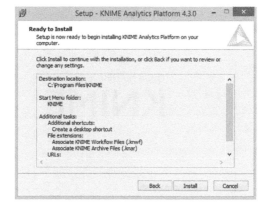

Figure 1.13 Installing KNIME (2).

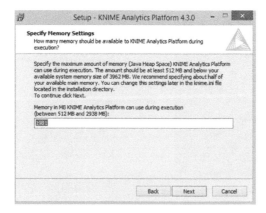

Figure 1.14 Specifying memory for KNIME.

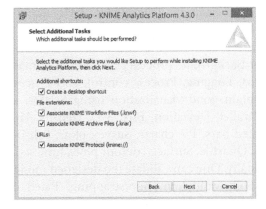

Figure 1.15 Finalizing the installation of KNIME.

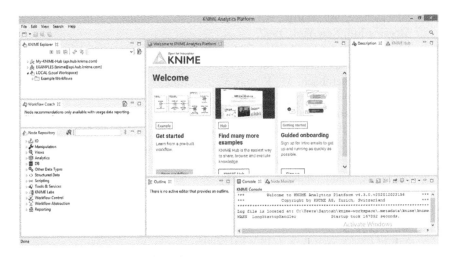

Figure 1.16 Initial screen of KNIME.

1.7.3   Rapid Miner

One can visit https://rapidminer.com/products/studio/ for further instructions to download this tool. Its main features are as follows speedy creation of predictive models; Rich set of libraries to build the model like *Bayesian modeling, Regression, Clustering, Neural networks, Decision trees.* A rapid miner comes with templates, which are provided for guidance. One can use any data source like *MS-excel, Access, CSV, NoSQL, MongoDB, Microsoft*

SQL Server, MySQL, Cassandra, PDF, HTML, XML. Rapid Miner Supports ETL (extract–transform–load), multiple file types, and Data exploration using exact statistical analysis. The Code control & management module is responsible for Background process execution, Automatic optimization, Scripting, Macros, Logging, Process control, and Process-based reporting. One can obtain good visualization using Scatter, scatter matrices, Line, Bubble, Parallel, Deviation, Box, 3-D, Density, Histograms, Area, Bar charts, stacked bars, Pie charts, Survey plots, Self-organizing maps, Andrews curves, Quartile, Surface/contour plots, time series plots, Pareto/lift chart. And finally, One can validate the designed model before deployment through Split validation, Bootstrapping, Batch cross-validation, Wrapper cross-validation, Lift chart, and Confusion matrix [24].

References

1. Silberschatz, A., Korth, H.F., Sudarshan, S., *Database system concepts*, Mcgraw-hill, New York, 1997.
2. Fayyad, U., Piatetsky-Shapiro, G., Smyth, P., From data mining to knowledge discovery in databases. *AI Mag.*, 17, 3, 37–37, 1996.
3. Tan, P.-N., Steinbach, M., Kumar, V., *Introduction to data mining*, Pearson Education India, New Delhi, 2016.
4. Sumathi, S. and Sivanandam, S.N., *Introduction to data mining and its applications*, vol. 29, Springer, Berlin Heidelberg, 2006.
5. Mehrotra, S., Rastogi, R., Korth, H.F., Silberschatz, A., A transaction model for multidatabase systems, in: *ICDCS*, pp. 56–63. *Mining, What Is Data. "Data mining: Concepts and techniques*, vol. 10, pp. 559–569, Morgan Kaufmann, 2006.
6. Pyo, S., Uysal, M., Chang, H., Knowledge discovery in the database for tourist destinations. *J. Travel Res.*, California, USA, 40, 4, 374–384, 2002.
7. Gehrke, J., Ginsparg, P., Kleinberg, J., Overview of the 2003 KDD Cup. *ACM Sigkdd Explor. Newsl.*, 5, 2, 149–151, 2003.
8. Shafique, U. and Qaiser, H., A comparative study of data mining process models (KDD, CRISP-DM, and SEMMA). *Int. J. Innov. Sci. Res.*, 12, 1, 217–222, 2014.
9. Mennis, J. and Peuquet, D.J., The role of knowledge representation in geographic knowledge discovery: A case study. *Trans. GIS*, 7, 3, 371–391, 2003.
10. Mahmood, M.R., Patra, R.K., Raja, R., Sinha, G.R., A Novel Approach for Weather prediction using forecasting analysis and Data Mining Techniques, in: *7th International Conference on Innovations in Computer Science and Engineering on 27–28 July 2018*, 2018.
11. Han, J., Kamber, M., Pei, J., *Data mining concepts and techniques*, third edition, *The Morgan Kaufmann Series in Data Management Systems*, vol. 5(4), pp. 83–124, Elsevier, Massachusetts, USA, 2011.

12. Zhang, S., Zhang, C., Yang, Q., Data preparation for data mining. *Appl. Artif. Intell.*, 17, 5–6, 375–381, 2003.

13. Agarwal, S., Data mining: Data mining concepts and techniques. *2013 International Conference on Machine Intelligence and Research Advancement,* IEEE, 2013.

14. Pathak, S., Raja, R., Sharma, V., Ramya Laxmi, K., A Framework Of ICT Implementation On Higher Educational Institution With Data Mining Approach. *Eur. J. Eng. Res. Sci.*, 4, 5, 2019.

15. Barbará, D. and Jajodia, S. (Eds.), *Applications of Data Mining in Computer Security,* vol. 6, Springer Science & Business Media, Berlin Heidelberg, 2002.

16. Chen, M.-S., Han, J., Yu, P.S., Data mining: An overview from a database perspective. *IEEE Trans. Knowl. Data Eng.*, 8, 6, 866–883, 1996.

17. Tanveer, S.K., Mining regular patterns in transactional databases. *IEICE Trans. Inf. Syst.*, 91, 11, 2568–2577, 2008.

18. Pathak, S., Bhatt, P., Raja, R., Sharma, V., Weka vs Rapid Miner: Models Comparison in Higher Education with these Two Tools of Data. *SAMRIDDHI: A J. Phys. Sciences, Engineering, Technol.*, 12, Special Issue (3), 183–188, 2019.

19. Gabriel, R., Gluchowski, P., Pasta, A., *Data warehouse & data mining,* W3l GmbH, Münster, Germany, 2009.

20. Bowles, M., *Machine learning in Python: Essential techniques for predictive analysis,* John Wiley & Sons, New York, USA, 2015.

21. Nagwanshi, K.K., Atulkar, M., Durugkar, S., *Learn Python by Experiments,* Educreation Publishing, New Delhi, 2021.

22. Raj, A.P., Raja, R., Akella, S., A New Framework for Trustworthiness of Cloud Services. *Int. J. Res.*, 04, 1, 639–643, December 2017.

23. https://www.anaconda.com/download/

24. https://www.knime.com/

25. https://rapidminer.com/products/studio/

2

Classification and Mining Behavior of Data

Srinivas Konda[1]*, Kavitarani Balmuri[1] and Kishore Kumar Mamidala[2]

*[1]Department of Computer Science and Engineering, CMR Technical Campus,
Kandlakoya, Hyderabad, India
[2]Department of Computer Science and Engineering, Vivekananda Institute of
Technology and Science, Karimnagar, India*

Abstract

Behavior information is Information created by, or because of, a client's commitment to a business. This can incorporate things like site visits, e-mail recruits, or other significant client activities. Regular wellsprings of conduct information incorporate sites, versatile applications, CRM frameworks, promoting computerization frameworks, call focuses, help work areas, and charging frameworks. Clients can either be purchasers, organizations, or people inside a business. However, conduct information can generally be tied back to a solitary end-client. Note that this client can be a known individual (signed in) or unknown (not signed in). Complex practices are broadly observed in fake and characteristic insightful frameworks, on the web, social and online systems, multi-operator frameworks, and mental frameworks. The inside and out comprehension of complex practices has been progressively perceived as a pivotal method for uncovering inside main impetuses, causes, and effects on organizations in taking care of many testing issues. Notwithstanding, customary conduct demonstrating primarily depends on subjective techniques from conduct science and sociology points of view. The purported conduct examination in information investigation and adapting regularly centers around human segment and business use Information, in which conduct situated components are covered up in regularly gathered value-based Information. Subsequently, it is inadequate or even difficult to profoundly investigate local conduct expectations, lifecycles, elements, and effects on complex issues and business issues.

Keywords: Data mining, knowledge discovery, web indexes, complex datasets, high-dimensional information, data organizations, data filtering, fleeting information

---

*Corresponding author: phdknr@gmail.com

Rohit Raja, Kapil Kumar Nagwanshi, Sandeep Kumar and K. Ramya Laxmi (eds.) Data Mining
and Machine Learning Applications, (21–56) © 2022 Scrivener Publishing LLC

2.1   Introduction

In simple words, data mining is defined as a process often used to replace valuable data from a broad array of raw data. It suggests metadata design ideas in enormous data groupings using at least one computing. Data mining applies in different fields related to scientific facts and assessment. With mining techniques, organizations could even familiarize themselves with their customers and develop more successful processes recognized with different market capacities, thus influencing assets in a more ideal and adroit way. This makes organizations closer to their goal and better choices. Data mining techniques contain feasible information assortment and storage almost as Console preparation. To deform data and predict the risks of future occasions, information mining uses advanced quantitative measurements. Data mining is also known as Knowledge Discovery in Data (KDD).

With huge Information right now accessible and being gathered, acquiring admittance to Information is only occasionally the worry. Data is being created and put away at an exceptional rate, and progressively, a significant part of the large Information being gathered is about human conduct. This kind of Information is ordinarily made and put away as an "occasion," which means a move that was made, with "properties," which means metadata used to depict the occasion. For instance, an occasion could be "site visit," and property for that occasion could be "gadget type." It might assist with considering occasions the "what" and the properties as the "who, when, and where."

Our conduct is caught in the Data that we give from utilizing web indexes, e-business stages, informal community administrations, or online training. Filtering through this Information and determining bits of knowledge on human conduct empowers the stages to settle on more viable choices and offer better support. Nonetheless, customary conduct demonstrating depends on subjective strategies from conduct science and sociology viewpoints. There is an incredible requirement for computational models for assignments, for example, design examination, forecast, proposal, and abnormality recognition, on enormous scope datasets.

The information economy requires information mining to be more objective situated so more substantial outcomes can be created. This necessity infers that the semantics of the Information ought to be consolidated into the mining cycle. Information mining is prepared to manage this test since ongoing advancements in information mining have demonstrated an expanding enthusiasm for mining complex Information (as exemplified by chart mining, text mining, and so on). By consolidating the connections of the Information alongside the Information itself (instead of zeroing in on the Information alone), complex Information infuses semantics into the mining cycle, subsequently improving the capability of improving commitment to an information economy. Since the connections between the Information uncover certain social viewpoints hidden in the plain Information, this move of mining from straightforward Information to complex Information flags a key change to another phase in the exploration and practice of information disclosure, which can be named conduct mining. Conduct mining likewise has the capability of binding together some other ongoing exercises in information mining. We talk about significant viewpoints on conduct mining and examine its suggestions for the eventual fate of information mining.

This examination subject reports creative answers for issues of client conduct information scale in a wide scope of uses, for example, recommender frameworks and dubious conduct discovery. It covers information science and measurable ways to deal with information disclosure and demonstrating, choice help, and forecast, including AI and AI, on client conduct information. Potential settings incorporate Mining dynamic/streaming information, Mining diagram and system Information, Mining heterogeneous/multi-source information, Mining high dimensional information, Mining imbalanced information, Mining media information, Mining logical information, Mining successive information, Mining interpersonal organizations Mining spatial and transient Information.

2.2   Main Characteristics of Mining Behavioral Data

2.2.1   Mining Dynamic/Streaming Data

An information stream is a succession of unbounded, constant information things with an extremely high information rate that can just peruse once by an application [1, 2]. Information stream investigation has, as of

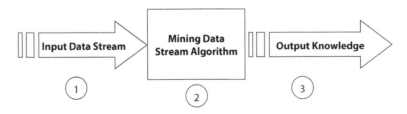

Figure 2.1 Process of mining data stream.

late, stood out in the exploration network. Calculations for mining information streams and progressing ventures in business and logical applications have been created and talked about in [3, 4]. The vast majority of these calculations center around creating estimated one-pass strategies is shown in Figure 2.1.

Two ongoing progressions propel the requirement for information stream handling frameworks [5, 6]:

I.   The programmed age of an exceptionally nitty gritty, high information rate succession of information things in various logical and business applications. For instance: satellite, radar, and cosmic information streams for logical applications and securities exchange and exchange web log information streams for business applications.

II.   The requirement for complex investigations of these rapid information streams, for example, grouping and exception location, arrangement, regular item sets, and checking continuous things.

There are two techniques for tending to the issue of the fast idea of information streams. Information and yield rate variation of the mining calculation is the primary procedure. The rate transformation implies controlling the information and yield pace of the mining calculation as indicated by the accessible assets. The calculation estimate by growing new light-weight strategies that have just one glance at every information thing is the subsequent system. The principal focal point of mining information stream methods proposed so far is the structure of surmised mining calculations that have just one disregard or less the information stream [7].

2.2.2   Mining Graph & Network Data

As an overall information structure, charts have gotten progressively significant in displaying complex networks and their connections, with wide applications, including compound informatics, bioinformatics, PC vision, video order, text recovery, and Web investigation. Digging regular subgraph designs for additional portrayal, separation, grouping, and bunch investigation turns into a significant errand. Also, diagrams that connect numerous hubs may frame various types of systems, for example, media transmission systems, PC systems, organic systems, and Web and social network systems. Since such systems have been concentrated widely with regards to informal communities, their investigation has

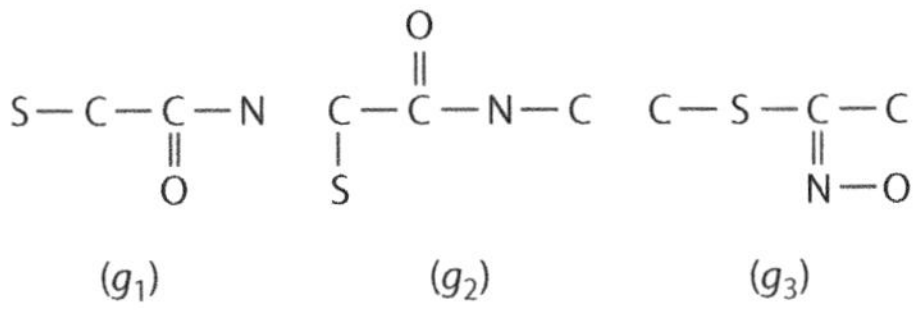

Figure 2.2 Sample of graph data set.

frequently been alluded to as interpersonal organization examination. Besides, in a social information base, objects are semantically connected over numerous relations. Mining in a social information base frequently requires mining over different interconnected relations, which is like mining in associated diagrams or systems. Such sort of mining across information relations is considered multi-relational information mining is represented in Figure 2.2.

Illustrations increasingly become important for presentations of inter-connected structures, such as network, circuit, XML, images, papers, working practices, mixtures of substances, natural processes, informal communities, and protein sequences. Many diagram search calculations have been created in synthetic informatics, PC vision, video order, and text recovery. With the expanding request on the investigation of a lot of orga-nized Information, diagram mining has become a functioning and signifi-cant topic in information mining [8].

Even though chart mining may incorporate mining incessant subgraph designs, diagram order, bunching, and different examination undertak-ings, in this segment, we center around mining continuous subgraphs. We take a gander at other strategies, their expansions, and applications.

2.2.3   Mining Heterogeneous/Multi-Source Information

Subsequent instance processing is a data mining topic concerned with find-ing factually applicable examples between information models that express the attributes in a series [9]. Finding consecutive examples from a huge information base of successions is a significant issue in the field of infor-mation revelation and information mining [10]. The issue is to find afteref-fects, among a lot of information successions, that is continuous where the arrangements containing them has a higher help than a client determined the least help [11]. Typically, arrangement designs are related to various conditions, and such conditions structure a numerous dimensional space. It is fascinating and valuable to successive mine examples related to multi-dimensional data [12].

2.2.3.1   Multi-Source and Multidimensional Information

A wellspring of data could furnish Information with various types, As examined in [13, 14], various types of Information are considered as various measurements; along these lines, a wellspring of Information gives at least one measurements. Such sort of Information is called multidimensional Information is represented in Figure 2.3.

In specific cases, the Information doesn't originate from a similar wellspring of data; in any case, it originates from various sources and is assembled in one dataset. Such sort of Information is called multi-source Information. Information could be of similar kind or various types among various sources. Consequently, each wellspring of data could give multidimensional Information, which makes the Information mind-boggling and heterogeneous.

2.2.3.2   Multi-Relational Data

There could be relations between the measurements that originate from the equivalent or various sources. Each measurement could have a connection between at least one different measurement. The measurements for this situation are interrelated [15]. This sort of Information is called multi-social Information that can be spoken to in multi-social information bases as depicted [16]. Accordingly, multi-social Information digging is

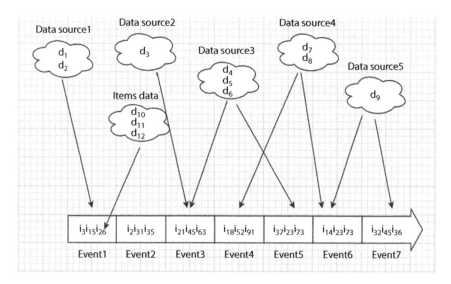

Figure 2.3 Multi-source & multidimensional information.

utilized for this sort of Information. Multi-social information-digging approaches search for designs that include various tables (relations) from a social information base [17].

2.2.3.3   Background and Connected Data

Utilizing foundation information in the area of continuous example mining can help to find designs, just as finding new examples that start from joining the first Information with extra foundation information [18]. Subsequently, including foundation and connected Information as extra data to the central Information that as of now exists in the dataset helps in acquiring more productive outcomes or better clarifying the outcomes got. Extra Information could be at least one measurement from the multidimensional Information, and hence it could be from at least one source that is now existing or new.

2.2.3.4   Complex Data, Sequences, and Events

Complex datasets are information assortments in which the individual information things are not, at this point, "straightforward" (nuclear in information base phrasing) values. However, are (semi-)organized assortments of Information themselves [19]. A sequence is a progression of occasions happening continuously, where an occasion is either a thing or a thing set (requested or unordered) happening at a specific time stretch. An arrangement is perplexing when the components in each time-stamp are mind-boggling, which implies that there is more than one thing where there can be a few attributes between things, for example, requests and other potential connections between them [20]. An unpredictable grouping could likewise be various occasions happening all the while.

Complex occasions can be as a few occasions happening (multi-factors) one after another space regarding different spans (e.g., hours, days, and weeks) [21]. There could be extra Information originating from outside sources connected to every occasion in an arrangement. This Information gives extra data about things or thing sets. The Information could be at least one measurement and from at least one information source.

2.2.3.5   Data Protection and Morals

Certain exploration spaces require treating clients' Information which could contain some close-to-home data about clients; they are all the more explicitly the areas that give results that are customized to every client. Nonetheless, when managing such sort of Information, certain proportions of secrecy and security ought to be contemplated because this Information is dependent upon some protection strategies and guidelines and should regard information morals. Thus, while treating this sort of Information, the genuine personality of the client is covered up and couldn't be recognized, and this is done either by anonymization or pseudo-anonymization [22].

2.2.4   Mining High Dimensional Data

Bunching high-dimensional Information has been a significant test because of the innate sparsity of the focuses. Most existing grouping calculations become generously inefficient if the necessary likeness measure is registered between Information focuses on the full-dimensional space. Grouping calculations ordinarily utilize a separation metric (e.g., Euclidean) or a similitude measure to parcel the information base with the goal that the Information focuses on each segment are more comparable than focuses in various partitions. The usually utilized Euclidean separation, while computationally basic, requires comparable articles to have close qualities in all measurements. Be that as it may, with the high-dimensional Information usually experienced these days, the idea of closeness between objects in the full-dimensional space is frequently invalid and, for the most part, not accommodating. Late hypothetical outcomes [23]. uncover that Information focuses on a set will, in general, be all the more similarly separated as the element of the space increments, as long as the segments of the information point are I .i.d. (autonomously and indistinguishably dispersed). Even though I .i.d. condition is infrequently satisfied in genuine applications, it despite everything turns out to be less important to separate Information focuses dependent on a separation or a closeness measure processed utilizing all the measurements. These outcomes clarify the terrible showing of traditional separation put together grouping calculations for such information sets. Feature determination procedures are generally used as a preprocessing stage for bunching to defeat the scourge of dimensionality. The most useful measurements are chosen by wiping out unessential and excess ones. Such procedures accelerate grouping calculations and improve their presentation [24]. By and by, in certain applications, various bunches may exist in various subspaces crossed by various measurements. In such cases, measurement decrease utilizing a regular element determination strategy that may prompt considerable data misfortune [25].

2.2.5   Mining Imbalanced Data

Actuating classifiers from informational collections having slanted class appropriations is now and again experienced in the information mining measure. In various applications, the family member, as well as the supreme number of certain classes, maybe intensely dwarfed by the recurrence of others. A few models are charge card extortion recognition, where the quantity of fake activities is a lot of lower than the quantity of non-deceitful ones [26]; uncommon sickness clinical findings, where the quantity of patients having the illness is extremely low in the populace [27]; and persistent shortcoming checking assignments where non-flawed cases vigorously dwarf broken cases, to name yet a few. This issue is regularly alluded to in writing as the "class irregularity" issue, as various investigations bring up corruption in the execution of the models extricated from slanted areas, particularly while foreseeing the low spoke to (minority) classes. This horrible showing to the minority classes is entirely bothersome, as they are frequently the classes we are more inspired by. Even though class irregularity is an issue vital in information mining, a total comprehension of how this issue affects the classifiers' presentation isn't clear yet.

2.2.5.1   *The Class Imbalance Issue*

Learning calculations are broadly utilized during the example extraction period of the information mining measure. As this cycle manages "genuine world" information, a few issues of applying existing and settled learning calculations to genuine Information have developed. Among them, a pertinent handy issue is learning within sight of uneven class characters. Many learning calculations were planned, expecting even class circulations, for example, no significant differences in class earlier probabilities. In any case, this isn't generally the situation in genuine Information where one class may be spoken to by countless models, while the others are spoken to by just a few. Generally, the issue of imbalanced informational indexes happens at whatever point one class speaks to a delineated idea, while the difference speaks to the partner of that idea, so models from the partner class intensely dwarf models from the positive idea class. For this situation, the inductive predisposition of learning calculations which are not extraordinarily intended to manage uneven class characters, will in general concentrate in the class which is spoken to by the biggest number of models [28].

2.2.6   Mining Multimedia Data

Late advancement in the field of electronic imaging, video gadgets, stock-piling, systems administration, and PC power show that the measure of mixed media has developed immensely, and information mining has become a mainstream and a simple method of finding new Information from such an enormous informational index, for example, differing information bases. Note that for mining interactive media information, the mix of at least two information types, for example, text and video, or text, video, and sound, should be done, which is anything but a primary strategy [29]. One arrangement is to create mining instruments to work on the sight and sound Information straightforwardly is represented in Figure 2.4.

Interactive media information mining alludes to the mining of Multimedia content. In different words, it is an investigation of a lot of sight and sound data to discover designs or measurable connections. When Information is gathered, PC programs are utilized to break down it and search for important associations. This Data can be utilized in advertising to find shopper propensities. However, it is predominantly utilized by governments to improve social systems. Multimedia information mining will, in general, find designs, extract rules, and alludes to Information obtaining from mixed media information base mining, specifically, different angles [30].

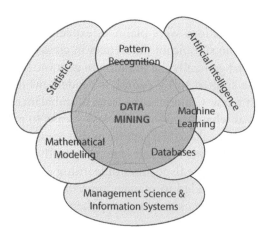

Figure 2.4 Shows the data mining process of multimedia data.

2.2.6.1   Common Applications Multimedia Data Mining

When sight and sound are exhumed for data, one of the most widely recognized utilizations for this proof is to foresee standards of conduct or patterns. Data can be isolated into classes also, which permits various gatherings, for example, people or Sundays and Mondays, to be broken down independently. Information can be bunched or assembled by sensible relationship, which can help track purchaser fondness for a specific brand over another. Sight and sound information digging for traffic video groupings—Example: Traffic camera film to dissect traffic stream. This would prove to be useful while arranging new lanes, growing existing roads, or occupying traffic. The equivalent can be utilized by the Government associations and city organizers to assist traffic with streaming all the more easily and rapidly. Digital Libraries Mixed Media Data Mining—the digital library retrieves, stores, and configures profound understanding. For this purpose, hence the need to modify different data organizations, such as text, images, video, audio, etc. Hence, during the time spent change of the mixed media records in the libraries, the information mining strategies are well known. Data-mining technologies for diagnostic object recognition medical research application—a proliferation of radio and TV broadcasting—make telecommunications companies pursue more different strategies for projects and the evaluation of their material [31].

2.2.6.2   Multimedia Data Mining Utilizations

2.2.6.2.1   Customer Insight

It incorporates gathering and summing up data about client's sentiments, items or administrations, clients' gripes, client's inclinations, and the degree of consumer loyalties of items or administrations. Numerous organizations have help work areas or consider focuses that acknowledge calls from the clients. The sound Information fills in as a contribution for information mining to seek after the accompanying objectives [32]:

   a) Topic discovery
   b) Resource task
   c) Evaluation of nature of administration.

2.2.6.2.2   Reconnaissance

Reconnaissance comprises of gathering, breaking down, and summing up sound, video, or varying media data about a specific region, for example, combat zones, timberlands, horticultural territories, expressways, parking garages, structures, workshops, shopping centers, retail locations, workplaces, homes, and so on, which are related with Insight, security, and law requirement and the significant employments of this method are discussed in the succeeding sections.

2.2.6.2.3   Versatility Prediction for Delay Reduction in WLAN Utilizing Location Tracking and Data Mining

Forecast of the versatile way of a portable hub is vital since it diminishes the handoff delays brought about during the handoff strategy. The proposed framework is called Predictive Mobility Management conspire. We track the development of portable hubs by area following and information mining. In the area following, we persistently screen the development of a portable hub. The development of versatile hubs can be anticipated by the course of development of portable hubs and past way history, which can be gotten by information mining procedures. The information mining strategy is utilized to look through the way history of a versatile hub, and the method utilizes this Data to foresee the future development of a portable hub. NG pruning plan can be utilized for expectation alongside area following. In NG pruning, we will reject examining passages that are not reachable. In this manner, the filtering postponement can be limited to a huge degree. Utilizing the expectation plot, we can limit the postponements during handoff, track a versatile hub, and so on. At the point when a hub connects to the range zone, Information sending to the hub is coordinated to the AP, which was chosen by expectation where the hub will get associated.

2.2.6.3   *Multimedia Database Management*

As of late, media has been a significant concentration for some scientists around the globe, and numerous advances are proposed for speaking to, putting away, ordering, and recovering sight and sound Information. The vast majority of the investigations done are bound to the Information separating the venture of the KDD cycle. Reference [33] exhibited how KDD strategies can be utilized to examine sound Information and eliminate commotion from old accounts. Sight and sound information mining allude to design revelation, rule extraction, and information procurement from mixed media data set, as talked about in paper [34]. In present work [35] used information-based AI methods to help picture preparing in a huge picture data set created from the Galileo crucial.

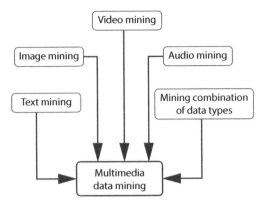

Figure 2.5 Mining of multimedia data.

Sight and sound data mining structure model, Multi-Media Min combines the creation of a solid digital media shape that promotes various dimensional investigations of media content, ultimately based on visual material, and the extraction of various kinds of Information, such as collection, association, sorting, connection and buckling is represented in Figure 2.5 [36].

A. Text Mining: Text mining is an emerging new area that aims to collect relevant Information from a distinctive text document. Combined and the kind of data held in data sets, the document is unorganized, unidentifiable, and difficult to handle algorithmically. In today's society, the text is the most commonly known medium for traditional data trading. The field of text mining, as a rule, manages text whose power is the contact of actual data or evaluations, and the reason for trying to extract Information from such material is, of course, compelling, irrespective of whether accomplishment is fairly significant [37].

B. Picture Mining: Image mining frameworks that can naturally remove semantically significant data (Information) from picture information are progressively popular. The core test in picture mining is how low-level, pixel representation found in a rough image or image layout can be treated to identify high-level structural articles and relationships.

C. Video Mining: Video contains a few sorts of mixed media information, for example, text, picture, meta information, visual and sound. It is broadly utilized in many significant potential applications like security and reconnaissance, amusement, medication, training projects, and sports. The target of video information mining is to find and depict fascinating examples from the colossal measure of video information as it is one of the center issue zones of the information mining research network [38].

D. Sound Mining: Audio mining is a procedure by which the substance of a sound sign can be consequently investigated and looked at. It is most regularly utilized in the field of programmed discourse acknowledgment, where the investigation attempts to distinguish any discourse inside the sound [39].

2.2.7   Mining Scientific Data

Data investigation procedures supporting conventional logical cycles were planned for dealing with a genuinely modest quantity of low dimensional Information through a guess and test worldview. These amazingly work escalated procedures are getting infeasible for the examination of tremendous logical datasets acquired at a lot higher speed and lower cost utilizing improved or novel information assortment advances. Lately, space experts, geoscientists, natural chemists, high vitality physicists, and different researchers gather colossal and high measurement datasets utilizing progressed telescope advances [40], multi-phantom far off sensors on satellites [41], coordinating worldwide situating frameworks with high goal sensors on the ground [42], growing greatly equal instruments like microarrays that create quality articulations for whole creatures without a moment's delay [43], and utilizing other cutting edge innovations.

For instance, in Earth sciences, notwithstanding a system of geostationary and polar circling climate and meteorological satellites, the novel arrangement of satellites have been as of late presented that give consistent information stream from different sensors to achieve further comprehension of atmosphere and natural changes . Specifically, the NASA Earth Observation System, comprising of a few low-elevation satellites, is the main watching framework to offer coordinated estimations of the Earth's cycles. It upholds an organized arrangement of polar-circling and low-tendency satellites for long-term worldwide perceptions of the land surface, biosphere, strong Earth, air, and seas. Its Landsat 7 instrument has an information pace of 150 Mbps while the Terra instrument produces Information arranged by 1 TB every day.

Another wellspring of huge datasets in science is the consequence of utilizing quick computational offices in reenactments of astronomy, liquid elements, auxiliary mechanics, compound building, atmosphere displaying, and different fields. For instance, the Reanalysis Project, together sought after by the National Center for Environmental Prediction and the National Center for Atmospheric Research has an objective to create new barometrical examinations utilizing verifiable Information just as to deliver investigations of the ebb and flow climatic state [44].

This exertion results in 55 GB/year of handled Information, containing a few worldly atmosphere and climate traits at a standard 3D spatial framework for 50+ long periods of barometrical fields. The Information has been utilized in different spaces, including climatology, ranger service, and natural sciences [45] too to make preview yearly CD-ROMs containing reviews of crude reanalysis information.

Likewise, inventive information mining strategies were created to address certain parts of explicit logical issues that are particular from common business applications and were utilized in other logical areas. At the 1996 report of the Workshop on Scientific Data Management, Mining, Analysis, and Assimilation, it was underscored that paying little heed to a specific space, logical informational indexes share a ton of normal properties and need a brought together way to deal with effectively tackle various basic issues including Information stockpiling, association, access, and information disclosure [46]. Terabyte scale issues were proposed for assessing logical information mining innovations at this workshop. For instance, one of the detailed applications was focused on the investigation of 3 TB of radio space science information for deciding the size and appropriation of articles. To break down this Information in a short time would require Information taking care of framework with an entrance pace of 10 gigabytes for every second to the put-away Information. In later logical information mining workshops [47] and somewhere else [48], testbed issues were expanded to Petabytes of Information [49] circulated among different areas.

Notwithstanding critical advances in information mining and related fields of far off detecting, information bases, AI, worldly, spatial, and spatial-transient measurements [50], there is a dire requirement for extra logical information mining exercises to make a certified change in outlook in science a reality [51]. Difficulties that need more consideration are various. Some of the significant logical information mining issues that won't be considered in this article include:

a) Learning with earlier information;
b) Gradual learning;
c) Taking care of short perception history;
d) Incorporating data from numerous sources;
e) Performing viable information enrollment to relate data from different subjects.

2.2.8   Mining Sequential Data

Sequential Data is inescapable. Client shopping groupings, clinical treatment information, and Information identified with cataclysmic events, science, and building measures Information, stocks and markets Information, phone calling designs, weblog click streams, program execution arrangements, DNA successions, and quality articulation and structures Information are a few instances of grouping information.

Given an example p, the backing of the arrangement design p is the number of groupings in the information base containing the example p. An example with help more prominent than the help limit min_sup is known as a regular example or an incessant consecutive example. A consecutive example of length l is called an l-design. Successive example mining is the assignment of finding the total arrangement of regular aftereffects given a lot of groupings. Countless conceivable consecutive examples are covered up in information bases.

A consecutive example mining calculation ought to:

a) locate the total arrangement of examples, whenever the situation allows, fulfilling the base support (frequency) limit,
b) be profoundly productive, versatile, including just a few information base outputs,
c) have the option to fuse different sorts of explicit client limitations.

2.2.9   Mining Social Networks

Social advertising is an exceptional data source and a perfect correspondence point. Individuals and organizations should do their best, not just share their photos and videos on stage. The stages give customers the ability to communicate efficiently and phenomenally with their objective gathering. Whether it's a meeting or a set-up company, both face obstacles to keep

Figure 2.6 Shows social media mining.

positive also with the web-based advertising industry. However, via digital media, customers can highlight or create their image or material with others is shown in Figure 2.6.

Online media mining incorporates web-based media stages, interpersonal organization investigation, and information mining to give a helpful and predictable stage for students, experts, researchers, and venture supervisors to comprehend the essentials and possibilities of web-based media mining. It proposes different issues emerging from online media information and presents crucial ideas, developing issues, and viable calculations for information mining and system examination. It incorporates different degrees of trouble that upgrade Information and help in applying thoughts, standards, and strategies in unmistakable web-based media mining circumstances.

As per the "international digital survey," the overall amount of dynamic clients through online advertising stages worldwide in 2019 is 2.41 billion, and it increases to 9% year-on-year. For all-inclusive use of social networking sites stages through the web, a considerable way of measuring content is provided. Web-based media stages incorporate numerous fields of study, for example, humanism, business, brain science, amusement, legislative issues, news, and other social parts of social orders. Implementing data mining techniques to online advertising will provide an energetic point of view on human behavior and affiliation. Data mining can be used in combination with online advertising to understand client assessments of a topic, differentiate a community of people among all the majority of a population, examine bunch changes after a while, find convincing human beings, and even strongly suggest a product or response to an individual.

For example, throughout 2008, the presidency political decision endorsed outstanding use of online advertising stages in the U.S. Online media stages, including Facebook, YouTube which assumed an essential function in raising assets and getting voters' messages from competitors. Professional's abolished blog evidence to express associations among web-based media stage measurement used by competing products and the 2008 presidential task eventual winner is shown in Figure 2.7.

This convincing design illustrates the prospects for online media data mining to evaluate community-level results. Data mining web-based media can also develop corporate and individual benefits.

Web-based media prospecting relates to social registration. Social registration is characterized as "Any figuring interface where the configuration is used as a legislator or social relationship center." Social ability to process application is used for genuine feedback, much like evaluation and investigation tasks recognized with "computational social research" or social etiquette.

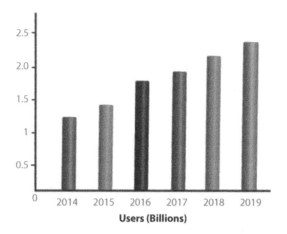

Figure 2.7 Shows total facebook users per year.

For e.g., through well-known traditional newspapers, radio, print, and TV, communication is one-way from the newspaper source or promoter to the media shoppers' mass as shown in Table 2.1. Web 2.0 developments and online media stages have changed the scene from one-way media

Table 2.1 Shows social media network applies to various data services.

Category	Examples
Blogs	Blogger, LiveJournal, WordPress
Social news	Digg, Slashdot
Social bookmarking	Delicious, StumbleUpon
Social networking platform	Facebook, LinkedIn, Myspace, Orkut
Microblogs	Twitter, GoogleBuzz
Opinion mining	Epinions, Yelp
Photo and video sharing	Flickr, YouTube
Wikis	Scholarpedia, Wikihow, Wikipedia, Event

communications powered by media providers to where almost everyone can transmit composite, sound, video, or image content to the community.

This broadcast situation fundamentally affects company communications with their clients. It offers people incredibly exceptional opportunities to interact incredibly rapidly with a large number of people in classes. The links available on the web and emerged via the web-based media stage are computerized sets of web-based media stages on a scale. The frequently reviewed provides great open doors for rationalism and bits of expertise for buyers to undertake and encourage a variety of applications linked to comparative areas.

The application and number of subscribers via web-based sufficient to lead is unbelievable. Consider, for example, the most tempting online media website, Facebook. Mostly during the initial six years of operation, Facebook came to over 400 million diverse clients and grew rapidly. The figure shows Facebook's rapid growth over the initial six years. According to the study, Facebook is placed second on the planet for sites that rely on customers' traffic on the web everyday day.

The wide use of web-based media stages is not limited to one world geological venue. Orkut, a popular person-to-person contact stage operated by Google, has the majority of external U.S. customers, and the usage of online media by Internet customers is currently common in various parts of the globe, including Asia, Africa, Europe, South America, and the center east. Online media also cause major organizational changes, and the company needs to choose its approaches to remain up to this digital technology.

2.2.9.1   Social-Media Data Mining Reasons

The Information accessible through the social media stage can give us bits of Insight about interpersonal organizations and social orders that were previously unplausible in size and degree. This developed media will alter objective world constraints to consider interpersonal interactions and help small networks measure well-known political and social beliefs without an analytical solution. Digital media tracks viral trends and is the best way to effectively see and influence effect factors. In any case, it is very hard to increase important data from long-range interpersonal communication destinations Information without executing information mining methods because of explicit difficulties.

Information Mining procedures can help viably in managing the three essential difficulties with web-based media information. Initially, online media informational collections are huge. Consider the case of the most well-known web-based media stage Facebook with 2.41 billion dynamic clients. Without robotized Information handling to investigate online media, web-based media information examination gets distant to some extent sensible phase period.

Second, knowledge indexes of social networking platforms can be uproarious. For example, spam web journals are huge in the media world, just like meaningless Twitter tweets.

Third, evidence from online web-based media stages is dynamic; ordinary changes and updates over a short period are not normal, but instead, a massive perspective to recognize when trying to manage web-based media information.

Trying to apply data mining techniques to enormous data databases will boost action if needed for daily web crawlers, acknowledge determined business purposes, assist therapists in evaluating behavior, customize shopper site administration, give sociologists new bits of knowledge in the social system and enable us all to discern and prevent spam. Furthermore, open access to Information gives specialists an outstanding measure of knowledge to develop expertise and optimize data-mining practices. Advancing data mining relies on exceptionally enormous databases. Web-based media is an optimal knowledge outlet for promoting and evaluating additional knowledge mining techniques for academic and related data mining researchers.

2.2.10 Mining Spatial and Temporal Data

Reality is omnipresent parts of perceptions in various spaces, including atmosphere science, neuroscience, sociologies, the study of disease transmission, Earth sciences, transference, and criminology. The knowledge storm is rapidly evolving. Since this process contributes measures concentrated in these spaces are innately Spatio-temporal, various data assortment theories were structured to report the temporal and fleeting details of each estimate in the Information, thus alluding to as spatial-transient (ST) data is shown in Figure 2.8. For example, in neuroimaging details, estimated

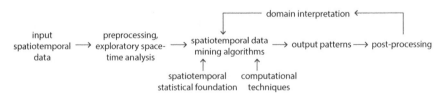

Figure 2.8 Shows the spatiotemporal data mining process.

action from the human mind is group dynamic the spatial area from which the behavior was calculated and when the estimate was made. Thus, web-search demands on Google staff have a geographic area and time from which they are made. Effective analysis of such increasingly pervasive ST knowledge is guaranteed to propel the best in class in a few logical commands.

2.2.10.1   Utilizations of Spatial and Temporal Data Mining

Enormous volumes of ST information are gathered in a few application spaces, for example, online media, medical care, farming, transportation, and atmosphere science. In this segment, we quickly portray the various wellsprings of ST information and the inspiration for breaking down ST information in various application spaces.

a) *Atmosphere Science:* Remarkable and strong natural and aquatic factors (e.g., temperature, heat, wind, and humidity) are gathered and concentrated in atmospheric science [52]. Despite observational information 1 from climate stations and space-grided dataset data [53], replicated knowledge provided using environmental models [54] is also concentrated in this room. The purpose of analyzing this knowledge is to give references and instances in atmospheric science that progress our understanding of the Earth's environment and allow us to better prepare for potential hostile circumstances by recommending variance, moreover, promptly.

b) *Neuroscience:* For example, functional magnetic resonance imaging (fMRI), electroencephalogram (EEG), and magneto-encephalography (MEG) are concentrated in neuroscience [55]. The approximately spatial target of neural activity using these technologies is not the same as another. For example, neural action is estimated from a large number of areas in fMRI information, whereas it is measured from several areas due to EEG information. The worldly goal of the Information gathered utilizing these advancements is additionally very extraordinary. For instance, fMRI regularly gauges movement for like clockwork, while the fleeting goal of EEG information is commonly 1 ms. The reason for examining this Information is to comprehend the administering standards of the mind and subsequently decide the interruptions to typical conditions that emerge on account of mental issues [56]. Finding such disruptions can aid in the preparation of therapeutic procedures and the development of patient care strategies.

c) *Ecological Knowledge:* Analyzing data about climate, water, and the environment is one of the ecological science destinations. Although air quality is estimated to be dependent on the proximity of pollutants, such as particulate matter, carbon monoxide, nitrogen dioxide, sulfur dioxide, ozone, and so on, water quality is expected to be dependent on elements such as broken down oxygen, conductivity, turbidity, and PH. Air quality sensors are typically placed on lanes or at the head of buildings, and water quality sensors are installed in lakes. Notwithstanding the safety of air and water, Information on sound pollution is also collected. These natural information indexes are focused on identifying changes in the levels of contamination, discerning the causal elements that contribute to the contamination, and organizing effective approaches [57] to reduce the different forms of radioactivity.

d) *Crop Monitoring:* wide-frequency high-goal (attempting to run between 0.25 and 1 m) areal or satellite data pictures of huge homes are taken on regular stretches (e.g., week after week). One of the reasons behind collecting and considering this knowledge is to differentiate between plant ailments [58] and the impact of a few variables, for example, misinterpretation of compost, soil erosion during cultivating, and weeds on crop yield, as well as their interconnections. With this Information, steps can be taken in future yield cycles to alleviate the dangers due to the elements that adversely affect crop yields.

e) *The study of disease transmission/Health care:* Electronic wellbeing record information that is generally put away in emergency clinics gives segment data relating to patients also determination made on patients at various time focuses. This dataset can be spoken to as a spatial-fleeting dataset where every determination has a spatial area and a period point related to it. One can build such spatiotemporal cases for various kinds of ailments, for example, malignancies and diabetes, just as for irresistible sicknesses, for example, flu. This Information is concentrated to find spatial-transient examples in various illnesses [59] and examining the spread of a scourge. This Information is additionally utilized related to natural, atmosphere science informational collections to find connections between ecological components and general wellbeing [60]. The revelation of such connections will permit strategy producers to create successful approaches that will guarantee the prosperity of the populace.

f) *Web-based media:* Web-based media entry users, e.g., Twitter and Facebook, post their engagement with a given place and time. Each web-based content post captures a client's experience at a time and location. Using this Data, one may consider cumulative user engagement with a given spot for a given period [61]. One may also capture the spreading of pestilence, e.g., influenza or Ebola, depending on customer messages. Moreover, there is increased enthusiasm for the dissemination of social and political trends using online media knowledge [62]. Occurrences, including tremors, waves, and flames, can also be detected from this knowledge.

g) *Traffic Dynamics:* Large-scale shuttle finds/drop-off information is freely available to several large urban populations worldwide [63]. This Information includes details on each taxi administration customer excursion, including time and area of getting and drop-off, and GPS areas for each second during the taxi trip. This knowledge can be used to see how a city's population shifts spatially as a portion of time and the effect of indirect variables such as traffic and climate. Moreover, this knowledge can also be optimized to examine traffic elements based on taxicabs' aggregate growth instances. This will enable transport architects to plan effective gridlock approaches. Furthermore, the behavior of taxi drivers can also be investigated using this knowledge so that effective procedures can be aimed at identifying irregular behavior, increasing the likelihood of attracting new travelers, and taking an ideal course for a target.

h) *Heliophysics:* Heliophysics discusses the Sun's moments and their influence on the Solar System. The publicly available Heliophysics Occurrences electrical potential [64] offers various definitions of sun-oriented occasions and their feedback for a coherent scheme. These occasions' models include Active Local, Evolving Transformation, Filament, Flare, Sigmoid, and Sunspot. Additionally, the time and area where these occasions were seen on the Sun are given in the knowledge base. Spatial and worldly details are combined alongside different expectations to find designs on sun-oriented occasions. Also, the Heliophysics knowledge base empowers analysis of the impact of sun-powered occasions and the Earth's atmosphere structure. False Information: law enforcement offices store data on exposed breaches in various urban areas, and this Data is freely available in the open-information soul [65]. This Information generally has the kind of wrongdoing (e.g., pyromania, assault, theft, burglary, robbery, and defacement), just as the wrongdoing time and region. Examples of wrongdoing and the effect of law enforcement policies on assessing misconduct in a community may be seen using this evidence to minimize negligence.

2.3   Research Method

The vitality utilization of structures depends not just on the deterministic angles, for example, building material science and plan of HVAC frameworks, yet additionally on the stochastic perspectives, for example, inhabitants' conduct. In any case, so far, the inhabitant's practices have not been displayed enough. Therefore, field test contemplates have demonstrated disparities among genuine and reenacted execution of building. On the outskirts of clever structure research, one of the most significant highlights that could demonstrate a structure to be 'savvy' is powerful communication with its tenants [66]. With a superior comprehension of individuals' standards of conduct, the structure control framework could create custom-made methodologies for its tenants. Along these lines, it is basic to comprehend tenants' conduct and their inspiration from genuine records are represented in Figure 2.9.

It depicts by and large in what capacity will the information 'stream' all through the entire cycle and characterizes the fundamental squares and their functionalities. Right off the bat, the related dataset was extricated from the checking program information base, including climate information, indoor condition information, and tenant conduct records. After fundamental information cleaning and planning, the calculated relapse

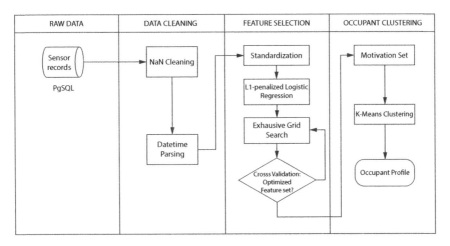

| RAW DATA | DATA CLEANING | FEATURE SELECTION | OCCUPANT CLUSTERING |

Figure 2.9 Shows the schematic outline of the information mining-based strategy.

model was then prepared to discover the inspiration blend. At last, the inspiration sets from various individuals were looked at and gathered into a few tenant profiles. To discover the motivation behind why individuals change ventilation could be viewed as an element determination question from the viewpoint of information mining. Numerically, it's conceivable to assemble a model to foresee individuals' conduct under a specific condition and afterward quantitatively assess the significance of each component. L1-regularized calculated relapse is a hearty answer for this reason by training. Up to the network level, contrasting various examples and gathering ones and likenesses is called grouping in the information mining area. This sort of calculations, for example, broadly utilized K-implies, could gather various examples into a few bunches with the best improved in-group closeness and between bunch distinction. In the accompanying of this segment, the strategy referenced will be quickly presented. Calculated relapse, regardless of its name, is a straight model for the arrangement as opposed to relapse. It is likewise referred to in writing as logit relapse, most extreme entropy characterization (MaxEnt), or the log-direct classifier. This is a standard direct relapse formula

$$h_\theta(x) = \theta^t x \qquad (2.1)$$

where x is a progression of highlights, it is a vector containing coefficients for each component and speaks to the relapse result. While in strategic relapse, since we need to do a grouping rather than relapse, the direct relapse condition is fitted into a sigmoid capacity

$$g(z) = \frac{1}{1+e^{-z}} \qquad (2.2)$$

Finally, the condition of calculated relapse becomes

$$h_\theta(x) = \frac{1}{1+e^{-\theta^t x}} \qquad (2.3)$$

The capacity is plotted in Figure 2.10. It could be seen that the scope of calculated relapse yield is somewhere in the range of 0 and 1. A limit, say 0.5, could be picked to isolate two distinct classifications (for example, whenever output <0.50, anticipate the case to be in class 0, else foresee classification 1). In the wake of preparing with the dataset, which planned for finding improved θ to limit the cost work, the model is acclimated to limit the expectation mistake dependent on the preparation set and the coefficients of each component.

$$J(\theta) = -\frac{1}{m} \sum_{i=1}^{m} y^i \log(h_\theta x^\theta) + (1-y^i)\log(1-h_\theta x^i) \qquad (2.4)$$

Depending on its direct existence, the function of each variable in a planned, measured regression model is utilized to determine its importance.

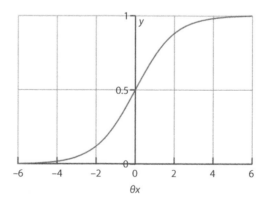

Figure 2.10 Calculated regression output.

Most counterpart experts have accepted the sufficiency, extensibility, and heartfeltness of this technique; however, in this role, the operational regression component used is with L1-standard regularisation, which means an additional punishment element arising from the L1-st. The model runs over and over λ to render a matrix scan. At last stops at the boundary blend, which gives the highest approval accuracy,

$$J(\theta) = -\frac{1}{m}\sum_{i=1}^{m} y^i \log(h_\theta x^\theta) + (1 - y^i)\log(1 - h_\theta x^i) + \sum_{i=1}^{n} |\vartheta_i|$$

$$(2.5)$$

As direct model punished with the L1 standard will, in general, give inadequate arrangements. For example, a large number of its assessed coefficients would be zero. Subsequently, it will make the element choice more critical has become one of the least intrusive equations in independent learning, able to take care of the grouping problem with great usability. It plans to parcel n perceptions into k bunches where each perspective does have the nearest mean only with the group. The category allocations with high market share-bunch similarity and lower academic consistency would be considered an appropriate performance. In particular, measurement gives a similar method to bundle a specified data index through several classes. The fundamental concept is to initially classify k centroids, one for each group, which should be placed in a crafty manner because distinctive area causes diverse outcomes. The next stage is to bring each specific to an available data set and match it to the nearest centroid. Since no point arrives, the initial phase is stopped and an early gathering is done. Now we have to re-evaluate k new centroids as the knowledge guide's barycenter getting a position to a particular bunch due to past advances. Since we have these new centroids, another pairing between similar knowledge collection focuses and the closest new centroid should be possible. The circle was formed so far. As a result of this circle, we can see that the centroids change their area bit by bit until no change. At the end of the day, centroids pass nothing else after several circles. Finally, this estimate aims to restrict the target function, a square blunder function for this situation.

$$J = \sum_{i=1}^{k} \sum_{i=1}^{n} \left\| x_i^j - c_j \right\|^2 \qquad (2.6)$$

where $\left\| x_i^j - c_j \right\|^2$ is the picked separation measure amongst an information point and the group place it has a place with. For this situation, we pick

Euclidean separation as the separation measure technique. In this examination, the K-implies bunching is utilized to aggregate inhabitants from 10 unique houses into a few kinds. This methodology has been approved likewise via the exploration commencing.

2.4   Results

The method is developed to predict how much a development/decrease adjustment will occur based on input factors such as time and inner situation. In the time leading up to measurement, the planning set was standardized, meaning that all highlights are rescaled to zero mean and unit-fluctuation dispersions. At that point, the dataset is cared for in an L1-punished strategic relapse classifier, which will streamline the cost capacity to predict the response of residents in a particular situation. As the portion scale is normalized, the prepared straight model coefficient may show the overall meaning of the compared element. For example, Figure 2.11 Indicates the importance of each trigger factor for tenant No. 1, with the model being 86% inter-approved.

It could be seen that the less instructive highlights for this inhabitant were sifted through with zero coefficients, while the remaining shows the indoor CO_2 focus and dampness are the most significant inspirational drivers for this tenant to change the ventilation stream rate. By this

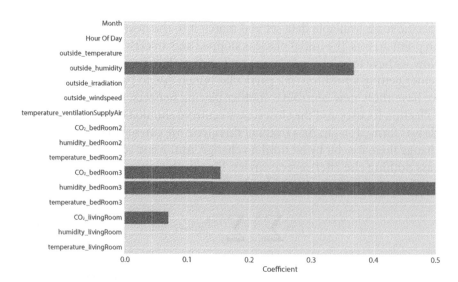

Figure 2.11 Highlight significance yield.

methodology, the primary driver for inhabitant No. 1 to alter ventilation flowrate is distinguished.

2.5   Discussion

Learning identical models for each tenant could reveal the individual level's fundamental motivating led components. Nevertheless, it may be common for different individuals to have different inclinations and not to carry on likewise. Subsequently, expanded to a network level, a bunching investigation might gather inhabitants into a few designs of trigger behavior. The most educational list of capabilities, with its coefficients, is omitted from the yield of the measured relapse model. All the key-driven elements fall into two classifications: time-related components including month, non-weekend day/weekend, hour-day data, and condition-related variables including indoor temperature, relative humidity, CO_2 emphasis, and outside climate information. According to these two measures and with essential resizing, Figure 2.12 may address the tenants involved in the study. The flat hub speaks to the significance of indoor condition factors

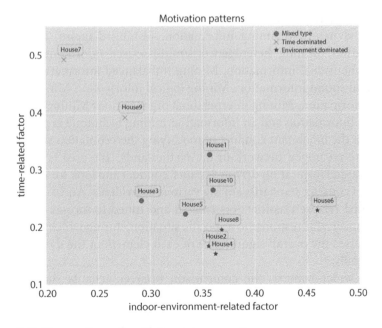

Figure 2.12 Cause patterns of ventilation system operations.

in determining the actions of tenants, while the vertical hub speaks to the significance of time-related factors.

K-Means calculation shows three distinct kinds of tenants:

- Indoor condition touchy inhabitants (plotted in star): 2, 4, 6, 8
- Time delicate tenants (plotted in the cross): 7, 9
- Mixed sort inhabitants (plotted in specks): 1, 3, 5, 10.

The unpredictability of inhabitants' conduct cause example could be seen from the information mining results. The Indoor condition touchy tenants are bound to cooperate with their ventilation control board when they feel somewhat unsatisfied about the indoor solace, while the time-delicate inhabitants are bound to carry on with fixed schedules (e.g., when they wake up or return from work and so forth, they modify the ventilation). There are likewise a few people in the middle of, as blended kind tenants, their practices are affected impressively by the two elements in a similar time.

2.6   Conclusion

In this chapter, we considered the expected properties of Data mining like Mining dynamic/streaming information, Mining diagram, and system information, Mining heterogeneous/multi-source information, Mining high dimensional information, Mining imbalanced information, Mining sight and sound Information, Mining logical information Mining consecutive information, Mining interpersonal organizations Mining spatial and fleeting Information and an information mining technique is proposed to examine the inhabitant conduct of modifying the ventilation stream in an as of late revamped network in the Netherlands. The goal is to uncover the shrouded inspiration driving tenants' conduct and look for conceivable personal conduct standards among various individuals. An L1-regularized calculated relapse classifier was created and tuned to foresee the inhabitant's conceivable response to a specific situation, during which it additionally assesses the overall significance of each element in the dynamic cycle numerically.

In a wider context, the comparison between tenants showed three impressive inspiring examples. To be particular the earth-driven sort, contrasting the tenants who are more touchy to the ecological variables, the time-driven sort corresponds to the occupants who have relatively set temporal tendencies, just like the occupants of the merged kind, whose behavior is far more unpredictable with no single tendency design that is clear on the situation and transient aspects.

The information-based strategy to explore tenants' conduct presented in this investigation empowers additional opportunity to use the BMS information. The taking in drawn from the investigation could be utilized either to display individuals' conduct all the more unequivocally in the structure reproduction program just as to add to the improvement of the insightful structure. Additionally, other than the customary ways to deal with exploring individuals' conduct by directing a study or meeting, the algorithmic technique is more strong with less man-made aggravations.

References

1. Babcock, B., Babu, S., Datar, M., Motwani, R., Widom, J., Models and issues in data stream systems, in: *Proceedings of PODS*, 2002.
2. Golab, L. and Ozsu, M.T., Issues in Data Stream Management. *SIGMOD Rec.*, 32, 2, 5–14, June 2003.
3. Henzinger, M., Raghavan, P., Rajagopalan, S., Computing on data streams. Technical Note 1998-011, Digital Systems Research Center, Palo Alto, CA, May 1998.
4. Muthukrishnan, S., Data streams: Algorithms and applications. *Proceedings of the Fourteenth Annual ACM-SIAM Symposium on Discrete Algorithms*, 2003.
5. Muthukrishnan, S., *Seminar on Processing Massive Data Sets*, Available Online: http://athos.rutgers.edu/%7Emuthu/stream-seminar.html, 2003.
6. Garofalakis, M., Gehrke, J., Rastogi, R., Querying and mining data streams: You only get one look a tutorial. *SIGMOD Conference 2002*, p. 635, 2002.
7. Kargupta, H., CAREER: Ubiquitous Distributed Knowledge Discovery from Heterogeneous Data. *NSF Information and Data Management (IDM) Workshop*, 2001.
8. Muthukrishnan, S., Data streams: Algorithms and applications. *Proceedings of the Fourteenth Annual ACM-SIAM Symposium on Discrete Algorithms*, 2003.
9. Pinto, H., Han, J., Pei, J., Wang, K., Chen, Q., Dayal, U., Multidimensional sequential pattern mining, in: *Proceedings of the Tenth International Conference on Information and Knowledge Management*, ACM, pp. 81–88, 2001.
10. Mabroukeh, N.R. and Ezeife, C.I., A taxonomy of sequential pattern mining algorithms. *ACM Comput. Surv. (CSUR)*, 43, 1, 3, 2010.
11. Garofalakis, M.N., Rastogi, R., Shim, K., Spirit: Sequential pattern mining with regular expression constraints, in: *VLDB*, vol. 99, pp. 7–10, 1999.

12. Agrawal, R. and Srikant, R., Mining sequential patterns, in: *Data Engineering, 1995. Proceedings of the Eleventh International Conference*, IEEE, pp. 3–14, 1995.
13. Echo, E., Raïssi, C., Ienco, D., Jay, N., Napoli, A., Poncelet, P., Quantin, C., Teisseire, M., Healthcare trajectory mining by combining multidimensional components and itemsets, in: *International Workshop on New Frontiers in Mining Complex Patterns*, Springer, pp. 109–123, 2012.
14. Yu, C.-C. and Chen, Y.-L., Mining sequential patterns from multidimensional sequence data. *IEEE Trans. Knowl. Data Eng.*, 17, 1, 136–140, 2005.
15. Raïssi, C. and Plantevit, M., Mining multidimensional sequential patterns over data streams, in: *International Conference on Data Warehousing and Knowledge Discovery*, Springer, pp. 263–272, 2008.
16. Padhy, N. and Panigrahi, R., Multi relational data mining approaches A data mining technique. International Journal of Computer Applications (0975 – 8887) Volume 57– No.17, pp. 23-32, November 2012, arXiv preprint arXiv:1211.3871, 2012.
17. Džeroski, S., Multi-relational data mining: An introduction. *ACM SIGKDD Explor. Newsl.*, 5, 1, 1–16, 2003.
18. Paulheim, H., Exploiting linked open data as background knowledge in data mining. *DMoLD*, vol. 1082, 2013.
19. Siebes, A. and Struzik, Z., Complex data: Mining using patterns, in: *Pattern Detection and Discovery*, pp. 24–35, Springer, Berlin, 2002.
20. Fahed, L., Brun, A., Boyer, A., Extraction de règles d'épisodes minimales dans des séquences complexes. *EGC*, pp. 545–548, 2014.
21. Wu, C.-W., Lin, Y.-F., Yu, P.S., Tseng, V.S., Mining high utility episodes in complex event sequences, in: *Proceedings of the 19th ACM SIGKDD International Conference on Knowledge Discovery and Data Mining*, ACM, pp. 536–544, 2013.
22. Huang, K.-Y. and Chang, C.-H., Efficient mining of frequent episodes from complex sequences. *Inf. Syst.*, 33, 1, 96–114, 2008.
23. Beyer, K., Goldstein, J., Ramakrishan, R., Shaft, U., When Is Nearest Neighbor Meaningful? *Proc. of the 7th International Conference on Database Theory*, pp. 217–235, 1999.
24. Liu, H. and Yu, L., Toward Integrating Feature Selection Algorithms for Classification and Clustering. *IEEE Trans. Knowl. Data Eng.*, 17, 3, 1–12, 2005.
25. Raja, R., Sinha, T.S., Dubey, R.P., Soft Computing and LGXP Techniques for Ear Authentication using Progressive Switching Pattern. *Int. J. Eng. Future Technol.*, 2, 2, 66–86, 2016.
26. Raja, R., Sinha, T.S., Dubey, R.P., Orientation Calculation of human Face Using Symbolic techniques and ANFIS. *Int. J. Eng. Future Technol.*, 7, 7, 37–50, 2016.

27. Cohena, G., Hilariob, M., Saxc, H., Hugonnetc, S., Geissbuhler, A., Learning from imbalanced data in surveillance of nosocomial infection. *Intell. Data Anal. Med.*, 37, 1, 7–18, 2006.

28. Czyzewski, Mining Knowledge in Noisy Audio Data, in: *Proc. 2nd Int. Conf. on KD and Data Mining*, pp. 220–225, 1996.

29. Wang, D., Kim, Y.-S., Park, S.C., Lee, C.S., Han, Y.K., Learning-Based Neural Similarity Metrics for Multimedia Data Mining. *Soft Comput.*, 11, 4, 335–340, February 2007.

30. Chien, S., Fisher, F., Mortensen, H., Lo, E., Greeley, R., Using Artificial Intelligence Planning to Automate Science Data Analysis for Large Image Databases, in: *Proc. 3rd Int. Conf. on Knowledge Discovery and Data Mining*, pp. 147–150, 1997.

31. Zaïane, O.R., Han, J., Li, Z.-N., Chee, S.H., Chiang, J.Y., MultiMediaMiner: A System Prototype for MultiMedia Data Mining, in: *Intelligent Database Systems Research Laboratory and Vision and Media Laboratory report*, 2009.

32. Witten, I.H., Text mining, in: *Computer Science*, University of Waikato, Hamilton, New Zealand, 2005.

33. Ordenoz, C. and Omiecinski, E., Discovering association rules based on image content, in: *ADL '99: Proceedings of the IEEE Forum on Research and Technology Advances in Digital libraries*, IEEE Computer Society, Washington, DC, p. 38, 1999.

34. Vijayakumar, V. and Nedunchezhian, R., A study on video data mining. *Int. J. Multimed. I Inf. Retr.*, 1, 3, 153–172, Publisher Springer-Verlag, October 2012.

35. Brunner, R.J., Djorgovski, S.G., Prince, T.A., Szalay, A.S., Massive Datasets in Astronomy, in: *Handbook of Massive Datasets*, J. Abello, P. Pardalos, M. Resende, (Eds.), p. 931, Kluwer Academic Publishers, New York, 2002.

36. NASA, *Science Data Users Handbook*, Landsat Project Science Office. Goddard Space Flight Center, Greenbelt, 2002.

37. NASA, *EOS Reference Handbook, A Guide to NASA's Earth Science Enterprise and the Earth Observing System*, EOS project science office, Greenbelt, 1999.

38. Vucetic, S., Fiez, T., Obradovic, Z., Analyzing the Influence of Data Aggregation and Sampling Density on Spatial Estimation. *Water Resour. Res.*, 36, 12, 3721–3731, 2000.

39. Han, J., Altman, R.B., Kumar, V., Mannila, H., Pregibon, D., Emerging Scientific Applications in Data Mining. *Commun. ACM*, 45, 8, 54–58, 2002.

40. Brown, M.P.S., Grundy, W.N., Lin, D., Cristianini, N., Sugnet, C.W., Furey, T.S., Ares Jr., M., Haussler, D., Knowledge-based Analysis of Microarray Gene Expression Data By Using Support Vector Machines. *Proc. Natl. Acad. Sci.*, 97, 262–267, 2000.

41. Barrett, E.C. and Curtis, F.L., *Introduction to Environmental Remote Sensing*, Stanley Thornes Pub. Ltd, Cheltenham, UK, 1999.

42. Kar, K. and Raja, R., A Review on Weather Prediction using Data Mining Techniques. *International Conference on New Frontiers of Engineering Science,*

Management and Humanities (ICNFESMH-2017) Associated with national Institute of Technical Teachers Training and Research Program (NITTTR), 21 May 2019.

43. Kar, K., Raja, R., Chopra, J., Extreme Weather Event Change Prediction using CDF. *International Conference on Advancement in Engineering, Applied Science and Management (ICAEASM-2017) at Centre for Development of Advanced Computing (C-DAC)*, Juhu, Mumbai, Maharashtra (India), pp. 448–452.

44. Nogues-Paegle, J., Mo, K., Paegle, J., Predictability of the NCEP-NCAR Reanalysis Model During Austral Summer. *Mon. Weather Rev.*, 126, 3135–3152, 1998.

45. Kamath, C., Introduction to scientific data mining. *Presented at Mathematical Challenges in Scientific Data Mining, Short Program at Institute for Pure and Applied Mathematics*, Univ. of California Los Angeles, 2002.

46. Pallavi, S., Ramya laxmi, K., Ramya, N., Study and Analysis of Modified Mean Shift Method and Kalman Filter for Moving object Detection and Tracking, in: *3rd International Conference on Computational Intelligence and Informatics (ICCII-2018)*, held during 28–29 Dec 2018, 2018.

47. Burl, M., Kamatch, C., Kumar, V., Namburu, R., *Third Workshop on Mining Scientific Datasets. First SIAM Int'l Conf. Data Mining*, Chicago, IL, 2001.

48. Kumar, V., Burl, M., Kamatch, C., Namburu, R., *Fifth Workshop on Mining Scientific Datasets, Second SIAM Int'l. Conf. Data Mining*, Arlignton, VA, 2002.

49. Grossman, R.L., Creel, E., Harinath, S., Mazzucco, M., Reinhart, G., Turinskiy, A., Terabyte Challenge 2000: Project DataSpace. *Workshop on Mining Scientific Datasets*, University of Minnesota, Minneapolis, MN, 2000.

50. Kumar, S., Jain, A., Shukla, A.P., Singh, S., Rani, S., A Comparative Analysis of Machine Learning Algorithms for Detection of Organic and Non-Organic Cotton Diseases. *Math. Probl. Eng., Special Issue—Deep Transfer Learning Models for Complex Multimedia Applications*, vol. 1, pp. 1–18, 2021.

51. Lazarevic, A. and Obradovic, Z., Knowledge Discovery in Multiple Spatial Databases. *Neural Comput. Appl.*, 10, 4, 339–350, 2002.

52. Roddick, J.F. and Spiliopoulou, M., A Bibliography of Temporal, Spatial, and Spatio-Temporal Data Mining Research. *SIGKDD Explor.*, 1, 34–38, 1999.

53. Han, J., Altman, R.B., Kumar, V., Mannila, H., Pregibon, D., Emerging Scientific Applications in Data Mining. *Commun. ACM*, 45, 8, 54–58, 2002.

54. Niyogi, P., Girosi, F., Poggio, T., Incorporating Prior Information in Machine Learning by Creating Virtual Examples. *Proc. IEEE*, 86, 11, 2196–2209, 1998.

55. Domingos, P. and Hulten, G., Mining High-Speed Data Streams. *Knowl. Discovery Data Min.*, 2, 71–80, 2000.

56. Pokrajac, D., Hoskinson, R.L., Obradovic, Z., Modeling spatiotemporal Data with a Short Observation History. *Knowl. Inf. Syst.*, 5, pp. 368–386, 2003.

57. Hall, D. and Llinas, J., *Handbook of Multisensor Data Fusion*, CRC Press, Boca Raton, 2001.

58. Lester, H. and Arridge, S.R., A Survey of Hierarchical Non-Linear Medical Image Registration. *Pattern Recognit.*, 32, 129–149, 1999.

59. Calì, D., Andersen, R.K., Müller, D., Olesen, B.W., Analysis of occupants' behavior related to the use of windows in German households. *Energy Build.*, 103, 54–69, 2016.

60. Andersen, R.V., Olesen, B.W., Toftum, J., Modeling window opening behavior in Danish dwellings. *Proceedings of Indoor Air*, 2011.

61. Sahu, A.K., Sharma, S., Tanveer, M., Internet of Things attack detection using hybrid. Deep Learning Model. *Comput. Commun.*, 176, 146–154, 2021, https://doi.org/10.1016/j.comcom.2021.05.024.

62. Mahmood, M.R., Patra, R.K., Raja, R., Sinha, G.R., A Novel Approach for Weather prediction using forecasting analysis and Data Mining Techniques, in: *7th International Conference on Innovations in Computer Science and Engineering*, 27–28 July 2018.

63. Shi, S. and Zhao, B., Occupants' interactions with windows in 8 residential apartments in Beijing and Nanjing, China. *Build. Simul.-China.* Tsinghua University Press, 9, 2, pp. 221–231, 2016.

64. D'Oca, and Hong, T., A data-mining approach to discover patterns of the window opening and closing behavior in offices. *Build. Environ.*, 82, 726–739, 2014.

65. Dodge, Y., *Statistical data analysis is based on the L1-norm and related methods*, Birkhäuser, Berlin, 2012.

66. Moore, *K-means and Hierarchical Clustering—Tutorial Slides*, School of Computer Science. Carnegie Mellon University, 2007.

3

A Comparative Overview of Hybrid Recommender Systems: Review, Challenges, and Prospects

Rakhi Seth* and Aakanksha Sharaff

National Institute of Technology Raipur, Chhattisgarh, India

Abstract

Recommender System (RS) helps to find the items according to user interest and provides various suggestions that help in the decision-making process. These suggestions depend on distinct recommendation techniques. These approaches are divided into different categories like Collaborative, Content, Demographic, Utility, Knowledge-based, and Hybrid. Collaborative RS works on the concept of "people to people co-relation". Content-Based RS suggests the idea of recommendation in which next item for a user is similar to the item that user like in the past. Demographic RS categorized the attributes based on the demographics of the user or item and make recommendations based on these demographics classes. Utility-based RS is a concept which depends on the estimation of the utility for a user for each item by using a specific utility function. Knowledge-Based RS works on "a particular user needs that how it meets with the item". Hybrid RS is a combination of two or more recommendation strategies in a distinguished way to create a better and more personalized experience for the individual user like one of the recent study suggested the novel approach of solving sentimental issues faced in recommendation system by combining the two models of collaborative filtering i.e., by taking the rating score from memory-based and tagging (vital role in describing user feelings using Matrix Factorization (MF)) approach from model-based. So our objective is to find out how the hybrid approach is better and also understand the different types of solutions using the hybrid recommender systems and demonstrating new challenges and future scope of the hybrid system. The basic and widely discussed problem of the traditional RS technique is cold start problem and the problems associated with demographics, the utility is also

*Corresponding author: rakhisethcsit1990@gmail.com

Rohit Raja, Kapil Kumar Nagwanshi, Sandeep Kumar and K. Ramya Laxmi (eds.) Data Mining and Machine Learning Applications, (57–98) © 2022 Scrivener Publishing LLC

considered for the study and how the Hybrid based approach is used to analyze and solve these problems.

Keywords: Recommender system, matrix factorization, root mean square, mean absolute error

3.1   Introduction

Initially, recommendation plays a supporting role but with time as the internet grows, more and more people ask queries through the internet and the evolution of the recommender system has done. In this evolution process, various types of recommendation techniques are introduced in different fields like medicine, movies, music, e-commerce based recommendation, and many others.

A conversational RS [1] is one of the approaches described as a more one-to-one user preference got attention at the time of conversation and become a more personalized one for each user. In this paper [1] the RS provides the differential diagnosis to schizophrenia, schizoaffective and bipolar diseases by using fuzzy implications. In Health care, there is not only the conversational RS that is useful but also the web page RS is very helpful for those users who have any previous record and on that basis, they want to take suggestion from the internet but the problem is that the recommended data is in a very scattered way [2] so researcher suggests the new idea of Web Page based RS for web pages in one place provided to patients so that patient get very precise and related information regarding his/her disease.

Sentiment Analysis is one of the fields that is also explored in RS; we need to understand that in RS each review that a user provides connects to some emotions either positive or negative. So from the text we need to understand the sentiment of the user [3]. The authors propose the model called a stochastic model of HMM (Hidden Markow Model) for the customer reviews that come in various marketing portal like Amazon, Flipkart and others. Through this, the author achieves the higher precision and accuracy of analyzing the sentiment of the customer in reviews. Now there is another type of recommendation system which is built on trust. Trust is one of the major issues or aspects of interaction with the user [4]. So for achieving this goal, the researcher built the system which not only works on privacy but also sees the multi-dimension reputation of the user like what contribution as well as what are the social link and rating among similar users.

There are several recommendations that are provided when one visits a web portal for a specific item like carwale, cardekho, OLx, and magicbricks. All these are examples of how interactive and advanced this system works. Now the question arises as to how this recommendation system works. For that we need to understand the evolution of RS [5]. The recommender systems are categorized into three generations: basic one, knowledge-based one, and Sentiment or emotion-based recommender systems have been developed. As evolution has been done in three different generations we can understand it through Figure 3.1.

The recommender system belongs to the domain of Data Mining which is used to store and manipulate data. Different methods are used in data mining for processing the dataset and valuable information. One can understand how the recommender system works from Figure 3.2. First, Data, which is meaningful information, is collected from the legal source, and then pre-processing starts in which cleaning of that data has been done by removing the noisy redundant data and making the information clear and useful for further work.

The next step is model learning which means to classify according to the dataset and how one wants to see the model working in the real-world as well as according to challenges one is finding in the existing model. There are many aspects of model learning in which different testing and verification strategies are applied. In classification, there are some issues related to the classification that is discussed [6] in this paper, the authors focus on one of the issues of dodging spam filters by spamming. When a high dimensionality of email is sent or received then the main challenge is to train the classifier in a way that prediction may not be compromised and the author gives the solution for this type of classification. The last step is

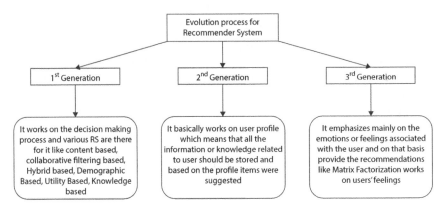

Figure 3.1 Evolution process of RS.

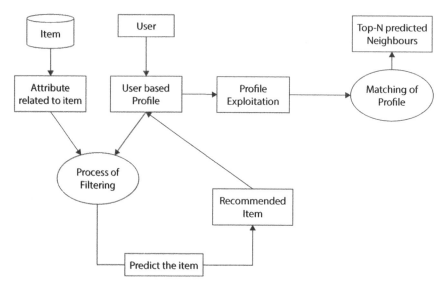

Figure 3.2 Recommender systems.

testing and validation in which RMSE and MAE are the evaluation measures that evaluate which RS gives the best result between the predicted and measured interest.

3.2 Related Work on Different Recommender System

The RS are classified into six different types and the working of all the approaches is different from one another. The types are as follows:

Collaborative Filtering: CF is an automatic filtering technique used for prediction. It means that recommendation for any user (as per his/her interest criteria) is done through preferring the ratings of many users who rate similar items. CF works on recommendations that focus on user liking about the item and then finds the pattern and rating for each item and then classified according to user interest.

For example: If user X1 likes item Y1, Y2, and Y3.

If user X2 likes item Y1, Y3, Y4

If user X3 likes item Y1?

So there are higher chances that person X3 gets a recommendation for an item liked by X1 and X2.

When we talk about CF then we have two models: one is memory-based, which is also known as neighborhood filtering, user-item rating which is directly used to predict the new-items. It works on similarity measures such as cosine similarity and correlation coefficient. But there is a problem in the [7] technique is that the rating is not uniform and some user ratings are stringent and some are lenient. So how do we suggest the items to a set of users who are stringent and to predict the rating values for each user. The authors provide the solution for it by an algorithm called NCFR (Normalization based Collaborative filtering) which finds the average user per item and does the user count then normalize it with min–max normalization.

The other one is model-based CF, which works on learning the predictive model by using rating as input; for modeling a parameter the characteristics of user and item are used. In this paper [8] the authors discuss this CF in phases, the first one is a factorization-based model and the other is a NN (neural network) based model.

Content-Based (CBRS): This method is based on the profile of different users as well as different items. First CBRS matches basic data of the user with all similar items rated and if not then bases on the profile of the items that are recommended [9]. It follows certain steps as given below:

    a. *Content Analyzer:* It is used at the initial step when there is no structure and we need only relevant data so pre-processing is done and only data items can be used when important features are extracted. It works as input for profile learners and filtering components.

    b. *Profile learner:* In this step, the user profile is created by taking preference data and tries to generalize those data, for example feedback-based recommender system, in which positive and negative feedbacks could be learned and according to that recommendation that the user makes.

    c. *Filtering Component:* Here the matching item related to the item list will be found out and this will be done by calculating cosine similarity between the item and prototype vector. Through a diagrammatic view, we understand its working process better.

When we talk about RS data it is one of the major focuses and creates a problem too because maintenance and cleaning the data is not an easy task. The most important thing is how one will retrieve the data as per the user interest or preferences [10] The authors give the solution through the method which uses POS-taggers to format the dataset. By using the NLTK (Natural language processing kit) framework taggers it is not the first time to be used by anyone as it has been used many times like in blogs, Facebook, and Instagram for categorizing the data and making the search easy for the user.

Demographic Recommender System (DRS): It works on the demographic profiles of the user as we can see in Figure 3.3. Now what does the demographic mean. It means that it works on a different attribute like age, gender, occupation for recommendation purposes. Half-trusted means third parties use this technique for recommendation purposes on individual users. It also solves the problem of cold start and it works on the concept of "People to People" correlation but uses dissimilar data. In [11] the author gives an idea for developing more personalized RS and provides a better fitting recommendation. Demographic approach is used in the music-based dataset. The author is proposing the feature modeling approach by using Term Frequency-Inverse Document Frequency (TF-IDF) for an

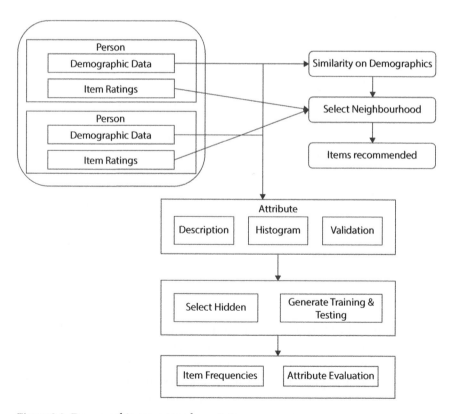

Figure 3.3 Demographic recommender systems.

artist based listening information as well as tags combined with extracted features (user-traits prediction).

Utility-Based Recommender System (UBRS): This RS works on the computation of utility to the user of each item as shown in Figure 3.4 but the problem is how to understand the utility of individual users. So the solution is the utility function which can be extracted from the rating of items and apply it to the objects [12]. Multi-attribute utility concept is a systematic as well as a quantitative method for utility-based RS which helps in decision making. There is one method called critiquing [13] defined as the method used in the Conversational recommender where the recommendation is based on the user preference feedback regarding item attributes and associated with constraint and utility-based methods. One implementation is in conversational RS [13] which combines the utility-based method with a deep learning framework and recommendation is done based on preference feedback regarding item attributes as well as constraint associated with it.

Knowledge-Based Recommender System (KBRS): KBRS uses knowledge about users and products to make recommendations in Figure 3.5. Using Knowledge acquisition means that acquired knowledge must be in some

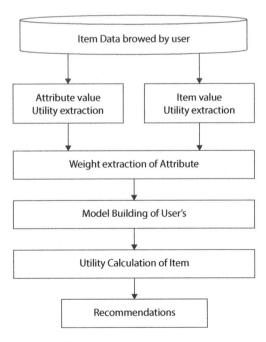

Figure 3.4 Utility recommender system.

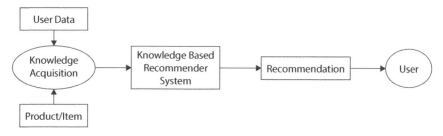

Figure 3.5 Knowledge-Based RS.

structured machine-readable form. Knowledge-based RS works on the definite realm of knowledge about how users' needs are met with items' features and generate preferences on how a particular item is appropriate to a particular user. In these, a similarity function estimates how much the user's needs match the recommendation. These identity or similarity scores can precisely be explained as the recommendation for the user. In recent years, as the author proposed [14] recommendation system which works with the knowledge graphs. It is a heterogeneous graph where node functions as entities and edge works as the relation among nodes. There are many KG based RS present which work better in real-time. One more problem is how we do the decision making in a Knowledge-based system [13]. Here the authors provide the idea of argumentation-based RS in which competing argument is the center of user's query answering process. This approach handles multiple arguments for understanding and improving the reasoning capabilities. In this paper, [15] provide the recommendation for higher education in which system saw the past publication, research interest, education background to generate the best scholarship plan for student as per the suitable faculty whose data is also maintained

Hybrid Recommender System: All the methods that we mentioned have their advantages and disadvantages so researchers adopted a new technique which results to two or more recommendation techniques as seen in Figure 3.6. Collaborative Filtering can't handle the new item problems. In content-based, this problem will be handled through item description so there are several ways of combining the basic RS technique to provide the new improved version of the recommendation technique. We saw in the above mentioned diagrams how two distinguished RS approach works; here we combine content and collaborative filtering and understands the more useful as well as advantageous approach. Here also deep learning is used [16] with the hybrid approach as a solution to the overfitting problem by installing the learning for user and items based on Latent-factors for non-linear data set. Reference [17]

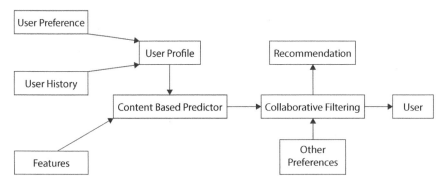

Figure 3.6 Hybrid recommender system.

proposed RS use the tagging feature for this semantically related tags which are extracted from the WordNet lexical database and then by using CF's the implicit rating is found out using similarity measures. In an online system [18] many influencers bribe the different users to change their ratings so that sellers' reputation may increase. Here the solution is provided by using a novel technique called matrix completion algorithm using hybrid memory-based collaborative filtering that uses an approximation of Kolmogorov complexity to be used for bribery resistance approach.

3.2.1   Challenges in RS

The recommender system faces many challenges [19, 20] that may affect the working of the system, and finding a solution for these challenges is the main task of research.

1. *Novelty:* When the user has no clear idea about items and is not known to the user or a new item is also used for the emotional replay of users towards the suggestion.
2. *Cold Start problem:* This problem is generated when a site has a new user and a new item then the first issue is how one would recommend items to the new user and as we don't know about the user interest. The second issue is new item is not rated yet so how we recommend this item to any user.
3. *Serendipity:* When RS accidentally suggests novel items that are unexpected but useful for users but the problem is that the quality of RS may suffer.
4. *Sparsity Problem:* This problem is generated when a large number of users focus on a few items and don't rate every item they buy as well as some items are always untouched.

5. *Scalability:* It measures the system's ability to work effectively when information grows with high performance.
6. *Over Specialization Problem:* Items recommended to the user are already known.
7. *Correctness:* It calculates or evaluates the degree to which how close the measured value is to each other. It gives truthfulness.
8. *Diversity:* It shows the correlation between the recommended items. It can be measured by using the objective difference. It answers the question "How unrelated are the suggested item".
9. *Stability:* It evaluates the level of consistency and reliability among the predictions made by the recommendation algorithm. It answers the question "How reliable is the system for making recommendations".
10. *Privacy:* It is one of the main concerns in RS because user data collected from different sources are in two forms: one is explicit and the other one is implicit and this dimension affects the scalability and accuracy. It answers the question "Is there any issue or hazard with the user privacy?".
11. *Gray Sheep:* It occurs when the opinion of the user doesn't fit with any group and as a result, the RS will not work for that user it happens in collaborative filtering.
12. *Usability:* It aims to provide a well-organized and effective recommendation that gives the result to some degree that satisfies the user and gives the answer to the question that "how functional is an RS?".
13. *User Preference:* It is a way through which one can monitor the choices and the items preferred which can discriminate from those that are not preferred. It simply means that users perception of the recommended approach.
14. *Shilling attack:* When any malicious user comes into the system and gives false ratings so that items get popular or decreasing the value of the item.

3.2.2   Research Questions and Architecture of This Paper

Based on our study we explore the following research questions not only this. In Table 3.1 we discuss the different filtering techniques and what the advantages and disadvantages are of each technique and also we provide the architecture of this paper in Figure 3.7.

Table 3.1 Show the advantage and disadvantage of different types of RS.

No.	Types	Advantage	Disadvantage
1	Collaborative Filtering	1. This filtering doesn't use the demographic for recommending the items. 2. There is a proper match between users and items. 3. This system recommends the items to the user outside their preferences.	1. The highest rating of any item in the dataset determines the quality. 2. One of the major problems seen in this recommendation system is the "Cold Start" problem that the system doesn't provide recommendations for new users.
2	Content-Based Recommender System	1. It uniquely characterizes each user profile. 2. The system can recommend a new user based on the similarity between item specifications.	1. For creating a recommendation list one needs to create all features of items which is one of the complex tasks. 2. In Content-based user-item rating is not included so one cannot determine the quality of the recommendation system.
3	Demographic Recommender System	1. It is based on the demographics of the user so without rating also recommends items.	1. One of the major issues is that every customer is not comfortable in sharing personal data as well as it's a privacy issue. 2. Stability vs. plasticity problem.
6	Utility-Based Recommender System	1. It works on utility function so it becomes closer to user interest 2. Prioritize the item.	1. How to find the utility of any user.

(Continued)

Table 3.1 Show the advantage and disadvantage of different types of RS. (*Continued*)

No.	Types	Advantage	Disadvantage
5	Knowledge-Based Recommender System	1. It provides qualitative preferences based on feedback. 2. It also handles the changes in preferences.	1. A knowledge database is required. 2. The suggestion ability is static.
4	Hybrid Recommender System	1. This approach mainly targets the advantage of one system and is used for other systems so by combining one get a better recommendation system. 2. Its main focus is a content-related description and user evaluation. 3. The Hybrid approach works on a specialized solution. 4. Improve customer satisfaction rates.	1. Early Rater problem for products. 2. Sparsity problem.

1. RQ1: Up to which level the existing individual approach like Collaborative filtering can provide recommender systems according to the users' best interest in the requested field.
2. RQ2: To what extent do existing algorithm handles the problem like cold start problem (like new users), data sparsity, scalability, diversity, and stability.
3. RQ3: How the hybrid approach comes into the role of overcoming the drawbacks of the existing algorithms based on a research perspective.

3.2.3   Background

There is a rapid increase of global research community on the recommender system findings and everyday new development is coming based

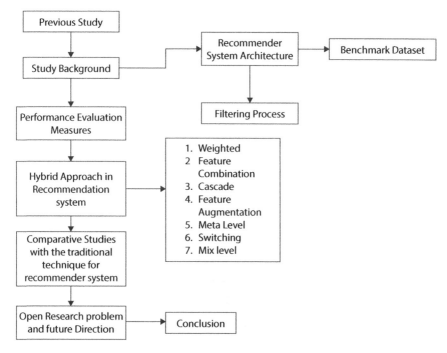

Figure 3.7 Architecture of this paper.

on different aspects or attributes used for recommendation. Here in Table 3.2, we discuss the technique used and what the drawbacks are of those algorithms. Through this, we also understand that for which technique which evaluation criteria are used for performance measure. In this section, we also understand the architecture of the hybrid approach.

3.2.3.1 *The Architecture of Hybrid Approach*

Here we discuss the different approaches of applying Hybridization according to the challenges faced by the researchers where we need to understand the problems and what they are the different possible solutions of it. There are several **Hybridization Methods (HM)** which are as follows:

1. *Weighted:* A single recommendation will be provided from the score of several recommendation technique ex-P-Tango systems.
2. *Switching:* It is a method which switches between different recommendation techniques depending on the situation

Table 3.2 Shows which technique, evaluation criteria are used in different RS.

Paper name	Type of RS	Technique	Evaluation metric	Drawback/Future work
Panda, S.K., *et al.* [7]	CF	Normalization based collaborative filtering	1. Recall 2. Precision 3. Mean Absolute Error (MAE) 4. F-Score 5. FMI 6. Root Mean Square Error (RMSE)	1. The rating matrix used in the suggested algorithm is static. 2. The authors have not observed user and item biases in the proposed algorithm. 3. The proposed algorithm is not exhibited using a standard dataset due to the inclusion of rigid users.
Amara, S., *et al.* [10]	Content-Based RS	Tagger-User Profile-Tree	1. Precision	1. The tag-based system updates over a while. 2. It shows that profiling through this algorithm is much better than personal and content-based filtering.

(Continued)

Table 3.2 Shows which technique, evaluation criteria are used in different RS. (*Continued*)

Paper name	Type of RS	Technique	Evaluation metric	Drawback/Future work
Deng, F., [12]	Utility-Based RS	IU-GA (Item Utility-Genetic Algorithm) extracts the utility functions based on user behavior while browsing not one attribute. This utility function is multi-attribute and then the genetic algorithm is used.	1. Precision 2. Recall 3. F1	1. This recommendation system works on limited context online.
Ullah, F., *et al.* [21]	Collaborative Filtering	A novel Deep Neural Collaborative Filtering	1. RMSE 2. MAE 3. Similarity measure 4. Predicted Score	1. The side information and other contextual data in the educational service recommendation.

(*Continued*)

Table 3.2 Shows which technique, evaluation criteria are used in different RS. (*Continued*)

Paper name	Type of RS	Technique	Evaluation metric	Drawback/Future work
Feng, C., *et al.* [22]	Collaborative Filtering	Uses the model that integrates the rating matrix with neighbors information and this model is called the Fusion probability Matrix Factorization model	1. MAE 2. RMSE	1. In the future, the author wants to use the incremental learning approach with the proposed CF model i.e. Fusion based.
Zarzour, H., *et al.* [23]	Collaborative Filtering	A trust-based model implemented through collaborative filtering	1. RMSE	1. This collaborative filtering method established on a method called dimensionality reduction which can be paired with a clustering algorithm.
Mustaqeem, A., Anwar, *et al.* [24]	Collaborative Filtering	Cluster-Based Modular Recommendation System	1. Precision 2. Recall 3. MAE	1. It dealt with only one type of patients. 2. The dataset will be extended by adding more patients and partitioned based on demographics.

(Continued)

Table 3.2 Shows which technique, evaluation criteria are used in different RS. (*Continued*)

Paper name	Type of RS	Technique	Evaluation metric	Drawback/Future work
Zhang, B., *et al.* [25]	Collaborative Filtering	Residual Convolution CF (Work on Combined approach of PMT + CNN)	1. RMSE	1. Current work is on textual features, in the future latent factor features can also be considered.
Gu, Y., Zhao, B., *et al.* [26]	Content-Based RS	An approach that learns (Supervised Learning) simultaneously how to find optimal global term weight and finds the similarity on the multiple text features between user and item profiles.	1. Area under ROC(Receiver operating characteristics) 2. Precision 3. Recall 4. Area under precision-recall curve.	2. The proposed approach improves AUC up to 17% but in the future efficiency can be increased. So this unified framework provides an overall relevance model.
Zheng, Y., [27]	Utility-Based RS	It uses a Multi-criteria utility-based algorithm.	1. Pearson correlation 2. Cosine similarity 3. Euclidean distance	1. There is an issue called over expectation, which may contribute to finger-grained recommendation models.

(*Continued*)

Table 3.2 Shows which technique, evaluation criteria are used in different RS. (*Continued*)

Paper name	Type of RS	Technique	Evaluation metric	Drawback/Future work
Huang, S.L., *et al.* [28]	Utility-Based RS	A decomposed and holistic utility-based based method.	1. Accuracy 2. Time Expense	1. In this paper, only 96 students as subjects the limited no of participants decrease the credibility of the research. 2. Utility-based can be compared with collaborative filtering too. 3. Research finds that content-based work on nominal attributes, decomposed one will work better with numerical attributes and holistic will work in different contexts.
Patro, S.G.K., *et al.* [29]	Knowledge-based RS	Based on domain knowledge, the preference is created and a learning model is prepared with an adaptive neuro-fuzzy model	1. Mean absolute percentage error 2. Root Mean Square Error 3. Mean Absolute Error 4. Precision 5. F1-score	1. This algorithm works in three steps first one is clustering then decomposition and then prediction any step error may affect the prediction.

(Continued)

Table 3.2 Shows which technique, evaluation criteria are used in different RS. (*Continued*)

Paper name	Type of RS	Technique	Evaluation metric	Drawback/Future work
Dong, M., et al. [30]	Knowledge-Based RS	Interactive Knowledge-based Design Recommender System	1. Rate of satisfaction	1. It can be enhanced by learning different design cases.
Bobadilla, J., et al. [31]	Demographic RS	Obtaining different demographic features from the different latent factors by using the gradient localization method	2. Accuracy	1. This algorithm cannot be able to work on zip code or salary as user demographic feature. 2. Detection of unreported minority users, as well as items, is still one of the limitations which can be solved in the future.
Yang, C., et al. [32]	Collaborative Filtering	Neural Collaborative filtering approach i.e. Gated and Attentive (GANCF)	1. Hit ratio 2. Normalized Discounted Cumulative Gain (NDCG)	1. In the future, explore the area of social networks and how users trust this platform. 2. The list of interests of the user is realized in the online recommender system.

(*Continued*)

Table 3.2 Shows which technique, evaluation criteria are used in different RS. (*Continued*)

Paper name	Type of RS	Technique	Evaluation metric	Drawback/Future work
Huang, X.Y., *et al.* [33]	Collaborative Filtering	Logo (Local and global) online CF algorithm	1. RMSE 2. MAE	1. Implicit and explicit feedback can be used in the recommendation. 2. Assumptions for each rating vector can be a mixture of some distributions.
Cami, B.R., *et al.* [34]	Content-Based RS	A New Extended Distance Dependent CRP (Chinese Restaurant Process)	1. Precision 2. Recall 3. F1-measure	1. Incorporating a collaborative approach with the current technology provides a richer user profile.
Bagher, R.C., *et al.* [35]	Content-Based RS	A Bayesian framework works on the non-parametric area is known as DPMM (Dirichlet Process Mixture model)	1. Precision 2. Recall 3. F1-measure 4. DCG (Discounted cumulative Gain)	1. User rate feedback can be used as a parameter. 2. For improving the diversity measure one can use the CF.

like Netflix initially content-based is there and after that, it switches to collaborative filtering.

3. *Mixed:* Different recommendation methods are present and used over the same time.

4. *Feature Combination:* Using different features that come as the result of different recommendation data and put it into one recommendation algorithm.

5. *Cascade:* It follows the staged process in which first produces the coarse ranking of user and items as well and refines the recommendation with other techniques.

6. *Feature augmentation:* It is a technique in which the output of one is the input of another recommendation technique

7. *Meta-level:* Here the model learned by one recommender is used as input to another.

As we all know that recommender system is increasingly used in the field of e-commerce, movies, music as well as education and health sectors. Hybrid is a solution for all the individual recommender system which comes with certain inbuilt problems [16] As we all know, collaborative filtering has one major problem which is the cold start problem "problem of Recommendation in which no past interaction provided for the user as well as for an item". The categorization of cold start is of two types which are as follows:

1. User Cold Start
2. Item Cold Start.

Both the above mentioned cold start problems are fixed by using the side information about users and items into a deep neural network. Also, resolves the problem of the linear latent factors, the solution is learning through no-linear latent factors of users and items. This is not the only way to handle the problems of different recommender systems there are [36] which focuses on the item targeting problem means "best as per user interest" so it finds the solution through a hybrid approach in which the Bayesian recommender model is being created which shows the advantages of memory-based and model-based collaborative filtering. Individually, Model-based CF has better fitting operations as well as works when data is missing (data sparsity). Matrix factorization is one of the techniques used for latent factors as well as it solves the problem of cold start. The Hybrid approach comes with several advantages that are useful for solving existing problems:

a) It increases the interaction between user and item as most as possible for making a better recommendation system.

b) Researchers work on merging several recommendation models like factor-based, item-based, and user-based collaborative filtering models as a hybrid for artist based recommender system it improves the user-item interaction.

c) For the item identification problem, the hybrid approach works to propose a model called the "Bayesian inference-based model".

As the author is focusing on serendipity [37] which is one of the challenges we discussed in an earlier section of the paper, the author provides the hybridization method to face this challenge. This is more subjective than the attribute-based so a large set of data set has been taken and find the following criteria:

1. *Content difference:* It is defined as a movie that is not searched by the user in past and gets the recommendation.

2. *Genre accuracy:* For the short term of preference for the movie for the user.

3. *Serendipity:* It shows both attractiveness and surprise based on Content difference and Genre accuracy.

4. *User elasticity:* It is the ability to accept the difference from past behavior.

5. *Movie elasticity:* It is the possibility of being adopted by a different user.

6. *Relevance network:* It is a network that shows the asymmetric association between different nodes; this node is nothing but the movies and users.

3.2.4   Analysis

3.2.4.1   Evaluation Measures

How will one find out which recommender system is better than the other? So for that we need appropriate evaluation criteria or metric through which one can understand there are different evaluation metrics like Accuracy, Adaptability, and Reliability which are all not used in all the RS. It depends on the models which evaluation criteria provide the performance analysis. Recommender systems can be evaluated through various evaluation metrics; it is based on the experimental setup for various research studies. It can be understood through these terms:

a) *Hypothesis:* Before starting an experiment, a hypothesis is built up like any algorithm X is better than algorithm Y so we need to be precise about these hypotheses and only use one measure to find and prove this hypothesis is "prediction accuracy". The researcher doesn't require any other factor for this hypothesis. The major drawback is the researcher becomes restrictive.

b) *Controlling Variable:* So when according to variable the result may change and we can't just depend on prediction accuracy because dataset is never static as it changes from time to time and we can't publish the fact that results differ because of algorithm or dataset so we require more evaluation measures.

c) *Generalization Power:* It is generalizing the experiments based on different datasets. When one will deploy or develop any new algorithm it should not be specific to any one application; it must be beyond that application for that generalization of results are necessary.

How one will decide which recommendation system is to select or better so the answer different parameters that affect the properties of the recommender system is used to evaluate and these measures get affected based on user experience.

Prediction Accuracy: It is one of the properties of RS and it provides more accurate predictions according to the user's interest. PA evaluates the accuracy of item ratings displayed by users.

Measuring Rating Prediction Accuracy

a. *Root Mean Square Error:* When the true ratings are known and the system produces predicted ratings for a test of user-item pairs.

$$RMSE = \sqrt{\sum_{i=1}^{n} \frac{(\hat{y}_i - y_i)^2}{n}}$$

Where, $\hat{Y}1$, $\hat{Y}2$... $\hat{Y}i$ is predicted values

Y1, Y2…..Yi is the observed value

N is no. of observation.

b. *Mean Absolute Error:* The average of all absolute errors in the definition of MAE. An absolute error is a difference between the measured value and the true value.

$$(\Delta x) = x_i - x$$

Where x_i is the measurement, x is the true value.

$$MAE = \frac{1}{n} \sum_{i=1}^{n} |x_i - x|$$

Where, n = the number of errors, $|x_i - x|$ = the absolute errors

Measuring Usage Predication

A dataset consisting of items that each user used is known as usage prediction and inside these various measures are works based on True Negative, False Positive, False Negative, True positive. Now, these four types are based on the actual value and predicted value as we can see in Table 3.3.

a. *Precision:* When fractions of positive number of cases among the total number of positive cases in the system are retrieved then it is known as positive class prediction which is another name of precision. When it predicts yes the person likes cats, how often is it correct?

$$\text{Precision} = \frac{tp}{(tp + fp)}$$

Table 3.3 Base of usage predication.

Conditions	Actual value	Predicted value
True Negative	False	False
False Positive	False	True
False Negative	True	False
True Positive	True	True

b. *Recall:* Number of positive class predictions out of positive class in the dataset. It answers the questions that when it is actually yes the person likes cats, how often does it predict correctly?

$$\text{Recall} = \frac{\text{tp}}{\text{tp} + \text{fn}}$$

c. *F-measure:* It is a measure that takes both precisions and recalls into account and when one finds out the weighted average of precision and recall then it is known as F-measure and it also defines as a parameter that makes a compromise to be reached concerning precision and recall.

$$f1 = \frac{2(\text{precision} * \text{recall})}{(\text{precision} + \text{recall})}$$

Measuring Ranking of Items
Normalized Distance-Based Performance Measure: When there is a need for information retrieval then this measure is used and it distinguishes correct and incorrect orders of pairs and ties.

$$\text{NDPM}(I, \succ_1, \succ_2) = \frac{\beta_{\succ_1, \succ_2}(I)}{m(\succ_1)}$$

3.2.5   Materials and Methods

Recommender System is a part of Data mining. As we see in recommender systems the main focus is on sampling, dimensional reduction, and classification, clustering technique in RS. Also there is association rule discovery and RS is also implemented through deep learning so in this section we understand different algorithm works on the above-mentioned concept.

Sampling is the concept of selecting a small amount of relevant data i.e. subset from a large dataset. This subset is used for training and testing purposes. When a task like model fitting is there then a training dataset is used. When one wants to see how the model generalizes then a testing dataset is used. Various sampling techniques are there like random sampling, stratified sampling. The approach used for sampling is with replacement means items can be removed from the population once they get selected and without replacement means that no item gets removed.

A *dimension reduction* is a technique that helps to overcome the problem by changing high-dimensional space into lower dimensionality. There is a various method of doing so, PCA, Matrix factorization (like SVD) is one of the most common and powerful techniques of dimensionality reduction.

Denoising is a very important part of pre-processing in which removal of the unwanted effect on data when widening of information is done; in simple words we define unwanted artifacts as noise.

A *classifier* is of two types: supervised and unsupervised. It is defined as the mapping between label space and feature space. Now here feature means elements characteristics for proper classification and for representing classes label space is used. For example, Hospital RS classifies into two categories i.e. either good or bad based on features that are associated with it.

Instance-Based Classifier: It is defined as the classifier that works on the training and uses it to forecast the labels of unseen cases. It learns the entire set of training and classifies when a new record matches the training example.

kNN classifier is one of the most used classifiers not only in the recommender system but in machine learning too. It is also known as lazy learners and one of the advantages of this technique is that it doesn't require learning and maintaining a given model and in RS it is used in Collaborative filtering. *Nearest Neighbor* is used in CF to find like-minded users but this approach is also get challenged by other approaches called Matrix completion.

Decision Tree: It is a type of Nearest Neighbor and as the name suggests it creates a tree based on the target class. A single attribute-value is represented as a Decision node and is tested to find which branch of leaf nodes indicates the target value. Different methods are used for the decision tree like Hunt's Algorithm. Hunt algorithm works on test conditions implemented on the specified attribute that inclines the observations by their target value. The Decision tree for ranking has also been used.

Rule-Based Classifier works based on various "if...else rules " and thus this classifier is used to develop the descriptive models and the condition used with "if" is called precedent and the predicted class for each rule works as a consequence. To implement the Rule-based classifier is a classifier that extracts rules directly over different data some examples are Ripper, CN2.

Logistic Regression is the basic probabilistic classification model; it is a type of classifier but then also it is called regression because of the legacy used for linear regression. Linear regression is used for linear equations. In one paper [38] the author uses the regression technique and other non-linear techniques like AI and made the comparison between which model works better for weather prediction so the researcher can analyze the performance of both linear and non-linear methods. In the regression model, a regular value comes as output but on other hand, the classifier has the output in the form of a class label. Logistic Regression work on the decision boundary many other classification methods that work on a similar concept like SVM (Support Vector Machine).

$$F(x) = \begin{cases} 1 \ w.x + b \geq 1 \\ -1 \ w.x + b \leq -1 \end{cases}$$

$$\text{Margin} = \frac{2}{\|w\|^2}$$

A *Support Vector Machine* is a classifier that is a user to find the linear hyperplane which separates the data with maximum margin. Here a linear separation is w.x + b = 0 and the other two are separated by using the class separation function which is based on minimum distance but when the condition arises of non-linearly item then SVM (Support Vector Machine) provides the solution of *soft margin classifier* by introducing a new variable called "*Slack Variable*". Now condition arises of non-linear decision boundary so for that data to change into higher dimensional space it can be done through the help of a mathematical transformation called "*Kernel Trick*".

A *Bayesian classifier* is used to solve the classification problem which works on the concept of a probabilistic framework. Some researchers say that this classifier is the fastest and the gradient boost model is the most accurate algorithm. It is used to represent the uncertainty among the relationship learned from data. It considers each of the attribute and class labels as random variables. It not only uses in collaborative filtering but also in a hybrid approach the example of this is [36] the method calculates or computes the probability through which the user rate the item. When we talk about the hybrid approach it includes all clustering and classification algorithms in a certain way.

Artificial Neural Network is an accumulation [39] of interconnected nodes and these nodes are known as a neuron. The simplest case is the perceptron model when we specify an activation function as a threshold function. Another most common approach is feed-forward ANN.

An *Ensemble of Classifiers* is a classifier that creates training data from a set of classifiers and does the prediction based on class labels. The two most common techniques used in ensemble learning is Bagging and Boosting.

Bagging is defined as performing the sampling with reinstatement and built the classifier on each step of bootstrap.

Boosting is an adaptive change of distribution in training data by giving importance to the previous misclassified records. In this initially, all records are of equal weights, and then wrongly classified records have higher weights have their weights increased, and those which are correctly classified with lessen weights. Adaboost is one of the algorithms that is used for boosting an ensemble classifier. This classifier is most commonly used in the hybrid approach RS.

In this *clustering technique*, the researcher [2] proposed a new algorithm that works on the semantics information of the web page, and pages are set into clusters by using a clustering algorithm and builds upon the similarity of semantics with the user. In this, the author provides the user agent which works as an interface where the user can input and gets output. The knowledge base is also created to classify the information as the user model there is a behavior model that precisely suggests the behavior of each user and all this model help in finding a better recommendation system.

In this paper, [24] the author gives the new method applied on supervised data in four different classes of disease retrieved by using the Kmean clustering and this method is implemented on each partition separately, and once the query patient is partitioned into the correct class of disease then it requires the similarity scores for reduced sub-clusters so it means that a separate recommendation is used for each class of disease and the whole process is known as modularization.

In this paper [40] the author suggests the solution for the issue of classifying the text to a discrete set of predefined categories it helps in identifying the categorical terms present in emails for this author uses the LDA modeling approach. The author [41] built the two datasets for evaluation: first one is transaction data and the other one is demographic data (personal data of user transaction data is calculated through similarity matrix and demographic data works on the cluster-product rating matrix by using K mean clustering technique. Fuzzy logic is an application-based approach that is used for classification [42]; the author proposed the idea for text summarization, fuzzy logic is used to normalize the unspecific reasoning of human ability. As the author proposed the Fuzzy logic based on the triangular member function which maps the input space points to membership functions and by using this method improvement takes place on the present model which is evaluated through different measures like precision and recall.

3.2.6   Comparative Analysis With Traditional Recommender System

When we say comparative analysis it means that what are the problems in one system and how it is solved by any other system through which better RS we get and we understand it through various evaluations metric in Table 3.4. Dataset of different types shows different results so we can't say that if one algorithm is working in one data set so it will work for another so the size of the data set also matters at the time of implementing any new algorithm.

3.2.7   Practical Implications

As per Research Questions (RQ), we find the answers to these questions:

1. RQ1 (Answer): When we talk about collaborative filtering then there are various challenges we face in an existing system like the cold start problem as well as gray sheep problem (discussed in challenges) are present prominently and if we say what are the practical implications are there so the solution is tagging as well as using content-based or feature-related extraction and make a recommendation through that main problem with collaborative is it depends on rating matrix either it is user-based or item-based but recommendations explored by many researchers says that accuracy and precision not only based on this, it depends on the ranking scheme and user profile through this we get better results so by combining all this approach in a different way hybrid approach arises and all the paper we read hybrid gives a better result than the individual traditional approach.
2. RQ2 (Answer): If we talk about existing solutions through the existing traditional approach of RS then for cold start content-based work as a solution, for data-sparsity one can provide the solution like building a trust-based model, one

Table 3.4 Comparative study of hybrid approach with traditional approach.

Paper name	Proposed technique	Evaluation metric	Comparison with traditional approach	Limitations
Kiran., *et al.* [16]	Embedding and content based combined and make a hybrid approach	1. RMSE 2. MAE 3. R-squared 4. MSE 5. MAE	1. Global average 2. User Average 3. Item Average 4. User K-Nearest Neighbor (KNN)-Cosine, Item-KNN-Cosine 5. SVD 6. Biased MF 7. SVD++ 8. Non-Deep NN	1. In collaborative filtering cold start case. 2. It allows the learning of non-linear latent features but the problem is that system handles the problem of rating prediction based but not the ranking based.
Riyahi, M., *et al.* [17]	Discussion group uses the tagging feature for more precise recommendation. Relevance of tags on the basis of Semantics is extracted through WordNet database.	1. Precision 2. Recall 3. F-measure	1. Collaborative Filtering 2. Content-Based Filtering technique	1. It is only focusing on discussion groups.

(Continued)

Table 3.4 Comparative study of hybrid approach with traditional approach. (*Continued*)

Paper name	Proposed technique	Evaluation metric	Comparison with traditional approach	Limitations
Ramos G., *et al.* [18]	Matrix Completion Algorithm which performs hybrid Collaborative filtering.	1. RMSE 2. Normalized Discounted cumulative gain	1. Singular Vector Decomposition(SVD) 2. SVD++ 3. KNN	1. When we talk about bribing it comes from various sources in this paper not all dynamic sources covered
Ngaffo, A.N., *et al.* [36]	A hybrid model-based approach this method shows the probability between user-item based features. i.e. (Bayesian Inference Hybrid Recommender System)	1. Normalized discounted cumulative Gain 2. Recall 3. Precision 4. RMSE 5. MAE	1. UPCC (user-based similarity Pearson Correlation Coefficient) 2. IPCC (Item-based similarity Pearson Correlation Coefficient) 3. Spearman-CF 4. NBCF(Naive Bayesian Collaborative Filtering) 5. PMF (Probabilistic Matrix Factorization) 6. BNMF(Bayesian Non-negative Matrix Factorization)	1. This strategy takes the model-based and memory-based which works on rating not on the content so this one of the limitations of this working model.

(Continued)

Table 3.4 Comparative study of hybrid approach with traditional approach. (*Continued*)

Paper name	Proposed technique	Evaluation metric	Comparison with traditional approach	Limitations
Li, X., *et al.* [37]	Serendipity is one of the challenges which is solved through a model called HAES (Hybrid Approach for movie recommendation with Elastic Serendipity)	1. Genre accuracy 2. Content Difference 3. Micro-F1 4. Average Hamming distance 5. Diversity	1. ACC (Accuracy based approach) 2. NOV (Novelty based method) 3. POP (Popularity-based recommendation) 4. RAND (Random Based algorithm)	1. There is an improvement but still, there is a limitation of those users who have short-term demands, and representing this type of preference is not included based on global preference. 2. Threshold filtering causes the fluctuation in the prediction performance.
Oyebode, O., *et al.* [41]	Implicit rating for transactional data and dynamic weighting method that is used for predicting user-item ratings.	1. Root Mean Square Error 2. Mean Absolute Error	The Proposal method is compared with existing 1. Item-based collaborative filtering 2. Demographic-based approach	1. It is an offline evaluation of the proposed technique so it becomes a static evaluation. 2. It can be evaluated through dynamic customer feedback.

(Continued)

Table 3.4 Comparative study of hybrid approach with traditional approach. (*Continued*)

Paper name	Proposed technique	Evaluation metric	Comparison with traditional approach	Limitations
Lee, Y., *et al.* [43]	Hybrid CF model with Doc2Vec algorithm using search keywords	1. F1-score 2. Precision 3. Recall	1. Collaborative filtering technique	1. In the conventional methods, there is a sparsity problem. 2. Purchase patterns across customers were insufficient and empirical analysis is done on sampled data which becomes a limitation of the proposed technique.

(Continued)

Table 3.4 Comparative study of hybrid approach with traditional approach. (*Continued*)

Paper name	Proposed technique	Evaluation metric	Comparison with traditional approach	Limitations
Pradhan, T., *et al.* [44]	A diversified yet integrated Social Network analysis and Contextual –similarity-based venue recommender system	1. Precision 2. Accuracy 3. Mean Reciprocal Rank 4. Recall 5. F-measure 6. Normalized discounted cumulative again 7. Diversity 8. Stability 9. Average-Venue Quality	Compared with 1. Collaborative Filtering 2. Personal Venue rating based recommender system. 3. Content-Based Filtering 4. Friend based model 5. Co-authorship network-based model 6. Random walk with re-start models 7. Hybrid (CF + CBF) 8. Personalized academic Venue recommendation model	1. The proposed technique works worst in EJF in the sub-domain of ML. 2. During content similarity, the author extracts keywords from papers only.
Walek, B., *et al.* [45]	Monolithic Hybrid System is known as Predictory model	Precision Recall F1-measure	Compared with traditional approaches 1. Collaborative 2. Content-Based approach 3. Hybrid Based approach	1. It takes a small no of users 2. Some hybrid system is very complex and robust which hampers the recommendation.

(*Continued*)

Table 3.4 Comparative study of hybrid approach with traditional approach. (*Continued*)

Paper name	Proposed technique	Evaluation metric	Comparison with traditional approach	Limitations
Shanmuga Sundari, P., *et al.* [46]	Integrating tag data with a rating score that predicts the overall impression and sentimental analysis on the tag.	1. Mean Absolute Error 2. Root Mean Square Error 3. Precision 4. Recall 5. F1-Score 6. Time	Comparison with 1. RSVD 2. Tri-Fac uses PMF 3. PCA + Kmeans 4. Item-specific uses Neighborhood Model 5. Proposed Iter_ALS	1. Is the proposed method tested with Apache spark to achieve stability? 2. Does it support the batch processing 3. Normalized the opinion bias rather than creating a trust user model.
Pérez-Marcos, J., *et al.* [47]	Provide the implicit rating from the hours of play, and content-based is used for deciding the similarity measure of active user	1. Mean Absolute Error 2. Root Mean Square error. 3. Normalized root mean square error	1. Compared with Pacula	1. It is based on the individual choice of the game but when it adds the friend's choice means the demographic dataset provides more accuracy.

(*Continued*)

Table 3.4 Comparative study of hybrid approach with traditional approach. (*Continued*)

Paper name	Proposed technique	Evaluation metric	Comparison with traditional approach	Limitations
Logesh, R., *et al.* [48]	Personalized Context-Aware Hybrid Travel Recommender System	1. RMSE 2. Coverage 3. F1-measure	Various Recommendation Algorithms like Location-Based Collaborative filtering (LBCF) PCAHTRS (personalized Context-Aware Hybrid Travel Recommender System)	1. Traditional approaches suffer from scalability, cold start problem, and sparsity.
Waqar, M., *et al.* [49]	The combined approach of Collaborative, Content, and Demographic uses the novel adaptive algorithm to provide the doctors ranking by using the ranking function.	1. Precision 2. Recall 3. F1-measure 4. Mean Absolute Error	No comparison	1. It works in the healthcare domain only.

(Continued)

Table 3.4 Comparative study of hybrid approach with traditional approach. (*Continued*)

Paper name	Proposed technique	Evaluation metric	Comparison with traditional approach	Limitations
Pereira, N., et al. [50]	It uses the technique consists of a hybrid approach that combines collaborative and demographic filtering.	1. Recall 2. Precision 3. TF-IDF item-item 4. TF-IDF user-user 5. Markow Chain	Comparison of ROC curve for TF-IDF item-item, TF-IDF user-user, Markow Chain ranking	1. It suggests an individual. 2. It implements an online evaluation.

of the challenges of diversity is solved through the hybrid system [36]. The scalability problem is solved through a context-aware strategy.

3. RQ3 (Answer): After exploring and understanding the above two research we concluded that the hybrid approach is one of the most flexible and by taking a different approach and combined in a distinguished way and gives a better result.

3.2.8   Conclusion & Future Work

The hybrid approach solves the problem of the traditional filtering technique and improves the effectiveness of recommendation by using different classifiers and clustering techniques. Many significant works have been done in this field to give users a recommendation based on their interests. In various traditional approaches there are some drawbacks like collaborative filtering suffers from data sparsity, cold start and scalability problems in demographic, there is a problem of breaching user privacy and in utility-based how to find that which product is more utilized for user and knowledge base create a complex system to understand and maintain. In all these, we have various other issues regarding dataset not in all dataset proposed algorithm works appropriately and accurately. Training and testing are one of the fields that may change the experiment results so all these will become the discussion point shortly that how researcher decides what the percentage of testing data is and what the percentage of training data will be present. Also Hybrid approach includes the deep neural network concept which also provides better results in terms of precision and recall.

A hybrid approach is the most flexible and most used approach of research which shows how many different ways one can use the traditional approaches and solve all the disadvantages of an individual approach but the problem is that how one will find that which two combination works better than the other.

References

1. Cordero, P., Enciso, M., López, D., Mora, A., A conversational recommender system for diagnosis using fuzzy rules. *Expert Syst. Appl.*, 154, 113449, 2020.
2. Manikandan, R. and Saravanan, V., A novel approach on Particle Agent Swarm Optimization (PASO) in semantic mining for web page recommender

system of multimedia data: A health care perspective. *Multimed. Tools Appl.*, 79, 5, 3807–3829, 2020.

3. Soni, S. and Sharaff, A., Sentiment analysis of customer reviews based on hidden markov model, in: *Proceedings of the 2015 International Conference on Advanced Research in Computer Science Engineering & Technology (ICARCSET 2015)*, pp. 1–5, 2015.

4. Ardissono, L. and Mauro, N., A compositional model of multi-faceted trust for personalized item recommendation. *Expert Syst. Appl.*, 140, 112880, 2020.

5. Sinha, B.B. and Dhanalakshmi, R., Evolution of recommender system over the time. *Soft Comput.*, 23, 23, 12169–12188, 2019.

6. Sharaff, A. and Srinivasarao, U., Towards classification of email through selection of informative features, in: *2020 First International Conference on Power, Control and Computing Technologies (ICPC2T)*, IEEE, pp. 316–320, 2020.

7. Panda, S.K., Bhoi, S.K., Singh, M., A collaborative filtering recommendation algorithm based on normalization approach. *J. Ambient Intell. Hum. Comput.*, 1–23, Springer, 2020.

8. Pujahari, A. and Sisodia, D.S., Model-Based Collaborative Filtering for Recommender Systems: An Empirical Survey, in: *First International Conference on Power, Control and Computing Technologies (ICPC2T)*, IEEE, pp. 443–447, 2020.

9. Mohamed, M.H., Khafagy, H.M., Ibrahim, M.H., Recommender systems challenges and solutions survey, in: *International Conference on Innovative Trends in Computer Engineering (ITCE)*, IEEE, pp. 149–155, 2019.

10. Amara, S. and Subramanian, R.R., Collaborating personalized recommender system and content-based recommender system using TextCorpus, in: *6th International Conference on Advanced Computing and Communication Systems (ICACCS)*, IEEE, pp. 105–109, 2020.

11. Krismayer, T., Schedl, M., Knees, P., Rabiser, R., Predicting user demographics from music listening information. *Multimedia Tools Appl.*, 78, 3, 2897–2920, 2019.

12. Deng, F., Utility-based recommender systems using implicit utility and genetic algorithm, in: *International Conference on Mechatronics, Electronic, Industrial and Control Engineering (MEIC-15)*, Atlantis Press, 2015.

13. Wu, G., Luo, K., Sanner, S., Soh, H., Deep language-based critiquing for recommender systems, in: *Proceedings of the 13th ACM Conference on Recommender Systems*, pp. 137–145, 2019.

14. Guo, Q., Zhuang, F., Qin, C., Zhu, H., Xie, X., Xiong, H., He, Q., A survey on knowledge graph-based recommender systems. *arXiv preprint arXiv:2003.00911*, 2020.

15. Samin, H. and Azim, T., Knowledge based recommender system for academia using machine learning: A case study on higher education landscape of Pakistan. *IEEE Access*, 7, 67081–67093, 2019.

16. Kiran, R., Kumar, P., Bhasker, B., DNNRec: A novel deep learning based hybrid recommender system. *Expert Syst. Appl.*, 144, 113054, 2020.

17. Riyahi, M. and Sohrabi, M.K., Providing effective recommendations in discussion groups using a new hybrid recommender system based on implicit ratings and semantic similarity. *Electron. Commer. Res. Appl.*, 40, 100938, 2020.

18. Ramos, G., Boratto, L., Caleiro, C., On the negative impact of social influence in recommender systems: A study of bribery in collaborative hybrid algorithms. *Inf. Process. Manage.*, 57, 2, 102058, 2020.

19. Anwar, T. and Uma, V., A review of recommender system and related dimensions, in: *Data, Engineering and Applications*, pp. 3–10, 2019.

20. Kumar, B. and Sharma, N., Approaches, issues and challenges in recommender systems: A systematic review. *Indian J. Sci. Technol.*, 9, 1–12, 2016.

21. Ullah, F., Zhang, B., Zou, G., Ullah, I., Qamar, A.M., Large-scale Distributive Matrix Collaborative Filtering for Recommender System, in: *Proceedings of the 2020 International Conference on Computing, Networks and Internet of Things*, pp. 55–59, 2020.

22. Feng, C., Liang, J., Song, P., Wang, Z., A fusion collaborative filtering method for sparse data in recommender systems. *Inf. Sci.*, 521, 365–379, 2020.

23. Zarzour, H., Jararweh, Y., Al-Sharif, Z.A., An Effective Model-Based Trust Collaborative Filtering for Explainable Recommendations, in: *2020 11th International Conference on Information and Communication Systems (ICICS)*, IEEE, pp. 238–242, 2020.

24. Mustaqeem, A., Anwar, S.M., Majid, M., A modular cluster based collaborative recommender system for cardiac patients. *Artif. Intell. Med.*, 102, 101761, 2020.

25. Zhang, B., Zhu, M., Yu, M., Pu, D., Feng, G., Extreme residual connected convolution-based collaborative filtering for document context-aware rating prediction. *IEEE Access*, 8, 53604–53613, 2020.

26. Gu, Y., Zhao, B., Hardtke, D., Sun, Y., Learning global term weights for content-based recommender systems, in: *Proceedings of the 25th International Conference on World Wide Web*, pp. 391–400, 2016.

27. Zheng, Y., Utility-based multi-criteria recommender systems, in: *Proceedings of the 34th ACM/SIGAPP Symposium on Applied Computing*, pp. 2529–2531, 2019.

28. Huang, S.-L., Designing utility-based recommender systems for e-commerce: Evaluation of preference-elicitation methods. *Electron. Commer. Res. Appl.*, 10, 4, 398–407, 2011.

29. Patro, S.G.K., Mishra, B.K., Panda, S.K., Kumar, R., Long, H.V., Knowledge based preference learning model for recommender system using adaptive neuro-fuzzy inference system. *J. Intell. Fuzzy Syst.*, 39, 3, 4651–4665, 2020.

30. Dong, M., Zeng, X., Koehl, L., Zhang, J., An interactive knowledge-based recommender system for fashion product design in the big data environment. *Inf. Sci.*, 540, 469–488, 2020.

31. Bobadilla, J., González-Prieto, Á., Ortega, F., Lara-Cabrera, R., Deep learning feature selection to unhide demographic recommender systems factors.

32. Yang, C., Miao, L., Jiang, B., Li, D., Cao, D., Gated and attentive neural collaborative filtering for user generated list recommendation. *Knowledge-Based Syst.*, 187, 104839, 2020.

33. Huang, X.-Y., Liang, B., Li, W., Online collaborative filtering with local and global consistency. *Inf. Sci.*, 506, 366–382, 2020.

34. Cami, B.R., Hassanpour, H., Mashayekhi, H., User preferences modeling using Dirichlet process mixture model for a content-based recommender system. *Knowledge-Based Syst.*, 163, 644–655, 2019.

35. Bagher, R.C., Hassanpour, H., Mashayekhi, H., User trends modeling for a content-based recommender system. *Expert Syst. Appl.*, 87, 209–219, 2017.

36. Ngaffo, A.N., El Ayeb, W., Choukair, Z., A Bayesian Inference Based Hybrid Recommender System. *IEEE Access*, 8, 101682–101701, 2020.

37. Li, X., Jiang, W., Chen, W., Wu, J., Wang, G., Haes: A new hybrid approach for movie recommendation with elastic serendipity, in: *Proceedings of the 28th ACM International Conference on Information and Knowledge Management*, pp. 1503–1512, 2019.

38. Sharaff, A. and Roy, S.R., Comparative analysis of temperature prediction using regression methods and back propagation neural network, in: *2018 2nd International Conference on Trends in Electronics and Informatics (ICOEI)*, IEEE, pp. 739–742, 2018.

39. Ricci, F., Rokach, L., Shapira, B., Introduction to recommender systems handbook, in: *Recommender Systems Handbook*, pp. 1–35, Springer, Boston, MA, 2011.

40. Sharaff, A. and Nagwani, N.K., Identifying categorical terms based on latent Dirichlet allocation for email categorization, in: *Emerging Technologies in Data Mining and Information Security*, pp. 431–437, Springer, Singapore, 2019.

41. Oyebode, O. and Orji, R., A hybrid recommender system for product sales in a banking environment. *J. Bank. Financ. Technol.*, 1–11, Springer, 2020.

42. Sharaff, A., Khaire, A.S., Sharma, D., Analysing Fuzzy Based Approach for Extractive Text Summarization. *International Conference on Intelligent Computing and Control Systems (ICCS)*, pp. 906–910, 2019.

43. Lee, Y., Won, H., Shim, J., Ahn, A Hybrid Collaborative Filtering-based Product Recommender System using Search Keywords. *J. Intell. Inf. Syst.*, 26, 1, 151–166, 2020.

44. Pradhan, T. and Pal, S., A hybrid personalized scholarly venue recommender system integrating social network analysis and contextual similarity. *Future Gener. Comput. Syst.*, 110, 1139–1166, 2020.

45. Walek, B. and Fojtik, V., A hybrid recommender system for recommending relevant movies using an expert system. *Expert Syst. Appl.*, 158, 113452, 2020.

46. Shanmuga Sundari, P. and Subaji, M., Integrating sentiment analysis on hybrid collaborative filtering method in a big data environment. *Int. J. Inf. Technol. Decis. Mak.*, 19, 2, 385–412, 2020.

47. Pérez-Marcos, J., Martin-Gomez, L., Jiménez-Bravo, D.M., López, V.F., Moreno-García, M.N., Hybrid system for video game recommendation based on implicit ratings and social networks. *J. Ambient Intell. Hum. Comput.*, 11, 11, 4525–4535, 2020.

48. Logesh, R. and Subramaniyaswamy, V., Exploring hybrid recommender systems for personalized travel applications, in: *Cognitive Informatics and Soft Computing*, pp. 535–544, 2019.

49. Waqar, M., Majeed, N., Dawood, H., Daud, A., Aljohani, N.R., An adaptive doctor-recommender system. *Behav. Inf. Technol.*, 38, 9, 959–973, 2019.

50. Pereira, N. and Varma, S.L., Financial planning recommendation system using content-based collaborative and demographic filtering, in: *Smart Innovations in Communication and Computational Sciences*, pp. 141–151, 2019.

4

Stream Mining: Introduction, Tools & Techniques and Applications

Naresh Kumar Nagwani

*Computer Science & Engineering, National Institute of Technology Raipur,
Raipur, India*

Abstract

Stream mining is a key research area in big data analytics, where mining operations are applied on the input streamed data. There are numerous modern applications of it, particularly after the invention of the Internet of Things (IoT), which generates the real time streamed data from various sources. Storage of the streamed input data in a local system is not feasible because it enters in continuous fashion and volume of the data is very high, so an analysis of this data requires the single pass processing. Data selection and summarization are the major challenges in mining streamed data. This chapter provides an overview of stream mining and provides a brief introduction of various tools and techniques available for implementing mining operations on streamed data. Major stream mining techniques such as sampling and sketching from data streams, concept drift detection, classification, clustering, frequent set mining and outlier detection techniques are discussed in this chapter. A, overview of tools for processing the data stream in Java, Python and R programming languages is also presented. Some of the key application areas of stream mining are also discussed.

Keywords: Stream mining, stream clustering, stream implementation, applications of stream mining, tools and technologies for stream mining

Email: nknagwani.cs@nitrr.ac.in

Rohit Raja, Kapil Kumar Nagwanshi, Sandeep Kumar and K. Ramya Laxmi (eds.) Data Mining and Machine Learning Applications, (99–124) © 2022 Scrivener Publishing LLC

4.1   Introduction

Stream mining or data stream mining is a key research area in big data analytics which takes the streamed data as input for data analysis. A data stream is an ordered sequence of data over a period of time. The biggest challenge in handling data streams is volume and velocity of the incoming data apart from the other issues [1]. As the data in a stream comes in a continuous flow over the span of a time, practically it is impossible to store the entire data and process it on the local system. So it is expected to process the input data stream in just a single pass and discard it as soon as it is processed by the analysis algorithms.

The overview of a typical data stream processing system is shown in Figure 4.1. Input data is data streams that reach the stream processing module where processing of streams is carried in three major phases. In the first phase data reduction is performed from the input data stream using suitable sampling techniques. Sketching or data reduction can also be performed as an alternate technique for sampling with the input data stream in the first phase. Then in the second phase a suitable data stream mining algorithm is applied on the samples or sketches selected from the data stream from phase one. The choice of a particular stream mining algorithm depends on the type of pattern discovery from the data streams. Then pattern generation and representation of output is made in the third phase and the output is stored in the local storage unit for future work and applications. After processing the steam, the rest part of the stream is

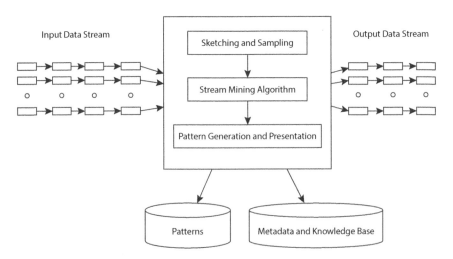

Figure 4.1 Overview of data stream processing system.

discarded as it takes a huge amount of memory to store the data stream. Along with *ad hoc* results, metadata and summary of data streams can also be stored in the local storage unit for any future stream analysis task.

4.2   Data Reduction: Sampling and Sketching

Data reduction is applied in typical data mining systems to minimize the amount of input data to the data mining algorithms to get the faster output from the mining algorithms. Generation of histograms, sketching algorithms and sampling techniques are major approaches of data reduction in data streams [2]. In this section an overview of sampling and sketching techniques is presented in brief.

4.2.1   Sampling

Sampling is a popular technique of data reduction in data mining and the same can be applied to the data streams also. But at the same time, it is the big challenge in the data stream systems. As stream is the continuous flow of data and practically it is not possible to store the entire data streams for mining, sampling plays a key role in mining of data streams. If suitable samples can be selected from the data streams then data stream analysis can be more perfect and accurate. The overview of sampling techniques for data streams is presented in this section.

The sampling techniques are in two major categories [3–5] namely, uniform and biased sampling. Technically it can be categorized as fixed window sampling and sliding windows sampling techniques. Uniform sampling is further classified as reservoir sampling and Bernoulli sampling techniques, whereas biased sampling is further categorized as count and weighted sampling. In this section an overview of various commonly used sampling techniques for data streams is presented in brief.

The first category of sampling techniques in data stream sampling is known as sampling from a fixed length of window. Major sampling techniques in this category are simple random sampling technique, systematic sampling, stratified sampling, uniform sampling, Bernoulli sampling, reservoir sampling, sequential sampling and concise sampling techniques.

Simple Random Sampling (SRS) is the oldest and popular sampling technique in which data samples are selected randomly from a data stream. In Systematic Sampling, samples are selected from the pre-identified data chunks or segments for a data stream. In stratified sampling, samples are selected from a start which is created from the data streams. Weighted random sampling is the variation of random sampling technique in which weights are assigned to data elements in a particular window. Uniform sampling is performed using uniform distribution of the data from a data stream. Samples from each uniform distribution are selected randomly with equal likelihood. Bernoulli sampling works on the basis of sampling rate and a known probability of samples. Reservoir sampling is the popular sampling technique in data stream mining. It uses a window of fixed length and then randomly selected data points are added to the window initially as the samples, later on using probability functions the windows are updated with most suitable values of samples. Sequential sampling is a special type of reservoir sampling for a known window size in advance. Concise sampling is a type of random sampling technique in which a map (key-value pair) is stored as the samples where the key value indicate the data sample and value part indicates the frequency of the data sample. These key-values pairs are maintained for the samples having the frequency value of more than one, for remaining only values are stored as samples without keys.

The second major category of sampling technique is designed on the basis of sampling from sliding windows. The sliding window can be generated using timestamp also in this case it is known as timestamp based windows. The major techniques in this category of sampling techniques are chain sampling, backing sampling, priority sampling, random pair sampling and StreamSamp sampling techniques.

Chain sampling is a special type of reservoir sampling technique in which samples are taken from the recent items present in the data streams. It provides a uniform sampling using the recently traversed data items from the data stream. Backing sampling technique is a special type of reservoir sampling technique in which a sample is added to the reservoir and then after skipping a fixed number of samples another is added to the reservoir as a sample. Using priority sampling technique priority is decided to predict the next tentative sample to be selected from the data stream. In the random pairing sampling technique uniform sampling is done by choosing the samples from a fixed size sliding window. StreamSamp sampling technique is a type of simple random sample technique in which samples are selected from a sample summary from a sliding window. Summary from the window can be generated using suitable techniques.

4.2.2 Sketching

Sketching is the unique technology for processing of data streams. It provides the way for generating the summary from an incoming data stream and also provides the data structures to store the summary of the data streams.

The development of sketching algorithm depends on the types of analysis queries to be addressed in the data streams. In this section an overview of some popular sketching algorithms is presented in brief. Sketching algorithms present a way for summarizing the data streams [2]. The generated summary is also known as synapses. The stream analysis is then performed on the summary of the data streams to make the analysis faster. Sketching can be performed in many ways one simple is by using aggregate operators and functions. Sketching is used primarily as a data reduction tool for data streaming as an alternate technique for sampling.

Cormode and Muthukrishnan [6] presented a sketching algorithm namely, count-min sketch which is based on a sublinear space data structure. The proposed sketching algorithm works in two steps. In the first step data streams elements are counted in a chunk and then in the second step a minimum subset of the chunks is selected as a sketch of the data stream. Another sketching algorithm for software switches is presented by Liu et al. [7]. The proposed sketching algorithm is designed to generate the summaries from the software switches for network traffic analysis as an alternate approach of packet sampling in network traffic analysis. The proposed sketching algorithm is named as NitroSketch that performs sketching of network traffic (packet) in two major stages. In the first stage multiple hash arrays are generated from the network traffic and then in the second stage sketch is generated from a reduced number of hash functions and arrays selected from the previous stage.

4.3   Concept Drift

Concept drift represents a cut-off point in the data stream which can impact the data stream analysis tasks. When there are some changes on input data streams and behavior of the stream start going different then obviously the analysis output from the data stream will also start varying, the point from which the changes takes place is called as the concept drift. Concept drift detection is also a key area in stream data mining and researchers have carried lot of recent work in the direction of detection of concept drift in the incoming input data stream.

Wares et al. [8] have summarized the previous work carried in the direction of concept drift detection in stream mining. Wares et al. [8] broadly categorized the concept detection techniques in the four major categories. These categories are statistical based concept drift detectors, window-based detectors, block-based ensemble detectors and incremental ensemble detectors. In statistical based concept drift detectors, various statistical techniques along with supporting logical operations are used for detection of concept drifts in a stream.

A comparative study on concept drift detectors is carried by Gonçalves *et al.* [9]. Gonçalves *et al.* [9] have discussed that concept drift detection techniques can be classified using speed of change and reason of change. Using speed of change the concept drift detectors can again classified into two categories, abrupt concept drift occurs in case of sudden data changes and gradual concept drift occurs in the case of smooth data changes. On the other side, using reason of change technique the concept drift detectors are categorized into two categories, real concept drift when target labels are changed for incoming instances and virtual concept drift when data distribution is changed.

Gonçalves *et al.* [9] have compared eight concept drift detectors namely, DDM (Drift Detection Method), EDDM (Early Drift Detection Method), PHT (Page–Hinkley Test), STEPD (Statistical Test of Equal Proportions), DoF (Degree of Drift), ADWIN (Adaptive Windowing), Paired Learners, and ECDD (Concept Drift Detection). DDM uses a classifier to categorize and compare the incoming instance of the stream with the target labels and compute the error rate, based on the error rate it predicts about the concept drifts. EEDM is just like the DDM, the only difference is this technique uses distance error rate rather than error rate for detecting concept drifts. PHT computes the mean of observed values and is fails to classify the incoming instance in case of concept drift occurs as classifier accuracy will fall suddenly. ADWIN is the windows based concept drift detection technique, where depending on the window size the concept drift is detected. Based on the incoming instances the window will grow and shrink, a sudden change in the window size will indicate a concept drift. Paired Learners is the concept drift detector uses a pair of classifier learners, one classifier is called the stable learner and other is called as reactive learner. Based on the accuracy change in both of the learners the concept drift is detected. ECDD is the probability based concept drift detection technique where exponential weighted moving average values of random variables on incoming input instance is used to detect the concept drift. STEPD algorithm compares the accuracy of the most recent instances with the average accuracy of the classifier to predict the concept drifts. DoF processes the incoming instances chunk by chunk and the using nearest neighbor technique for previous chunks measures the similarity and predicts the concept drifts. The comparisons are made using the performance parameters accuracy, evaluation time, false alarm and miss detection rates. It was shown that DDM is the best concept drift algorithms using most of the performance parameters.

4.4   Stream Mining Operations

Various analysis tasks can be performed over the data streams but most commonly tasks includes frequent set mining, stream classification and clustering and outlier detection. Other tasks are summarizing of the data stream and identification of outliers in the data streams. In this section an overview of key stream mining tasks namely, stream clustering, classification, frequent set mining and outlier detection is discussed.

4.4.1   Clustering

Data stream clustering is the process of identifying the group of similar data elements from the incoming data streams. Major challenges and issues in data stream mining are discussed by Alothali *et al.* [10]. Alothali *et al.* [10] have presented a comparative study on various clustering and classification algorithms available for clustering and classification of data streams. Clustering is the process of grouping the similar objects in a collection of objects. Clustering algorithms are categorized as partitioning based, density based, hierarchical and model based algorithms. A study on the impact of dimensionality of incoming data stream for clustering analysis is also carried by Nagwani [11], where it is shown that most of the clustering algorithms perform better irrespective of the dimensionality of data stream.

In partitioning based methods there are four major techniques for data stream clustering namely CluStream (Clustering on Stream), HPStream (High Dimensional Projected Stream Clustering), DSCSTREAM and StreamKM++. CluStream pyramidal time pattern is used for identifying micro clustering in online and macro clusters in offline mode for a data stream. HPStream projection based clustering algorithm for data stream clustering. DCSTREAM uses a divide and conquer approach in which first subset generator is done then micro clustering is performed and splitting and merging of clusters is made in the third phase. StreamKM++ algorithm is K-Means based clustering algorithm for data stream clustering.

Three density-based method clustering techniques for data stream clustering are DenStream, CEDAS and FStream algorithms. DenStream and D-Stream use a fading function to weigh the micro clusters and generate the global clusters. CEDAS first micro clusters are generated then overlapping micro clustering defined based kernel regions and clusters are generated for data stream. FStream algorithm finds initial clusters then assign streams to the closet cluster discovered earlier.

Another category of clustering algorithms is hierarchical clustering in which a hierarchy of data items also known as Dendogram is created for clustering. Three examples of hierarchical clustering algorithms for data stream clustering are ODAC (Divisive-Agglomerative Clustering), E-Stream (Evolution-based technique for stream clustering) and HUE-Stream (Evolution-Based Clustering Technique for Heterogeneous Data Streams with Uncertainty) algorithms. ODAC online binary tree structure hierarchy, is an incremental clustering technique based on time series analysis. E-Stream and HUE-Stream self evolution merge and split. HUE is an extension of E-stream with the handling of uncertainty in the incoming data in data stream.

Any clustering technique not discussed previously falls under model based clustering technique, where any suitable mathematical model is developed for data clustering. Four such model based data stream clustering algorithms are CluDistream, SWEM, SNCStream and AFTER-STREAM algorithm. CluDistream and SWEM both are expectation maximization based clustering algorithms. CluDistream is Gaussian mixture model for data stream clustering whereas SWM is time based sliding window approach. The SNCStream on line clustering technique is particularly designed for social networks but can also be used for data streams. It groups the people with similar characteristics in a social network. It can be modified to use for data streams. AFTER-STREAM uses Chebyshev test to remove outliers and then merge the suitable clusters.

4.4.2   Classification

Classification is the process of categorizing the objects into various predefined categories. Stream classification techniques are used for categorizing the data streams. Data stream classification based technique is categorized into five major categories namely, tree based, rule based, ensemble based, nearest neighbors based and statistical measure based [10].

Tree-based classifiers use a dedicated tree based data structure to classify the data streams. The base data structure is called as a decision tree which is modified to handle stream data and an incremental version of decision tree is used for data stream classification. Two main classifiers in this category are Hoeffding tree or VFDT (Very Fast Decision Tree) and CVFDT (Concept drift—Very Fast Decision Tree).

Hoeffding tree or VFDT is the incremental decision tree based classifier specifically designed for data stream classification. It keeps track of a minimum number of incoming instances in data stream for deciding the splitting criteria of decision tree for data streams. CVFDT (Concept drift—Very Fast Decision Tree) is a variation of the VFDT classifier with the support of handling concept drift in the data stream.

In rule-based classifiers, focus is given on generating the classification rules using which classification decision can be taken for any object. Two major algorithms in this category are On-demand stream classifier and SimC (Similarity-based Data Stream Classifier) classifier. On-demand stream classifier uses micro-clusters to classify the data stream along with handling of concept drifts. SimC classifier is a similarity based instance based learning classifier.

In ensemble-based classifier, more than one classifier is used for classification purpose. A combination of classifiers is arranged in such a manner that it is optimized to take a classification decision in a better way than a single classifier can take. Four popular ensemble-based classification algorithms are SAE2 (Social Adaptive Ensemble 2), SFN (Scale-free Network Classifier), CBCE (Class Based Ensemble for Class Evolution) and KME (Knowledge Maximized Ensemble).

SAE2 is the extension of the classifier Social Adaptive Ensemble (SAE). In this classifier a connection between the classifiers are made if the classifier has the common predictions. SFN Classifier is based on weighted majority voting ensemble learning method. CBCE uses under sampling for class imbalance problem and KME evaluates the weights of classifiers to enhance classification It is able to handle different types of concept drifts in a data stream.

Nearest Neighbors classifiers work on the basis of similarity of surrounding neighbors. The similar surrounding neighbors may belong to the same category. Anytime Nearest Neighbors is a distance based data stream classifier and as the name suggests the input data stream can be interrupted at any time to get more accurate classes of data streams.

Statistical classifiers use statistics measures and parameters to design the classifiers. SAL (Stream based Active Learning algorithm) is a type of statistical classifiers which is a Bayesian classifier based on probability theory and can support the multi-class classification of data stream. It is capable of handling concept drifts in a data stream.

4.4.3   Outlier Detection

Outlier detection is a technique by which abnormal data can be eliminated from a data stream, in other words if for some data points in stream the typical characteristics of data is different from the entire stream it can be marked as an outlier and eliminated from stream for stream analysis as it indicates noise in the data stream. The main challenge in identifying the outliers in streamed data is the handling of concept drifts, uncertainty, transience and temporal context of data [12, 13]. Various issues in outlier detection for data stream is also discussed by Sadik and Gruenwald [14]. In this section some of the outlier detection techniques discussed by Yu *et al.* [12] are summarized in brief.

Yu *et al.* [12] have discussed that the outlier detection techniques in a data stream can be classified as sliding window based techniques, distance based techniques, density based techniques, statistical based models, kernel density models and clustering based techniques for identification of outliers in a data stream. In sliding window based technique, data stream is processed in a fixed size window (data chunk) from which tentative outliers are identified. As discussed earlier, it is practically not possible to analyze the entire stream so it is a good choice to process the stream in segments and hence sliding window based techniques are a popular choice for analysis tasks such as outlier detection. Various parameters are calculated for a window such as average medians and the calculated value is passed to the next windows for detecting outliers in window based outlier detection techniques. In distance based outlier detection techniques, various distance measures are considered for outlier detection and far away distance elements are marked as outliers in a data stream. In density based outlier detection techniques, the non-dense region of data elements is focused for determining the outliers. A sense region indicates the population of the general data elements and considers them as non-outlier data. Density functions are used to identify the non-dense regions and marking outliers. Statistical based models of outlier detection are parametric models which are driven by various analysis parameters from which the outlier decision can be made. Kernel density based models are nonparametric models which are driven by probability density functions of random variables also known as kernel functions to estimate the outliers in a data stream. The last category of outlier detection technique is the oldest and popular technique called as clustering based models for outlier detection. In this type of technique clusters are created from the data stream and data points which do not fall under any clusters are treated as outliers in the data streams.

4.4.4   Frequent Itemsets Mining

Nasreen *et al.* [15] have compared the five algorithms for finding frequent patterns in data streams. The five frequent pattern mining algorithms are: Apriori algorithm, Frequent Pattern (FP) Growth algorithm, Rapid Association Rule Mining (RARM), ECLAT (Equivalence CLAss Transformation) algorithm and Associated Sensor Pattern Mining of Data

Stream (ASPMS) algorithm. Apriori is the oldest, popular and simplest algorithm for finding the frequent itemsets from a database or from a data stream. It uses the concept of apriori property which states that all the subsets of a frequent itemset are also frequent or it can also be stated that if any subset is not frequent then all its supersets can also be non-frequent. Using this property and counting the frequency of individual items in the database or data stream frequent itemsets can be generated. The only problem with apriori algorithm is more numbers of database scans are required. FP growth algorithm only takes two scans of database for finding the frequent itemsets. It works on a special data structure called a frequent pattern tree (FP-Tree) which stores the items along with its frequencies from which frequent itemsets are mined. RARM computes tries itemsets for finding the frequent itemsets, using the tries generated from the input data stream frequent itemsets are generated. In Equivalence CLAss Transformation (ECLAT) algorithm items along with the list of transactions are maintained and processing is performed on the basis of list of transactions rather than on items. ASPMS algorithm is specifically designed for the wireless sensor network data which uses a specific data structure known as sensor pattern stream tree. Then using a suitable size of window and batch by batch processing frequent patterns can be generated from the sensor pattern stream tree. It is shown that the algorithm performance and selection depends on number of parameters such as number of database scans, execution time and memory requirements.

4.5   Tools & Techniques

In this section various tools and techniques available on different platforms are discussed for implanting the stream data mining operations. Almost every platform supports the following essential functionalities for implementing stream data mining operations:

1. Stream Generation: Stream generation is an important activity provided in stream data mining tools, using its various types of streams can be generated for simulating the stream data mining operations.
2. Classification: Various types of classification algorithms provided for categorizing the data streams.
3. Clustering: Various types of clustering algorithms provided for grouping the data streams. Few tools also provide the

functionalities of outlier detection in stream data to handle noise in data streams.

4. Concept Drift Detection: Concept drift detection is a critical operation in handing data streams. As discussed earlier data streams take a theoretically infinite memory so processing it is a complex task and an analyst needs to identify the cut-off points (known as concept drifts) from where the stream changes and make impact on stream mining operations. So concept drift detection mechanism is also provided by most of the data stream mining tools.

Apart from the above mentioned functionalities, a few other utilities and supporting operations are also provided in the tools dealing with the data stream mining.

4.5.1   Implementation in Java

Stream mining implementation in Java is provided through a MOA platform which is developed by Bifet *et al.* [16]. MOA is Massive Online Analysis platform and is developed by the Waikato University who has earlier developed the WEKA (Waikato Environment for Knowledge Analysis) tool. MOA provides a standard framework for stream mining and includes most of the basic operations for stream mining such as classification, regression, cluster analysis, detection of concept drifts and generation of data streams.

Stream Generators in MOA—MOA supports a number of stream generation algorithms. It includes the Agrawal Generator, Hyperplane Generator, LED Generator, Random RBF Generator, Random Tree Generator, SEA Generator, Stagger Generator and Waveform Generator. In order to generate a particular data stream using any generator some configuration settings are required where user needs to set the value of few parameters. Typically the settings of configuration parameters are namely, instance limit, time limit, sample frequency, memory check frequency, width and alpha are required for generating a particular data stream. A snapshot of configuring settings for generating a data stream is shown in Figure 4.2.

Classifiers—Classification is a key operation in data mining. It is used for categorizing data elements in a collection of data. Various classification models available in MOA are shown in Figure 4.3. It provides the implementation of all standard and popular classification algorithms such as Naive Bayes, SAMkNN, OzaBag, Adaptive Random Forest and Hoeffding Tree.

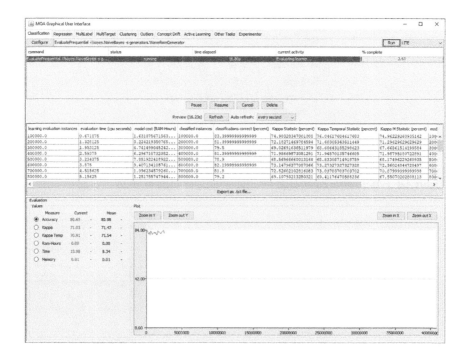

Figure 4.2 Configuration settings for stream generators in MOA.

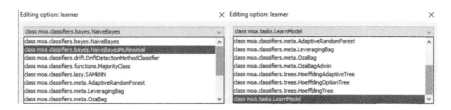

Figure 4.3 Learning models for various classifiers in MOA.

Parameters—In order to evaluate the performance of classifiers in MOA, various performance measures are supported. Evaluation measures are shown in Figure 4.4. Performance parameters accuracy, Kappa, time and memory can be evaluated for the selected stream classifiers.

Clustering—Clustering is the process of grouping the similar objects. For stream mining, clustering can be applied to create the groups of objects coming from a stream. The clustering window of MOA is shown in Figure 4.5. User can select the stream generator, clustering algorithm and performance parameter from this window.

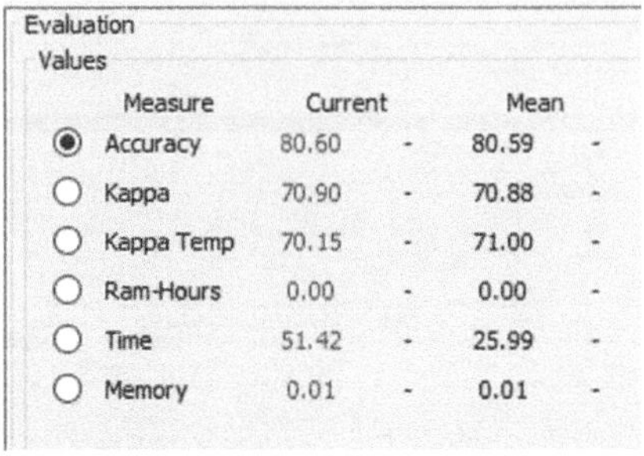

Figure 4.4 Performance Parameters for Evaluating Classifiers in MOA.

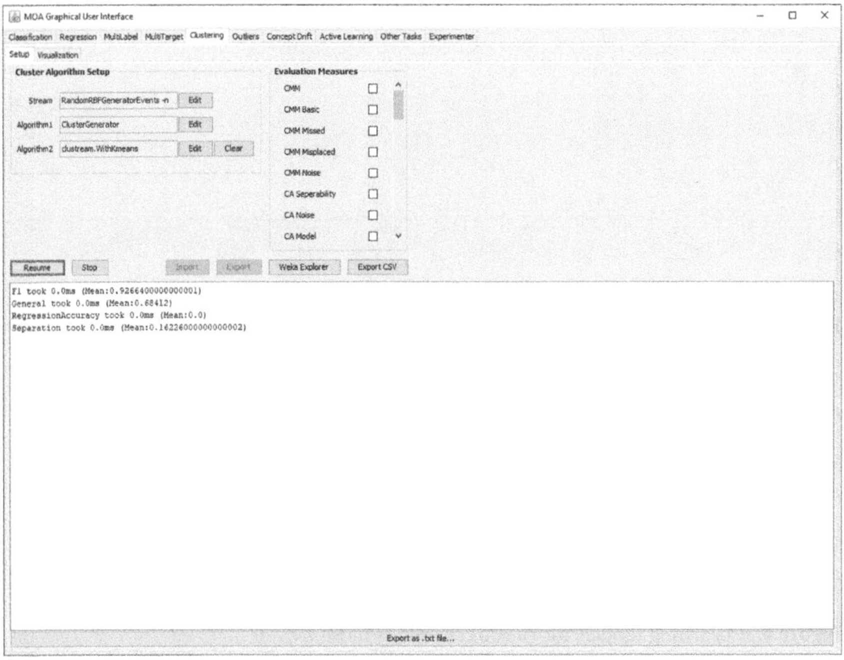

Figure 4.5 Clustering window of MOA for data stream clustering.

Clustering algorithms available in MOA are presented in Figure 4.6. MOA provides the implementation of clustering algorithms like Cluster Generator, CobWeb, ClusTree, Clustream, StreamKM, etc.

Parameters—In order to evaluate the performance of clustering algorithms, numerous parameters are provided by MOA. The list of clustering performance parameters are shown in Figure 4.7. Performance parameters namely, CMM, entropy, purity, precision, recall, number of clusters, time,

Figure 4.6 Clustering algorithms available in MOA.

Figure 4.7 Performance parameters for evaluating clustering in MOA.

memory and sum of square error, etc. can be evaluated for evaluation of clustering algorithms in MOA.

Apart from the clustering algorithms and performance parameters, MOA also provides the visualization of stream clusters with the help of clustering visualization window shown in Figure 4.8. Cluster centers, population density and cluster overlapping kind of information can be visualized using the visualization tool of MOA in Java.

Concept Drift—Concept drift window of MOA implementation is shown in Figure 4.9. User can select a particular concept drift detection technique for a data stream and evaluate the performance of it.

Active Learning—MOA also supports the implementation of active learning algorithms shown in Figure 4.10. User can generate any type of data stream, apply the active learning algorithm and select the performance parameters for evaluating the algorithms in this window.

Outlier Detection—Outlier detection and outlier visualization window in MOA is shown in Figures 4.11 and 4.12 respectively. Here user can also select any outlier detection algorithm and stream generator to evaluate any outlier detection technique in a data stream. Just like cluster visualization interface, outlier visualization interface is also provided in the Java MOA for outlier visualization in a data stream.

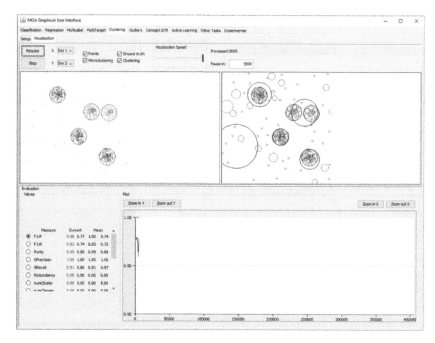

Figure 4.8 Clustering visualization in MOA.

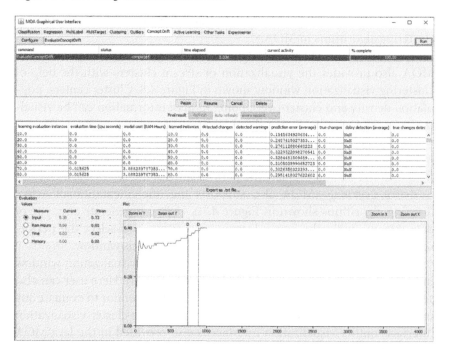

Figure 4.9 Concept drift detection techniques in MOA.

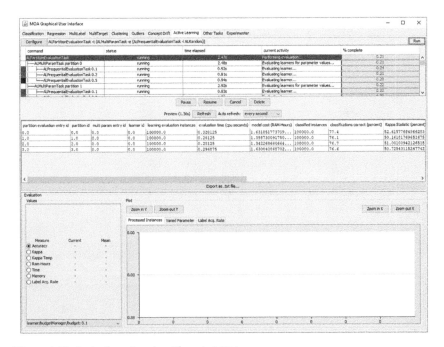

Figure 4.10 Active learning algorithms in MOA.

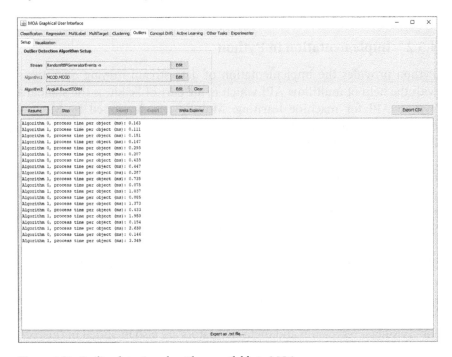

Figure 4.11 Outlier detection algorithms available in MOA.

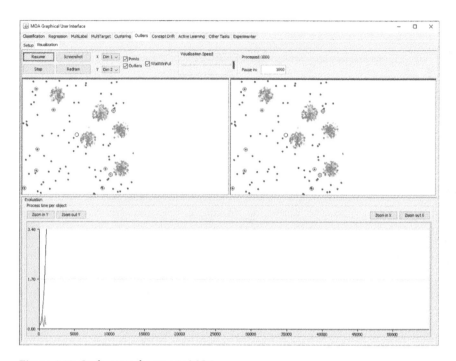

Figure 4.12 Outlier visualization in MOA.

4.5.2   Implementation in Python

Python provides the implementation of data stream mining operations with the help of multiflow API which is the part of Scikit, is the standard python API for machine learning. Multiflow is developed by Montiel *et al.* [17]. In order to use the python stream mining API, user needs to first install the multiflow package using pip or conda command like:

pip install -U scikit-multiflow

Just like Java MOA API, multiflow also provides a standard framework for implementing data stream mining operations. The multiflow API is broadly managed in seven major sections, namely, core, data, learning methods, drift detection, evaluation, transformation and miscellaneous API.

Core—The core module of multiflow API includes the base classes for all the major data stream mining operations classes. For example base estimator class for compatibility with scikit-learn package is included in it to make the multiflow data stream mining operations compatible with the basic python analysis and learning operations. Similarly, mix-in classes for classifiers, regression and meta estimators are also included in the core package of the multiflow package.

Data—Stream generation in python is performed using data module of multiflow. It provides the option to create a stream from data source or files. It also provides the option of stream generation with concept drift or with temporal data stream. It has several algorithms for generating streams to name a few key algorithms are LED stream generator, Hyperplane generator, random RBF generator, random tree generator, SEA generator, Sine generator, Stagger generator, Wave generator, Multilabel generator and Regression stream generators.

Learning methods—Learning methods module includes the implementation of anomaly detection methods, probability based Naive Bayes classifier, lazy learning methods, and ensemble methods. Lazy learning methods further include the implementation of KNN classifier, KNN classifier with ADWIN change detector, self-adjusting memory coupled KNN classifier and KNN regressor classifier. Ensemble methods further include the implementation of accuracy weighted classifier, adaptive random forest, additive expert classifier, classifier chains with multi label learning, Monte Carlo sampling classifier, dynamic weighted majority classifier, Learn++ classifier, online AdaC2 classifier, online boosting classifier, online CSB2 classifier, online CSB2 classifier, online SMOTE bagging classifier, Oza bagging classifier, Oza bagging with ADWIN change classifier, regressor chains of multi output classifier and streaming random patches ensemble classifiers.

Neural Networks—The neural network module provides the implementation of mask for Perceptron algorithm for handing stream data with the help of neural network.

Prototype-based methods—This prototype provides the implementation of robust soft learning vector quantization algorithm for both stream and non-stream data.

Rules-based methods—Very fast decision rule classifier is provided in the rule based methods in multiflow.

Trees-based methods—Multiflow module also provides the implementation of tree based learning methods for stream mining operations. The key algorithms available in it are: Hoeffding adaptive tree classifier, Hoeffding tree or very fast decision tree classifier, extremely fast decision tree classifier, label combination Hoeffding tree classifier with multi label classification, Hoeffding tree regressor, Hoeffding adaptive tree classifier, incremental structured output prediction tree and stacked single target Hoeffding tree regressor algorithm.

Drift Detection—Drift detection module provides the implementation of various concept drift detection technique in python through multiflow module. It includes the implementation of ADWIN algorithm, drift detection method, early drift detection method, and drift detection using Hoeffding bounds with moving average and weighted average method, Kolmogorov–Smirnov Windowing method and Page–Hinkley method for concept drift detection.

Evaluation—For evaluation of data stream mining operations in multiflow, three evaluation strategies are present in the multiflow API. These evaluation methods are holdout evaluation, prequential evaluation and prequential evaluation delayed method. Parameters accuracy, kappa, precision, recall, f-measure and gmean are used for the evaluation of classification algorithms in multiflow API. For multi target classification parameters hamming score, hamming loss, exact match and j index are used. For Regression techniques mean square error, mean absolute error and average root mean square error are used. For multi target regression average mean squared error, average mean absolute error and average root mean square error are used.

4.5.3 Implementation in R

Stream data mining in R programming language is provided using stream package. Stream package is developed by Hahsler *et al.* [18] and provides a simple and nice way for clustering and animation of stream clustering. A sample code snippet for performing data stream clustering is presented in Figure 4.13 along with the output. The cluster visualization sample output is shown in Figure 4.14.

Another code snippet for cluster animation in R is shown in Figure 4.15 and animation output is shown in Figure 4.16.

Stream Generation and Clustering algorithms—BICO (K-means coresets algorithm), BIRCH (Balanced Iterative Reducing Clustering using Hierarchies), DBSCAN (density based clustering algorithm), DBSTREAM, D-Stream, Evolutionary Algorithm, Hierarchical Micro cluster re-clusterer

```
>stream <- DSD_Gaussians(k=5, d=2)
>dstream <- DSC_DStream(gridsize=0.05, Cm=1.5)
>update(dstream, stream, 500)
>plot(dstream, stream)
>evaluate(dstream, stream, measure=c("numMicro","numMacro","purity", "crand", "SSQ"),
+        n=100)
Evaluation results for micro-clusters.
Points were assigned to micro-clusters.

numMicroClusters numMacroClusters     purity      cRand        SSQ
    25.0000000        5.0000000    0.9145658   0.1286303   0.4904225
```

Figure 4.13 Code snippet for demonstrating stream package from R for stream clustering.

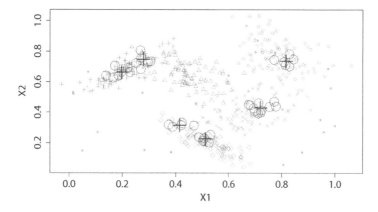

Figure 4.14 Output of stream package from R for stream clustering.

```
>stream <- DSD_Gaussians(k=5, d=2)
>dstream <- DSC_DStream(gridsize=0.05, lambda=0.1)
>animate_cluster(dstream, stream, horizon=100, n=5000,
+        measure=c("crand"), type="macro", assign="micro",
+        plot.args = list(type="both", xlim=c(0,1), ylim=c(0,1)))
```

Figure 4.15 Code snippet for clustering animation from stream package in R.

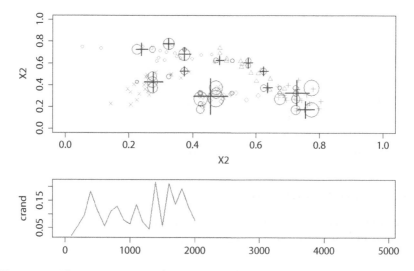

Figure 4.16 Clustering animation from stream package in R.

algorithm, K-means, Sample (fixed size sample from data stream), Window (sliding window from a data stream) and Bars and Gaussians generator.

In order to evaluate the performance of stream data clustering numerous performance parameters are included in the stream package. The key parameters included for evaluating stream clustering are number of micro clusters, number of macro clusters, and number of classes.

Three noise related parameters namely, Number data points predicted as noise, Number of data points which are actually noise and Precision of the predicting noise are provided in the package.

Stream clustering evaluation parameters are broadly categorized into two categories namely, internal evaluation measures and external evaluation measures. Stream package of R provides both types of performance parameters implementation. The internal evaluation measures are within cluster sum of squares, silhouette index, average distance between clusters, average distance within clusters, maximum cluster diameter, minimum cluster separation, within clusters sum of squares, Goodman and Kruskal's Gamma coefficient, Pearson Gamma correlation, Dunn index and entropy of the cluster memberships. The external evaluation measures are precision, recall, F1 measure, purity, Euclidean dissimilarity, Manhattan dissimilarity, Rand index, Adjusted Rand index, Normalized Mutual Information, Katz–Powell index, maximal cosine of the angle between the agreements, maximal co-classification rate, Fowlkes and Mallows's index, Jaccard index, Prediction Strength and variation of information.

4.6 Applications

With the invention of the Internet of Things and development of advanced internet based online applications a huge amount of continuous data are generated as a data stream. Mining of such data stream can yield useful knowledge and patterns using which smart and intelligent systems can be developed for various applications. Some of the major applications of data stream mining are discussed in this section.

4.6.1 Stock Prediction in Share Market

Stock market is the area where not only machine learning techniques but also the advance technologies like deep learning, etc. are utilized to forecast the stock prices. Since stock market is volatile in nature and every moment (off course during the working hours) the price of a particular stock fluctuates. These fluctuations are due to various factors and the price data works as a data stream or continuous flow of price data over a period of time so stream mining techniques can also be utilized for effective analysis of the stock price stream. Prediction of the stocks can be made by mining the stream of the stock prices. Oğuz *et al.* [19] have proposed a work in the field of predicting stock market price movement using technical indicators. The concept of data stream mining is used by the authors.

4.6.2   Weather Forecasting System

Weather forecasting is another area where a lot of data impacting the weather is generated every moment. Earlier weather forecasting was carried by deploying sensors at various places particularly at weather stations, but nowadays with the help of advanced satellite systems images are produced and analyzed for making the forecasting of weather. Since there is no limit on data capturing either from the sensors or by the satellites so these input data can be treated as the data stream for weather data which can be analyzed using stream mining technique to forecast and categorize the weather data for a particular location. Concept drift detection with application to weather data stream is proposed by Namitha [20].

4.6.3   Finding Trending News and Events

There are so many news collaborators available on the Internet today. News are captured from various news websites and made available to the users through websites and mobile apps. Thus news data also generates a data stream of text data consisting of news information. With the help of stream data mining, trending news and event information can be mined and other major analysis tasks such as grouping the similar news contents and categorizing it can be done. A recent work in this direction is carried by Liu *et al.* [21] where an event extracting and breaking news identification approach is proposed. Another work in the similar directions is proposed by Mele *et al.* [22] where event mining and analysis of news stream is performed.

4.6.4   Analyzing User Behavior in Electronic Commerce Site (Click Stream)

Electronic commerce sites are also getting popular day by day as users are now tending to buy most of the items through online shopping sites. The user data from these sites are analyzed for a number of analysis tasks such as deciding combo offers, seasonal offers and recommending new products.

Users can interact in many ways on these online shopping sites particularly browsing the items, which also generated huge amount of data at real time can be captured as data stream of user's interaction with the electronic commerce sites. With the help of stream data mining numerous analysis tasks can be carried out for better analysis of the users behavior and product information analysis. A survey on user behavior in digital marketing is performed by Padigela and Suguna [22] using clickstream data mining.

4.6.5   Pollution Control Systems

Just like the weather forecasting systems now a day's pollution monitoring systems consisting of number of sensors are deployed in most of the cities of the world. With the help of IoT (Internet of Things) technologies the sensor data from pollution monitoring systems can fed to the server instantaneously and causes the generation of data stream for the pollution data.

Data stream mining is not only applicable to the above systems but it also has numerous applications to various other applications such as Healthcare systems, financial applications, and many other real world applications where data is continuous coming all the period of time.

4.7   Conclusion

An overview of data stream mining is presented in this chapter. Major tasks in data stream mining such as sampling and sketching, concept drift detection, classification, clustering and outlier detection in a data stream are discussed. Tools and techniques for data stream mining in Java, Python and R programming languages are also covered to demonstrate the implementation part of stream mining tasks. Some of the key applications of data stream mining are also discussed in the chapter.

References

1. Gaber, M.M., Zaslavsky, A., Krishnaswamy, S., Mining data streams: A review. *ACM Sigmod Rec.*, 34, 2, 18–26, 2005.
2. Ahmed, M., Data summarization: A survey. *Knowl. Inf. Syst.*, 58, 2, 249–273, 2019.

3. Hu, W. and Zhang, B., Study of sampling techniques and algorithms in data stream environments, in: *IEEE 2012 9th International Conference on Fuzzy Systems and Knowledge Discovery*, pp. 1028–1034, 2012.

4. El Sibai, R., Chabchoub, Y., Demerjian, J., Kazi-Aoul, Z., Barbar, K., Sampling algorithms in data stream environments, in: *IEEE 2016 International Conference on Digital Economy (ICDEc)*, pp. 29–36, 2016.

5. Haas, P.J., Data-stream sampling: basic techniques and results, in: *Data Stream Management*, pp. 13–44, Springer, Berlin, Heidelberg, 2016.

6. Cormode, G. and Muthukrishnan, S., An improved data stream summary: the count-min sketch and its applications. *J. Algorithms*, 55, 1, 58–75, 2005.

7. Liu, Z., Ben-Basat, R., Einziger, G., Kassner, Y., Braverman, V., Friedman, R., Sekar, V., Nitrosketch: Robust and general sketch-based monitoring in software switches, in: *Proceedings of the ACM Special Interest Group on Data Communication*, pp. 334–350, 2019.

8. Wares, S., Isaacs, J., Elyan, E., Data stream mining: Methods and challenges for handling concept drift. *SN Appl. Sci.*, 1, 1412, 2019, https://doi.org/10.1007/s42452-019-1433-0.

9. Gonçalves Jr., P.M., de Carvalho Santos, S.G., Barros, R.S., Vieira, D.C., A comparative study on concept drift detectors. *Expert Syst. Appl.*, 41, 18, 8144–8156, 2014.

10. Alothali, E., Alashwal, H., Harous, S., Data stream mining techniques: A review. *Telkomnika*, 17, 2, 728–737, 2019.

11. Nagwani, N.K., Impact of Dimensionality on the Evaluation of Stream Data Clustering Algorithms. *Fifth International Congress on Information and Communication Technology ICICT*, London, UK, 2020.

12. Yu, K., Shi, W., Santoro, N., Ma, X., Real-time Outlier Detection over Streaming Data, in: *2019 IEEE SmartWorld, Ubiquitous Intelligence & Computing, Advanced & Trusted Computing, Scalable Computing & Communications, Cloud & Big Data Computing, Internet of People and Smart City Innovation (SmartWorld/SCALCOM/UIC/ATC/CBDCom/IOP/SCI)*, pp. 125–132, 2019.

13. Chen, L., Gao, S., Cao, X., Research on real-time outlier detection over big data streams. *Int. J. Comput. Appl.*, 42, 1, 93–101, 2020.

14. Sadik, S. and Gruenwald, L., Research issues in outlier detection for data streams. *ACM Sigkdd Explor. Newsl.*, 15, 1, 33–40, 2014.

15. Nasreen, S., Azam, M.A., Shehzad, K., Naeem, U., Ghazanfar, M.A., Frequent pattern mining algorithms for finding associated frequent patterns for data streams: A survey. *Proc. Comput. Sci.*, 37, 109–116, 2014.

16. Bifet, A., Holmes, G., Pfahringer, B., Kranen, P., Kremer, H., Jansen, T., Seidl, T., Moa: Massive online analysis, a framework for stream classification and clustering, in: *Proceedings of the First Workshop on Applications of Pattern Analysis*, pp. 44–50, 2010, https://moa.cms.waikato.ac.nz/ (Last accessed on 01/07/2020).

17. Montiel, J., Read, J., Bifet, A., Abdessalem, T., Scikit-multiflow: A multi-output streaming framework. *J. Mach. Learn. Res.*, 19, 1, 2915–2914, 2018, URL https://scikit-multiflow.github.io/ (Last accessed on 01/07/2020).
18. Hahsler, M., Bolanos, M., Forrest, J., Introduction to stream: An extensible framework for data stream clustering research with r. *J. Stat. Softw.*, 76, 1, 1–50, 2017.
19. Oğuz, R.F., Uygun, Y., Aktaş, M.S., Aykurt, İ., On the Use of Technical Analysis Indicators for Stock Market Price Movement Direction Prediction, in: *IEEE 2019 27th Signal Processing and Communications Applications Conference (SIU)*, pp. 1–4, 2019.
20. Namitha, K., Concept Drift Detection in Data Stream Clustering and its Application on Weather Data. *Int. J. Agric. Environ. Inf. Syst. (IJAEIS)*, 11, 1, 67–85, 2020.
21. Liu, B., Han, F.X., Niu, D., Kong, L., Lai, K., Xu, Y., Story Forest: Extracting Events and Telling Stories from Breaking News. *ACM Trans. Knowl. Discovery Data (TKDD)*, 14, 3, 1–28, 2020.
22. Mele, I., Bahrainian, S.A., Crestani, F., Event mining and timeliness analysis from heterogeneous news streams. *Inf. Process. Manage.*, 56, 3, 969–993, 2019.
23. Padigela, P.K. and Suguna, R.A., Survey on Analysis of User Behavior on Digital Market by Mining Clickstream Data, in: *Proceedings of the Third International Conference on Computational Intelligence and Informatics*, Springer, Singapore, pp. 535–545, 2020.

5

Data Mining Tools and Techniques: Clustering Analysis

Rohit Miri[1], Amit Kumar Dewangan[2]*, S.R. Tandan[1], Priya Bhatnagar[3] and Hiral Raja[4]

[1]Department of CSE, Dr. C.V. Raman University Bilaspur, Chhattisgarh, India
[2]IT Department, G.G.V. (Central University) Bilaspur, Chhattisgarh, India
[3]Department of CSE, VNR VJIET, Hyderabad, India
[4]CMR Engineering College, Hyderabad, India

Abstract

The whole research focuses on a range of techniques, challenges, and different areas of investigation that are useful and identified as an important field of data mining technology. Even though we know, many MNCs and huge organisations are working in better places in different countries. Each place of action can generate huge amounts of data. Corporate executives grant access from every solitary source and make vital choices. The Information Distribution Center is often used in an enormous business sense by enhancing the viability of the administrative dynamic. In an uncertain and deeply serious development business, the approximation of important data frameworks, for example, is nevertheless successfully viewed in the existing business situation. Efficiency or frequency is not the key to intensity. This kind of tremendous amount of information is available as a tera-to-petabyte that has completely changed in the scientific fields and specification. To analyze, monitor, and resolve the selection of this massive quantity of information, we require methodology based Data Mining, that will change in a lot of areas. The whole paper also observes focusing on the current characterization and data recovery strategies to use a computation that will acquire a lot of reports. Accordingly, the unfurling of information in writings is chosen as the best possible philosophy

**Corresponding author*: amit.nitrr@gmail.com

Rohit Raja, Kapil Kumar Nagwanshi, Sandeep Kumar and K. Ramya Laxmi (eds.) Data Mining and Machine Learning Applications, (125–150) © 2022 Scrivener Publishing LLC

to be followed, and the means are disclosed to arrive at the order of the solo report. In the wake of leading a trial with three of the most known strategies for unaided records arrangement and the evaluation of the outcomes with the Silhouette list, it could be seen that the better gathering was with four gatherings whose principle trademark was to manage subjects, for example, data the executive's data, frameworks the board, man-made reasoning, and advanced picture preparing.

Keywords: Data mining tasks, data mining application, document clustering, data mining life cycle, data mining methods

5.1   Introduction

With its simplest design, Data Mining mechanizes the recognition of prominent features in the data source, using characterized methods and computations to researches have been proposed and severe data that could then be analyzed to predict future trends. Just like data mining tools recognize potential practices and knowledge by browsing data sets for hidden case studies, they allow organizations to make comprehensive, information-driven decisions and response identify that were previously too cumbersome to identify.

Data Mining has a lengthy tradition, with strong roots in quantification, human-made justification, AI, and the development of the existing data. Data Mining is a step in the public disclosure from the knowledge Base (KDD) measure that involves the use of data collection and audit computations to create a particular verification of illustrations (or models) over relevant data.

Data Mining is a way of eliminating data from alternative views and summarizing it in useful data that can be used to generate revenue, reduce costs, or both. Data Mining computing is one of the relevant forensic systems for the interpretation of information. It enables consumers to analyze data from a wide variety of observations or edges, requests it, and summarizes the distinctive contacts. Data Mining is a place to explore links or examples between so many areas in the huge social baseline performance. Data Mining originally comes from the resemblance between searching for relevant information in an immense set of data and searching a cliff for an important metal vein. The two phases permit, be it sorting through such a vicious measure of the substance or smartly investigating it, to find out where the value resides.

Data Mining, or disclosure of data, is the CP that assisted the process of digging through and collapsing large reverse structures and then trying to separate the significant data. The concepts of KDD and Data Mining are exceptional. KDD relates to the "cycle of discovering useful information from information." Data Mining refers to finding new examples of the explosion of data in the baseline performance by tuning on the computations to differentiate valuable information.

The KDD measure consists of adaptive achieve sustainability as described in the following:

1. Selection: choosing the relevant data for the evaluation assignment from the existing data;
2. Pre-processing: removal of concussion and inaccurate statements; consolidation of extraction of knowledge;
3. Transformation: converting data into appropriate data mining systems;
4. Data Mining: selecting a Data Mining computation that is appropriate for the layout of the data;
5. Translation/Evaluation: analyzing descriptions into data by removing extra or meaningless instances; trying to interpret the strongest overall inhumanly acceptable terms.

Data Mining is indeed an ability to share an apparatus that incorporates structures for the data source, AI, evaluation, recognition of data analytics, and other orders. Data Mining modified retrospective approach is a non-partisan section of the organization that promotes description, forecasting, and targeting. Data Mining can often help in forecasting future opportunities. Data Mining could even make use of essential recorded data and provides vital information.

Steps for Mining the Data:
With ventures, multidimensional geographic areas, multi-information base digging is getting significant for successful and educated dynamics. The accompanying Data Mining strategies will assist you in improving your mining:

Stage 1: Handling of unstructured information
Unstructured information influences exactness and successful Data Mining. The accompanying strategies are viable for working with such sort of information.

- The ISOM-DH method is beneficial in identifying relevant details and imagining that it took good care of high-dimensional data through the use of an available section investigative process (ICA) and self-assessment guides (SOMs). A further structure relies on the structures gathered using parametric and nonparametric ascription methods or evolutionary computations to construct a design.

- Organization approaches dependent on performing multiple task learning utilized for design grouping, with missing sources of info, can be contrasted and agent methodology utilized for taking care of inadequate information on two notable informational indexes.

Stage 2: Provide successful Data Mining Algorithm
Expertise is required for the utilization, execution, support, and execution of compelling Data Mining applications. These strategies may help:

- Implementation of Data Mining designs.
- The network authorizes Data Mining requests through not at all intercession arranged the submission adjacent.
- Decide on versatile Data Mining.
- Eliminate hindrances.

Stage 3: Mining of enormous Databases
Use join set structural with information base frameworks. Such Data Mining strategies could include:

- An embodiment of the Data Mining calculation.
- Reserving the information, at that point, mining.
- Tight-coupling with client characterized capacities.
- SQL executions for DBMS.

Stage 4: Handling of Data types
It's hard to build up a framework for intelligent mining of different levels of information in enormous data sets and information distribution centers. This requires the tight coupling of systematic online preparing with a wide range of Data Mining capacities, including characterization, affiliation, order, forecast, and grouping. The framework ought to encourage question-based, intelligent mining of multidimensional information bases by actualizing a lot of advances Data Mining incorporates:

- Multidimensional investigation
- Data Mining refined information

- Meta-mining, and information and information perception
- Assessing Data Mining results
- Analyzing chart information bases
- sub-chart histogram portrayal.

Stage 5: Handling Heterogeneous condition
Heterogeneous data set frameworks are mainstream ones in the data industry in 2011. Information stockrooms must help information extraction from numerous data sets to stay aware of the pattern.

5.2   Data Mining Task

5.2.1   Data Summarization

Summarization is the speculation or reflection of information. A lot of significant information is disconnected and summed up, coming about a little set that gives an overall diagram of information. For instance, the significant distance calls of the client can be summed up to add up to minutes, absolute calls, complete spending, and so forth rather than itemized calls. Correspondingly the calls can be summed up into neighborhood calls, STD calls, ISD calls, and so forth.

5.2.2   Data Clustering

Bunching is distinguishing comparable gatherings from unstructured information. Bunching is the order of gathering of several articles in just such a way that objects in the very same selection are almost like one another and then that in various gatherings. When the groups are chosen, the articles are named their comparative bunches, and the normal highlights of the items in the bunch are summed up to form a class portrait. For example, a bank can connect its customer to several meetings that rely heavily on the similarity of their income, age, sex, home, and so on, as well as the request features of customers in a meeting could be used to depict that collection of customers. This will make it easier for the bank to understand its customers and therefore provide modified offices.

5.2.3   Classification of Data

The portrayal is learning decisions that can only be exposed to specific data and therefore will ordinarily be incorporated after developments:

pre-preparing data, scheduling, training/highlighting, and authorization/ evaluation. Request anticipates all of its consistently valued capabilities. For example, we can use a grouping model to order a bank credit application as either sheltered or unsafe. The arrangement is the induction of a framework that takes the class of a product that is completely reliant on its composes. A considerable amount of articles is given as a set of preparations whereby each product is referred to and along with its team by a vector of attributes. Besides attempting to break down the link between the features and the class of the items in the preparation set, a grouping model can be developed. That very clustering method can be used to organize future posts and to construct a greater knowledge of the courses of products in the existing data. For example, from either the configuration of progress issuers (Name, Age, and Income) who bring in as set-up, a request model can be built that decides to close the bank loan application either as sheltered or hazardous (On the off chance that age = Youth, at that point Loan choice = hazardous).

5.2.4   Data Regression

Relapse is discovering capacity with an insignificant blunder to display information. It is a factual system that is frequently utilized for the numeric forecast. The relapse investigation is widely used for expectations and guidance, whereby the user does have a significant impact mostly on the AI field. The relapse test has also been used to understand if any of the independent variables are recognized with both the parameter needed and to evaluate the forms of such connexions. Throughout specific circumstances, the relapse investigation may be used to establish causal relationships between both the available and ward aspects. Even so, it might lead to desires or false connexions, so advise smartly [1], for instance, the relationship doesn't suggest causation.

5.2.5   Data Association

Affiliation is searching for a connection between factors or items. It plans to remove intriguing affiliation, relationships, or easy-going structures among the articles, for example, the presence of another arrangement of articles [2]. The affiliation rules can help promote where the board, publicizing, and so forth. Affiliation rule learning is a central feature and an all-around researched methodology for discovering fascinating connexions among variables with specific regard to exceptionally enormous units. This is designed to recognize strong rules discovered in baseline performance utilizing different quantities of benefit [3] and reliant on the concept of sound specifications presented in [4], the association regulations for discovering values and attitudes among items in the vast scope of information exchange recorded by retail location (POS) frameworks in general stores. For example, the norm {Onions, potatoes} {burger} prevalent in the general store's business data will indeed show that if the consumer buys onions and potatoes together, the person in question is likely to buy hamburger meat in the same way. That very information may be used as a basis for choosing decisions about undertakings, e.g., time-limited evaluation or product accommodations. Despite the apparent above-mentioned model of market container investigatory affiliation rules are currently applied in several implementation areas, which include internet use mining, interference recognition, constant generation, and computational biology.

5.3   Data Mining Algorithms and Methodologies

Various calculations and methodologies, such as Classification, Artificial Intelligence, Genetic Algorithms, Neural Networks, Nearest Neighbour Strategy, Association, Rules Clustering, Regression, Decision Trees, and so on, are used for disclosing information from baseline performance.

5.3.1   Data Classification Algorithm

The framework is perhaps the most frequently used Data Mining method, which uses a large set of pre-characterized tutorials to develop a classifier that can set the number of individuals in broken archives. Recognition of fraud and credit-hazard technologies are particularly suitable for the type of investigative process. This method of analysis often uses selected tree or cognitive organization-based character development computations. Measures for the informational collection involve learning and clustering. In Learning, the preparedness data are evaluated by analysis measurement. Test information is used to measure the accuracy of the clustering rules. The mostly on-off possibility that the truthfulness is adequate the regulations can be applied to new data vertices. For something like a misappropriation identifying implementation, it would also utilize total data of both false and significant activities finally agreed on a database-by-record assumption. The classifier-preparing calculation uses these pre-grouped guides to determine the boundaries required for legitimate separation. The calculation at that point encodes these limits into a model called a classifier.

5.3.2 Predication

The relapse technique can be adapted for the predictive model. The relapse investigation could be used to show the connexion among at least one independent component and the clinic factor. In Data Mining Free variables, credits are known and the response variables are what we need to predict. Unfortunately, a few of the actual concerns are not always anticipated. For illustration, agreements on volumes, stock costs, and item failure rates are generally difficult to predict on the premises that they can rely on changes that occurred of several indicators. Along those same lines, the most mind-boggling methods (e.g., calculated relapse, choice of trees, or neural networks) may be essential for forecasting future attributes. Actual performance against standards sorts can be used frequently for both relapse and portrayal. For example, the CART (Classification and Regression Trees) tree selection calculation can be used to organize both place trees (to characterize exact reaction factors) and relapse trees (to estimate persistent reaction factors). Neural organizations also can develop both tend-to-group and relapse designs.

5.3.3 Association Rule

Affiliation and connexion is usually the discovery of frequent inventions among the vast amounts of data and information. But that kind of discovery specific problem to decide on deliberate changes, such as inventory installation, cross-showing, and customer shopping. Affiliation Rule computations should have the alternative of establishing rules with the assurance that it is short of what might be. In any case, the number of feasible Association Rules for a set of data is usually immense, and a high degree of guidelines is usually of the little (considering) accomplishment.

5.3.4 Neural Network

The cognitive organization is a huge amount of related input/yield components, and each affiliation has its mass. Mostly during the learning phase, the network can learn by changing loads to be allowed to predict the correct type of information of the knowledge data points. Neural organizations have a tremendous opportunity to acquire significance from jumbled or inaccurate data and can be used to differentiate instances and to recognize patterns that are too troubling to be shown in any manner, either through individuals or by other Computer processes. Those were suitable for prolonged valued information sources and products. For example, translated character reconfigure, for the preparation of a Computer for the articulation of English decision and various real business issues, has just been efficiently implemented in a range of companies. Neural organizations are ideally equipped to recognize instances or trends of data and to meet expectations or implement the strategy.

5.3.4.1   Data Clustering Algorithm

Data Clustering could be said to be an ID of the relative classifications of products. By using clustering methods, we can further differentiate dense and scanty regions in the spatial domain and, therefore, can normally find examples of scattering and connexions between data assigns. Structure methodology can also be used for efficient techniques of recognition of collections or electives of items, but it transforms out to have been extraordinarily high so that clustering can be used as a pre-processing strategy for identification and characterization of subsets. For example, to form the collection of customers completely reliant on the purchase of design elements, to classify quality with similar relevance is represented in Figures 5.1 and 5.2.

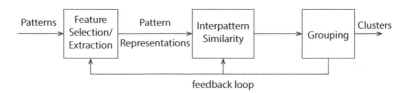

Figure 5.1 Shows different data clustering stages.

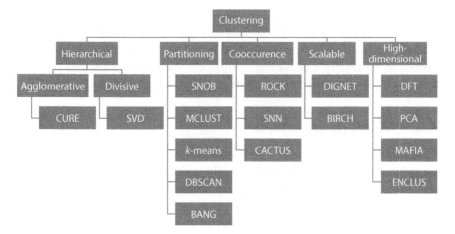

Figure 5.2 Shows clustering techniques classifications.

5.3.5   In-Depth Study of Gathering Techniques

Even if all is said to have been completed, considerable clustering methodologies could be organized in the functional process.

5.3.6   Data Partitioning Method

Assume there are n objects in the first informational collection; dividing techniques split the first informational index into k allotments.

- Relegate each object to the group related to the nearest centroid;
- Register the new situation of every centroid by the mean estimation of the items in a bunch.
- Rehash steps 2 and 3 until the methods are fixed [5].

A fuzzy clustering categorization measurement receives a lone package of data instead of a particular construct, e.g., a significantly more active provided by a progressive method. Methodologies are of benefit to implementations, including large-scale information compilations in which the advancement of a graph is computational complexity unfeasible [6]. The problem regarding the use of a partial measurement is the choice of the amount of the potential acquisition clumps. The primary research sets out the path for this having promised selection. Partitional methodologies probably contain communities by enhancing the tasks of a regime characterized whether regionally (on a subset of examples) or across the world (characterized over a whole number of instances).

The combined advancement of the design of possible labels for the optimal assessment of a method of measuring is computational complexity restrictive. Technically speaking; therefore, the measurement is normally produced on multiple occasions to different starting regions, and the system model obtained from that series is used as a gathering of returns.

5.3.7   Hierarchical Method

This strategy gives the tree connection among bunches and creates a dendrogram speaking to the settled gathering relationship among objects. On the off chance that the bunching chain of importance is shaped from the base up, toward the beginning, every information object is a group without anyone else, at that point, little bunches are converged into greater bunches at each degree of the progressive system. This kind of progressive technique is called agglomerative. The contrary cycle is called disruptive [7].

The entity measurement of this kind is systematic bundling, which would be modified into the well-known mathematical computing of MATLAB [8]. This measurement is a fuzzy clustering measurement that has several variations that depend on the measurement used only to calculate the separations between the clusters. Euclidean separation is typically used as a special emphasis. There are still no known methods to be used for community splitting, and the database seems to be unmistakably assisted. One of the most commonly used variants of liberal bundling, depending on the various surface steps, is [9] shown in Figure 5.3:

- *Normal linkage bunching:*
  The uniqueness between bunches is determined by utilizing normal values. The normal separation is determined from the separation between each point in a group and all different focuses in another group. The two groups with the most reduced normal separation are consolidated to frame the new bunch.
- *Centroid linkage grouping:*
  This variety utilizes the gathering centroid as the normal. The centroid is characterized as the focal point of a haze of focuses.
- *Complete linkage bunching (Maximum or Furthest-Neighbor Method):*
  The difference between two gatherings is equivalent to the best divergence between an individual from group I and an individual from group j. This technique will in general, deliver tight groups of comparable cases.

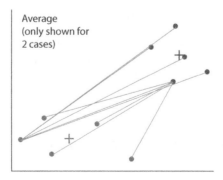

Figure 5.3 Shows centroid linkage clustering.

- *Single linkage grouping (Minimum or Nearest-Neighbor Method):*
  The divergence between two bunches is the base uniqueness between individuals from the two bunches. This technique creates long chains that structure-free, irregular groups.
- *The Stake technique:*
  Cluster membership is distributed by testing the actual totality of standard different from the mass average. The justification for the configuration is that the smallest feasible increase in the accumulated error of the distributions will be given.

5.3.8   Framework-Based Method

This procedure gauges the item space into a limited number of cells that structure a lattice structure on which the entirety of the tasks for bunching is performed [10]. It depends on bunching-focused question replying in staggered network structures. In upper-level stores, examination of the data of it's after that level, accordingly, the networks make cells between the associated levels.

5.3.9   Model-Based Method

Model-put together bunching procedure is based concerning the best conjecture that information is produced by a mix of hidden likelihood disseminations, and they enhance the fit among the information and some numerical model.

5.3.10   Thickness-Based Method

The thickness-based strategies follow the growing of the bunch until a thickness limit is reached [11]. For these techniques, an "area" must be characterized, and the thickness must be determined by the number of substances in the area.

5.4   Clustering the Nearest Neighbor

As proximity comprises a vital aspect of the impulsive thinking of a lot, the nearest - neighbor variations will serve as the basis of a sorting technique. An experimental procedure has been suggested in Lu and Fu 1978;

it assigns every unmarked instance to a lot of its closest-marked neighbor nature, provided that the distinction of the identified neighbor is below a limit. The process begins till all samples are called or no additional marks are made. Popular neighborhood affection (portrayed above concerning the removal of measurement) could also be used to establish close-neighbor communities.

5.4.1 Fuzzy Clustering

Customary grouping methodologies create allotments; in a segment, the respective example has a place with on and just one bunch. Consequently, the groups in hard bunching are disjoint. Fuzzy grouping stretches out this thought to relate each pattern [12] with each bunch utilizing a participation work. The performance of such measurements is a collection but not a package shown in Figure 5.4.

5.4.2 K-Algorithm Means

The K-means measurement, probably the first one of the suggested sorting measurements, focuses on a simple idea: given the majority of explanatory bundles, assign one of them to every one of the highlights, at a certain stage, each category position is replaced by the basis on the bundle [13]. Such two important developments have been reshaped until around the association. A value is assigned to the category that is similar to the Euclidean separation. Even though K-means does have an extraordinary chance to impress of being anything other than hard to prove, there are two major setbacks [14]. To begin with, it can be quite complicated because,

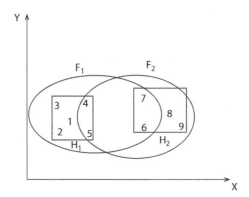

Figure 5.4 Show fuzzy clustering.

for each development, the distinction between both the highlights within each group needs to be calculated but can be rather costly in the view of an immense database. Second, this approach is genuinely applicable to the developmental classes, even though, lately, this topic has appeared to have some level of performance.

5.5   Data Mining Applications

Different fields utilize Data Mining innovations in light of quick access to information and important data from the tremendous measure of information. Data Mining innovations have been applied effectively in numerous regions like advertising, media transmission, misrepresentation recognition, and account, clinical, etc. A portion of the application is recorded underneath.

Budgetary Data Analysis: The fiscal knowledge in the banking and related financial industries is generally sound and outstanding, which promotes the methodological analysis of information and Data Mining. Here are a few frequent cases: the design and development of knowledge management centers for the multifaceted analysis of data processing and Data Mining: advance payment requirements and assessment of the client's credit policy. Request an assortment of customers to concentrate on exhibiting—detection of fraudulent tax evasion and other money linked to corruption.

Retail Industry: Data Mining seems to have an outstanding scope in the retailing business as it collects large quantities of knowledge on sales, consumer purchasing background, transport products, usage, and management. It is common to practice that the amount of information collected will continue to increase exponentially due to the increased convenience, availability, and popularity of the web. Data Mining in the retail sector helps to understand consumer buying habits and trends. This leads to an increased essence of customer service and good service and fulfillment of the customer. And here's a list of the data mining cases in the retail sector:

- Design and development of knowledge delivery centers that draw on the benefits of Data Mining. Multidimensional analysis of transactions, customers, objects, duration, and region.
- Analysis of adequacy of deals crusades.
- Customer Retention.
- Product proposal and cross-referring to of things.

Media transmission: Technology sector nowadays, the telecommunications industry is amongst the most evolved businesses providing help and assistance, e.g., fax, pager, wireless, Internet courier, images, e-mail, site details, and so on. The broadcast communications industry is rising rapidly as a result of the development of new PCs and correspondence technologies. This would be the inspiration for how and why Data Mining has become important to support and understand the process. Data Mining in the telecommunications industry helps to differentiate broadcast communications models, get inaccurate experiments, to use properties, and to enhance the administrations. Here are the frameworks in which Data Mining increases media communications advantages and also

- Multidimensional Analysis of Telecommunication information.
- Fraudulent example examination.
- Identification of unordinary designs.
- Multidimensional affiliation and successive examples of investigation.
- Mobile Telecommunication administrations.
- Use of perception apparatuses in media transmission information investigation.

Natural Data Analysis: These days, we expect major developments in the field of science, such as genomics, proteomics, functional bioinformatics, and medical research. Natural Data Mining is an integral aspect of genomics. Below are the contexts in which the mining of data contributes to the review of organic data:

- A functional mixture of interconnected, distributed functional genomics sets of data.
- Multiple nucleotide successions have been associated, organized, scanned for correlation, and related investigations.
- Exploration of supplementary descriptions and examination of inherited organizations and protein processes.

Certain Scientific Technologies: The above-mentioned applications would generally deal with relatively limited and culturally diverse informative databases in which the empirical approaches are sufficient. Immense measurements of knowledge are being obtained from logical fields such as geoscience, space science, and so forth. There is indeed a tremendous amount of informative samples created due to rapid computational recreations in various fields, e.g., atmospheric and environmental show, material construction, fluid components, and so on. The followed are the use of Data Mining in the process of science technologies.

5.6   Materials and Strategies for Document Clustering

Collecting and Pre-processing Texts: This is the initial step of the cycle and comprises of removing the plain data that shows up in a lot of reports that have been recently gathered [15]. Since all the proposals from the staff are in PDF design, it was important to discover a component to snatch text from these records. To remove text from PDF records, a specialist library called PDFBox was utilized [16]. This library offers a wide scope of pre-processing assignments, for example, text extraction, blending different reports into a solitary one, changing over plain content into a PDF record, making PDF records from pictures, printing archives, and others. From every one of these highlights, it was chosen to work with the extraction of text from a PDF document to plain content, where it will be simpler to manage. Notwithstanding this library, it was utilized another library called FontBox contains different kinds of text styles to make the PDFBox library text styles viable with the most ordinarily known typefaces.

Lexical examination: Once the content from the reports has been gotten, the main tasks to be pre-framed on the content comprise sectioning enormous chains into comparing words. This cycle is known as the partition of lexical segments [17]. These tokens (which are only the words contained in the content) are acquired utilizing the clear space characters for dividing the entire content into autonomous words.

Filtering and eliminating stop-words: A subsequent advance is to channel all non-in order characters, for example, numbers and accentuation marks, since they don't give pertinent data to the arrangement. At that point, all the content is revised in lowercase, this will be valuable to recognize a similar word, notwithstanding it is capitalized or lowercase, be related to a similar word. A short time later, another separating is performed to kill those words that don't include pertinent data, for example, pronouns, articles, and conjunctions. These words are known as stop-words [18]. A rundown of Spanish and English stop-words was taken structure to dispense with those words from the pursuit.

Standardization: stemming: When the prevent words are taken out from the content, the lexemes of the rest of the words are looked for to eliminate those words got from a similar stem. Words that share a similar lexeme are treated as though they were a similar word, and this is particularly valuable for words that have a diverse number and sexual orientation since they share a similar significance [19].

To discover the lexemes from each word, Java-based programming was utilized. This product is Snowball [20] which is utilized in a few regions of data recovery and supports numerous dialects, including Spanish and English. A case of its capacities shows up in Table 5.1.

An immediate outcome of the utilization of the product is that it permits us to keep sifting the content since every one of those words and their varieties that fundamentally mean the equivalent are stifled. This influences things, modifiers, action words, and intensifiers, yet not conjunctions and relational words since they were recently separated as stop-words.

Notice that the words having a similar lexeme are considered as a similar word. Else, it would be harder to track down connections among records since words contrasting in only one letter would be viewed as various words. This would make it hard to achieve if we think about the variations of an equivalent action word in various forms.

Unique word list: To recognize the arrangement of archives, it must be made an in the order arranged word list having the words from all records, the main prerequisite is that a similar word ought not to be rehashed. To eliminate rehashed words, a sequentially arranged word rundown will think

Table 5.1 The transformation from word to lexeme.

Words	Lexemes
Run	runs
Take	taken

Table 5.2 Transformation to an extraordinary word list.

Words	Stem
runs	run
running	
taken	take
take	

about rehashed words, and in this manner, they will be taken out from the rundown of words. To make a one of a kind word list, the technique utilized is to produce a rundown for each archive with halfway single words, that is, the place there are neither rehashed words or at least two words with a similar lexeme or stop-words-later, the word list is sequentially orchestrated. In Table 5.2, we convert words into their root word (which is known as stem word).

In the wake of doing this with every one of the reports, a novel worldwide word list is drawn up for all records utilizing the recently produced records from incomplete words in each archive. By making an individual cycle for each record, it is quicker to make a rundown of special words because, in this cycle, there have been many sifted words that give a great deal of additional preparation.

5.6.1   Features Generation

Toward the finish of the last segment, a premise of a vector space was gotten to speak to every one of the records. It is sufficient to consider the occasions a word shows up in a given report framing a vector with an equivalent length to the entire word list. This idea is frequently called the term recurrence (tf). Table 5.3 shows the portrayal of a printed corpus in the vector space [20], where the recurrence of a term t in an archived is the total of the occasions it shows up in the report.

Notwithstanding, not all words are similarly applicable to victimize among the records since there are words that are normal to all reports and, in this way, don't serve to recognize an archive from others.

Because the past vector portrayal for each archive is adjusted, so those words that don't serve to recognize reports are not considered. For that it is applied the TF-IDF (Term Frequency-Inverse Document Frequency) is characterized in the accompanying equation:

Table 5.3 Vector portrayal of a report corpus.

	Term$_1$	Term$_2$	...	Term$_m$
Document$_1$	tf$_{d1}$(t$_1$)	tf$_{d1}$(t$_2$)	...	tf$_{d1}$(t$_m$)
Document$_2$	tf$_{d2}$(t$_1$)	tf$_{d2}$(t$_2$)	...	tf$_{d2}$(t$_m$)
...	...	...	...	...
Document$_n$	tf$_{dn}$(t$_1$)	tf$_{dn}$(t$_2$)	..	tf$_{dn}$(t$_m$)

$$TF - IDEF(t,d) = tf_d(t) * \frac{\log N}{df(t)} - 1 \qquad (5.1)$$

Where N is the, all outnumber of archives in the corpus, and df (report recurrence) the quantity of records from the whole corpus wherein that word shows up. Consequently, we see that if a word shows up in all reports (for example, Sp. "tener"), after this change, its incentive in the table is invalid. The word consider was performed utilizing a reference to the remarkable word list that had been recently created. A sequentially masterminded word list serves to investigate each archive and locate the occasions each word is rehashed in the content.

Toward the finish of this content, preparing a framework with an exceptional number related with a comparing related number will be utilized for additional investigation and order. This network is called the word-reports framework and signified by the letter. M, it has exceptionally huge information and depends on the arrangement of records.

5.7   Discussion and Results

In this part, the qualities of the arrangement of records on which the experimentation is completed are nitty-gritty. The trial convention is clarified, portraying the calculations used to play out the grouping of the archives. At that point is characterized by the assessment metric to break down the aftereffects of the experimentation.

The Portrayal of the Corpus of Documents
The FCI (Faculty of Computer Science) has a continually expanding store of theories in advanced configuration. It has archives dating from the graduation of CSE, class of 2006. These archives are in PDF design, so it was looked to manage this arrangement.

PDF (Portable Document Format) is a record stockpiling design created by Adobe Systems. It is exceptionally intended for archives that can be printed. This configuration is multi-stage since it very well may be seen in all major working frameworks (Windows, Unix\Linux, or Mac) without changing either the appearance of the structure of the first archive. It likewise fills in as the norm (ISO 19005-1: 2005) for electronic records containing reports planned to be safeguarded for a long haul.

Since the scholastic year 2010–2011 to 2018–2019, Computer Engineering at the FCI UNICA has put away more than 235 theories, 209 are confirmation papers, and 25 bosses' postulations (see Table 5.4).

Table 5.4 The portrayal of the corpus utilized in this examination.

Researcher year	Thesis of engineering	Thesis of masters	Total
2010–11	05	00	05
2011–12	06	00	06
2012–13	07	05	12
2013–14	16	01	17
2014–15	18	16	34
2015–16	29	18	47
2016–17	47	19	66
2017–18	63	20	83
2018–19	18	17	35
Total	209	96	305

Protocols of Experiment:
To locate the ideal approach to gather report recognition papers, a correlation is performed among the various calculations for gathering archives k-means, SOM, and Hierarchical Agglomerative in its variations Single-Link, Complete-Link, and Centroid.

The fundamental impediment of these calculations is that they need to set the underlying number of gatherings. In many applications, and in this specific case, there are no rules to effectively indicate this worth. This is because the Corpus of Diploma Papers of Computer Engineering at UNICA isn't named in gatherings.

To take care of the issue of accidental the quantity of gatherings to get, a fundamental boundary to apply grouping calculations. These calculations were run in a scope of 2 to a fourth of the number of documents to be clustered $\frac{N}{4}$ that is, a sum of $\frac{N}{4} - 1$ run was made for every calculation.

Afterward, to decide the best gathering technique, it was essential to investigate the outcomes with a list of interior approval. As per a few creators a standout amongst other performing lists in such a manner is the Silhouette list.

The Silhouette record is a pointer of the ideal number of gatherings. A higher estimation of this list demonstrates a more attractive number of gatherings. The outline coefficient for a set is given as the normal coefficient of each item outline test, s(i). this list can be utilized for both: a gathering of items (bunch) or for each article. The outline coefficient for an item x is:

$$s(i) = \frac{b(i) - a(i)}{\max\{a(i),\, b(i)\}} \qquad (5.2)$$

Where an (i) is the normal good ways from the item, I to all different articles in their gathering, and b(i) is the normal good ways from the article I to all different articles in the closest gathering. The estimation of s(i) can be acquired by joining the estimations of a(i) and b(i) as demonstrated as follows:

$$s(i) = \begin{cases} 1 - \dfrac{a(i)}{b(i)} & \text{if } a(i) < b(i) \\[2mm] 0 & \text{if } a(i) = b(i) \\[2mm] \dfrac{b(i)}{a(i)} - 1 & \text{if } a(i) \geq b(i) \end{cases} \qquad (5.3)$$

As indicated by the estimation of the Silhouette outline gatherings (structures) discovered they can be arranged into:

- 0.71–1.0, the structures are strong.
- 0.51–0.70, the structures are sensible.
- 0.26–0.50, the structures are feeble and will, in general, be fake interchange techniques ought to for information examination.
- <0.25, no structures are found.

An estimation of s(x) close to zero demonstrates that article x is on the fringe of two gatherings. If the estimation of s(x) is negative, at that point, the item ought to be appointed to the closest gathering. This can be seen in Figure 5.5 with values framing outlines B, C, and D bunching with the arrangement of purposes of (A).

As it very well may be seen, outline esteems are featured in the realistic with shading esteems for various gatherings. A normally utilized rule for a superior gathering is the normal estimation of the layout of all articles in all gatherings.

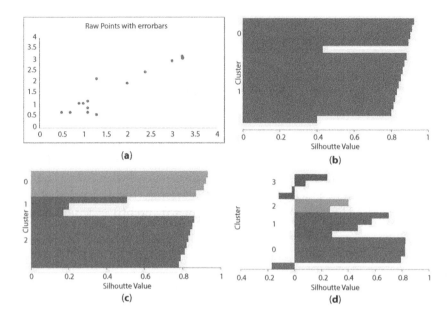

Figure 5.5 Shows silhouette's graphical representation of clusters. (a) Represents the discrete points, (b) Represents the two clusters, (c) Represents the three clusters and (d) Represents the four clusters.

For this situation, the more noteworthy Silhouette worth will be picked as the best gathering.

5.7.1   Discussion

To accumulate records in connection with their substance, the K-means, SOM, and various leveled Agglomerative calculations are applied in blends SingleLink, Complete-Link, and Centroid on the information network attributes got from the Corpus of Diploma Papers. The information boundaries utilizing these calculations are the arrangement of information that is needed for gathering. At the yield of every calculation, a vector containing the names is acquired with the gathering it has a place with every one of the archives, as it tends to be found in Figure 5.6.

The all outnumber of reports in the Corpus is 305. It was important to complete 76 runs for every calculation for a scope of the number of gatherings of 2 to 77. Table 5.5 shows the ten best estimations of Silhouette for every calculation and the number of gatherings acquired for each situation.

As it tends to be found in the table, the K-implies calculation was the most noteworthy estimation of the outline acquired (0.7680) shaping four

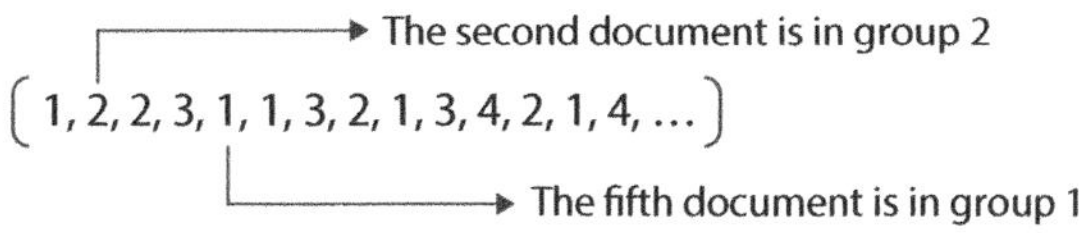

Figure 5.6 Shows Output vectors of Algorithm.

Table 5.5 Groups with various Silhouette an incentive for every calculation.

K-Means		SOM		Single		Complete		Centroid	
Index	Groups	Index	Groups	Index	Groups	Index	Groups	Index	Groups
.7680	04	.7115	03	.7089	04	.5288	02	.7279	04
.7083	03	.5657	04	.6670	03	.5168	03	.5539	03
.7072	02	.4827	05	.5015	02	.3233	04	.4826	02
.6512	73	.4656	06	.3070	05	.1365.	76	.4260	06
.6291	74	.4270	07	.2109	06	.1259	77	.3710	05
.6270	76	.3815	08	.1819	76	.1084	74	.3080	07
.6185	75	.2725	13	.1810	75	.0995	74	.2959	08
.6109	78	.2516	12	.1739	73	.0734	72	.2880	09
.6087	70	.2305	10	.1689	76	.0665	73	.2781	11
.6049	73	.2200	09	.1605	74	.0521	06	.2509	10

gatherings. It was trailed by the progressive agglomerative Centroid-Link calculation which likewise got four gatherings however with a normal estimation of outline a little lower (0.7279). thirdly, the various leveled agglomerative Single-Link calculation plays out a gathering of four gatherings yet additionally with a normal outline (0.7089).

Similarly, on the off chance that we plot the three best outline esteems for every calculation on the number of bunches got, it shows that the framed bunches are made out of two, three, four, and five gatherings. Three out of the five calculations utilized in experimentation got the best incentive in outline for a bunch comprising of four gatherings. K-implies calculation is the best worth got. These outcomes can be found in Figure 5.7.

To see more unmistakably the importance of this Silhouette esteem, use Figure 5.8 where the outline of reports having a place with various gatherings can be seen, that is, the records having a place with a similar gathering, show up together in a square.

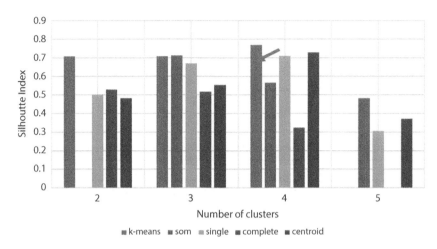

Figure 5.7 Shows realistic of the three Silhouettes with a various number of groups esteems acquired by every calculation.

The Silhouette an incentive for each report is a separation that takes after how each archive is like different records inside their gathering. When contrasted and the archives from different gatherings, taking qualities inside the scope of −1 to 1. As appeared in Figure 5.8, the outline of the items from a similar gathering (for the four gatherings got) has near 1 positive quality and is wide, which is a pointer of value in the gathering. Just gathering 2 has a couple of articles with negative figures.

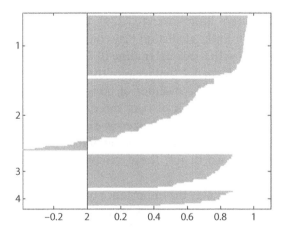

Figure 5.8 Shows Silhouette estimation using K-Means Algorithm archives by the four clusters.

5.7.2   Conclusion

Data Mining has importance in the quest for instances, in the determination, in the disclosing information, and so on, in various business units. Data Mining techniques and estimates, e.g., order, classification, etc., try people to identify indications of how to establish potential trends in organizations. Data Mining being commonly used in almost every sector wherever knowledge is generated, which is why Data Mining is regarded among the most important natural areas in information sets and data frameworks are one of the most promising collaborative advances in technology. We considered that Clustering is among the key content digging strategies for information extraction from huge assortments of unlabelled archives. In this paper, we applied the Knowledge Discovery in Texts (KDT) system, and we use bunching to group Documents accessible. We assessed the various outcomes as per an inside bunch legitimacy file, which permits us to acquire a top-notch grouping. The best outcome relates to k-Means calculation, with four groups. The acquired groups speak to records with various subjects, which are: data the executive's frameworks, endeavor the board frameworks, man-made reasoning, and advanced picture preparing.

References

1. Kaur, R., Kaur, S., Kaur, A., Kaur, R., Kaur, A., An Overview of Database management System, Data warehousing and Data Mining. *IJARCCE*, 2, 7, 130, July 2013.
2. Fu, Y., Shih, M., Creado, M., Ju, C., Reorganizing Web Sites Based on User Access Patterns. *Int. J. Intell. Syst. Account. Finance Manage.*, 11, 1, 130, 2002.
3. Maheshwar, K. and Singh, D., A Review of Data Mining based instruction detection techniques. *Int. J. Appl. Innov. Eng. Manage.*, 2, 2, 13, Feb. 2013.
4. Ramamohan, Y., Vasantharao, K., Kalyana Chakravarti, C., Ratnam, A.S.K., A Study of Data Mining Tools in Knowledge Discovery Process. *Int. J. Soft Comput. Eng.*, 2, 3, 131, July 2012.
5. Pande, S.R., Sambare, S.S., Thakre, V.M., Data Clustering Using Data Mining Techniques. *Int. J. Adv. Res. Comput. Commun. Eng.*, 1, 8, 134, 2012.
6. Patra, R.K., Raja, R., Sinha, T.S., Extraction of Geometric and Prosodic Features from Human-Gait-Speech Data for Behavioral Pattern Detection: Part II, in: *Advanced Computational and Communication Paradigms. Advances in Intelligent Systems and Computing*, S. Bhattacharyya, N. Chaki, D. Konar, U. Chakraborty, C. Singh (Eds.), vol. 706, Springer, Singapore, 2018.

7. Zaïane, O.R., Foss, A., Lee, C.H., Wang, W., On data clustering analysis: scalability, constraints, and validation. In: M.S. Chen, P.S. Yu, B. Liu (eds), *Advances in Knowledge Discovery and Data Mining*. PAKDD 2002. Lecture Notes in Computer Science, vol 2336. Springer, Berlin, Heidelberg, 2002, https://doi.org/10.1007/3-540-47887-6_4

8. Salton, G., *Automatic text processing: the transformation. Analysis and Retrieval of Information by Computer*, Addison-Wesley Longman Publishing Co., Boston, MA, United States, 1989.

9. Raj, A.P., Raja, R., Akella, S., A New Framework for Trustworthiness of Cloud Services. *Int. J. Res.*, 04, 1, 135, December 2017.

10. Jain, A., Murty, M., Flynn, P., Data clustering: A review. *ACM Comput. Surv.*, 31, 264–323, 1999.

11. Mu, T., Goulermas, J., Korkontzelos, I., Ananiadou, S., Descriptive document clustering via discriminant learning in a co-embedded space of multilevel similarities. *J. Assoc. Inf. Sci. Technol.*, 67, 1, 106–133, 2016.

12. Lenka, R.K., Rath, A.K., Tan, Z., Sharma, S., Puthal, D., Simha, N.V.R., Tripathi, S.S., Prasad, N., Building Scalable Cyber-Physical-Social Networking Infrastructure Using IoT and Low Power Sensors. *IEEE Access*, 6, 1, 30162–30173, 2018.

13. Na, S. and Xumin, L., Research on k-means Clustering Algorithm. *IEEE Third International Conference on Intelligent Information Technology and Security Informatics*, 2010.

14. Cios, K.J., Pedrycz, W., Swiniarsk, R.M., Data Mining methods for knowledge discovery. *IEEE Trans. Neural Networks*, 9, 1533–1534, 1998.

15. Mu, T., Goulermas, J., Korkontzelos, I., Ananiadou, S., Descriptive document clustering via discriminant learning in a co-embedded space of multilevel similarities. *J. Assoc. Inf. Sci. Technol.*, 67, 1, 106–133, 2016.

16. Apache PDFBox, A Java PDF Library, https://pdfbox.apache.org/, September 2016.

17. Nalawade, R., Samal, A., Avhad, K., Improved Similarity Measure For Text Classification And Clustering. *Int. Res. J. Eng. Technol. (IRJET)*, 3, 6, 140, 2016.

18. Kanan, T. and Fox, E., Automated Arabic Text. Classification with PStemmer, Machine Learning, and a Tailored News Article Taxonomy. *J. Assoc. Inf. Sci. Technol.*, 67, 140, 2016.

19. Swapna, N. and Raja, R., An Improved Network-Based Spam Detection Framework for Review In online Social Media. *Int. J. Sci. Res. Eng. Manage. (IJSREM)*, 03, 09, 141, Sep 2019.

20. Tang, B., He, H., Baggenstoss, P., Kay, S., A Bayesian classification approach using class-specific features for text categorization. *IEEE Trans. Knowl. Data Eng*, 28, 6, 1602–1606, 2016.

21. Sahu, A.K., Sharma, S., Tanveer, M., Internet of Things attack detection using hybrid Deep Learning Model. *Comput. Commun.*, 176, 146–154, 2021, https://doi.org/10.1016/j.comcom.2021.05.024.

6

Data Mining Implementation Process

Kamal K. Mehta¹, Rajesh Tiwari²* and Nishant Behar³

¹Computer Science & Engineering, MPSTME NMIMS, Shirpur, Maharashtra, India
²Computer Science & Engineering, CMR Engg. College, Hyderabad,
Telangana, India
³Computer Science & Engineering, S.O.S. (Engg. & Tech.), G.G.V. Bilaspur,
Chhattisgarh, India

Abstract

Data mining assumes a significant job in different human exercises since it removes obscure valuable examples (or data). Because of its abilities, data mining has become a basic assignment in a huge number of use spaces, for example, banking, retail, clinical, protection, bioinformatics, and so on. To take an all-encompassing perspective on exploration patterns in the region of data mining, a far-reaching study is introduced in this paper. This paper presents an efficient and thorough study of different data mining errands and procedures. Further, different genuine utilization of data mining is introduced in this paper. The difficulties and issues in the region of data mining research are additionally introduced in this paper.

Keywords: Data mining implementation, data mining techniques, data mining calculations, data mining applications

6.1 Introduction

The advancement of knowledge in various fields of human life has contributed to vast amounts of information accumulating in numerous gatherings, such as documents, books, images, sound accounts, chronicles, coherent information, and various new information systems. The information assembled from different applications requires a genuine part of removing information/information from immense files for better uniqueness. Information divulgence in information bases (KDD),

---

*Corresponding author: raj_tiwari_in@yahoo.com

Rohit Raja, Kapil Kumar Nagwanshi, Sandeep Kumar and K. Ramya Laxmi (eds.) Data Mining and Machine Learning Applications, (151–174) © 2022 Scrivener Publishing LLC

normally called information mining, centers around the disclosure of significant information from tremendous arrangements of data [1]. Different methods and calculations are used to discover and concentrate on the occurrences of defined-aside information [2]. Leading to its vastness in special, data mining and knowledge exposure applications have a rich emphasis since the last twenty years and have become a critical part of major associations. The area of data mining was competitive and implemented with different compromises and styles of advancement in the fields of Statistics, Machine Learning, Artificial Intelligence Databases, Computation Limits, and Pattern Reorganization, etc. The distinctive application regions of information mining are LS (Life Sciences), CRM (Customer Relationship Management), Manufacturing, Web Applications, Competitive Intelligence, Banking/Retail/Finance, Security/Computer/ Network, Monitoring, Forecasting of Climate, Teaching Support, showing, Behavioral Ecology & Astronomy and so on. Essentially every field of human life has become information heightened, which made information mining a basic section. Consequently, this paper reviews various examples of information mining and its relative areas from past to present and researches its future zones.

6.2   Data Mining Historical Trends

The data mining system squared is a region for occurrences of various approaches, consolidating database management systems (DBMS), Figures, Machine Learning (ML), and Artificial Intelligence (AI). In the year 1980, the hour of data mining techniques was envisaged essentially by research-driven tools concentrated on single tasks [3]. Early-day data mining techniques are database patterns in initial days, knowledge digging estimates function best for qualitative knowledge gathered from a specific data repository, and distinctive information-digging techniques have advanced for level libraries, daily and social information collections where information is held in clear context. Later, with a fork in the road of simulations and artificial intelligence techniques, numerous datasets advanced to explore non-statistical data and social information computing patterns. The development of mining techniques was enormously driven by the concept of fourth-period computing affiliations and identifiable finding processes. At the beginning of data mining, almost all of the statistics utilized strictly definable methods. Soon they progressed with various techniques, including AI, ML, and sequence reconfiguration. Various data processing methods (induction, compression, and approximation) and estimates of enormous quantities of diverse data set aside in knowledge stores.

6.3   Processes of Data Analysis

The data mining phase is divided into two parts: data structure or pre-processing and data mining. The data planning step involves data cleaning, data reconciliation, data collection, and data adjustment while the next stage involves information gathering, design evaluation, and information extraction [4].

6.3.1   Data Attack

During the data mining era, the data is cleaned up. As we all know, data is loud and aggressive, contradictory, and scattered. This integrates different approaches. For example, filling in missing qualities consolidated register. The yield of data cleaning measure is satisfactorily cleaned data [5].

6.3.2   Data Mixing

During this period, data mining measures were incorporated into a set of data from different sources. In the same way, the dataset occurs in different configurations in an alternative field. Designers could maintain data in databases, text records, spreadsheets, files, 3D data squares, etc. Even though we may say the data mix is so complex, unstable, and challenging. This is because, as a rule, the information does not coordinate various sources [6].

Researchers practice metadata to diminish faults in data joining measures. An alternative concern threatened is data repetition. In this case, identical data may be found in a common database in different tables. Data combination tends to reduce redundancy to the most severe possible degree, without compromising the unfailing consistency of the data.

6.3.3   Data Collection

It is a loop during which analysis data is retrieved from the database. This cycle needs massive amounts of reported data for analysis. Mostly along these lines, a data archive with structured data contains considerably more data than needed. Open data should pick and store exciting details [7].

6.3.4   Data Conversion

In this step, we must modify and merge data into different structures. Mining must be fair. This process usually involves standardization, confluence, speculation, etc.

A data table accessible as −5, "37, 100, 89, and 78" could be updated as −0.05, "0.37, 1.00, 0.89, and 0.78." Here data seems to be more appropriate for data mining. Open data is prepared for data mining after variation.

6.3.4.1   Data Mining

In this period of Data Mining measure, we have applied strategies to extricate designs from data as these techniques are mind-boggling and wise. Likewise, this mining incorporates a few assignments—for example, arrangement, expectation, bunching, time arrangement investigation, etc. [8].

6.3.4.2   Design Evaluation

The example assessment recognizes genuinely fascinating examples. So this is data based on different interesting steps. An instance is seen as interesting in the circumstance that it is feasibly beneficial. In contrast, people are effectively fair. It also supports several of the concepts. That everyone wants to verify a certain degree of belief in the existing research.

6.3.4.3   Data Illustration

During the Data Mining measurement era, we have to engage in talking to customer data. Similarly, information is sourced from data. Similar methods should be followed to yield.

6.3.4.4   Implementation of Data Mining in the Cross-Industry Standard Process

The common benefits-industry system involves six phases. It's also a repeated loop.

Data mining measure is a revelation through huge informational collections of examples, connections, and experiences that guide undertakings estimating and overseeing where they are and anticipating where they will be later on. A huge measure of data and data sets can emerge out of different data sources and might be put away in various data warehouses. Furthermore, data mining procedures, for example, AI, man-made brainpower (AI), and

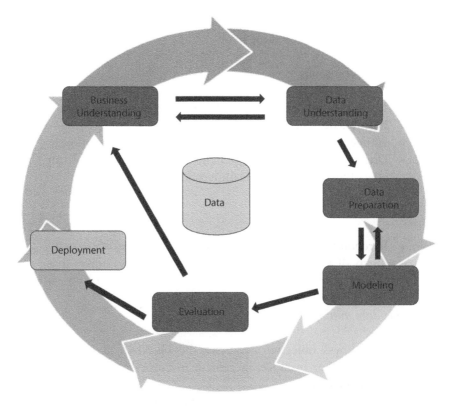

Figure 6.1 Data mining implementation process.

prescient demonstrating can be included. The data mining measure requires duty. However, specialists concur, overall enterprises, data mining measure is equivalent. What's more, it ought to follow a recommended way [9] (Figure 6.1).

Here are six fundamental strides of data mining measure:

6.3.5   Business Understanding

In business getting stage, in any case, it is expected to understand business objections clearly and find what the business needs are.

It centers on understanding venture objectives and prerequisites, structures a business perspective, then, turning the data into an information mining problem, a starting plan is aimed at achieving the objectives [10].

Assignments:

- Decide business goals
- Access circumstance

- Decide data mining objectives
- Produce an undertaking plan.

Decide business goals:

- It understands undertaking targets and essentials from a business perspective.
- Altogether comprehend what the client needs to accomplish.
- Uncover noteworthy components, at the beginning, it can affect the aftereffect of the undertaking.

Access circumstance:

- It requires a more definite examination of realities pretty much all assets, imperatives, presumptions, and others that should be thought of.

Decide data mining objectives:

- A business objective expresses the objective of business wording. For instance, increment inventory deals with the current client.
- A data mining objective portrays task goals. For instance, it expects what number of articles a client will purchase, given their socioeconomics subtleties (Age, Salary, and City) and cost of things in recent years.

Produce a task plan:

- Expresses its emphasis on market and data mining plans.
- This undertaking strategy ought to characterize the normal arrangement of steps to be performed during the remainder of the venture, including the most recent strategy and better determination of devices.

6.3.6   Data Understanding

Information understanding begins with a unique information assortment and continues with tasks to get acquainted with information, to information quality issues, to discover better knowledge in information, or to distinguish intriguing subsets for covered data theory [11].

First, "gross" or "surface" products of knowledge gained should be cautiously revealed. Furthermore, data can be discussed by answering data mining issues that could be used to answer, discover, and represent. Finally, information quality must be investigated by tending to some critical requests, for instance, "Is the gotten information complete?", "Are there any missing characteristics in obtained information?"

Assignments:

- Gathers beginning data
- Depict data
- Investigate data
- Check data quality.

Gather the beginning data:

- It procures the data referenced in venture assets.
- It incorporates data stacking, if necessary, for data understanding.
- It might prompt unique data readiness steps.
- On the off chance that different data sources are gained, at that point, coordination is an additional issue, either here or at the ensuing phase of data arrangement.

Depict data:

- It inspects the "gross" or "surface" attributes of the data acquired.
- It gives an account of the results.

Investigate data:

- Tending to data mining issues that can be settled by questioning, imagining, and detailing, including:
- Conveyance of significant attributes, consequences of straightforward conglomeration.
- Set up a connection between a modest number of traits.
- Qualities of significant sub-populaces, straightforward statical investigation.
- It might refine data mining destinations.
- It might contribute or refine data depiction and quality reports.
- It might take care of change and other vital data arrangements.

Check data quality:

- It inspects the data quality and tending to questions.

6.3.7   Data Preparation

The information status regularly exhausts about 90.00% of the great importance of errands. The after effect of the information plan stage is the last information record. At the point when open information sources are remembered, they ought to be picked, cleaned, formed, and planned into the ideal structure. The information examination task at a more unmistakable significance may be passed on during this phase to see topics reliant on business understanding [12].

Assignments:

- Select data
- Clean data
- Build data
- Incorporate data
- Arrangement data [13].

Select data:

- It chooses which data to be utilized for assessment.
- In data, choice measures incorporate hugeness to data mining destinations, quality, and specialized constraints, for example, data volume limits or data types.
- It covers the choice of attributes and decisions of archives in the table [14].

Clean data:

- It might include the choice of clean subsets of data, embeddings proper defaults, or more eager strategies, for example, assessing missing data by demonstrating [15].

Build data:

- It contains a Constructive data arrangement, for example, creating inferred attributes, total new records, or changed estimations of current qualities [16].

Incorporate data:

- Incorporate data alludes to the strategies whereby data is consolidated from different tables or archives to make new records or qualities.

Configuration data:

- Designing data allude basically to etymological changes delivered to data that doesn't modify their criticalness; however, it may require a demonstrating apparatus [17].

6.3.8 Modeling

In displaying, different demonstrating techniques are chosen and applied, and their boundaries are estimated to ideal qualities. A few techniques gave specific prerequisites for the type of information. Hence, venturing back to the information arrangement stage is important [18].

Assignments:

- Select displaying strategy
- Produce test structure
- Fabricate model
- Access model.

Select the modeling strategy:

- It chooses a genuine displaying technique that will be utilized—for instance, choice tree, neural system.
- On the off chance that different techniques are applied, then it plays out this assignment exclusively for every strategy [19].

Produce test Design:

- Produce a strategy or component for testing the legitimacy and nature of the model before developing a model.
- For instance, in the grouping, mistake rates are typically utilized as quality data mining models.
- Consequently, regularly separate data index into train and test set, form the model on a train set, and evaluate its quality on the different test sets [20].

Build model:

- To make at least one demonstration, we have to run display-ing instruments on readied data collection.

Assess model:

- It deciphers the models as indicated by its space ability, data mining achievement rules, and necessary plan.
- It evaluates the achievement of the utilization of displaying and finds strategies all more actually.
- It contacts business examination and area pros later to talk about the results of data mining in a business setting.

6.3.9   Evaluation

At the remainder of this stage, a choice on the utilization of information mining results ought to be reached. It assesses the model proficiently, and survey means executed to manufacture the model and to guarantee that business destinations are appropriately accomplished.

The fundamental goal of assessment is to decide some noteworthy business issue that has not been respected satisfactorily. At the remainder of this stage, a choice on the utilization of information mining results ought to be reached [21].

Assignments:

- Assess results
- Survey measure
- Decide the following stages [22].

Evaluate results:

- It evaluates how much the model meets the association's business goals [23].
- It tests the model on test applications in genuine execution when time and spending constraints grant and evaluates other data mining results created.
- It reveals extra challenges, proposals, or data for future directions.

Survey measure:

- The survey cycle does a more nitty-gritty assessment of data mining commitment to decide when there is a huge factor or errand that has been in one way or another overlooked [24].
- It surveys quality affirmation issues.

Decide on the following stages:

- It concludes how to continue at this stage.
- It concludes whether to finish the undertaking and proceed onward to sending when fundamental or whether to start further cycles or set up new data-mining initiatives.
- It incorporates assets investigation and spending that impact choice.

6.3.10   Deployment

It incorporates scoring an information base, using results as organization rules, intuitive web scoring. The data gained should be composed and introduced in a manner that can be utilized by the customer. Nonetheless, the sending stage can be as simple as delivering. Likewise, the transmitting step can be as simple as producing a report or as confused as implementing a consistent data mining algorithm across connections [25].

These six stages represent the Cross-Business Standard Data Mining Cycle, defined as CRISP-DM. That is an application platform period design representing standard methods and techniques used by data mining specialists. Very commonly used test design.

Assignments:

- Plan organization
- Plan observing and upkeep
- Produce the last report
- Audit venture.

Plan deployment:

- To convey data mining results into a business takes appraisal results and closes a methodology for an organization.

- It alludes to the documentation of the cycle for later sending [26].

Plan observing and upkeep:

- It is significant when data mining results become some portion of everyday business and its condition.
- It assists with maintaining a strategic distance from pointlessly extensive stretches of abuse of data mining results.
- It needs a point-by-point investigation of the checking cycle.

Produce the last report:

- The last report can be drawn up by the undertaking chief and his group.
- It might just be an outline of the task and its experience.
- It might be a last and exhaustive introduction to data mining.

6.3.11   Contemporary Developments

The data mining industry has turned out to be a direct product of its great accomplishment in terms of deepening application achievements and a steady improvement in learning. Distinguishable data mining technologies have been extensively applied in different areas such as medicinal operation, currency, marketing, marketing communication tool, misinformation detection, risk assessment, etc. Accurately increasing challenges in different fields, and progress enhancements have resulted in new data mining problems; various difficulties are linked to a variety of data frameworks, data from various districts, progress in assessment and corporate resource structures, research and legitimate fields, constant creation of business difficulties, etc. Sorts of advancement in data mining with different blends and implications of procedures and tools have shaped current data mining solutions to solve numerous issues, current examples of data mining techniques [27].

6.3.12   An Assortment of Data Mining

The table presents a range of data mining techniques commonly being used marks for several an out plans in different application divisions.

6.3.12.1   Using Computational & Connectivity Tools

Data mining has expanded with the use of authentic strategy and operating system tools such as Parallel, Distributed, and Grid propellers. Comparable data mining applications have been created using parallel processing, and basic equivalent information mining technologies use probabilistic reasoning numbers [25]. Equivalent figuring and scattered information mining are both composed in Grid headways [26]. Grid-based help Vector Machine framework is being used for process improvement processing [27]. Starting late, unique, fragile enlisting methodologies have been applied in information digging, for instance, fleecy basis, disagreeable set, neural frameworks, formative figuring (Genetic Algorithms and Genetic Programming), & sponsorship vector machinery towards exploring several courses for the action of the information set aside in appropriated informational indexes achieves a more sharp and enthusiastic structure giving a human-interpretable, ease, estimated game plan, when stood out from standard techniques [28] for exact assessment, a generous preprocessing system, versatile information planning, information assessment and dynamic.

6.3.12.2   Web Mining

The development and utilization of the World Wide Web will keep increasing, the production of substance, structure, and use of data and the estimate of Web mining will seek to grow. The investigation must be performed to develop the correct arrangement of web measurements and their calculation systems, to distinguish measured variables from usage data, seeing how different sections of the cycle model impact different web quantities of interest, seeing how cycle models adjust due to various changes that are made—to modify client updates, to establish web mining procedures to boost different performance [29].

6.3.12.3   Comparative Statement

The following table represents the general announcement of the various trends of data mining from past to future.

6.3.13   Advantages of Data Mining

- Used for retrieval of information (Table 6.1).
- It can be used as a tool which can segregate the information according to the user requirements in no time.

Table 6.1 Data mining developments qualified statement.

Data mining patterns	Algo./ techniques utilized	Data designs	Computing resources	Prime territories of uses
Past	Statistical, Machine Learning Techniques	Numerical data and organized data put away in customary data sets	Evolution of 4G PL and different related strategies	Business
Current	Statistical, Machine Learning, Artificial Intelligence, Pattern Reorganization Techniques	Heterogeneous data designs incorporate organized semi-organized and unstructured data	High-speed systems, High end stockpiling gadgets and Parallel, Distributed figuring, and so on	Business, Web, Medical analysis, and so on
Future	Soft Computing methods like Fuzzy rationale, Neural Networks, and Genetic Programming	Complex data objects incorporate high dimensional, fast data streams, succession, commotion in time arrangement, chart, Multi-case objects, Multi-spoke to articles and worldly data, and so on	Multi-operator advancements and Cloud Computing	Business, Web, Medical finding, Scientific and Research investigation fields (bio, distant detecting, and so forth.), Social systems administration, and so on

- It can be used for building a model from the past experiences.
- It can be use in operational and manufacturing industry to identify the faulty equipment.

- It can be helpful for the government by analyzing the financial details of individual and build a patter so that it can be helpful to identify the criminal and money laundering activity [30].

6.3.14   Drawbacks of Data Mining

Information mining programs are difficult to write and at the same time difficult to manage. Therefore it always requires advance skills to manage.

- The information mining strategies are not definite; in this way, they can cause certifiable outcomes in explicit conditions.
- Nowadays internet and social media is a common platform which everyone uses therefore there is always a concern of privacy of the information. It is always possible that unethically someone retrieve that information and use the information in a bad way and it create a trouble to others.

6.3.15   Data Mining Applications

Table 6.2 represents different applications and usage of data mining.

Table 6.2 Shows application and usage of data mining.

Applications	Usage
Communications	Data mining methods can be used as a tool to segment the customers according to their targets and interests.
Insurance	It can used as tool in the insurance industry to identify the gain of the company, analysis the existing policies and interest of the customers in these policies.
Education	Data mining methods can be used for the classification and prediction of the student's performance for the course and programs. It can be used as a tracker to improve the student teaching learning process, also used for helping the students for choosing the course efficiently.

(Continued)

Table 6.2 Shows application and usage of data mining. (*Continued*)

Applications	Usage
Manufacturing	It can be use in operational and manufacturing industry to identify the faulty equipment. They can analyze and manage their resources with the help of mining tools.
Banking	Data mining can be used in banking sector. Using data mining model banks can analyze the financial behavior of the customers. Using this data bank professional can identify the faulty customers and the loyal customers.
Retail	Data mining is helpful for the retail industry because it can collect large amount of customer data, sales data, history of customer purchase and their consumption. This data is always increasing because easy availability of data and continuous usage of wed applications for shopping. This model can help the retail industry to make the better relationship with the customers.
Administration Providers	Most of the service based telecommunication company can use this as an analysis tool. It can be used to identify that why customers are leaving their services and check the customers grievance. They can improve the services from user point of view.
E-Commerce	Most of the e-commerce sites are using data mining tools to attract the customers by offering various stratigical plan.
Super Markets	Super markets can also use this as data analysis tool. E.g. They can observe their daily customers like: their gender, age, and product. Suppose most of the female customers are visiting the supermarket then they can focus on the products like: Facial creams, Shampoos, Baby products, sanitary products, etc.,
Wrongdoing Investigation	Data Mining can be used for the investigation purpose also. Investigation officers can track the people who try to cross boarders, LOC and the deatis can send to the local police officers.
Bioinformatics	It can also be used in the science and Biomedical field.

6.3.16   Methodology

An audit cum preliminary methodology is used. Through the expansive request of composition and discussion with pros on understudy execution, different components that are considered to have sway on the introduction of an understudy are perceived. These affecting variables are arranged as data factors. For this work, progressing genuine information is assembled from the optional school. Information can be filtered out using manual methods. Further, it can be changed into the standard format used by WEKA tool. Starting now and into the foreseeable future, features and limits assurance are perceived.

By then, examination of recognized limits and use is performed on gadgets. After successful execution, results are compared and analyzed. The stepwise representation is shown in Figure 6.2 and it recorded 152.00 understudies of auxiliary school which is used as a dataset and understudy related elements are described in Table 6.3 close by their space regards.

Tools and Techniques Utilized:
The different data mining methods are used to understand the concept of educational Data Mining. The various methods are: classification, density

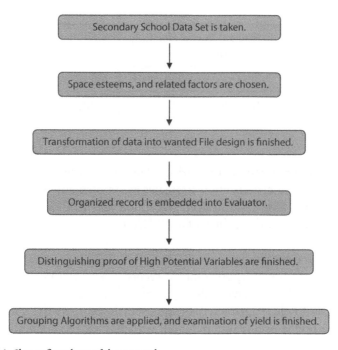

Figure 6.2 Shows flowchart of the research.

Table 6.3 Understudy related factors.

Variable name	Depiction	Area
SEX	Sex of Student	M,F
INS-HIGH	High-Level Institution	Government, Private
TOB	Board's Type	CBSE, State Board
MOI	Supervision's Medium	English, Hindi
TOS	School Type	Girls, Co-ed, Boys
PTUI	Cost of Coaching	No, Yes
S-AREA	School's Locality	Rural, Urban
MOB	Students have cellphones/ tablets	No, Yes
COM-HM	Students have Computer/ Laptop	No, Yes
NETACS	Students have internet	No, Yes
ROLL NO	Roll no. of Student	Specified through school administration
INT-GR	Evaluation of understudy internally	A A+, B, C
ATTN	Students Attendance tally	School's Attendance record
CLASS (Response Variable)	If eligible or not	Q, NQ

estimation and regression. The various datasets are used for analysis purpose and different classification strategies are implemented such as: Naïve Bayes classifier, SMO, Multi-layer perception and REPTree and J48. The execution is done with the help of a WEKA tool.

Reproduction Case Study:
For the investigation purpose total 152 records are taken into consideration [31]. For the quality analysis Chi-Squared, info Gain, Symmetrical Uncert attribute, and ReliefF characteristic are used. To estimate the rank, ranker search method is used. High potential variables are recorded underneath close by their situations in Table 6.4.

Table 6.4 High potential variables.

Variable rank value's name	Values of rank
INT-GR	01.650
ATTN	02.2250
SEX	03.600
PTUI	03.5250
MOB	05.3750
INS-HIGH	05.9250
COM-HM	08.3250
NET-ACS	09.200

6.3.17 Results

The experiments are performed on different classifier and results are represented in Table 6.5. The various parameters are used to check the performance of the model and these parameters are also mentioned in Table 6.5.

As per the analysis, the precision of the multilayer perception method is 74.99% and it is better than other methods. Table 6.6 represents comparative analysis of various classifiers with their precision rates.

Table 6.5 Analysis of various classifiers.

Classified algorithm's name	Student's class	Rate of TP	Rate of FP	Precision	F-Measure	Recall	Area of ROC
Multi-layer Perception	NQ	0.830	0.440	0.808	0.823	0.830	0.770
	Q	0.550	0.163	0.606	0.577	0.553	0.774
Naive Bayes	NQ	0.760	0.595	0.742	0.752	0.761	0.647
	Q	0.400	0.238	0.432	0.418	0.404	0.648
SMO	NQ	0.880	0.766	0.721	0.795	0.886	0.56
	Q	0.230	0.114	0.478	0.314	0.314	0.56
J48	NQ	0.810	0.574	0.761	0.789	0.819	0.713
	Q	0.420	0.181	0.513	0.465	0.426	0.713
REPTree	NQ	0.830	0.681	0.733	0.762	0.838	0.667
	Q	0.310	0.162	0.469	0.38	0.319	0.667

Table 6.6 Comparative analysis of various classifiers with their precision rates.

Technique for mining	Precision
Multi-layer perception	74.99%
Naïve Bayes	65.09%
SMO	68.39%
J48	69.80%
REPTree	67.80%

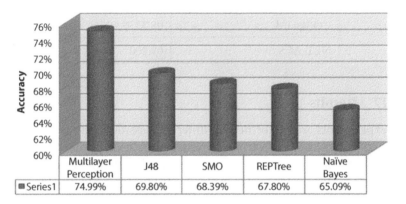

Figure 6.3 Exactness classifier's comparison.

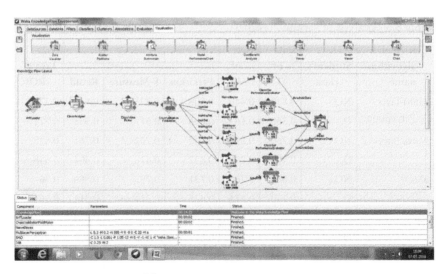

Figure 6.4 Datastream model.

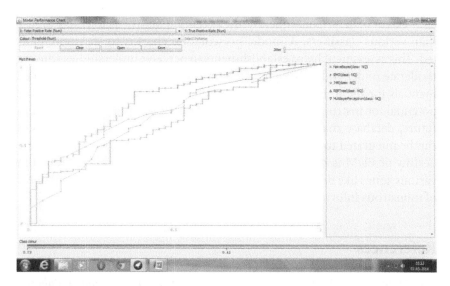

Figure 6.5 Model execution graph.

Figure 6.3 shows exactness classifier's comparison and Figure 6.4 represents Datastream model. Ensuing to stacking information record run the model and a model show chart as shown in Figure 6.5 for various classifiers, for instance, Multilayer Perceptron, Naive Bayes, J48, REP Tree & SMO. Figure 6.5 shows the region of mixing twist (ROC) for each classifier.

6.3.18   Conclusion and Future Scope

In this chapter, we immediately kept an eye on distinctive information mining designs from their root to what exactly to come. This review would be valuable to authorities to focus on various issues of information mining. In the future course, we will review distinctive gathering estimations and the vitality of the extraordinary figuring (innate programming) approach in arranging gainful portrayal computations for information mining.

We, in like manner, dismember, request strategies are used for conjecture on a dataset of 152 understudies to foresee, and research understudy's introduction likewise moderate understudies among them. In this assessment, a model was made reliant on some picked understudy-related information factors accumulated from the veritable world. According to the comparative studies the performance of the Multi-Layer Perception is better with 74.99% accuracy. Therefore it can be concluded that MLP winds up being perhaps practical and capable classifier. Furthermore, the connection of all of the five classifiers with the help of the WEKA experimenter is similarly made; for this circumstance in like manner, MLP winds up being best with an F-extent of 82%. Consequently, the execution of MLP is tolerably higher than various classifiers. A model presentation chart is furthermore plotted. This assessment helps establishments to perceive understudies who are moderate understudies, which further offers a base for picking exceptional manuals for them. EDM is in its beginning phases, and it has part of the potential for instruction. It can be used as a tool for future assessment. In future, database management system, e-learning tools and mining tools can be integrated to find the better precision and results. Accordingly, the destiny of EDM is promising for extra investigation. It can be applied in various zones like drug, sports, and offer market as a result of the openness of monstrous information bases.

References

1. Manila, H., *Data mining: Machine learning, statistics, and databases*, IEEE, 1996.
2. Fayad, U., Piatesky-Shapiro, G., Smyth, P., *From Data Mining To Knowledge Discovery in Databases*, AAAI Press/The MIT Press, Massachusetts Institute of Technology, Springer, Berlin, Heidelberg, 1996.
3. Piatetsky-Shapiro, G., The Data-Mining Industry Coming of Age. *IEEE Intell. Syst.*, 14, 32–34, 1999.
4. Romero, C., Educational Data Mining: A Review of the State-of-the-Art. *IEEE Trans. Syst. Man Cybern.—Part C: Appl. Rev.*, 40, 6, 601–618, 2010.
5. Zaïane, O., Web usage mining for a better web-based learning environment. *Proceedings of Conference on Advanced Technology For Education*, pp. 60–64, 2001.
6. Zaïane, O., Building a recommender agent for e-learning systems. *Proceedings of the International Conference on Computers in Education*, pp. 55–59, 2002.
7. Baker, R.S., Corbett, A.T., Koedinger, K.R., Detecting Student Misuse of Intelligent Tutoring Systems. *Proceedings of the 7th International Conference on Intelligent Tutoring Systems*, pp. 531–540, 2004.
8. Tang, T. and McCalla, G., Smart recommendation for an evolving e-learning system: Architecture and experiment. *Int. J. E-Learn.*, 4, 1, 105–129, 2005.
9. Merceron, A. and Yacef, K., A web-based tutoring tool with mining facilities to improve learning and teaching. *Proceedings of the 11th International Conference on Artificial Intelligence in Education*, pp. 201–208, 2003.
10. Romero, C., Ventura, S., De Bra, P., Castro, C., Discovering prediction rules in aha! Courses. *Proceedings of the International Conference on User Modelling*, pp. 25–34, 2003.
11. Beck, J. and Woolf, B., High-level student modeling with machine learning. *Proceedings of the 5th International Conference on Intelligent Tutoring Systems*, pp. 584–593, 2000.

12. Dringus, L.P. and Ellis, T., Using data mining as a strategy for assessing asynchronous discussion forums. *Comput. Educ. J.*, 45, 141–160, 2005.

13. Lenka, R.K., Rath, A.K., Tan, Z., Sharma, S., Puthal, D., Simha, N.V.R., Raja, R., Tripathi, S.S., Prasad, M., Building Scalable Cyber-Physical-Social Networking Infrastructure Using IoT and Low Power Sensors. *IEEE Access*, 6, 1, 30162–30173, 2018.

14. Nguyen, T.-N., Busche, A., Schmidt Thieme, L., Improving Academic Performance Prediction by Dealing with Class Imbalance. *Ninth International Conference on Intelligent Systems Design and Applications*, 2009.

15. Arockiam, L., Charles, S., Kumar, A. *et al.*, Deriving Association between Urban and Rural Students Programming Skills. *Int. J. Comput. Sci. Eng.*, 02, 03, 687–690, 2010.

16. Salmon, S. *et al.*, Ubiquitous Secretary: A Ubiquitous Computing Application Based on Web Services Architecture. *Int. J. Multimed. Ubiquitous Eng.*, 4, 4, 53–70, October 2009.

17. Hsu, J., Data Mining Trends and Developments: The Key Data Mining Technologies and Applications for the 21st Century. *The Proceedings of the 19th Annual Conference for Information Systems Educators (ISECON 2002)*, http://colton.byuh.edu/isecon/2002/224b/Hsu.pdf.

18. Krishnaswamy, S., Towards Situation-awareness and Ubiquitous Data Mining for Road Safety: Rationale and Architecture for a Compelling Application. *Proceedings of Conference on Intelligent Vehicles and Road Infrastructure 2005*, pp. 16–17, 2005, Available at: http://www.csse.monash.edu.au/~mgaber/CameraReadyI.

19. Kotsiantis, S., Kanellopoulos, D., Pintelas, P., Multimedia mining. *WSEAS Trans. Syst.*, 3, 3263–3268, 2004.

20. Abdulvahit, T. and Eminem, D., Using spatial data mining techniques to reveal the vulnerability of people and places due to oil transportation and accidents: A case study of Istanbul strait. *ISPRS Technical Commission II Symposium*, 1st edition, Addison–Wesley, Vienna, 2006.

21. Jain, S., Mahmood, Md.R., Raja, R., Laxmi, K.R., Gupta, A., Multi-Label Classification for Images with Labels for Image Annotation. *SAMRIDDHI: A Journal of Physical Sciences, Engineering and Technology*, 12, Special Issue (3), 183–188, 2020.

22. Mitchell, T.M., Generalization as Search. *Artif. Intell.*, 18, 2, 203–226, 1982.

23. Michalski, R., Mozetic, I., Hong, J., Lavrac, N., The AQ15 Inductive Learning System: An Overview and Experiments. *Reports of Machine Learning and Inference Laboratory*, MLI-86-6, George Mason University, University of Illinois at Urbana-Champaign, 1986.

24. Tiwari, L., Raja, R., Awasthi, V., Miri, R., Sinha, G.R., Alkinani, M.H., Polat, K., Detection of lung nodule and cancer using novel Mask-3 FCM and TWEDLNN algorithms. *Measurement*, 172, 108882, 2021.

25. Baker, Z.K. and Prasanna, V.K., Efficient Parallel Data Mining with the Apriori Algorithm on FPGAs. Submitted to the *IEEE International Parallel and Distributed Processing Symposium (IPDPS '05)*, 2005.
26. He, J., Advances in Data Mining: History and Future. *Third International Symposium on Information Technology Application*, 978-0-7695-3859-4/09 IEEE, 2009.
27. Meligy, A., A Grid-Based Distributed SVM Data Mining Algorithm. *Eur. J. Sci. Res.*, 27, 3, 313–321, 2009, http://www.eurojournals.com/ejsr.htm.
28. Sahu, A.K., Sharma, S., Tanveer, M., Internet of Things attack detection using hybrid Deep Learning Model. *Comput. Commun.*, 176, 146–154, 2021, https://doi.org/10.1016/j.comcom.2021.05.024.
29. Mitra, S., Pal, S.K., Mitra, P., Data mining in soft computing framework: A survey. *IEEE Trans. Neural Netw.*, 13, 3–14, 2001.
30. Embrechts, M.J., Introduction to Scientific Data Mining: Direct Kernel Methods & Applications, in: *Computationally Intelligent Hybrid Systems: The Fusion of Soft Computing and Hard Computing*, pp. 317–365, Wiley, New York, 2005.
31. Han, J. and Kamber, M., *Data mining: Concepts and techniques*, Academic Press, Morgan-Kaufman Series of Data Management Systems, San Diego, 2001.

7

Predictive Analytics in IT Service Management (ITSM)

Sharon Christa I.L.[1*] and Suma V.[2]

[1]Dept. of Computer Science & Engineer, Graphic Era University, Dehradun, India
[2]Dept. of Information Science & Engineer, Dayananda Sagar College of Engineer,
Bengaluru, India

Abstract

Predictive analytics and applied machine learning techniques have taken a significant role in the state of the art in technology that make use of data mining techniques for knowledge extraction. It is observed that machine learning techniques perform and produce better results than what is achieved in hard computing techniques. Further, the IT service sector is a dominating component in the global market while machine learning techniques are most suitable to be applied in the areas of high uncertainty. Since client management and incident management aspects of IT service management are highly uncertain, integrating machine learning in IT service is a better choice as they can produce near accurate, robust results from uncertainty and partial truth. Services provided to the customers and efficiency of the service provider can be optimized in different ways using machine learning techniques. The different aspects of IT service sector and integration of machine learning techniques to enhance the productivity and quality of the deliverable using the machine learning techniques is presented in this chapter.

Keywords: Knowledge extraction, predictive analytics, machine learning, IT service, service maintenance

*Corresponding author: sharonchrista@gmail.com

Rohit Raja, Kapil Kumar Nagwanshi, Sandeep Kumar and K. Ramya Laxmi (eds.) Data Mining and Machine Learning Applications, (175–194) © 2022 Scrivener Publishing LLC

7.1 Introduction

Progression in technology has revolutionized the day to day activities of humans. Companies are embracing automation, artificial intelligence, Internet of Things, etc. Software systems are no longer used by experts but is embraced by common man in their day to day lives. Computing systems have a strong impact globally in varied domains and software systems are integrated to it directly or indirectly. According to the Institute of Electrical and Electronics Engineers (IEEE) Standard 610.12-990 [1] software is a condition or a capability needed by a user for problem solving/achieve a capability [1]. Therefore, the quality of software system depends on the stakeholders. The same is defined by Stephen H. Khan as an intangible concept that can be discussed, felt and judged from the customer's perspective [2].

If the software system meets the expectations of the customer and works as per the requirement, software systems are said to be successful [3]. The software systems come with a set of services and service level agreement. IT service management (ITSM) is the activities that are performed by an organization to design, plan, deliver, operate and control services associated with the software system offered to customers [4].

But what are IT services? All the services provided by your IT team can be termed—IT services. For example, Firewall Services, Cyber-security Services, Data Backup & Restoration, etc.

An IT Service Team is responsible for end-to-end management of these services and can rely on ITSM software like Freshservice to effectively manage these services. ITSM has detailed steps that need to be followed when a service request comes up or an incident occurs [5]. Figure 7.1 specifies the process followed when a ticket is raised by the customer that is defined by ITSM.

Therefore, failure in meeting the SLA clauses and resolving the incidents on time has a negative impact on the business strategy of the service providers. The demand on the improvement of software as well as the associated techniques are constantly rising and so is the need to recognize its consistency [6].

An effective ITSM not only benefits the company by creating processes to address each of the IT organization's most important functions, establishing what roles are required to deliver on each of those processes, clearly defining the responsibilities and participation of each role in the process but also establishes a process that supports the Service Catalog Management which establishes and maintains an up-to-date repository of all services

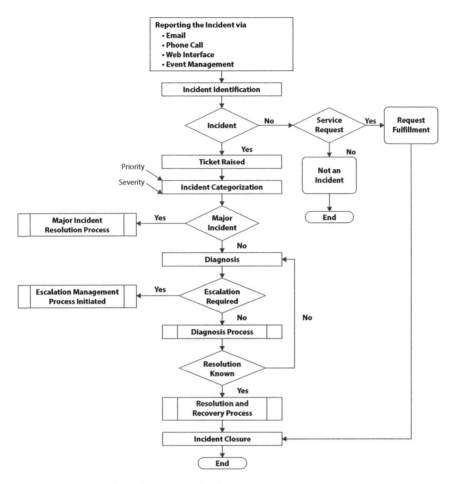

Figure 7.1 Process flow of incident and ticket.

that can be requested by the business and Knowledge Management process that maintain a knowledge base where they can document information and knowledge that is accrued through the delivery of IT services. This can be beneficial to the customers as well. The ITSM follows a process oriented approach which is reactive that can aid the organization in addressing incidents and performing manual operational tasks. This in turn can result in cost reduction. Further, the process provides consistent, standardized incident response service through a tracked ticketing system, structured service catalog and in turn better adherence to SLAs.

The ITSM cannot be replaced or removed since service providers need to address the glitches in the services provided and should be addressed.

The ITSM provides a framework to address the same. This can improve efficiency, control and governance over the various stakeholders and assets, collaboration and the most important customer satisfaction.

The significance of ITSM is undeniable and this chapter focuses on the aspects of predictive analytics that can impact the IT Service sector. Further, the chapter put forth a case study on ticket analytics based on the ticketing service offered as a part of ITSM [7].

7.2   Analytics: An Overview

Analytics is the process of deriving patterns from data. A systematic analysis and interpretation of existing data will in turn result in identifying the patterns in data. These can further be used in predicting the future events, risk analysis, process optimization, and overall improvement in business performance. While analysis of the data will give insights on what happened in the past and why it happened, analytics provide insights that can guide in decision making process. Analytics in fact is a multidisciplinary field involving mathematics, statistics, data modeling, computer programming, etc.

Data analytics is adopted in manufacturing sector to healthcare sector. The data related to downtime, work queue and run-time for various machines can be used by manufacturing companies to plan capacity management of machines. In the Six Sigma program, data analyzes the number of defects per million in a production line can be measured to derive its optimizing factor. Travel and hospitality on the other hand adopted data analytics for better turn around by collecting the customer data. Further, based on the insights on problems, steps can be taken to fix the same. Healthcare and retails industry generates a huge amount of structured and unstructured data. Healthcare data analytics can be used to predict the spread of diseases, care quality, diagnosis, etc. Further, the data can be used in detecting fraud insurance practices in the health care sector.

Retail industry on the other hand can identify the future trends, recommend products based on the trends, improve the supply chain accordingly and can increase the profit with an optimized data analytics. Another striking example of application of data analytics is in the gaming industry and content companies. User behavior data is used by game developers to maximize the gamer involvement, predict gaming bottlenecks, etc. whereas content analytics relies on the analysis of user behavior that predicts the engagement, clicks on various contents, etc. Adopting data analytics to the business model of an enterprise has manifold advantages like reduction in operating cost, optimizing performance, etc. Data can be used for analytics in order to identify the efficient ways of doing business, derive insights from customer trends and satisfaction and in turn better business decisions [8].

In order to perform data analytics, the primary step is to ask the right question like what are the insights the company is looking for or how the performance can be improved, etc. Once the goal is set, then the data requirements to answer the questions raised are to be identified along with the attributes that has to be considered. Further, the required data is collected through different sources. The data should be in an organized format in order to perform cleaning, duplication check, error detection, removing in- complete data, etc., and is then transferred for data analytics. A data analyst is responsible for deriving the conclusions based on the data presented to them. Data analytics can be broken down into four based on the value and difficulty and the question that it addresses. Figure 7.2 depicts the same in which Descriptive and Diagnostic analytics address what's happening in the enterprise based on the Root Cause Analysis (RCA). Predictive and Perspective analytics give a foresight on what may happen and how it can be made to happen [9].

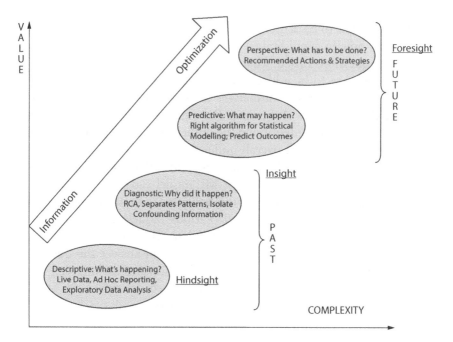

Figure 7.2 Process flow of incident and ticket.

7.2.1   Predictive Analytics

This chapter focuses on predictive analytics in IT Service Management and it is customary to give a brief on what is the whole idea. Predictive analytics is the amalgamation of a variety of statistical techniques like data mining, data modeling, machine learning, artificial intelligence, etc. A predictive model is developed using these techniques that captures the trends in the historical data. The model will be able to answer what can happen in the future using the real time data with a higher probability. The outcome is that, optimal decisions can be taken with the knowledge of the future and the desired outcomes; nothing but decision making [10]. Predictions are so hard to get right, so why exactly is it adopted by enterprises worldwide? Predictive analytics can identify which customers were likely to churn, which are the loyal customers, etc. and a coffee shop in New York could cut down 38% of the marketing cost by predicting exactly the same. A 10% increase in revenue was achieved by Rue La La by price optimization. A public service agency in the U.S. avoided budget overruns, predict consumer demand and could adapt to market changes based on models developed using historic data, demand study, market research, etc. [8].

To start with, identification of the anticipated result or outcome will be the first step towards embracing predictive analytics in the business model. What has to be achieved? In the case of the public service agency in the U.S., how to avoid budget overruns will be the right question. To answer the questions raised, what data is present? And with the data what can be done? Are to be addressed first. Further, exploratory data analysis is performed to that summarizes the data and gives an overview of the basic characteristics of the data. The outcome of EDA can help in the hypothesis generation, identifying the outliers and so on [11]. These steps were performed to get an overall understanding of the problem and the hypothesis. With a precisely defined problem statement and hypothesis, statistical model/AI based model or ML model can be developed using the historic data collected. The same is validated with the help of real time data to further calibrate the model. Various models can be developed that will best correlate with the historic data. The model is deployed to guide with the decision making process that can answer the questions. Poor design/validation of the models, poor decision making can result in more of negative impact than the anticipated outcome [12]. So how can IT Service Management gain from predictive analytics is presented in Section 7.3.

7.3   Significance of Predictive Analytics in ITSM

ITSM as mentioned in Section 7.1 is highly driven data. The ticketing system is used by IT service providers to address the service requests and other service related aspects. The service request effort estimation and incident resolution work-flow is depicted in Figure 7.3 and the overall incident management and ticket addressing process is depicted in Figure 7.7. The data generated as a result of these existing process is enormous. The data can be structured or unstructured. To give an overview, Table 7.1 gives the number of tickets raised by 24 different accounts due to the occurrence of an incident/service request, etc. and the number of tickets resolved on the same day. The data is provided by one of the world's top most service providers subjected to Non-Disclosure Agreement. An average of 1, 11,000 tickets were raised per day as per the data from 2016. With the adoption of technology, this number will be on a rise.

How can ITSM benefit from predictive analytics? Ticketing is a day to day process in ITSM and Ticket Analytics can be used to draw comparisons like Resolution time by Technology, Ticket Volumes by Technology, Resolution time by Industry Domain, Ticket Volumes by Industry Domains, Account wise Tickets resolved the same day, RCA, etc. The advantage of the same is that based on the analysis, the source of maximum tickets can be identified and it can be addressed, which type of tickets have

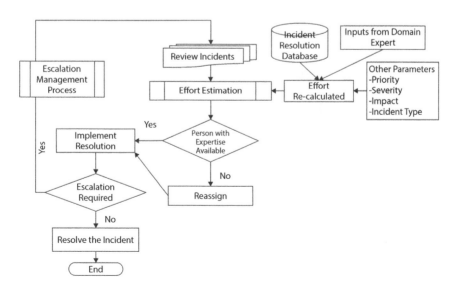

Figure 7.3 Service request effort estimation and incident resolution workflow.

Table 7.1 Number of tickets raised by 24 accounts/day and closed tickets/day: data from a leading service provider.

Account	Resolved same day	Total tickets
1	6,552	14,364
I2	5,436	8,316
3	3,632	36,100
4	2,603	2,696
5	2,532	7,672
6	2,390	5,251
7	1,610	6,452
8	1,423	3,208
9	1,383	3,598
10	1,197	2,522
11	713	909
12	331	3,232
13	273	3,266
14	273	1,287
15	254	2,412
16	250	2,172
17	220	396
18	191	460
19	158	3,244
20	65	2,618
21	29	1,174
22	16	60
23	3	23
24	1	180
Total	31,535	111,612

high resolution time can be identified and addressed. Predictive maintenance can be scheduled based on the identification of the root causes for incidents [13]. The insights like which industry domains will have major chunk of tickets can be mapped to the type of expertise required for the resolution and the amount of manpower. The time of arrival of tickets in different time zones and its severity and priority can also be mapped to the amount of manpower required for ticket resolution [14].

Figures 7.4 and 7.5 are the depiction of the analytics performed on the tickets. Priority of the raised tickets where the same is segregated based on

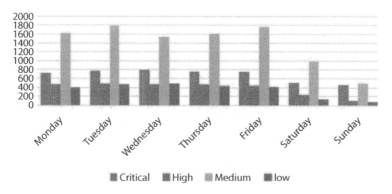

Figure 7.4 Ticket count vs. day of week based on priority of the tickets.

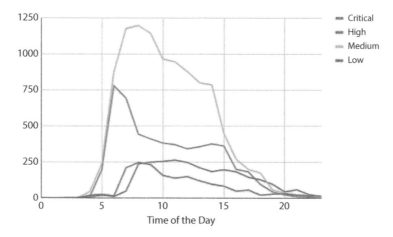

Figure 7.5 Ticket count vs time of the day in which it is logged based on priority of the tickets.

days of the week is performed. The time of the day is considered further and tickets logged with the same priority on different hours of the day are segregated to give an insight into the ticket occurrence rate during business hours [15].

Statistical analysis on tickets raised due to the occurrence of an incident is performed and Figure 7.6 depicts the result obtained. The number of tickets logged under different industry domains of each client of the IT Service industry is the first level of analysis performed and Figure 7.6 shows the result [16].

These are some of the sample analyses performed as a part of ticket analytics in the ITSM arena. So Ticket Analytics provides insight into ticket details and identifies potential root cause. Addressing the root cause brings down the incidents' volume and improves productivity. Reduced ticket volume and reduction in ticket resolution time is equal to improved client satisfaction. Further, delivery team gets insight to potential problem areas and can take proactive actions. An overall comparative analysis of productivity and ticket resolution time across accounts, industries, technologies, service areas will help in establishing performance baseline. This can improve day to day practices by addressing systemic issues. Furthermore, precision in capacity modeling and better review of SLA commitments are achieved. Higher accuracy in resolution, better insights into ticket arrival patterns and resolution time are all added advantages.

These can be beneficial to the enterprise since the ticket analytics have more to offer than the current practices like identification of the root causes

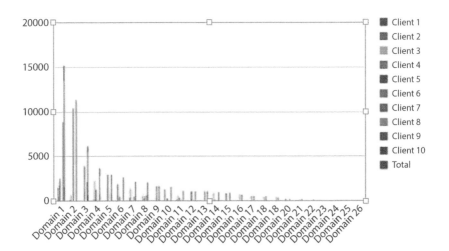

Figure 7.6 Industry domain by ticket volume.

through automated process, standardized productivity metrics, easy identification of tickets that can be moved to self-service and scope for automation. It will be easier to identify the accounts that need improvement and accounts that are giving good results. Also repetitive incidents can be identified and can be eliminated. As a fore-note the ticket analytics benefits reaped by two different clients are presented further.

Client 1

The questions raised by Client 1 was, "What will be the type of tickets that can be expected in the next 6 months and what will be the root cause of the majority of the tickets?" The insights from the ticket analytics performed on the tickets raised by the users of the services offered by Client 1 are as follows:

- five applications are responsible for the 54% of overall incidents
- In a 6-month period, three jobs failed more than 120 times
- The root cause of 137 failures in a single application is due to memory issue
- Data issue is the root cause of 60 failures in another application

Based on the insights corrective actions/decision were taken by the clients and was implemented. Issues in the areas of memory and data issues were addressed and preventive maintenance was performed. As a result, 25 applications moved to zero incident count and more productive work could be performed by the effort saved from avoiding these incidents. Issues in the areas of memory and data issues were addressed and preventive maintenance was performed.

Client 2

The questions raised by Client 2 were, what is the current volume of tickets under different areas and what caused the incidents?

The insights from the ticket analytics performed on the tickets raised by the users of the services offered by Client 2 are as follows:

- Higher than usual volume of ticket is generated by application under a specific area
- One of the major root causes for the occurrence on an incident is access related issues

Based on the insights corrective actions/decision were taken by the clients and were implemented. Application under the specific area was subjected to thorough code re-factoring and testing to address the recurring issues. Access control procedures were further reviewed and a reduction of 5 and 2% of total incidents were achieved respectively. Also resource optimization was performed that leads to a total savings of $4000/month.

Since, these models developed learning and modify as per the real time trends and data, remodeling and refitting of the data are not required. The insights can be based on the present data. Also automating the process can aid in acquiring the required insights from the model as and when it is required. Therefore, predictive analytics can completely reshape the way enterprise reporting is happening.

7.4   Ticket Analytics: A Case Study

An enterprise handling accounts in the Healthcare sector need insight on reducing the effort required to close a ticket raised due to an incident as a part of service maintenance. Based on the requirement, machine learning based predictive model that can predict required effort for each category of the ticket is modeled. The questions addressed are 1) How can effort be reduced while resolving an incident? and 2) Can effort required to resolve each category of incidents be predicted?

To answer the questions, the data is collected in the form of tickets and each recorded ticket has different fields and the format of a sample ticket is depicted in Figure 7.7. The collected tickets as a raw data are depicted in Figure 7.8.

Figures 7.8 and 7.9 depict the entire methodology followed for this case study.

INCIDENT ID	INC 1
SEVERITY	HIGH
STATUS	CLOSED
OPEN TIME	7/16/2015 6:55:25 AM
CLOSED TIME	7/17/2015 8:31:47 AM
ASSIGNEE NAME	JOHN DOE
ASSIGNMENT GROUP	ACCOUNT MANAGEMENT
DESCRIPTION	USER SUCCESSFUL TO LOGIN BUT UNABLE TO ACCESS SAP
:	:
RESOLUTION	FIND USER XXX PERMISSION
ESTIMATED TIME TO RESOLVE	30 MINS
RESOLUTION DATETIME	7/17/2015 8:31:47 AM

Figure 7.7 Sample ticket format.

Incident ID	IncidentActivit	Incident Activity	Assignment	# Reassigr	Handle Ti	# Related	Status	Business I	Severity	Priority
IM0000004	001A3689763	Reassignment	TEAM0001	26	3871	Other	Closed	4	4	4
IM0000005	001A5852941	Reassignment	TEAM0002	33	4354	Software	Closed	3	3	3
IM0000006	001A5852943	Update from cu:	TEAM0002	13	43	Operator	Closed	4	4	4
IM0000007	001A5849980	Operator Updat	TEAM0003	2	3383	Other	Closed	4	4	4
IM0000008	001A5849979	Assignment	TEAM0003	4	3383	Other	Closed	4	4	4
IM0000009	001A5852942	Assignment	TEAM0002	2	3703	Unknown	Closed	4	4	4
IM0000010	001A5852172	Closed	TEAM0003	5	3294	Other	Closed	4	4	4
IM0000011	001A5852173	Caused By CI	TEAM0003	2	0	Other	Closed	3	3	3
IM0000012	001A5849978	Reassignment	TEAM0003	6	3067	Software	Closed	4	4	4
IM0000013	001A5544096	Operator Updat	TEAM0003	8	1322	Software	Closed	4	4	4
IM0000014	001A4725475	Update	TEAM9999	5	1132	Software	Closed	4	4	4
IM0000015	001A4327777	Operator Updat	TEAM0003	17	66	Software	Closed	4	4	4
IM0000016	001A3689771	Reassignment	TEAM0001	1	3114	Data	Closed	3	3	3
IM0000017	001A5377163	Operator Updat	TEAM0003	3	2837	Other	Closed	4	4	4
IM0000018	001A4396943	Operator Updat	TEAM0003	1	1223	Other	Closed	4	4	4

Figure 7.8 Raw data collected from organization.

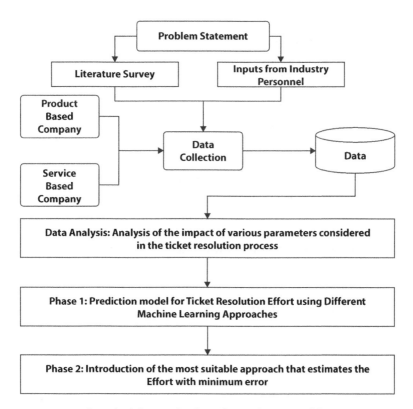

Figure 7.9 Research methodology to develop effort prediction model.

7.4.1 Input Parameters

As per EDA, the L2 and L3 severity and L2 and L3 priority tickets have more average TTR compared to high and low priority tickets, altogether, and the volume of tickets logged during weekdays from 8 AM to 6 PM is more. Therefore, further in this research, L2 and L3 level severity and priority tickets logged on weekdays from 8 AM to 6 PM will be considered. Insights obtained from related research and the opinions from expert reviews are considered further for the selection of input parameters for the modeling of prediction of effort required in resolving different incidents. Based on the preliminary analysis, the following input parameters are identified in the developing the predictive model for incident closure effort.

- Application: An overall of tickets logged under seven applications are considered that comes under custom and packaged product technologies.
- Priority: In this research priority levels 2 and 3 are considered.
- Severity: Tickets with severity levels 2 and 3 are considered in this research
- SLA Compliance: Both tickets that met and could not meet the SLA clauses are considered.
- Primary Technology: Five different primary technologies are considered.
- Root Cause: Six different root causes are present in the tickets that are used in the modeling.
- Complexity: Tickets with four levels of complexity were present in the ticket logs.
- No. of reassignments: The number of reassignments required to resolve an incident and close the associated tickets depends on the ticket type and the associated data is considered as such.
- Risk Assessment: tickets with Medium and High level risk factors are considered in the research.

7.4.2 Predictive Modeling

Effort prediction models for the tickets raised are modeled using random forest tree based algorithm. The same is presented further in this chapter. Further, analysis of the model is based on the result obtained.

7.4.3 Random Forest Model

Random Forest is a tree based ensemble model. Multiple trees are grown as per the training set data. Each tree is grown based on a subset of variables and a subset of data points. The process of growing the trees are called tree bagging. Its main advantage is that it overcomes over fitting of the model and change in the dataset has little effect on the outcome. Average of the trees when adopted in prediction will decrease the noise. Further, optimization is achieved using cross validation that estimates the level of fit. The algorithm for random forest is as follows:

Given a training dataset $X = x_1, x_2, x_3, ..., x_n$ and the response be $Y = y_1, y_2, y_3, ..., y_n$.

- Initialize B which is a random value and the number of times bagging should be repeated
- For $b = 1, 2, \cdots, B$:
  - Sample the dataset with replacement, training dataset from X, Y. X_b, Y_b be the sampled subsets of X and Y respectively.
  - Grow a regression tree f_b on X_b, Y_b

Prediction on test dataset x' is a function f(x') which is

$$f(x') = \frac{1}{B} \sum_{i=1}^{n} f_b(x') \qquad (7.1)$$

A total of 500 decision trees are randomly modeled using the training dataset. The development of the model is performed using the random Forest package meant for the classification and regression based on a forest of trees using random inputs. The Breiman and Cutler's Random Forests for Classification and Regression package [17] provides a randomForest() function that is used to build the model using training dataset and is further used in the prediction of incident resolution effort in the test dataset. Error measures like MAPE, MSE, RMSE and MAE tests are performed in order to validate the same.

The actual and the predicted effort by the developed models, for the training and test dataset are represented in Figures 7.10 and 7.11 for regression tree and random forest respectively.

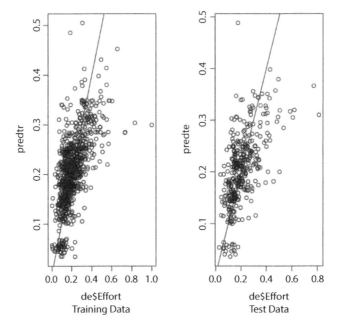

Figure 7.10 Effort values predicted vs. observed using training and test dataset.

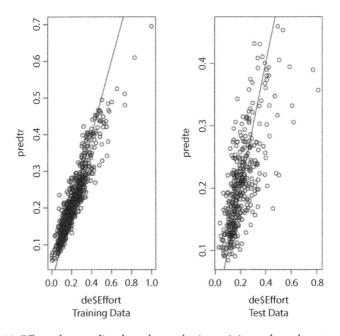

Figure 7.11 Effort values predicted vs. observed using training and test dataset.

Table 7.2 Overfitness, testing error and accuracy of the random forest model.

Model	Over fitting	Accuracy	Testing error
Random Forest	0.3475	0.88	0.3228

7.4.4 Performance of the Predictive Model

The tabulated results presented in Table 7.2 shows that the decision tree based predictive model can predict the effort required in resolving an incident with an accuracy of 88%. The overfittings value is less while considering random forest algorithm. But a general property of random forest is its inability to predict accurately in the presence of data values that are not present in the dataset. Therefore, this general property of random forest model makes it unsuitable for considering it as a predictive model for incident resolution effort. In such a situation, alternate approaches has to be adopted. Other machine learning based models can be developed in the similar way and its performance can be compared. Analyze the features that is required and whether it is suitable for the problem under consideration need to be addressed. An optimum model that will give more accurate result with the minimum error need to be deployed for predictive analytics and effort prediction.

7.5 Conclusion

All the services provided by your IT team can be termed—IT services and ITSM is a framework that has detailed steps that need to be followed when a service request comes up or an incident occurs. The data generated in the ITSM process is not friendly enough to easily produce metrics and reports. Adopting of predictive analytics can help in dealing with these issues. Increased speed of execution, cost reductions, improved customer experience, reduced human error, increased task adaptability, self-service are some of the advantages that predictive analytics offer enterprises when adopted with ITSM. Day to day operation in ITSM can further result in TTR effort pre-diction, root cause analysis, predicting occurrence of maintenance activity, track and manage the performance of IT assets efficiently, automated solutions, proactive prevention of tasks, automatic classification of incidents and service requests, predict SLA/contract violations, workload optimization, etc. This chapter further presents a case study on Ticket Analytics. The effort required to resolve an incident is predicted using Random Forest-based machine learning model. The process adopted is presented as a case study and why Random Forest model is not suitable is also presented. In such cases what can be the alternate approach that has to be adopted is also presented.

References

1. Radatz, J., Geraci, A., Katki, F., IEEE standard glossary of software engineering terminology. *IEEE Std*, 610121990, 121990, 3, 1990.
2. Kan, S.H., *Metrics and Models in Software Quality Engineering*, 2nd ed., Addison-Wesley Longman Publishing Co., Inc., Boston, MA, USA, 2002.
3. Sharma, J. and Rawani, A., From customers' requirements to customers satisfaction—quality function deployment in service sector. *Int. J. Product. Qual. Manage.*, 5, 4, 428–439, 2010.
4. IT Service Management (ITSM) software 2018 global market growth, opportunities and analysis, forecast to 2025, https://marketersmedia.com/it-service-management-itsm-software-2018-global-market-growth-opportunities-and-analysis-forecast-to-2025/292458. Accessed: 2018 [4] 12-31.
5. Sun, Y., Xu, Z., Zhang, T., On-board predictive maintenance with machine learning. Tech. Rep., SAE Technical Paper, WCX SAE World Congress, 2019.
6. Barafort, B., Betry, V., Cortina, S., Picard, M., Renault, A., St-Jean, M., Valdés, O., Luxembourg, *ITSM Process Assessment Supporting ITIL (TIPA)*, Van Haren Publishing, Luxembourg, 2009.
7. Christa, S. and Suma, V., Analysis of ticket severity: A case study, in: *2017 International Conference on Innovative Mechanisms for Industry Applications (ICIMIA)*, pp. 763–765, 2017.
8. Kubiak, P., Rass, S., Pinzger, M., IT-application behaviour analysis: Predicting critical system states on Openstack using monitoring performance data and log files. In *Proceedings of the 15th International Conference on Software Technologies (ICSOFT 2020)*, SCITEPRESS – Science and Technology Publications, Lda, pp. 589–596, 2020.
9. Hechler, E., Oberhofer, M., Schaeck, T., AI and change management, in: *Deploying AI in the Enterprise*, pp. 235–252, Springer, Germany, 2020.
10. Allamanis, M., Barr, E.T., Devanbu, P., Sutton, C., A survey of machine learning for big code and naturalness. *ACM Comput. Surv. (CSUR)*, 51, 4, 81, 2018.
11. dos Santos Messejana, J.D., *Predictive analysis of incidents based on software deployments*, Masters Dissertation, Department of Information Science and Technology, ISCTE - Lisbon University Institute, Lisboa, Portugal, August 2019.
12. Virata, A.J.A. and Niguidula, J.D., Mining it job-order services: Basis for policy formulation & it resource allocation, in: *International Conference on Big Data Technologies and Applications*, Springer, pp. 97–106, 2017.

13. Gupta, R., Prasad, K.H., Mohania, M., Automating ITSM incident management process, in: *2008 International Conference on Autonomic Computing*, IEEE, pp. 141–150, 2008.
14. Christa, S., Madhusudhan, V., Suma, V., Rao, J.J., Software maintenance: From the perspective of effort and cost requirement, in: *Proceedings of the International Conference on Data Engineering and Communication Technology*, Springer, pp. 759–768, 2017.
15. Christa, S. and Suma, V., An analysis on the significance of ticket analytics and defect analysis from software quality perspective, in: *Inventive Computation Technologies (ICICT), International Conference on*, vol. 1, IEEE, pp. 1–5, 2016.
16. Christa, S. and Suma, V., Significance of ticket analytics in effective software maintenance: Awareness, in: *Proceedings of the ACM Symposium on Women in Research 2016*, ACM, pp. 126–130, 2016.
17. Breiman, L., Cutler, A., Liaw, A., Wiener, M., Breiman and Cutler's random forests for classification and regression package 'randomforest'. Version 4.6-14, Software available at: http://stat-www.berkeley.edu/users/breiman/ RandomForests, 2012.

8

Modified Cross-Sell Model for Telecom Service Providers Using Data Mining Techniques

K. Ramya Laxmi[1]*, Sumit Srivastava[2], K. Madhuravani[1], S. Pallavi[1] and Omprakash Dewangan[3]

[1]*Department of CSE, Sreyas Institute of Engineering and Technology, Nagole, Hyderabad, India*
[2]*Dept. of Computer Science & Engineering Birla Institute of Technology, Mesra, Ranchi, India*
[3]*CSE, Kalinga University, Naya Raipur, India*

Abstract

Intensified competition and frequent shifting of the customer base for fixed-line telecom service providers, in recent years, has increased the necessity for better targeting and segmenting prospects and customers for cross-selling and up-sell of products and services. Telecom service providers now know and understand that old-fashioned marketing is no longer the option because of the abysmally low hit rates in the targeting of customers and the consequently low Return on Investment. Decision-makers in most fixed-line telecom operators are now of the view that better and accurate targeting of customers is only possible with accurate predictive analytics and data mining. A logistic regression algorithm has been used in this case study to identify those customers with the highest propensity to buy new products and services.

Keywords: Cross-sell model, data mining techniques, logistic regression algorithm

**Corresponding author*: kunta.ramya@gmail.com

Rohit Raja, Kapil Kumar Nagwanshi, Sandeep Kumar and K. Ramya Laxmi (eds.) Data Mining and Machine Learning Applications, (195–208) © 2022 Scrivener Publishing LLC

8.1 Introduction

A gold mine of the fixed-line telecom companies is their customer base. In the region across Asia Pacific, the telecom as a sector has witnessed dramatic changes in the past 15 years, owing to improvement in technology and socio-economic conditions. As a result, there has been a manifold increase in the customer base of the telecom providers [1].

In the past, the fixed-line telecom operators, particularly in the Asian region, rarely engaged in marketing activities to manage customer relationships. With the emergence of many new market players in the past decade and a half, catering to diversified bouquets and offerings, the need for customer focus has increased greatly. Intensifying competition and a multitude of choices have also resulted in frequent shifting of the customer base in the past few years [2, 3].

By better targeting and segmenting prospects and customers, fixed-line telecom operators can:

- Identify more sales-ready prospects.
- We are enhancing customer relationships and profitability.
- Capitalize on Marketing Return on Investment.
- Optimizes marketing campaign and performance
- Decision-makers in most fixed-line telecom operators are now of the view that all of the above is only possible with accurate predictive analytics and data mining [4, 5].

This work analyzes the problem of predicting students' academic performance, motivation, classroom management, and interaction, etc., that is increasingly investigated within the Educational Data Mining literature.

The proposed system having the following steps [6, 7],

- ➤ Dataset
- ➤ Pre-processing
  - ○ Splitting
  - ○ Data Cleaning
  - ○ Data Conversion
- ➤ Data Mining Feature Extraction
  - ○ Itemset
  - ○ Frequent Itemset
  - ○ Closed Frequent Itemset
  - ○ Support
  - ○ Confidence
  - ○ Lift

- ➢ Ranking
  - ○ Entropy
- ➢ Performance Analysis Training
  - ○ DH-DLNN
- ➢ Testing
  - ○ K-Fold Testing

1. Dataset

Data collection tools in the study include a self-structure questionnaire covering all the dimensions related to use of, increased access, knowledge building, learning, performance, motivation, classroom management and interaction, collaborative learning, and satisfaction [8].

Pre-processing: The first step in the proposed system is pre-processing of the dataset. Analyzing data must be done so that no misleading results are obtained [9].

Splitting: This is the first step in pre-processing phase. Splitting is done to part the values into words.

Data Cleaning: After that, unwanted words are removed from the dataset.

Data Conversion: Dataset having the attribute values in string format. The system can process only the numerical values. So that only, in the dataset the string will be converted into numerical values for corresponding strings [10].

2. Data Mining Feature Extraction

After pre-processing, the data mining features such as item set, frequent itemset, closed frequent itemset, support, confidence, lift are extracted from the dataset [11].

3. Ranking

After that, the Ranking will be calculated by using the features such as support, confidence, and lift with the help of the Entropy technique [12].

4. Performance Analysis Training

Finally, the performance will be analyzed by using the *DH-DLNN* algorithm. This algorithm trains the dataset depending upon the ranked features. Here the weight value was optimized using the *Deer Hunting Optimization Algorithm* to reduce the back propagation problem in the Artificial Neural Network algorithm [13–15].

5. Testing

After completion of the training process, the testing will be done. In this, 80% of the data will be given to training, and 20% of the data will be given for testing [16].

8.2   Literature Review

This chapter compares growth of the telecom industry, and the report is given by the ASA & Associates regarding Telecom Sector. Over the last few decades, significant expansion of the telecom sector was constantly increasing network coverage and catalysts for the growth in subscriber base. The objective of the telecom industry, according to growth story and potential, served new players in the industry. Top 10 risks in telecommunications 2014, Ernst & Young [17]. Predictive analytics for Telecommunications service providers, RED giant. Inc. Madison, WI 53713 USA, February 2012, the service provider has responsible for individual preferred the most disarble segments for economic growth [18].

The present paper 'Predictive Analytics: A Game-Changer for Telcos has explained the easy profit-making business and how revenue can be enhanced. There are many challenges to increased the number of subscribers; Modified cross-selling activities help them a lot to generate the revenue.

In the paper, telecom companies tap analytics for Growth WIPRO. Telecom service providers across the world face an enormous challenge. Analytics can help provide a solution by monetizing the huge data pools. Telecom service providers are looking at how best they can bundle their services and products and improve revenues and profitability (Knowledge@ Wharton—Wipro August 2014).

Determining the next offer for your customers using sophisticated analysis has been given Cross-Sell and Up-Sell for Telecommunications SAS. SAS integrates seamlessly with the other SAS intelligence solutions. OS upsell and cross-sell analysis are used in customer retention strategies for the rapid growth in the telecommunication industry.

In logical literature, the author [19] examines a few activities that attempt to classify the understudies to predict their last grade based on the highlights extracted from the recorded details in the insightful electronic frameworks. A variety of different classification models contributed to crucial progress in the implementation of specification by measuring the vectors of the component. The analysis directions of the developer through the Data-Mining rehearsals require discovering viable ways to provide the Managers of Specialized Education Institutions with enough knowledge to prepare a better explanation in a specific timeframe, which was in the past inflexible or impossible, taking into account huge datasets and prior techniques. Hence, the point is to advance an approach to comprehend the understudies' conclusions, fulfillments, and dissatisfaction in every component of the instructive cycle, and to anticipate their inclination in specific fields of study, the desire to continue with preparation, the advanced education failure, and to have an accurate connection among their perspective and the specifications of the labor market. Perhaps the fascinating data-mining initiatives in the informative sector are seen in the current section. The developer applies his ideas and applications to informative problems using specific data-mining techniques [20].

Information gives power in some genuine settings empowering and encouraging the protection of important legacy, new picking up, tackling mind-boggling issues, making center capabilities, and starting new circumstances for the two people and associations now and later [21]. The tremendous measures of information in data sets, which contain huge quantities of records, ascribes that while investigatomh to find helpful data and information, it makes manual examination unreasonable. All these variables show the requirement for shrewd and computerized information investigation procedures, which may find helpful information from information. Information revelation in data sets and Data mining has accordingly become critical apparatuses in understanding the target of insightful and robotized information examination [22, 23].

Data mining is a painstakingly arranged utilization of measurable and machine learning strategies and devices through the space of scientific procedures, which is considered as a cycle of choosing what will be generally helpful, promising, and uncovering. A definite survey of Data-Mining instruments and their applications can be found in, and Extensively, the significant undertakings of Data mining are prescient and expressive errands under disclosure situated Data-Mining framework [24, 25].

Data mining [26]:
Data mining is the center of the information disclosure measure, including the deducing of calculations that investigate the information, build up the model and find already obscure examples. Data mining is a multidisciplinary field that joins insights, AI, computerized reasoning, and data set innovation to extricate elevated level information from certifiable informational collections. Data mining includes deciding examples from or fitting models to noticed information. It is a complex information logical technique that concentrates upon investigation and develops new experiences for supporting dynamic. This separated data helps recognize patterns, frame a forecast or characterization model, and in summing up a data set.
Data-Mining Techniques [27, 28]:
The Data-Mining procedures include:

- Classification/Regression: the revelation of a model or capacity that guides objects into predefined classes (grouping) or reasonable qualities (relapse). The model/work is processed on a preparation set (regulated learning).

- Grouping: acknowledgment of the restricted structure of classification systems or categories for the representation of knowledge.
- Highlight: seeking a progressive description for a subsection of details, such as the approximation of breakdown or affiliate guidelines and the use of multivariate analysis method.
- Constraint Designing: seeking a local design that represents the necessary elements among variables or between the estimation methods of a variable in an informative set or part of a data set.
- Sequential Patterns: disclosure of incessant aftereffects in an assortment of arrangements (grouping information base), each speaking to a bunch of occasions happening at ensuing occasions. The requesting of the occasions in the aftereffects is pertinent.
- Update and Variance Identification: identifying the key improvements to the details from recent calculated or controlled estimations.

8.3   Methodology and Implementation

8.3.1   Selection of the Independent Variables

In most cross-sell or up-sell predictive modeling situations where either Logistic regression or some other competing data mining paradigm is the tool of choice, the analyst has several independent variables to choose from. These variables could either be there in the database or can be created from the existing variable list as newly derived variables [29].

Prediction of the dependent variable is made using Logistic regression variable on the basis of continuous and/or categorical independents and to determine the percent of the variance, and to rank the relative importance of explanatory/independent variables [30].

The simplest logistic regression equation is represented as Equation (8.1).

$$\text{Logit}(p) = \ln(p/1 - p) = a + bx, \text{ where } (p/1 - p) \text{ is the Odds ratio.}$$

$$(8.1)$$

The output from the PROC LOGISTIC program contains different tools for applying regression models to a dataset and assesses its results. The statistical significance of each of the independent variables, informs about both the overall fit of the model. Since cross-sell and up-sell efforts have an economic component, i.e., what it will cost to the X-cell product to a client and parameters, odds ratio makes it much easier for an cross-sell and up-sell effort to grasp the impact of parameters. The confusion matrix that PROC LOGISTIC generates provides an idea about model accuracy.

Model Process Life Cycle

For this project, we did not have real-time data, so we went ahead and created dummy data with dummy variables while incorporating real-time logic. The variables required for this model is decided based on extensive research like going through a lot of article and research paper, brainstorming with peers and from own experience is represented in Figure 8.1 [31, 32].

Two types of variables created for the modeling are:

- Dependent/response variable:
  - Propensity Buy—It has two values 1,0.
    - 1 indicates Customer who will buy new products (no. of products >1)
    - 0 indicates Customer who will not buy new products (no. of products >1)
- Independent variables:
  - The lists of independent variables are created based on extensive research and experience. These variables broadly fall under the following category:

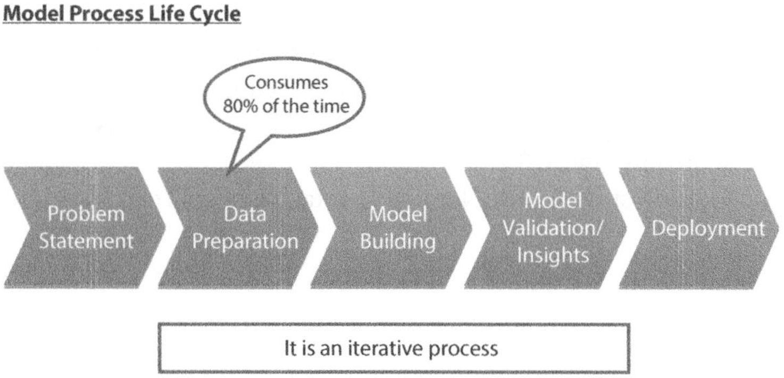

Model Process Life Cycle

Figure 8.1 Process life cycle.

- Basic customer information
- Demography
- Product usage
- Payment behavior
- Complaint variables.

- Data Exploration
  This stage usually starts with data preparation. This involves cleaning data, data transformations, selecting subsets of records, etc. Then, depending on the nature of the analytic problem, this first stage of the process of data mining may involve anywhere between simple or elaborate methods that are implemented in order to identify the most relevant variables. This is also used to determine the complexity and/or the general nature of models that can be taken into account in the next stage.
- Sampling
  Data sampling is an arithmetic and statistical data mining analysis technique used to select, manipulate and analyze a representative subset of data points to identify patterns and trends in the data set being examined as a whole.
  - ➢ *Logistic regression*—Using variables short-listed in the above step, a first-cut logistic regression model is developed. The model is developed in a step-wise fashion, introducing the significant variables one-by-one into the model in the order of their significance. The model will retain only those variables that have a significant effect on the probability to buy, controlling for the effects of all other variables in the model.
- Confusion Matrices
- Misclassification rate: The misclassification rate calculates the proportion of an observation being allocated to the incorrect group. It is calculated as follows and it is represented in Figure 8.2.
- (False Positive + False Negative) / Total Number of classification

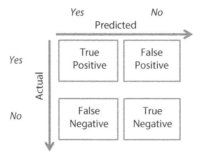

Figure 8.2 Confusion matrices.

8.4   Data Partitioning

Data partitioning provides mutually exclusive training and validation datasets and helps in validating the built model. Keeping industry best practices in mind, the data has been partitioned into Training and Validation on a 70:30 basis. The buyer and non-buyer counts in the training and validation datasets show approximately similar buyer count percentages (Table 8.1).

8.4.1   Interpreting the Results of Logistic Regression Model

The results of logistic regression on the training data set reveal that, out of the selected independent variables, seven variables are found to be significantly related to the Customer's propensity to be cross-sold or up-sold (Table 8.2).

Table 8.1 Buyer counts.

	Training		Validation	
Category	Frequency	Percentage	Frequency	Percentage
Buyer	996	14.23	402	13.40
Non-buyer	6,004	85.77	2,598	86.60
Total	7,000	100	3,000	100

Table 8.2 Analysis of maximum likelihood estimates.

Parameter	DF	Estimate	Standard error	Wald chi-Square	Pr >chiSq
Intercept	1	−7.5185	275.7	0.0007	0.9782
Number of late payments	1	−0.5611	0.0309	329.8319	<.0001
Proportion of bill paid	1	5.7902	0.3353	298.2068	<.0001
Location/ Geography	1	0.4348	0.0835	27.1011	<.0001
Mean bill complaint closure time	1	−1.3771	0.0967	202.9235	<.0001
(Repair time/ Assurance time) for bill complaint	1	−3.4687	0.4491	59.6525	<.0001
(Repair time/ Assurance time) for service complaint	1	−4.0633	0.4123	97.1184	<.0001
(Repair time/ Assurance time) for technical complaint	1	−0.2796	0.0906	9.5254	0.0020

8.5   Conclusions

The model has been very successful in classifying the best prospects from among the sample dataset of customers for cross-selling and up-sell campaigns. The expected rate of purchase for these prospects is approximately seven times more than the overall expected rate of purchase in the sample data. The predicted probability that these prospects would respond to a dedicated campaign is approximately 0.97, which means that 97 out of 100 prospects are likely to respond to a campaign positively. Most of the parameters that influence the Customer's propensity to purchase belong to the category of "Customer experience" with the service provider.

References

1. Srivastava, R., Bangle, J., Somaiya, K.J., Role of Competition in Growing Markets: Telecom Sector. *Indian J. Market.*, XXXVI, 9, 50–62, September 2006.
2. Sinha, S.K. and Wagh, A., Analyzing Growth of Cellular Telecom Sector and Understanding Consumer's Preferences and Choices on the Use of Cell phone. *Indian J. Market.*, VII, 9, 39–47, September 2008.
3. Anderson, J., Developing a route to market strategy for mobile communications in rural-India, *Int. J. Emerg. Mark.*, 3, 2, 22, 2008.
4. Banumathy, S. and Kalaivani, S., Customers' Attitude Towards Cell phone in Communication System. *Indian J. Market.*, VI, 3, 129–136, March 2006.
5. Shankar, R., *Innovation in the Indian Telecom Industry*, IJBARR and Banglore, India, Feb 2006.
6. Piatetsky-Shapiro, G. and Masand, B., Estimating campaign benefits and modeling lift. *Proceedings of KDD-99 Conference*, ACM Press, 1999.
7. Larose, D.T., *Data mining methods and models*, A John Wiley & Sons, Inc. Publication, Hoboken, NJ, USA, 2006.
8. Rusu, L. and Breşfelean, V.P., Management prototype for universities. *Annals of the Tiberiu Popoviciu Seminar, Supplement: International Workshop in Collaborative Systems*, vol. 4, Mediamira Science Publisher, Cluj-Napoca, Romania, pp. 287–295, 2006.
9. Shahiri, A.M. and Husain, W., A review on predicting student's performance using data mining techniques. *Proc. Comput. Sci.*, 72, 414–422, 2015.
10. Sinha, A.P. and Zhao, H., Incorporating domain knowledge into data mining classifiers: An application in indirect lending. *Decis. Support Syst.*, 46, 1, 287–299, 2008.
11. Sørebø, Ø., Halvari, H., Gulli, V.F., Kristiansen, R., The role of self-determination theory in explaining teachers' motivation to continue to use e-learning technology. *Comput. Educ.*, 53, 1177–1187, 2009.
12. Tomasevic, N., Gvozdenovic, N., Vranes, S., An overview and comparison of supervised data mining techniques for student exam performance prediction. *Comput. Educ.*, 143, 103676, 2020.
13. Tso, G.K.F. and Yau, K.K.W., Predicting electricity energy consumption: A comparison of regression analysis, decision tree and neural networks. *Energy*, 32, 1761–1768, 2007.
14. Universitatea Babes-Bolyai Cluj-Napoca, Romania. Programul Strategic al Universitatii Babes-Bolyai (2007–2011), Nr.11.366, 1 August 2006.

15. Vandamme, J.P., Meskens, N., Superby., J.F., Predicting Academic Performance by Data Mining Methods. *Educ. Econ.*, 15, 4, 405–419, 2007.

16. Vanderlinde, R., Aesaert, K., van Braak, J., Measuring ICT use and contributing conditions in primary schools. *Br. J. Educ. Technol.*, 46, 5, 1056–1063, 2015.

17. Vidya, Y. and Shemimol, B., Secured Friending in Proximity-based Mobile Social Network. *J. Excell. Comput. Sci. Eng.*, 1, 2, 1–10, 2015.

18. Waheed, H., Hassan, S., Aljohani, N.R., Hardman, J., Alelyani, S., Nawaz, R., Predicting academic performance of students from VLE big data using deep learning models. *Comput. Hum. Behav.*, 104, 106189, 2020.

19. Wan, S. and Lei, T.C., A knowledge-based decision support system to analyze the debris-flow problems at Chen-Yu-Lan River, Taiwan. *Knowledge-Based System*, 22, 8, 580–588, 2009.

20. Wang, H. and Wang, S., A knowledge management approach to data mining process for business intelligence. *Ind. Manage. Data Syst.*, 108, 5, 622–634, 2008.

21. Witten, I.H. and Frank, E., *Data Mining: Practical Machine Learning Tools and Techniques*, 2nd ed., Morgan Kaufmann series in Data Management Systems, Elsevier Inc., New Zealand, 2005.

22. Xu, J., Moon, K.H., Van Der Schaar, M., A machine learning approach for tracking and predicting student performance in degree programs. *IEEE J. Sel. Top. Signal Process.*, 11, 5, 742–753, 2017.

23. Yadav, R.S., Application of hybrid clustering methods for student performance evaluation. *Int. J. Inf. Technol.*, 21, 1–8, 2018.

24. Yousafzai, B.K., Hayat, M., Afzal, S., Application of machine learning and data mining in predicting the performance of intermediate and secondary education level student. *Educ. Inf. Technol.*, 25, 1–21, 2020.

25. Zughoul, O., Momani, F., Almasri, O.H., Zaidan, B.B., Alsalem, M.A., Albahri, O.S., Hashim, M., Comprehensive insights into the criteria of student performance in various educational domains. *IEEE Access*, 6, 73245–73264, 2018.

26. Pathak, S., Raja, R., Sharma, V., Ambala, S., ICT Utilization and Improving Student Performance in Higher Education. *Int. J. Recent Technol. Eng. (IJRTE)*, 8, 2, 5120–5124, July 2019.

27. Laxmikant Tiwari, R., Vaibhav Sharma, R., Miri, R., Adaptive Neuro-Fuzzy Inference System Based Fusion Of Medical Image. *Int. J. Res. Electron. Comput. Eng.*, 7, 2, 2086–2091.

28. Sumati Pathak, R., Vaibhav Sharma, R., Ramya Laxmi, K., A Framework Of ICT Implementation On Higher Educational Institution With Data Mining Approach. *Eur. J. Eng. Res. Sci*, 4.

29. Sumati Pathak, R. and Vaibhav Sharma, R., The Impact of ICT in Higher Education. *IJRECE*, 7, 1, 130–145, January–March, 2019.

30. Raja, R., Kumar, S., Rashid, Md., Color Object Detection Based Image Retrieval using ROI Segmentation with Multi-Feature Method. *Wirel. Pers. Commun. Springer J.*, 5, 1–24, https://doi.org/10.1 007/s11277-019-07021-6.

31. Raja, R., Shishir Sinha, T., Patra, R.K., Tiwari, S., Physiological Trait Based Biometrical Authentication of Human-Face Using LGXP and ANN Techniques. *Int. J. Inf. Comput. Secur.*, 10, 2/3, 303–320, 2018.

32. Raja, R., Patra, R.K., Sinha, T.S., Extraction of Features from Dummy face for improving Biometrical Authentication of Human. *Int. J. Lumin. Appl.*, 7, 3–4, Article 259, 507–512, 2017.

33. Raja, R., Sinha, T.S., Dubey, R.P., Soft Computing and LGXP Techniques for Ear Authentication using Progressive Switching Pattern. *Int. J. Eng. Future Technol.*, 2, 2, 66–86, 2016.

9

Inductive Learning Including Decision Tree and Rule Induction Learning

Raj Kumar Patra*, A. Mahendar and G. Madhukar

*Department of Computer Science and Engineering, CMR Technical Campus,
Kandlakoya, Hyderabad, India*

Abstract

Inductive learning empowers the framework to perceive examples and consistencies in past Data or preparing Data and concentrate complete expectations from them. Two basic classifications of inductive learning methods, what's more, tactics, are introduced. Gap and-Conquer calculations are often referred to as Option Tree calculations and Separate-and-Conquer calculations. This chapter first efficiently portrays the concept of option trees, followed by an analysis of prominent current tree calculations like ID3, C4.5, and CART calculations. A prominent example is the Rule Extraction System (RULES) group. A modern review of RULES calculations, and Rule Extractor-1 calculation, their strength just as lack are clarified and examined. At last, scarcely any application spaces of inductive learning are introduced.

A large portion of the current learning frameworks chips away at Data that are put away in inadequately organized records. This methodology keeps them from managing Data from the genuine world, which is frequently heterogeneous and gigantic and which requires data set administration instruments. In this article, we propose a unique answer for Data mining which incorporates a Fuzzy learning device that develops Fuzzy choice trees with a multidimensional database administration framework.

Keywords: Data mining, rules induction, RULES family, inductive learning, decision tree calculations

---

**Corresponding author*: patra.rajkumar@gmail.com

Rohit Raja, Kapil Kumar Nagwanshi, Sandeep Kumar and K. Ramya Laxmi (eds.) Data Mining and Machine Learning Applications, (209–234) © 2022 Scrivener Publishing LLC

9.1 Introduction

A further area of AI recognized as inductive learning was known to help enforce basic ideas and make predictions activities [1]. Inductive taking in is gaining from perception and prior Data by speculation of rules and ends. Inductive learning takes into account the distinguishing proof of preparing Data or prior Data examples and likenesses, which are then removed as summed up rules.

The distinguished and separated summed-up rules come to use in thinking and issue solving [2]. Data mining is one stage during the time spent Data revelation in Databases (KDD). It is conceivable to configuration computerized instruments for taking in rules from Databases by utilizing Data mining or other Data revelation techniques [3, 4]. There is a core value between data mining and AI, as both disassociate fascinating examples and database information [5].

Just as demonstrated by [6], data mining refers to using the database as a training collection in the learning process. In inductive learning, different strategies were proposed to collect system rules. These techniques and methods were divided into two simple classes: Divide-and-Conquer (Decision Tree) and Separate-and-Conquer (Covering). Split and resolve measurements, such as ID3, C4.5, and CART, are collection procedures that decide the overall ends of the option. Isolated and-Conquer calculations, for example, Class AQ, CN2 (Clark and Niblett), and RULES (Rule Extraction System), where laws are explicitly derived from a collection of facts. A choice tree speaks to one of the generally utilized methodologies in inductive AI. A lot of preparing models are normally used to shape a choice tree [7]. The tendency of option trees for inductive learning is due to structural flexibility in execution and understanding and lack of preparation methods like standardization. Option tree execution is appropriate and, therefore, can work well enough with enormous databases. Subsequently, the options tree can handle a colossal measure of assembling models due to its performance. Mathematical and unmitigated data are feasible in the selection binary tree.

Choice trees summarize superiorly for Data instances not yet seen until examined the feature confidence pair in the Data planning. Better description understanding depends on the features provided. The characteristic game plan on the option tree is now very widespread from the data available. The negative side of the option trees is that the summarized rules are usually aren't the most detailed. Therefore, a few calculations like AQ family calculations don't utilize choice trees. The AQ calculation family utilizes the disjunction of positive models to highlight esteems [8].

A major issue emerging in the area of partition and vanquish measurements are the difficulties with attempts to show those concepts in the tree. Constantly trying to prompt requirements that don't provide something for all intents and purpose with tree characteristics, and further confusion is the way that a few traits that show up are either monotonous or unnecessary [9]. Subsequently, these measurements triggered the repetition problem, where sub-trees can be repeated on different branches. It's tough to overcome a tree until it grows tall. Using isolated strategies on a giant tree will cause useless uncertainty.

As an outcome, analysts have of late taken a stab at improving covering calculations to think about or surpass the aftereffects of partition and overcome endeavors. This is wiser to function the criteria directly from the database within, as opposed to trying to provoke them from an option tree structure that is compiled onto four key characteristics as suggested [10]. Initially, utilizing portrayal, for example, "Assuming... THEN" makes the guidelines all the more handily comprehended by individuals. It is additionally a demonstrated truth that standard learning is a more powerful technique than utilizing choice trees.

Besides, the inferred rules can be utilized and put away effectively in any master framework or any Data based framework. Finally, it is additionally simpler to study and cause changes to decide that to have been actuated without influencing different guidelines since they are free of each other.

We additionally study Fuzzy choice tree-based strategies that give great devices to find Data from Data. They are equal to a lot of if rules and are explanatory since the classification they propose might be clarified. Additionally, the utilization of the Fuzzy set hypothesis permits the treatment of mathematical qualities in a more normal manner. Yet, most existing answers for build choice trees use records, and, notably, this methodology is sensible just if the measure of Data utilized for Data disclosure is somewhat small (for example, fits in central memory). Frequently, these techniques are not fitting for Data mining, which targets finding non-unimportant Data from huge genuine Data put away in Data stockrooms that require explicit apparatuses, for example, data set administration frameworks (DBMS).

At the point when Data are put away in a DBMS, there is a need to recover efficiently Data pertinent to Data mining measures dependent on inductive learning techniques. This is the motivation behind why the incorporation of inductive learning calculations is a pivotal point to construct proficient Data mining applications. On-Line Analytical Processing (OLAP) give intention to actualize answers for separating significant Data (for example, amassed Data esteems) from data sets.

In any case, it has been demonstrated that the social Data model doesn't fit the OLAP approach, and another model has risen: multidimensional databases [11]. Multidimensional Databases and OLAP give intention to execute extremely complex inquiries, chipping away at a lot of Data that are handled on an accumulated level and not as the individual degree of records. This sort of Database offers favorable execution circumstances, particularly for multidimensional total calculations, which are exceptionally fascinating on the off chance that we consider the programmed inductive learning, for example, choice tree development from Data.

9.2   The Inductive Learning Algorithm (ILA)

Although we have studied ID3 and AQ, we could go to ILA, another inductive calculation to generate several description rules for a collection of planning models. The factual information in an adaptive form, every focus finding a norm that includes numerous discrete class planning circumstances. Having discovered a law, ILA excludes the variants it occupies from the arrangement by marking them and attaches a version to its version collection. One's measurement keys for each class concept at the close of the day. For and class, guidelines are recommended to separate models in that class from models in all other classes. This produces arranged rules rather than an option tree. Computation gains can be defined as below.

- Values are in a suitable data analysis structural system; in specific, a representation of each category in the simplest way that enables it to be recognized from multiple categories.
- A standard set is requested in a more particular manner which empowers to zero in on a single standard at once. Choice trees are difficult to decipher, especially when the quantity of hubs is enormous.

Highlight space choice in ILA is stepwise forward. ILA additionally prunes any superfluous conditions from the standards.

ILA is very not at all like ID3 or AQ in numerous regards. The significant distinction is that ILA doesn't utilize a hypothetical data methodology and focuses on finding just applicable estimations of characteristics, while ID3 is worried about finding the property which is most important generally, although a few estimations of that quality might be unimportant.

Additionally, ID3 divides a specification set through subsystems without relation to the section type; ILA should differentiate each type.

ILA described in Section 9.3 starts arrangement of Data by separating the standard set in sub-tables for each exceptional class value. It then compares with estimates of an attribute for all sub-tables and defines their series of participants. ILA is designed to deal with discreet, indicative performance values seeking to overcome the problem of asset preference.

Mostly during selection tree or rule age, constantly valued attributes can be discreetly divided using cut-points. Most frequently, indeed, the reason for discretion is to boost the calculation's learning rate when consistent (numeric) characteristics are encountered.

9.3   Proposed Algorithms

- *Step 1:* Separation table containing m designs into n sub-tables. One panel for each imaginable class feature estimate. (* stages 2 over 8 are rehashed for individually sub-table *)
- *Step 2:* Initialize characteristic mix consider j = 1.
- *Step 3:* Also, for a feasible site table, split the feature list into indistinguishable blends, each combined with exceptional features.
- *Step 4:* For every blend of qualities, tally the quantity of events of trait esteems that show up under a similar mix of characteristics in plain lines of the sub-table feasible but yet not to appear under an identical set of other sub-tables. Name the key mixture with maximum series of events.
- *Step 5:* If max-mix = φ, increment j by one and go to Step 3.
- *Step 6:* Mark all lines of the sub-table viable, in which the estimations of max-mix show up as a group.
- *Step 7:* Connect a norm to R for whom the lower part includes consistency identities of peak combine with their values isolated by AND operator(s) and whose right side contains the selection feature confidence linked to the sub-table.
- *Step 8:* If certain lines are set apart while specified, then move to another sub-table and go to Phase 2. When there are still simple columns, go to Phase 4. If no sub-tables are available, exit with the regulations structures up until this.

9.4   Divide & Conquer Algorithm

Concise clarification of the idea of the choice tree and the notable partition and overcome calculations, for example, ID3, C4.5, and CART are introduced beneath.

9.4.1   Decision Tree

Choice trees, as suggested [12], sort instances by organizing them to arrange the core to a particular center of the tree. That's about labeling times. Any framework in the system refers to a practice of a particular case standard as each descending component from the hub talks to a possible feature interest. The figure below is a case of a choice tree formed based on the characteristic viewpoint. The distinctive perspective has three gloomy, sparkling, and downpour characteristics. Some attributes in Figure 9.1 have sub-trees like a downpour and radiant qualities. Model order in the unmistakable organization of possible categories is frequently called classification problems.

The early stages of the three models are categorization into awareness assemblies. The period following the design of the gathering the categorization period is the grading of these specific gatherings. Order trees and

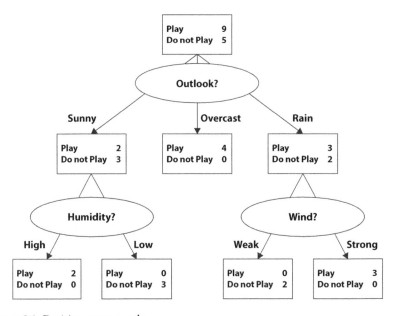

Figure 9.1 Decision tree example.

relapse trees are two tree model groups. A relapse braid, however, has a clear response component, has a statistical or qualitative utter and complete response factor. It is feasible to give a sense of decision trees as a recursive functional loop in which n observable units are placed in a collection. The way of putting the components in gatherings depends on a division law, and it's complex. The purpose of the separation rule is to improve the uniformity or calculate the response factor quality in its grouping as obtained. The division rule defines a system of separate experiences—division strategy in the process is subject to the illustrative variable requiring part and the division rule, making the division rule relevant. The very last plot of expectations is the primary effect of any option system.

9.5   Decision Tree Algorithms

Among the various selection tree measurements, J ID3 and C4.5. R. Quinlan, are the two commonly used. A further computation is Breiman's CART. A brief description of each of these is given below.

9.5.1   ID3 Algorithm

Ross Quinlan created recursive Dichotomiser 3 in 1986. It's sometimes termed approximation ID3. It's represented by the previous estimate. ID3 relies on Hunt's estimation. It's a simple tree learning estimate. The iterative inductive approach uses ID3 to segment images. The whole thinking in ID3 calculation creation is developed via the top-down inquiry of unique sets to look at the output from each hub in the tree [13, 14]. A calculation, Data benefit, may be the most important factor with the end goal of trait choice. Trait determination is an essential component of grouping sets. Data gathering encourages the portion of the investigations' importance. This needs to take into account reducing observations needed to define a learning collection. ID3's choice on the division character trait is related to data gain way of measuring. Claude Shannon concocted estimating data gain by entropy in 1948.

ID3's tendency to the trees developed. If formed, the tree should be smaller, and the place characteristics with lower entropies should be near the tree head. In building tree models, ID3 recognizes all land. It's the key loop ID3 acknowledges. Calculation ID3 update tree consecutively. Even then, the existence of ID3 disturbance doesn't even provide an accurate result. Therefore, ID3 wants to deliver comprehensive data preparation before its use in the tree structural model. These trees are usually used

[1] For each uncategorized trait, its entropy would be determined regarding the classified characteristic or end.

[2] The property with the most minimal entropy would be chosen.

[3] The Data would be partitioned into sets as per the property's estimation. For instance, if the trait 'Size' was picked, and the qualities for 'Size' were 'enormous,' 'medium' and 'little,' hence three sets would be made, partitioned by these values.

[4] A tree with branches that speak to the sets would be developed. For the above model, three branches would be made where the first branch would be 'huge,' the second branch would be 'medium,' and the third branch would be 'little'.

[5] Stage 1 would be rehashed for each branch, yet the as of now chosen property would be taken out, and the Data utilized was as it were the Data that exists in the sets.

[6] The cycle halted when there were no more ascribe to be thought of, or the Data in the set had a similar end; for the model, all Data had the 'Result' = yes.

Figure 9.2 Shows the ID3 algorithm.

for various purposes. Figure 9.2 shows the essential usage strategy of ID3 calculation as introduced.

ID3 computation problems exist. The resulting option tree for the configuration model is one problem. This is due to the systematic separation of entity split development instead of the whole tree's progress. The consequence of this method is selection trees that are overly accurate through the use of inconsistent or irrelevant circumstances. This outcome has consequences. This is the obstacle of categorizing cryptic models or models of scattered standard esteems. Tweaking is usually used to reduce the selection of trees. However, this approach does not work efficiently for inadequate knowledge collection requiring algorithms rather than straightforward classification [15].

Algorithm C4.5

Ross Quinlan, in 1993, modified an ID3 estimation. C4.5 ID3 redesign. C4.5 is like its predecessor, based on Hunt's measurement, which has a linear application. Tree pruning in C4.5 is post-creation.

If developed, it passes through the tree and helps to eliminate irrelevant branches by subordinating them with leaf centers [16]. Both nonstop and all-out traits are worthy in tree model structure in C4.5, not at all like in ID3. It utilizes categorization to handle consistent qualities. This categorization is finished by making a limit and isolating the characteristics dependent on their situation regarding this edge [17, 18]. Guarantee of the perfect separating feature, as in ID3, is per Data arrangement at-tree center. In C4.5, departing feature evaluation is the methodology of increasing the amount of polluting impact. C4.5 will begin to prepare data with insufficient attributes. It sees the insufficient attributes as "?" It also deals with different cost characteristics. C4.5 simply ignores the key qualities of benefit and entropy.

CART Algorithm
Order and relapse tree calculation, otherwise called CART, is an improvement by researcher. From its name, it can create arrangements and relapse model trees—truck parallel objects in definition trees arrangement. Like ID3 and C4.5, it focuses on Hunt's projections and can run sequentially.

Small analogy and continuous attributes are indeed sufficient in CART option tree construction. That's like C4.5 to work with lacking attributes in Results. The truck uses the Gini recording dividing test to assess the splitting product for tree construction of choice. It provides coupled parts parallel selection trees of its use of the double division of features. This seems to be special in ID3, and C4.5 split formation. Gini Index test, unlike ID3 and C4.5 estimates, does not use probabilistic suspicions. Finicky divisions are therefore replanted following expense intricacy. This increases tree accuracy.

9.5.2   Separate and Conquer Algorithm

Independent and -Conquer calculations, for example, AQ community, CN2, Rules Extractor-1 and RULES category of measurements whereby guidelines are prompted by a set of features.

RULES Implementation Family
The following is a succinct representation of all application community iterations.

RULES-1
Pham and Aksoy [19] developed RULES-1 (Rule Extraction System-1) [20]. RULES-1 execution tends to focus on entity rules incomparable class configurations—object has its attributes and characteristics, making them human. For example, if an object has Na as the number of attributes, then the norm can fall between one and Na standards. In a paper set, the whole of their qualities and benefits create a display. The shoe size is equivalent to all outnumbers, all being equivalent. Possibly there will be Na focus on traditional reporting.

In the corresponding framework, the system looks at each component to check whether that element as the situation can be appropriate for a norm. If any part in that circle applies to a solitary class, it may help structure a norm. Although it refers to more than one class, the primary indicators aspect is overlooked. When RULES-1 tests all parts, it re-evaluates all models against the up-and-comer rule to ensure all is set. Off chance that some models remain classified information, another cluster is formed with all unclassified models, and the following technique focus is initiated. If no more unclassified models, the research is finished. This continues before one or more cycles are correctly ordered Na. This period can be found below in Figure 9.3.

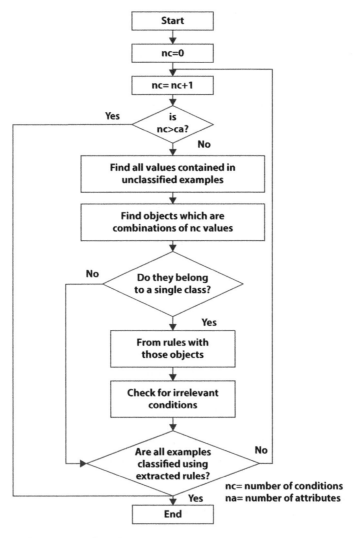

Figure 9.3 Shows RULES flow chart.

RULES-1's favorable conditions and limitations. A big advantageous position is that the problem of conditions is not superfluous due to the insignificant condition checking point. There's no remote management necessity provided that the Cpu doesn't have to track all models in the memory all the time. Nonetheless, the system has problems with disproportionately large amounts of rules chosen, as RULES-1 has no solution to sifting through sizes. Additionally, it has a long planning time linked to it when dealing with a problem with an enormous number of characteristics and attributes. A further flaw in RULES-1 that it cannot interact with computational attributes or faulty designs [21, 22].

RULES-2

After RUL1ES-1, Pham and Aksoy imagined RULES-2 in 1995. RULES-2 is similar to RULES-1 about how it defines rules; however, the key difference is that RULES-2 considers the approximation of one unclassified guide to establishing a norm for organizing that design as applied to the estimate of all unclassified models in each circle. Correspondingly, RULES-2 works better. It also gives the client some control over what series of regulations to extricate. A further favored role is the ability of RULES-2 to engage with unfinished designs and to deal with numerical and ostensible qualities when screening through non-significant systems and automatically away from redundant circumstances [23].

Stage 1 Define ranges for the characteristics, which have mathematical qualities and allot names to those reaches.

Stage 2 Set the base number of conditions (Ncmin) for each standard

Stage 3 Take an unclassified model

Stage 4 Nc=Ncmin−1

Stage 5 If Nc<Na then Nc=Nc+1

Stage 6 Take all qualities or names contained in the model

Stage 7 Form objects, which are blends of Nc esteems or then again marks taken from the qualities of names got in Step 6

Stage 8 If at any rate one of the items has a place with an interesting class at that point structure rules with those articles; ELSE go to Step 5

Stage 9 Select the standard, which arranges the most elevated number of models

Stage 10 Remove models arranged by the chose rule

Stage 11 If there are not any more unclassified models at that point, STOP; ELSE goes to Step 3.

(Note: Nc = number of conditions, Na = number of Traits).

Figure 9.4 RULES-3 calculation.

RULES-3

RULES-3 had been the effective development, building on the advantages of the preceding structures and implementing new highlights, for example, more simplified rule sets and methods to adjust how consistent the concepts outlined should be. RULES-3 clients can define the base set of responsibilities to create a norm. It is of interest—the criteria will be more precise, and not the same amount of activities based would be required to find the correct recommendation [24]. This cycle can be summed up as underneath in Figure 9.4 [25].

RULES3-Plus

In 1997 Pham and Dimov based upon RULES-3's capacity to shape rules in their production of RULES-3 PLUS calculation [26].

RULES-3 Plus is much more capable of looking at rules and regulations than RULES-3, applies the pillar search procedure rather than greedy exploration, and uses the so-called H metric to help select rules as to how appropriate and specific they are.

Nevertheless, RULES-3 Plus has its drawbacks—its efficiency is not an inevitable outcome, as it will usually train extensively to cover all info. Also, the H calculation is an incredibly disturbing measurement and does not achieve the most precise and specific results. Even though RULES-3 Plus discrete its enduring valued traits, its technique of discretion does not adhere to any fixed principles; it is self-assertive and does not attempt to discover any details in the Data, which hinders RULES-3 Plus' ability to learn new guidelines. The RULES-3 Plus standard framing scheme is illustrated in Figure 9.5 [27].

RULES-4

RULES-4 [28] offered the opportunity to progressively disassociate links in the RULES family by treating design in effect. From 1997, Pham and Dimov developed RULES-4 as the key gradual learning measurement in the RULES family. They developed it as a minor departure from RULES3 Plus, and it has some extra points of interest—particularly the ability to store models in short-term memory (STM) when they become accessible and ready. Another advantageous position of RULES-4 is the right of the customer to specify the scale of the STM supplying used to make specifications.

Once that database is complete, RULES-4 may draw new concepts on RULES-3 Plus' info. Pham and Dimov explain the incremental estimate 6.

STM consistently vacant, and it's initialized with a lot of analyzed models. LTM contained the recently removed guidelines or underlying principles characterized by the user. Figure 9.6 illustrates the RULE-4 incremental induction procedure.

Stage 1 Quantize traits that have mathematical qualities.

Stage 2 Select an unclassified model and structure cluster SETAV.

Stage 3 Initialize clusters PRSET and T_PRSET (PRSET and T_PRSET will comprise of mPREST articulations with invalid conditions and zero H measures) and set nco=0.

Stage 4 IF nco < na At that point nco= nco+ 1 and set m = 0; ELSE the model itself is taken when in doubt and go to
        Stage 7.

Stage 5 DO
                m=m+ 1;
                Structure of a variety of articulations (T_EXP). The components of this exhibit
                are mixes of articulation m in PRSET with conditions from SETAV that contrast
                from the conditions effectively remembered for the articulation m (the number
                of components in T_EXP is: an -NCO. Set k = 1;
        DO
                k=k+ l;
                Register the H proportion of articulation k in T_EXP;
                If its H measure is higher than the H proportion of any articulation in T_PRSET
                At that point supplant the articulation having the least H measure with
                articulation k;

                WHILE k < n_a–n_{co};
                        Dispose of the cluster T_EXP;
        WHILE m < mPREST

Stage 6 IF there are reliable articulations in T_PRSET At that point, pick when in doubt the articulation that has the most elevated H measure and disposes of the others;
                Imprint the models secured by this standard as ordered;
                Go to Step 7;
        ELSE duplicate T_PRSET into PRSET;
                Introduce T_PRSET and go to Step 4.

Stage 7 IF there are not any more unclassified models
                At that point, STOP;
                ELSE go to Step 2.

(Note: n_o = number of conditions, n_a = number of Attributes, T_EXP= an impermanent cluster of articulations, mPRSET= number of articulations put away in PRSET and it's given by the client, T_PRSET= a transitory cluster of incomplete principles of the equivalent measurement as PRSET)

Figure 9.5 Procedure of RULE-3 plus rule forming.

RULES-5

Pham developed RULES-5 from 2003, centered on RULES-3 Plus upsides. They tried to overcome some RULES-3 Plus shortcomings in their recently developed approximation titled RULES-5. It implements a policy to

Input: Short-Term Memory (STM), Long-Term Memory, scopes of qualities for mathematical characteristics, recurrence circulation of models among classes, one new model.
Output: STM, LTM, refreshed scopes of qualities for mathematical qualities, refreshed recurrence conveyance of models among classes.
Stage 1 Update the recurrence dispersion of models among classes.
Stage 2 Test, regardless of whether the mathematical qualities are inside their existing extents and if not update the reaches.
Step 3 Test whether there are decides in the LTM that characterizes or then again misclassify the new model and all the while updating their exactness quantifies (A measures) and H measures.
Stage 4 Prune the LTM by eliminating the principles for which the A measure is lower than a given prespecified level.
(edge).
Stage 5 IF the quantity of models in the STM is not exactly a prespecified limit THEN add the guide to the STM ELSE IF there are no guidelines in the LTM that group the new model THEN supplant a model from the STM that has a place with the class with the biggest number of presentations in the STM by the new model.
Stage 6 For every model in the STM that isn't secured by the LTM, structure another standard by applying the standard shaping methodology of Rules-3 Plus. Add the standard to the LTM. Rehash this progression until there are no models revealed by the LTM.

Figure 9.6 RULE-4 incremental induction procedure.

manage infinite attributes, so there is no quantification criterion [29]. The primary step in RULES-5 computation is to pick the state, and the technique for dealing with feature progresses. The developers explain this center measure as observes: RuleS-5 's rule abstraction loop considers only the conditions apart from the nearest model (CE) secured by the extricated Rule and has no position with the analytical class. Any data processing can integrate both income and discrete qualities. A test is used to record the distinction between any two types in the knowledge set, whether it integrates distinct qualities or continues with those.

The key benefit of understanding RULES-5 from past RULES calculations is its ability to generate very accurately fewer laws. This needs some effort and time [30].

RULES-6
RULES-6 originally developed by Pham and Afify in 2005, using RULES-3 Plus as a basis. RULES-6 is a fast method of discovering IF-THEN concepts from given models; it is also more straightforward in determining rules and how it manages emerging middle. Since Pham and Afify created RULES-6 to extend and enhance RULES-3 Plus by adding the ability to manage disturbance in the dataset, RULES-6 is both more reliable and

user-friendly and does not suffer similar log jams throughout the learning cycle as it is not hampered by needless subtleties. Making it significantly more efficient, RULES-6 uses more straightforward measures for qualifying rules and checking endless quality in measurements, which encouraged more improvement in calculation shows. Figure 9.7 represents the RULES-6 pseudo-code. The Induce One Rule technique completes a specific general search [31].

RULES3-EXT

Author [32] developed another inductive learning calculation called RULES3-EXT in 2010. Various real disservices exist in RULES-3 to resolve them effectively. The conceivable theory outcomes of RULES3-EXT are as follows: it is ideal for removing unnecessary models, enabling customers to make adjustments as needed in the form of a feature request, if any of the extricated rules cannot be sufficient certainty by an unmistakable model, the system can deal with slightly fire rules and can deal with less planned records to extricate a repository of two records. The key steps showing the RULES3-EXT deployment cycle are given below in Figure 9.8 [33].

RULES-7

The RULES class extended to Rules-7 [34] or RULe Extraction System Version 7, which improves its precedent RULES-6 by correcting a portion of its drawbacks. RULES7 uses a general specific data-gathering panel review to decide the best guideline. It selects a seed model progressively transferred by the Induce Rules method to the Induce One Rule method after calculating MS, which is the base number of cases to be protected by ParentRule. Two very different ParentRuleSet and ChildRuleSet are initialized to Empty.

```
Method Induce_Rules (TrainingSet, BeamWidth) RuleSet = Ø
While all the models in the training set are not secured
Do
Take a seed model s that has not yet been secured Rule = Induce_One_Rule (s, TrainingSet,
BeamWidth)
Imprint the models secured by Rule as secured.
RuleSet = RuleSet U {Rule}
End While
Return RuleSet
End
```

Figure 9.7 Pseudocode portrayal of RULES-6.

Stage 1 Define ranges for the traits, which have mathematical values, and appoint names to those extents.

Stage 2 Set the base number of conditions (Ncmin) for each standard.

Stage 3 Take an unclassified model.

Stage 4 Nc=Ncmin-1

Stage 5 If Nc<Na then Nc=Nc+1

Stage 6 Take all qualities or names contained in the model.

Stage 7 Form objects, which are blends of Nc esteems or names taken from the qualities or names acquired in Step 6.

Stage 8 If, at any rate, one of the items has a place with an extraordinary class at that point, structure rules with those items; ELSE go to Step 5.

Stage 9 Select the standard, which groups the most noteworthy number of models.

Stage 10 Remove models grouped by the chose rule.

Stage 11 If there are not any more unclassified models at that point, STOP; ELSE goes to Step 3.

(Note: Nc: number of conditions, Na: number of traits).

Figure 9.8 RULES3-EXT calculation.

The program called SETAV makes a precedent norm signifying all circumstances in the norm counterpart as non-existent. BestRule (BR) is the broadest concept generated by the SETAV methodology, and the ParentRuleSet is recognized for specialization. The loop constantly repeats until the ChildRuleSet is unclaimed, and there are no more values to replicate into ParentRuleSet. The RULES-7 estimation only recognizes certain criteria in the ParentRuleSet that contain more than MS. When the Rule is met, the standard adds a new "Legitimate" requirement by simply modifying the "exist" requirement banner from its original "no" to "yes" [35]. This form, called ChilRule (CR), will be tested for rule replication to assure ChildRuleSet is released from any replication. RULES-7 used an identifiable control system to correct a few flaws in RULES-6. Since the copy rule look at has just been conveyed, the calculation does not need to make more progress towards the conclusion to remove ChildRuleSet copy rules that help rescue massive time when compared to RULES-6 [36]. Figure 9.9 displays a RULES-7 process flow.

RULES-8

In 2012, Pham [3] developed another standard acceptance calculation called RULES-8 to interact with discrete and continuous factors without any pre-preparation need. It can also handle noisy data in data collection. RULES8 was suggested to fix its precursors' inconsistencies by selecting an up-and-comer opportunity rather than a seed guideline to define another level. It selects the user credit an opportunity to ensure the

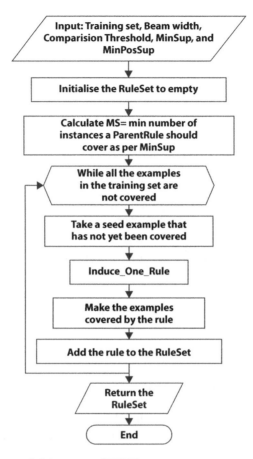

Figure 9.9 A disentangled depiction of RULES-7.

best recommendation is the created law. Choosing conditions depends on applying an explicit heuristic H test. The arrangement of parameters is rendered by continuously applying H-dependent conditions. This test surveys each recently formulated guideline's data content. There is also an enhanced disassociation approach applied to rules to provide more simplified utilizes the idea and decrease coverage between rules.

The sample feature value is called a requirement that is fitted to cover most models when applied to a norm. RULES-8 calculation, specific in comparison to its predecessors in the RULES family, initially selects a seed trait interest and then uses a specialization loop to locate an overall guideline by slowly adding new conditions. Figure 9.10 demonstrates RuLES-8 's normal forming techniques [37, 38].

Stage 1 In a given model set, the entropy is processed for each worth and each property.
Stage 2 Reformulated entropy esteems are figured. (The entropy estimation of each trait is duplicated with the number of the estimations of the trait).
Stage 3 The reformulated entropy esteems are put away in a rising way, and the model set is changed based on the arranging.
Stage 4 Odd number (n=1) mixes of the qualities in every model are chosen. Any estimation of which entropy rises to zero for n=1 might be chosen when in doubt. These values are changed over into rules. The grouped models are checked.
Stage 5 Go to stage 8.
Stage 6 Beginning from the main unclassified model, blends with n esteems are shaped by taking just one quality from the estimations of traits.
Stage 7 Each blend is applied to the entirety of the models in the arrangement of models. From the qualities made out of n blends, those coordinating with just one class are changed over into a standard. The grouped models are checked.
Stage 8 IF the entirety of the models are grouped THEN goes to stage 11.
Stage 9 Perform n=n+1 articulation.
Stage 10 IF n<N THEN go to stage 6.
Stage 11 IF there is more than one guideline speaking to the same model, the broadest one is chosen.
Stage 12 END.

(**Note:** N: number of Attributes, n: Number of Mixes).

Figure 9.10 REX-1 algorithm.

9.5.3   RULE EXTRACTOR-1

REX-1 (Rule Extractor-1) was rendered to obtain IF-THEN from either of the models. It is an innovative estimate for inductive learning and forgives the traps faced in RULES family measurements. Entropy confidence is used to give more motivation to major characteristics. REX-1 's rule enrolment period is as follows: REX-1 ascertains critical probability esteems and readjusted entropy esteems, at which point the assigns in hiking application are first set to deal with the lowest entropy esteem. Figure 9.11 displays the REX-1 formula below [39].

9.5.4   Inductive Learning Applications

Inductive learning calculations are space free and can be utilized in any errand, including characterization or example acknowledgment. Some of them are summed up below [40].

9.5.4.1   Education

Analysis of Data mining for use in learning is on the rise. This new software area, Educational Data Mining (EDM). Developing methods to

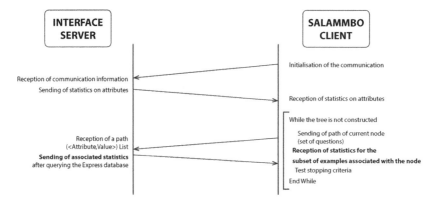

Figure 9.11 Construction procedure of fuzzy decision tree.

identify and focus data from instructive environments is EDM's fundamental concern. EDM may use Choice Trees, Neural Networks, Naïve Bayes, K-Nearest Neighbors, and various strategies. Through using this technique, different types of data are revealed, such as characterizations, association rules, and sorting. Recovered data can be used to establish different standards. For example, it appears to be used to forecast understudy enrolment in a particular course, expose anomalous qualities in the slips of the understudy performance, and decide the most suitable course for the understudies based on their past qualities and abilities. They may also help guide the learners on additional courses to benefit their show.

There are several choice tree creation measurements that are commonly used in all AI viewpoints practices, particularly in EDM. Occurrences commonly used in EDM are ID3, C4.5, Ride, CHAID, QUEST, GUIDE, CRUISE, CTREE, and ASSISTANT. J. Ross Quinlan's ID3 and substitute, C4.5, are among the most commonly used AI tree calculations C4.5 and ID3 are similar in their behavior, but C4.5 has better methods as compared to ID3.ID3 calculation bases, deciding the best data gain, and entropy concept. C4.5 manages unreliable data. This comes at the cost of a high classification blunder rate. The forklift is another notable calculation splitting the data into two subsets adaptively. This makes the information more precise in one sub-set than in the other sub-set. The wagon will restart until a stopping state or until the uniformity norm is attained.

9.5.4.2 *Making Credit Decisions*

Advance organizations regularly use polls to gather data about credit candidates to decide their credit qualifications. This cycle used to be manual yet has been computerized somewhat. For instance, American Express UK utilized a measurable choice system dependent on a separate investigation to dismiss candidates under a particular edge while tolerating those surpassing another. The staying fell into a "fringe" district and was changed to credit officials for additional consideration. Notwithstanding, advance officials were exact in anticipating expected default by marginal candidates close to half of the time.

These discoveries propelled American Express UK to attempt strategies, for example, AI, to improve dynamic measures. Michie and his partners utilized an enlistment strategy to create a choice tree that made exact expectations of about 70% of the marginal candidates. It doesn't just improve the precision however it causes the organization to give clarifications to the candidates.

9.5.5   Multidimensional Databases and OLAP

The social model of Data gives proficient instruments to store and manage the huge measure of Data at an individual level. The OLAP wording has been proposed for the sort of advances giving intends to gather, store, and manage multidimensional Data, with the end goal of conveying investigation measures. In the OLAP system, Data are put away in Data hypercubes (basically called solid shapes). A block is a lot of Data composed as a multidimensional cluster of qualities speaking to measures more than a few measurements. Pecking orders might be de ned on measurements to compose Data on more than one degree of collection.

A 3D shape B is assigned by methods form measurements, each measurement related with a space Di of qualities, and by a lot of components $S_B(d_1; :::; d_m)$(with $d_i \in D_i$; i= 1; :::; m) having a place with a set V of qualities. Mathematical activities have been characterized on hyper shapes to picture and examine them: move up, drill down, cut, dice, pivot, switch, part home, push furthermore, more traditional activities, for example, join, association, and so forth.

The union is utilized to accelerate inquiries. It comprises precomputing all or part of the shape with a conglomeration work. A portion of the most costly calculations are made before the question, and their outcome is put away in the Database to be utilized when required.

9.5.6   Fuzzy Choice Trees

Choice trees are notable apparatuses to speak to Data, and a few inductive learning techniques exist to develop a choice tree from a preparation set of Data. The utilization of the Fuzzy set hypothesis upgrades the under-standability of choice trees while thinking about mathematical qualities. Besides, it empowers to consider uncertain qualities. Choice trees can be summed up into Fuzzy choice trees while thinking about Fuzzy qualities as marks of edges of the tree. Along these lines, traditional strategies have been adjusted to deal with Fuzzy qualities either during their development or while characterizing new cases.

Let $A = \{A1; ::::; A_N\}$ be a lot of qualities and let $C = \{c1; ::::; c_K\}$ be a lot of classes. A and C empower the development of models: every model e_i is formed by a portrayal (an N-tuple of trait esteem sets $(A_j; v_{ol})$) related to a specific class c_k from C.

Given a preparation set $E = \{e_1; ::::; e_n\}$ of models, a (Fuzzy) choice tree is developed from the root to the leaves by progressive parceling of the preparation set into subsets. The development cycle can be part of three basics steps. An ascribe is chosen on account of a proportion of segregation H (stage 1) that arranges the credits as indicated by their exactness concerning the class. The parceling is finished by methods for a parting procedure P (stage 2). A halting rule T empowers us to quit parting a set and to develop a leaf in the tree (stage 3). To assemble Fuzzy choice trees, the usually utilized H measure is the star-entropy measure characterized as:

$$H^*(C|A_j) = -\sum_{l=1}^{L} P^*(v_{jl}) \sum_{k=1}^{K} P^*(c_k|v_{jl}) \log(P^*(c_k|v_{jl}))$$

where $v_{j1},\ldots\ldots, v_{jL}$ are values from E for characteristic A_j. This measure is acquired from the Shannon proportion of entropy by presenting Zadeh's likelihood measure P^* of Fuzzy occasions.

The calculation to develop Fuzzy choice trees is actualized in the Salammb framework. The yield of the framework is a Fuzzy choice tree that can be considered as a lot of found grouping rules.

9.5.7 Fuzzy Choice Tree Development From a Multidimensional Database

The multidimensional data set administration framework may either send just essential data on Data, or figure complex Fuzzy tasks and accumulations, or any of the middle arrangements.

In the primary case, the coordination of other inductive learning applications will be simpler. They in reality, all require at most reduced level straightforward total calculation, for example, check (for example, frequentist calculations). So the traded essential measurements we propose will even now be required. The various more unpredictable calculations will stay outside of the multidimensional Database administration framework, which will in this way be conventional. Then again, the subsequent arrangement upgrades the totals' calculations (for example, calculation of complex capacities as, for example, entropy proportion of a set) since multidimensional Database administration frameworks are intended for this sort of task.

In our framework, an interface is executed that comprises in trading, for every hub of the tree, measurements on the Data related to the current hub. These Data may either be singleton esteems or spans, which empower us to develop Fuzzy choice trees. These insights are figured utilizing OLAP questions to extricate a sub-shape from the Database and bringing measurements on it with accumulation capacities. As nitty-gritty beforehand satisfy, they either concern fundamental rely on the cells in the extricated Data 3D shape or may require more mind-boggling analytics, for example, entropy calculation. These insights are then utilized by Salammb to pick the best credit to proceed in the development of the tree. At that point, stage 1 of the choice tree development measure is supplanted by the accompanying cycle:

Step 1: Salammb sends an inquiry indicating the current hub to create in the tree. This inquiry is made by a set out of inquiries on estimations of properties that make the way from the root to this hub.

Step 2: The interface program inquiries the Data 3D shape and returns for each trait esteem, for each class esteem, the relating measurements registered from occurrences of the data set that satisfy the Salammb's question.

Step 3: Salammb gets the measurements and picks the best traits. Contingent upon the arrangement traded measurements are either frequentist tally of occasions or separation proportion of each trait.

9.5.8   Execution and Results

This framework has been created through customer/worker engineering, including a multidimensional Database administration framework (Oracle Express) on SunOS, an Oracle social data set worker on a PC under Microsoft Windows NT, a C++ interface on Windows NT, and Salammb running on a second SunOS station (Figure 9.12).

This proposed framework was assessed on Data from a Data distribution center of the French Educational Department, containing singular

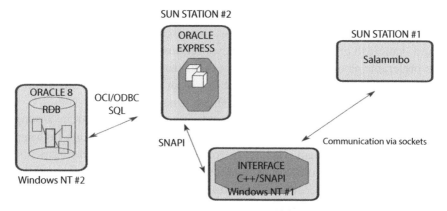

Figure 9.12 Offered multidimensional databases architecture from fuzzy data mining technique.

outcomes in secondary school declaration through two years (around 1,000,000 records). Examples of found guidelines are:

R1: If the secondary school is open, and the endorsement class is financial aspects, at that point, the extent of up-and-comers that prevail with notice (rather great, great, or awesome) is little.

R2: If the secondary school is private, and the scholastic year is 1996, and the strength of the understudy is unknown dialect 2, and the certificate is \STI", at that point the extent of applicants that prevail with notice (rather great, great, or awesome) is enormous.

9.6   Conclusion and Future Work

In this paper, another methodology is introduced to fabricate Fuzzy choice trees from a Data distribution center utilizing the OLAP innovation. This methodology prompts the meaning of a customer/worker engineering that relates the Salammb programming, a Fuzzy choice tree development framework, with Oracle Express, a multidimensional DBMS.

Designers also focused on how inductive learning encourages the system to interpret validity and reliability and instances in past data or data planning and emphasize necessary to characterize. This paper presented a description of inductive learning concepts as brief depictions of current calculations. Numerous characterization calculations were discussed in writing but, due to ease of usage, the options tree is the most widely used instrument, just as simple as other order calculations. Option tree calculations for ID3, C4.5, and CART were explained individually. Experts attempted to boost coverage estimates to overcome the effects of distance and -vanquish projects. Induce regulates genuinely from the database itself is preferable as opposed to collecting them from an option tree. The calculation of the RULES group is used to trigger several order rules from a range of styles for objects with one defined class.

Results are promising and urge us to start further research, among which the tests with different Databases, further examinations between the various arrangements we have introduced here to trade measurements, the incorporation of other learning techniques, the execution of an all the more well-disposed UI, and the treatment of Fuzzy Data (loose and additionally unsure) in the hypercubes.

References

1. Elgibreen, H.A. and Aksoy, M.S., RULES-TL : A Simple and Improved Rules. *J. Theor. Appl. Inf. Technol.*, 47, 1, 28–40, 2013.
2. Mohamed, A.H. and Bin Jahabar, M.H.S., Implementation and Comparison of Inductive Learning Algorithms on Timetabling. *Int. J. Inf. Technol.*, 12, 7, 97–113, 2006.
3. Trnka, A., Classification and Regression Trees as a Part of Data Mining in Six Sigma Methodology. *Proc. World Congr. Eng. Comput. Sci.*, vol. I, 2010.
4. Tolun, M.R. and Abu-Sound, S.M., *An Inductive Learning Algorithm for Production Rule Discovery*, pp. 1–19, Department of Computer Engineering Middle East Technical University, Ankara, Turkey, 2007.
5. Deogun, J.S., Raghavan, V.V., Sarkar, A., Sever, H., Data Mining : Research Trends, Challenges, and Applications, in: *Roughs Sets and Data Mining: Analysis of Imprecise Data*, pp. 9–45, Kluwer Academic Publishers, USA, 1997.
6. Khan, R. and Raja, R., Introducing L1—Sparse Representation Classification for facial expression. *Imp. J. Interdiscip. Res. (IJIR)*, 2, 4, 115–122, 2016.
7. Witten, I.H. and Frank, E., *Data Mining: Practical Machine Learning Tools and Techniques*, 2nd edition, Morgan Kaufmann, Burlington, Massachusetts, 2005.
8. Bahety, A., *Extension and Evaluation of ID3—Decision Tree Algorithm*, pp. 1–8, University of Maryland, College Park, 2009.
9. Stahl, F., Bramer, M., Adda, M., PMCRI : A Parallel Modular Classification Rule Induction Framework, in: *Machine Learning and Data Mining in Pattern Recognition*, pp. 148–162, Springer, Berlin, Heidelberg, 2009.
10. Kurgan, L.A., Cios, K.J., Dick, S., Highly scalable and robust rule learner: Performance evaluation and comparison. *IEEE Trans. Syst. Man Cybern. B. Cybern.*, 36, 1, 32–53, Feb. 2006.

11. Codd, E.F., Codd, S.B., Salley, C.T., *Providing OLAP (On-Line Analytical Processing) to User-Analysts: An IT Mandate*, Hyperion Solutions Corp, Sunnyvale, CA, 1993.

12. Mitchell, T.M., Decision Tree Learning, in: *Machine Learning*, pp. 52–80, McGraw-Hill, Singapore, 1997.

13. Baradwaj, B.K. and Saurabh, P., Mining Educational Data to Analyze Students' Performance. *Int. J. Adv. Comput. Sci. Appl.*, 2, 6, 63–69, 2011.

14. Rathee, A. and Prakash Mathur, R., Survey on Decision Tree Classification algorithms for the Evaluation of Student Performance. *Int. J. Comput. Technol.*, 4, 2, 244–247, 2013.

15. Pathak, S., Raja, R., Sharma, V., Ambala, S., ICT Utilization and Improving Student Performance in Higher Education. *Int. J. Recent Technol. Eng. (IJRTE)*, 8, 2, 5120–5124, July 2019.

16. Verma, T., Raj, S., Khan, M.A., Modi, P., Literacy Rate Analysis. *Int. J. Sci. Eng. Res.*, 3, 7, 1–4, 2012.

17. Yadav, S.K. and Pal, S., Data Mining: A Prediction for Performance Improvement of Engineering Students using Classification. *World Comput. Sci. Inf. Technol. J.*, 2, 2, 51–56, 2012.

18. Wu, X., Kumar, V., Quinlan, J.R., Ghosh, J., Yang, Q., Motoda, H., McLachlan, G.J., Ng, A., Liu, B., Yu, P.S., Zhou, Z.-H., Steinbach, M., Hand, D.J., Steinberg, D., Top 10 algorithms in data mining. *Knowl. Inf. Syst., Springer*, 14, 1, 1–37, Dec. 2007.

19. Pham, D.T. and Aksoy, M.S., RULES: A simple rule extraction system. *Expert Syst. Appl.*, 8, 1, 59–65, Jan. 1995.

20. Aksoy, M.S., A Review of RULES Family of Algorithms. *Math. Comput. Appl.*, 13, 1, 51–60, 2008.

21. Pham, D.T. and Dimov, S.S., An Efficient Algorithm For Automatic Knowledge Acquisition. *Pattern Recognit.*, 30, 7, 1137–1143, 1997.

22. Pham, D.T. and Dimov, S.S., An algorithm for incremental inductive learning. *Proc. Inst. Mech. Eng. Part B J. Eng. Manuf.*, 211, 3, 239–249, Jan. 1997.

23. Pham, D.T., Bigot, S., Dimov, S.S., RULES-5: A rule induction algorithm for classification problems involving continuous attributes. *Proc. Inst. Mech. Eng. Part C J. Mech. Eng. Sci.*, 217, 12, 1273–1286, Jan. 2003.

24. Pham, D.T. and Afify, A.A., RULES-6: A simple rule induction algorithm for supporting decision making. *31st Annu. Conf. IEEE Ind. Electron. Soc. 2005. IECON 2005*, p. 6, 2005.

25. Mathkour, H.I., RULES3-EXT Improvements on RULES-3 Induction Algorithm. *Math. Comput. Appl.*, 15, 3, 318–324, 2010.

26. Shehzad, K., EDISC: A Class-Tailored Discretization Technique for Rule-Based Classification. *IEEE Trans. Knowl. Data Eng.*, 24, 8, 1435–1447, Aug. 2012.

27. Pham, D.T., *A Novel Rule Induction Algorithm with Improved Handling of Continuous Valued Attributes*, Cardiff University, UK, 2012.

28. Akgöbek, Ö., Aydin, Y.S., Öztemel, E., Aksoy, M.S., A new algorithm for automatic knowledge acquisition in inductive learning. *Knowledge-Based Syst.*, 19, 6, 388–395, Oct. 2006.

29. Aksoy, M.S., Almudimigh, A., Torkul, O., Cedimoglu, I.H., Applications of Inductive Learning to Automated Visual Inspection. *Int. J. Comput. Appl.*, 60, 14, 14–18, 2012.

30. Rajadhyax, N. and Shirwaikar, R., *Data Mining on Educational Domain*, pp. 1–6, ArXiv, India, 2010.

31. Alhammadi, D.A. and Aksoy, M.S., Data Mining in Education—An Experimental Study. *Int. J. Comput. Appl.*, 62, 15, 31–34, 2013.

32. Quinlan, R., *C4. 5 : Programs for Machine Learning*, vol. 240, pp. 235–240, Kluwer Academic Publishers, Kluwer Academic Publishers, Boston. Manufactured in The Netherlands, 1994.

33. Langley, P. and Simon, H.A., *Applications of Machine Learning and Rule Induction*, ACM Digital Library, Palo Alto, CA, 1995.

34. Pathak, S., Raja, R., Sharma, V., Ramya Laxmi, K., A Framework Of ICT Implementation On Higher Educational Institution With Data Mining Approach. *Eur. J. Eng. Res. Sci.*, 4, 5, 2019.

35. Pathak, S., Raja, R., Sharma, V., The Impact of ICT in Higher Education. *IJRECE*, 7, 1, 1650–1656, January–March, 2019.

36. Agrawal, G.A. and Sarawagi, S., Modeling Multidimensional Databases, in: *Proc. of the 13th Int. Conf. on Data Engineering*, Birmingham, U.K., 1997.

37. Bouchon-Meunier, B., Marsala, C., Ramdani, M., Learning from Imperfect Data, chap. 8, in: *Fuzzy Information Engineering: A Guided Tour of Applications*, D. Dubois, H. Prade, R.R. Yager (Eds.), pp. 139–148, John Wiley and Sons pub., Hoboken, New Jersey, USA, 1997.

38. Bouchon-Meunier, B. and Marsala, C., Learning Fuzzy Decision Rules, chap. 4, in: *Fuzzy Sets in Approximate Reasoning and Information Systems*, J. Bezdek, D. Dubois, H. Prade (Eds.), pp. 279–304, Kluwer Academic Pub., Handbooks on Fuzzy Sets Series, Dordrecht, Netherlands, New York, NY, Norwell, MA, London, UK, 1999.

39. Chen, M.S., Han, J., Yu, P.S., Data Mining: An Overview from a Database Perspective. *IEEE Trans. Knowl. Data Eng.*, 8, 6, 866–883, 1996.

40. Harinarayan, V., Rajaraman, A., Ullman, J., Implementing data cubes efficiently, in: *Proc. of the 1996 ACM SIGMOD Int. Conf. on Management of Data*, pp. 205–216, 1996.

41. Marsala, C., Bouchon-Meunier, B., Ramer, A., Hierarchical Model for Discrimination Measures, in: *Proceedings of the IFSA'99 World Congress*, Taipei, Taiwan, August 1999, pp. 339–343.

10

Data Mining for Cyber-Physical Systems

M. Varaprasad Rao[1]*, D. Anji Reddy[2], Anusha Ampavathi[3]
and Shaik Munawar[4]

[1]*Department of Computer Science and Engineering, CMR Technical Campus,
Kandlakoya, Hyderabad, India*
[2]*Department of Computer Science and Engineering, Vaageshwari College of
Engineering, Karimnagar, India*
[3]*Department of Computer Science and Engineering, JB Institute of Engineering and
Technology, Moinabad, Hyderabad, India*
[4]*Department of Computer Science and Engineering, Annamalai University,
Chidambaram, India*

Abstract

The Cyber-Physical System (CPS) combines corporeal gadgets (i.e. sensors) through digital (i.e., illuminating) apparatuses to create an elusive structure that returns wisely towards complexing variations in actual circumstances. The fundamental aspect of the CPS is the analysis and evaluation of data from woody, challenging, and volatile external structures that can only be gradually transformed into usable knowledge. AI evaluation, such as neighborhood surveys, is being used to derive valuable data and insights from data obtained by smart objects, focusing on which various applications of CPS can be used to make informed choices. Throughout this paper, through the use of size and shape-dependent information stream sorting measurements, based on the Numerous Specimen Flocking Model, is suggested for the evaluation of large-scale details produced from various activities, e.g., system observation, well-being tests, sensor organizations. In the proposed method, the estimated findings are available on request at any time so that they are particularly well equipped for actual observation purposes.

Keywords: Checking applications, cyber-physical frameworks, information streams mining, stream grouping, AI evaluation

Corresponding author: varaprasadrao.cse@cmrtc.ac.in

Rohit Raja, Kapil Kumar Nagwanshi, Sandeep Kumar and K. Ramya Laxmi (eds.) Data Mining and Machine Learning Applications, (235–280) © 2022 Scrivener Publishing LLC

10.1   Introduction

Cyber-physical system (CPS) is accepting many considerations as of late with models including keen urban communities, savvy homes with the organization of machines, natural checking and transportation frameworks, shrewd network, and so on. These frameworks are furnished with an enormous organization of sensors circulated across various parts, which prompts a gigantic measure of estimation information accessible to framework administrators. Since these numbers are constantly collected over time, this can be used as a significant data analysis mechanism. Particular data can be derived from this huge amount of information and used to make better local economies, to provide better government, to carry out pre-scient inquiries, to obtain similar data by making several different demands. Most of this is feasible as a result of AI and data mining, where occurrences can be discovered in the number of alternatives given every moment. Collection and evaluation of source information [1] require novel calculations that can create models of the information in an online manner, taking a gander at every information record just a single time and inside a restricted measure of time. Albeit standard information examination and information mining calculations zone valuable beginning stage, people should be changed regularly to function in stream environments. In this particular situation, various leveled sorting is undertaken to carry out a bunch inspection of enormous information, to provide continuous and confined storage use. Even though information examination mining experts have successfully resolved a wide range of issues of major concern to enormous information, the region is still new and has many open issues. The multilayered existence of the CPS [2] arising from the variability of relevant parts (e.g. actuators and sensors), the necessarily appropriate nature of such devices, the shortage of performance efficiency, the immense difficulty and variety of situations, render a complicated activity to analyze information and carry out activities. We designed the Rainbow stage to resolve some of these issues. Rainbow shrouds uncertainty by presenting a concept to the Virtual Object and addresses the related definition of CPS through the provision of a distributed multi-specialist system (MAS). This promotes the manipulation of a variety of empirical techniques [3], where increasingly complex behavior emerges from encounters with simpler topics, working purely based on neighborhood information and without the need for a regional participant. MAS in Spectrum can be used for the methods used for data collection, data mixing, layout identification, analysis, and management.

Cyber-physical Systems (CPS) can change how we live and work. Shrewd urban communities, keen force frameworks, savvy homes with the organization of apparatuses, robots helped to live, nature observing, and transportation frameworks are instances of complex frameworks and applications [4]. In a CPS, the physical world is incorporated with detecting, correspondence, and figuring segments. These four parts have complex communications. The intricacy of CPS has brought about model-based plans and advancement, assuming a focal function in building CPS [5–7]. Normally the detecting part of CPS is basic to the demonstrating and the executives of CPS since it gives genuine operational information. The objective of detecting is to give top-notch information great inclusion of all segments requiring little to no effort. In any case, these objectives may not generally be feasible. For example, we can utilize high loyalty sensors, circle indicators, and radars to distinguish the traffic on the street, however, these sensors are costly and thus, can't be utilized to cover an enormous metropolitan zone. Savvy gadgets with GPS (for example, cell phones or GPS on taxis) can give great inclusion; however, their information quality is low [8]. Customarily, the plan of the detecting segment of a CPS zeroed in on the best way to convey a predetermined number of complex, solid, and costly sensors to streamline the inclusion of a domain or physical wonder [9]. Notwithstanding propels in detecting and correspondence advances in the course of the last 10–15 years have upset the customary way. Sensors have decreased and less expensive, and with the development of remote systems administration, we would now be able to send an enormous number of them to gather huge measure of information effortlessly. The Mobile Millennium traffic data framework wires information from GPS-empowered telephones and GPS in taxis with information from advanced sensors, for example, radar and circle finders, to gauge traffic in the San Francisco metropolitan territory. Today, easy, pervasive detecting is pushing a change in outlook away from asset compelled detecting towards utilizing large information examination to separate data and significant insight from the huge measure of sensor information [10, 11]. In this paper contend that the accessibility of huge observing information on CPS makes difficulties for conventional CPS demonstrating by breaking a portion of the presumptions, yet also gives chances to rearrange the CPS model ID task, accomplish proactive support, and manufacture novel applications by consolidating CPS displaying with information-driven learning and mining strategies.

The whole paper suggests the use of such an entire network sorting estimation [12] for the validation of programs. FlockStream focuses on a multi-operator structure that utilizes a decentralized basis to create a self-organizing technique for collecting potential information. Knowledge emphasizes it linked to specialists and sent to a 2D room, operating at the same time to determine an algorithm technique based on a bio-enlivened model known as a speeding design. Users go to space for a specific duration, and when different specialists undergo a pre-specified perception, they may want to go to maflock, if they are comparative. Herds can join in shaping multitudes of comparable gatherings. FlockStream is especially able for those applications that must screen a tremendous measure of information produced ceaselessly as a succession of occasions and originating from various areas because it enables the creation of the concept of clusters to be followed by showing the creation of specialists in virtual space. This empowers the client to discern outwardly the changes in the environment of the community and gives him little information because, at the end of the day, decisions and choices are constantly made in the light of the changing circumstances. An even more key advantage of FlockStream would be that it allows the users to obtain an estimated performance, very rapidly, by shortening the number that experts can pass to virtual space. This function should only be used when processing time is limited, as in many CPS apps. In comparison, if included in combination with any form of transition discovery [13], it is conceivable to recognize, as a consequence and on an ongoing basis, when the actions of the channel are changing.

10.1.1   Models of Cyber-Physical System

A CPS comprises of a firmly coupled joining of computational components with physical cycles. The computational components depend on sensors to screen and control the physical condition and cycles. The figuring asset controls the physical cycles utilizing an assortment of control goals, where input circles sway calculations also. Before summing up ways to deal with CPS displaying, we need to characterize our utilization of the terms demonstrating and investigation with regards to CPS. We utilize the term displaying to allude to a conventional way to deal with structuring and designing CPS [14], while investigation means learning and digging approaches for separating information from checking information, and this information can prompt significant insight [15]. We accept that displaying will keep on staying a basic piece of CPS plan, improvement, and activities, for example, large information examination will supplement not supplement CPS models. This is because models offer a few focal points [16] are

(1) they can have formal properties, for example, determinism that we can demonstrate,

(2) they can be utilized to catch a framework's development,

(3) they empower examination and reproduction to assist us with recognizing configuration deserts, and sometimes,

they can be utilized to naturally integrate executions (for example, code age).

The scholarly world and industry have manufactured a variety of devices for CPS displaying, for example, MATLAB Simulink and the Ptolemy suite. Nonetheless, with progressions in detecting, interchanges, and distributed computing, the term CPS presently additionally incorporates huge, complex frameworks, for example, the Internet of Things, keen urban communities, the force lattice, transportation organizations, and so on. Displaying these frameworks is testing and frequently includes making disentangling suspicions to accomplish manageability. In the most pessimistic scenarios, it probably won't be possible to fabricate exact models in any event when nitty-gritty and adequate measure of checking information are accessible. Enormous information investigation can be helpful in such situations [17].

The examination issues of CPS are generally new. In any case, many related themes, for example, recognizing defective sensor signals or target following, have been concentrated widely in the previous decades. The people group of information the executives and information mining likewise propose a few techniques to discover exceptions or abnormalities for sensor network applications. According to the scheme, important studies can generally be categorized into classes: observable model-based methodologies, spatial, and world-wide methods focused on proximity and highlighting recovery procedures.

10.1.2   Statistical Model-Based Methodologies

An enormous classification of factual models has been proposed to recognize flawed sensor information. Deficient knowledge is defined as something that does not obey the interpretation of these models. Researchers used time-differentiating multivariate Gaussian models to respond to preordained queries [18]. The unit responds to the predestined structure of the area of research, treating the sensor network as a knowledge base. Elnahrawy and Nath used the Bayesian Classifier (BC) to clean up the information [19]. They displayed the sensor information as a typical standard appropriation and produced the earlier information on the commotion model from preparing information as Koushanfar built up across the approval technique for Online False Alarm Detection (OFAD) because of different deficiency models [20]. Somewhat, those techniques can assist clients with sifting bogus sensor information. In any case, the vast majority of them need to prepare datasets or earlier information to develop the models and tune the boundaries. Such data isn't accessible in numerous genuine situations.

Additionally, with such numerous measurable models, it is difficult for the client to figure out which one is the most suitable. As referenced in [21], the current models are not sufficient, and the measurable models can't be good for some mind-boggling cases in genuine applications.

10.1.3   Spatial-and-Transient Closeness-Based Methodologies

The spatial-and-fleeting similitude put-together techniques are based in respect to the suspicion that there are solid connections between the sensor information and their neighbors (spatial likeness), just as their narratives (worldly comparability). Krishnamachari and Iyengar have exploited the structural and transient relationship of fragmented different sensors [22]. Jeffery et al. tried to manipulate both temporal and spatial relationships to fix inaccurate reports [23]. Their techniques agree that all details within each spatial and transient granule are uniform. The shortcoming recognition systems consider any high-value edge worthwhile outdoing as damaged and suggested a non-parametric outlier detection (NPOD) model for sensor data [24]. This system diffusely detects irregularities by testing the nearest neighbors of each sensor. Information circulations are measured by component volume function, and multifaceted variations are identified by testing heterogeneous readings. The system generates clumps of sensor readings and distinguishes variations by measuring the variance of the sensor to its neighbors. There are also some limits on this techniques: (1) The spatial similitude theory may not be legitimate in all the cases, the relationship of sensors are affected by different variables, including the organization of sensors, the general condition, and the objective development; (2) the worldly closeness suspicion may come up short in a few cases. The sensor's dependability may lessen after some time, e.g., the sensors may be harmed in the brutal condition, or run out of intensity [25].

10.2   Feature Recovering Methodologies

Feature recovering methods recognize defective information by contrasting distinctive highlights. Such techniques first endeavor a few information highlights like natural sort, associating degree, and fleeting examples, and afterward build classifiers to recognize various kinds of flaws. As Ni built up some regular highlights, including framework highlights, condition highlights, and information features [26]. They consolidated various highlights to characterize and distinguish regularly watched deficiencies. Ni and Pottie conveyed sensors to distinguish the presence of arsenic in groundwater [27]. A Fault Remediation System (FRS) is produced for deciding flaws and recommending arrangements utilizing rule-put together strategies and static limits to the water pressure and other area explicit highlights. Authors proposed a Pattern Growth Graph (PGG) based technique to distinguish varieties and channel clamor over advancing clinical streams [28]. The element of wave-design is proposed to catch the significant data of clinical information advancement and speak to them minimalistically. The varieties are identified by a wave-design coordinating calculation, and significant information changes are recognized from the clamor. Author proposed a two-phase way to deal with discovering inconsistencies in convoluted datasets [29]. The calculation utilizes a proficient deterministic space segment to kill clear, ordinary occurrences and produces a little arrangement of inconsistency competitors, and afterward checks every up-and-comer with thickness based various models to decide the conclusive outcomes. The element-based methodologies generally have preferable exhibitions over different techniques, yet they are more space explicit. Such techniques require clients to give nitty gritty setting data and characterizing the defective records cautiously. Versatility and adaptiveness are the serious issues that forestall their application in a more extensive scope of CPS.

10.3   CPS vs. IT Systems

In our view, four key contrasts make enormous information demonstrating and examination for CPS not the same as comparative issues in the universally useful processing space. The initial two are: (1) The tight connection of figuring components with the physical world through input control circles, and (2) A thorough designing cycle for crucial CPS when contrasted with standard programming building practice for IT applications, where specialists can't generally depend on steady programming updates to fix prior issues. These straightforwardly lead to a formalized model-based structure worldview [30, 31] exemplified by an assortment of building devices, for example, *Simulink/Stateflow*, Ptolemy, and so on. Third, CPS frameworks show a lot of additionally working modes contrasted with IT frameworks. We can think about a web administration working in various modes depending on the traffic design, for example, day versus night, however frequently, there are few such modes. With hardly any working modes, we can join space information and "savage power" search to decide the state change focuses and learn separate models. In any case, this methodology won't scale to numerous discrete states that are difficult to recognize, just like the case for complex CPS [32]. Fourth, we likewise expect the job and translation of investigation to be diverse in CPS. Regularly, when working with IT frameworks information, we can accomplish great speculation with standard AI methods by expanding the state space. For example, rather than utilizing just the quantity of solicitation appearances, we can likewise utilize its first and second subordinates as highlights. This may assist us in recognizing distinctive operational modes. Be that as it may, with the change in perspective to a minimal effort, omnipresent detecting such methodologies become craftsmanship—what number of and which factors to dissect? What do different changes (for example, subordinates, logarithms, and so forth.) speak to? Specially appointed examination approaches are probably not going to affect the CPS region halfway because of the need and entrenched custom of thorough model-based structure and advancement. Because of these distinctions, we accept that huge information demonstrating and investigation for CPS justifies further autonomous examination.

10.4   Collections, Sources, and Generations of Big Data for CPS

The wide variety of applications of sensors, for the most part for micro-electromechanical frames (MEMS, for example, open layout sheets [33] and modern production device designs and sections, have led to sensors

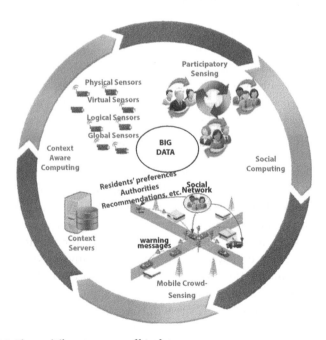

Figure 10.1 Shows different sources of big data.

becoming stronger for equipment worn from unyielding circumstances. Also, a large number of these sensors fuse actuators which are 1,000× quite impressive for their action than the one used with the Nintendo switch [34]. In this section, we discuss the wide variety of information sources and forms that have been identified by collecting them in the social analysis and setting up a careful registration procedure. The description is shown in Figure 10.1.

10.4.1 Establishing Conscious Computation and Information Systems

The ultimate sense of cognitive integration and device administration (CACN) was given in [35]. Creating attentive figuring may be known as a CACN operating in higher access management levels. The data collected by sensors for their unique service shall be regarded as original data, which have been legitimately gathered from the earth moving forward without any more handling. With crude information alone, it gets testing to break down and decipher them, and not to mention the enormous information created by the huge scope arrangement of sensors. With data and providing valid and efficiently understandable data, sensors need to participate in the careful registration process.; that is, sensors need to store prepared significant data, otherwise called "setting data", that is effectively reasonable [36, 37]. A reference to both the comparison among raw sensor data and establishing data will be insulin readings obtained by bio-clinical sensors on patient assemblies that are regarded as original data. At the stage where these measurements are processed with spoken to as the blood glucose level of the person, the data set is indicated. The presence of the perspective (QoC) metric will be used to assess relevance, reliability, quality, and existing structure data [38]. Establishing careful registration to protect, plan, delete, and think can be accomplished by applications themselves, by using libraries and toolboxes, or even by using a middleware stage [39]. The setting data can be additionally ordered into an essential setting and optional setting, which gives data on how the information was acquired. For instance, perusing RFID labels legitimately from various creation parts in mechanical plants is viewed as the essential setting, while at the same time getting similar data from the plant's information base is alluded to as the optional setting [40, 41].

10.5 Spatial Prediction

Collecting image data on objects in a good way is referred to as far away from detection (RS) [42]. RS is an important part of the analysis of the earth.

For context, space-borne and airborne detectors acquire multi-spatial and multi-transient RS information from a multinational environment to allow Earth monitoring and emission evaluation [43]. Numerous different remote sensing technologies comprise Google Earth, which provides images of the world's atmosphere, environmental degradation, traffic congestion, hydrology, and oceanography [44]. In [45], the creators proposed a major information diagnostic engineering for continuous RS information preparing utilizing earth observatory framework. The ongoing preparation incorporates filtration, load adjusting, and equal handling of the valuable RS information. The RS datasets are regularly geologically disseminated over a few server farms, prompting troubles in stacking, scheduling, and acquisition of experiences. In contrast, the computational complexity of RS information makes their ability and information access very confusing [46]. So that's why in [47] it suggested a wavelet shift to relate to RS large knowledge by crumbling variables into multi-scale detail coefficients that are measured using preference to improve the likelihood. In [48], the study compared the importance of RS data utilizing evidential extrapolation without using the former database information to deliver a reasonable validity advisor.

10.5.1   Global Optimization

Mostly with a touchy rise in smartphone use, portable information has experienced significant growth, conveying gigantic measures of data on client applications, network execution information, administration attributes, geographic data, endorser's profile, etc. [49]. This has prompted forming the idea of "enormous portable information", which, dissimilar to customary huge information in PC organizations, have their extraordinary attributes. One of these attributes is the capacity to segment versatile information in reality spaces, for example, in minutes, hours, days, area, etc. Moreover, because of the highlights of cell phones' utilization related activity, on the one side, could be almost assured of a grouping of followers in a given time and place; and, on the other hand, emotional connection supporters can demonstrate relative actions and connectivity designs, both of which can help to improve system performance [50]. Public authentication facilitates the convergence of these community activities and web-based contexts to help anticipate cultural characteristics that can execute activities, organize and support social remote organizations more efficiently than any other time [51, 52]. For example, because of high social connections and connections among supporters, an independent group association can be developed in which descriptions of motivation, interest, accessibility, and exchange can be used to create social network networks and disintegrate contact practices. However, one case of Client Social Deployment is the well-known Pokemon Go game, where Clients exchange constant references to the creation of Pokemon characters [53]. Another model where social registering can be useful is in crisis circumstances, for example, the spread of irresistible infections, where taking the suitable strategies by examining human communications and foreseeing the crisis' development can help secure the general well-being [54]. This paper [55] announced Cybermatics by way of a bigger visualization of IoT (exercise intensity increases-IoT) to solve scientific research problems in heterogeneous digital-physical social reasoning (CPST) hyperspace.

10.5.2   Big Data Analysis CPS

Cloud technology, beyond the data sorting, facilitates the fair management and implementation of undertakings and problems. Scheduling and planning of work activities in a multi-cloud condition improve monitoring and takes into consideration the great intellect of the management. In this area, we examine distributed computing, enormous information bunching, NoSQL, and mist registering for large information work processes preparing.

10.5.3   Analysis of Cloud Data

Mostly with an abundance of data in the exabyte order, it turns out to be almost impossible to manage data on a particular computer, irrespective of how amazing this is. Equal preparing of the information lumps on devoted workers, for example, the MapReduce apparatus proposed by Google offers preferences over regular handling strategies; anyway, it is as yet not exceptionally compelling to deal with a lot of information, primarily because of versatility, inertness, accessibility, and wasteful programming methods, including however not restricted to information base administration frameworks [56, 57]. One appealing answer for committed workers is the preparation on cloud focuses, which offers clients the capacity to lease processing and capacity assets in a pay-more only as costs arise way. Moreover, even though clients will be sharing typical equipment, the mutual assets seem selective to them through machine virtualization employing concealing the stage subtleties [58]. Nonetheless, this methodology can make issues in the pay-more only as costs arise condition because of untruthfulness, injustice, and failure of assets and the remaining task at hand exchanges [59]. The big distinction between parallelization approaches, along with

MapReduce and cloud services, would be that MapReduce uses map developers and modifiers to develop outcome variables and expected outcomes separately. Nevertheless, open mists offer clients of virtual machines (VMs) a highly flexible set of scores [60]. The capacity of Map is accountable for handling input key-esteem combines and creating middle key-esteem sets, while Reduce work is utilized to additionally pack the worth set into a littler set dependent on the halfway qualities with similar keys [61]. To amplify the inquiry pace of distantly found information trying to boost framework execution, the creators in [62] structured a unique asset designation calculation that considers the calculations of question streams over the hubs and the restricting number of assets accessible. Because of the volume and speed qualities of large information, streaming information handling and capacity may require distinctive pressure strategies to guarantee effectiveness and adaptability. Yang *et al.* proposed a novel low information precision misfortune pressure method for cloud information preparation and capacity. A comparability check was performed on parcelled information lumps, and pressure is led over the information pieces as opposed to the essential information units [63]. Another comparability registration pressure method was proposed in [64] utilizing weighted quick pressure separation. Combining cloud technology in IoT will take the planning of the monitoring of available data towards the next level and include pervasive monitoring of entities beyond the capability of autonomous individuals. At the point when joined with computerized reasoning, AI, and neuromorphic registering strategies, it is imagined that new applications will be created with robotized dynamics, which would alter the field of shrewd

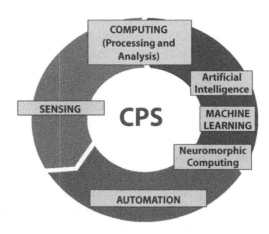

Figure 10.2 Show automated CPS cycle.

urban communities, modern plants, General statement, and so on (consider Figure 10.2). Cloud computing can support IoT applications with a minimized lack of mobility, resource utilization, and greater flexibility. The instances of such applications involve, but are not confined to, medical care, where patient information can be collected via a cloud-based system [65]. Cloud services are mists that are closer to customers to support the high implementation of idleness and to cause unreliable mists to be used [66]. Other cloud technology models represent traffic light system vehicles [67], genome research [68], earth's physical analysis [69], and some others.

10.5.4   Analysis of Multi-Cloud Data

In a variety of IoT logical applications, knowledge abundance and duration, measurement, planning, and examination are divided into the work process, consisting of various reporting products. Because of the information-escalated nature of IoT applications, the enormous scope of work processes should be circulated over various cloud communities [70]. To permit the help of numerous applications and to conquer the constraints of current systems that are devoted to a remarkable kind of uses, makers in [71] suggested a distributed implementation of the multi-cloud framework of the panel by using a domain-specific language (DSL) to increasingly represent technologies. In every event, the between cloud interchanges comprise a serious deal of the money-related expenses of handling work processes because of their enormous volume. In [72], to advance framework execution, Wu *et al.* proposed a spending plan that obliged work process planning in multi-cloud conditions. An effective on-demand cause condition for broadcasting massive information handling in multi-cloud conditions was suggested in [73] to provide a low cost of database load planning while at the same time magnifying the revenue of specialized network organizations. For building trust over various cloud focuses that work together on information stockpiling and preparing, in [74] proposed a trust-mindful observing design among clients and cloud focuses with various leveled criticism system to upgrade the power and dependability of the nature of administration of cloud suppliers, that mostly gives them ratings that rely on their confidence notoriety. It, therefore, helps users to choose domains from various cloud services that rely on reviews and past supporting documentation. In [75], Wang *et al.*'s Advanced Virtual Machinery (VM) in cloud computing server farms allows reducing the influence of records often used serious entities, such as the global survey. In all of these cloud environments, VMs are assigned to individual employees, granting users a high degree of management, but at the cost of higher productivity usage. The compromise between vitality utilization and the nature of administration is contemplated in the enhancement issue. The expense of information access and capacity restrictions of public cloud communities was considered in [76]. The creators utilized Lagrangian unwinding-based heuristics calculation to acquire the ideal server farms position that can decrease information access costs. The circulation of clients' undertakings on geologically appropriated cloud communities was tended to in [77], where the creators proposed major information the executives answer for amplify framework throughput with the end goal that reasonableness of restricted assets utilization by clients is ensured and the operational expense of specialist organizations is diminished. To identify client-focused multi-cloud properties, a multi-round combination two-fold closeout based method was proposed in [78] where the existing members and the server farms carried out bartering on separate VMs in many matches to ensure the highest level of safety.

10.6   Clustering of Big Data

Information bundling denotes the bundling of several features in separate sets of comparable papers and insights [79]. Information grouping turns out to be exceptionally helpful Comprehensive data applications where there is a substantial necessity to assess and evaluate the significant amount of data available. Analyzing the number of gatherings is becoming important as the arrangement promotes the movement of working frameworks, activities advancement [80]. Figure 10.3 shows two gatherings of bunching strategies investigated top to bottom in writing:

    i.   various leveled grouping, and
   ii.   centroid-based grouping.

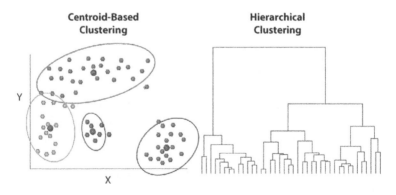

Figure 10.3 Show clustering of big data.

In different leveled clustering, close objects are more likely to be collected than far away items. Besides that, in the centroid-based bundling, the bundle of protests is mounted. The paper [81] looked at the ability to adapt the composition of the different conceptual and administrative groupings or the newly developed tensor-based multi-cluster system (TMCs). Among the most popular centroid-based groups are k means, analytical abilities, and narrow-intricacy usage. Notwithstanding, as the quantity of bunches builds, k-implies grouping experiences the vacant grouping issue and the expansion in the number of cycles for the union. This implies customary k-implies aren't appropriate for huge information applications. Various works have recommended upgraded adaptations of k-implies grouping for reasons for improving bunching quality, execution time, and precision. For example, in [82], the creators utilized an improved variant of the means bunching, where the underlying centroids of the group are not chosen arbitrarily however dependent on averaging the information focuses. This accomplishes higher exactness than ordinary k means. Another upgraded form of k-implies bunching was proposed in [83] to help dispose of the vacant grouping issue of customary k-implies. The selection process was based on several Fireworks, and algorithm-search estimates, with the descriptive focus was given as the centroids. In [84], the developers have used the centroid approximation algorithms to further boost the sorting performance by increasing the number of bunches. In [85], for example, the developers used proactive clustering in their suggested estimation, in which the number of participants was calculated as externally depending on the reorganized separating system. Learning tests were grouped to use a single link (SL) that divides large sorting tree centers into the main switching tree (MST). The estimate was shown to be unmatched in terms of bundling speed and efficiency relative to other labeling calculations as k-implies. A further radical bundling has been discussed throughout [86], where clients themselves characterize the number of groups dependent on various likeness estimates, for example, homogeneity and the overall populace of each bunch. This improves client fulfillment of the grouping calculation. A different leveled k-implies bundling method was presented in [87] to discover the smart approach of the centroids. The centroids have become reliant on the established work of the k-implies, which consists of a few levels, where the main level is the first dataset. Subsequent levels are compromised by smaller database sizes, which provide comparable examples as the first dataset. Fluffy bundling, another bundling technique, is like k-implies; in any case, an article may be connected to more than one single package, depending on its degree of involvement that is normally determined dependent on Euclidean separations between the item and the server farm [88]. Either broad data collection is the Class Highlights (CF) where the CF-tree incorporates a description of the data formats into the group. It utilizes a user limit to decide the quantity of the sized gatherings in the CF-tree. Consequently, this method can also have complexity and consistency problems, particularly with the amount of information that needs to be investigated and examined to build a graph. The design, which is focused on detailed assessment, allows the edge to be distinguishable for various miniature groups by equilibrium positions it by development and sustainability [89]. The grouping of diagrams aims to gather the information that is based on the layout of the organization and the relationships of hubs, where the similarities between hubs enable them to be correlated with the creation of a network. The system will establish a Tweet schematic for Twitter's social networking application where Tweets (hubs) with similarities (comparable URL count, comparable keyword quest, or corresponding username count) are linked to edges [90]. Throughout the long run, continuous mining helps to solve the rising challenges of network size and awareness growth by constantly updating groups without the need to duplicate them without any preparation. As far as the implementation of CPS is concerned [91], attempts have been made to incorporate structural CPS-based sensor groupings for reasons that reduce the vitality of the sensor organization. The sensor network is divided into small equivalent groups, each consisting of a lot of bunches, the sum of which is carefully chosen, focusing on the high-end segment of the delegate and its division to the core network, to accomplish resilience quality. In [92], the development teams sought to address the frustration of the CPS subnetworks by increasing the upper limit on the size of small groups to alleviate the frustration of the organizations, particularly once they are strongly connected. In [93], the authors proposed a safe grouping technique for CPS vehicles, where a trust metric is defined for each vehicle that is dependent on its transmission characteristics to generate secure bundles. Another safe grouping for CPS vehicles was proposed in [94], where the bundling problem is described as an alliance game thinking about the relative speed, location, and transmitting capability of vehicles. Moreover, motivating forces and punishment systems are recommended to keep egotistical hubs from corrupting the correspondence quality execution. A thickness-based stream information bunching for constant checking CPS applications was proposed in [95], where the creators utilized FlockStream calculation to amass comparative information streams. Every information point is related to an operator, and comparable specialists inside a perceptibility scope of one another in the virtual space, structure a group considering constant stream bunching.

10.7   NoSQL

Conventional social information base administration frameworks are not appropriate for heterogeneous large information preparing, as they comprise of severe information Predefined information technology and criteria model with a defined schematic [96]. NoSQL (Structured Query Language not only) loosens up a considerable lot of the social information bases' properties, for example, ACID conditional properties to take into consideration more noteworthy questioning adaptability, operational versatility and effortlessness, higher accessibility, and quicker read/compose activities of large unstructured information through repeating and parceling the information over a few hubs [97, 98]. NoSQL information bases can store information in three distinct structures: key-esteem stores, archive information bases, and section situated information bases [99]. In the archive information bases structure, the information is put away in a perplexing structure, for example, XML records. Section situated information bases store segments of information in information tables, permitting more prominent simplicity of adding and erasing segments contrasted with column arranged information bases. Also, there are two primary categories of NoSQL frameworks: Operating NoSQL structures. (The main difference between OLTP and DSSs though, is that it includes handling greater tables and, therefore, it implies the planning of difficult issues (verifying, entering, and totaling), while OLTP conducts reading/composing tasks for smaller parts in the knowledge base. For example, in [100], the developers used NoSQL for large-scale information work processes to enhance flexibility, synchronization primitives, and execution compared to the traditional MapReduce framework.

10.8   Cyber Security and Privacy Big Data

In the field of digital–physical systems, the close relationship between structural elements that collect and transmit a huge quantity of information puts safety hazards under the glare. With this enormous measure of knowledge that continues to flow through the enterprise, it is important to secure the system from cyber threats [101]. In this area, we give a diagram of the diverse security arrangements proposed for enormous information stockpiling, access, and investigation.

10.8.1   Protection of Big Computing and Storage

Cloud-based information storage provides the capacity for vindictive attacks, despite the possible security attacks by systems. This seriously undermines if cloud information storage is feasible, especially for administrative bodies and strategic companies. In [102] it suggested a strategy that would record parts into fragmented pieces and preserve them in a cloud-based transmitted workforce lacking clear access to client information from performance monitoring. In [103], the creators proposed that information ought to be scrambled and unscrambled before being sent to mists. The paper [104] focused on the potential applications for blending mode in iOS gadgets. In [105] it proposed a protected information move plot where clients scramble the information hinders before transferring to the cloud. Cloud information deduplication presents another test, particularly when information is shared among numerous clients. Even though synchronous replication can reserve 95% of the advantages offered for clinically tested and 68% for statistical data shows structures [106], it spends resources and consumes productivity and entangles the authority's knowledge. In [107], Yan *et al.* attempted to resolve virtualization concerns by introducing a proposal for clients to pass encoded information to the cloud with an information replication verification token that can then be used by specialised cloud organizations to verify if the content has also been deleted. A program to verify the presence of records has been placed in place to ensure the safe information of executives.

10.8.2   Big Data Analytics Protection

Supporting security and defense aspects of the large-scale information analysis has attracted the attention of established researchers, essentially for a range of factors. To start with, the information is more probable put away, handled, and broke down in a few cloud places prompting security issues because of the irregular areas of information. Second, large information examination comparably treats delicate information to other information without taking safety efforts, for example, encryption or visually impaired handling into thought [108]. Third, huge information calculations should be shielded from malignant assaults to protecting the trustworthiness of the separated outcomes. In the domain of CPS, a colossal measure of information make the reconnaissance of security-related data for oddity discovery a difficult undertaking for experts. In health care, for example, the security problems of extracting data from an immense availability of data and accurate analysis are of great significance. Delicate information recorded in information bases should be ensured through observing which applications and clients get gets to the information [109]. To ensure a solid secure large information examination, the accompanying undertakings can be performed [110]:

- Surveillance and checking of ongoing information streams,
- Implementation of cutting edge security controls, for example, extra confirmation and obstructing dubious exchanges,
- Anomaly identification in conduct, use, access, and organization traffic,
- Defending the framework against noxious assaults in realtime,
- Adoption of perception methods that give a full outline of organization issues and progress continuously.

The case of cellular organizations [111], vast information is seen as large pulling global integration of 1) an enormous number of control messages toensure unwavering consistency, protection, and communication skills; 2) major traffic information requiring traffic observation and analysis to change the network stack and streamline the system execution; 3) major area data given by GPS sensors; for example, transportation frameworks, open well-being, wrongdoing problem areas investigation, etc., 4) major radio waveforms information exuding from 5G huge MIMO frameworks to appraise clients' moving pace for motivations behind discovering relationship among communicated flags just as aid channel assessment, and 5) major heterogeneous information, for example, information rate, parcel drop, versatility, etc. that can be dissected to guarantee cybersecurity. The work [112] proposed a safe high-request bunching calculation through quick pursuit thickness tops on half and half cloud for the modern Internet of Things. AI provides a better response amongst these multiple networks to mechanize a substantial proportion of security-related undertakings, in general, the continuous production of movement from one place on a scale and wide-ranging design. Through the way toward preparing datasets, AI makes conceivable the location of future security peculiarities through distinguishing unordinary exercises in the respective authorities. To attain greater reliability, an incredible amount of repository planning is required, but this may be at the expense of each of those workloads and a conceptual approach. The method of preparing may be directed, either solo or moderately controlled, depending on whether the outcome of a particular data set is now recognized. Especially, the framework begins by characterizing comparable datasets into bunches to decide their inconsistency.

A human examiner would then be able to investigate and recognize any abnormal information. The result found by the examiner would then be able to be taken care of back to the preparation framework to make it more "directed" [112]. It will help the design process to adapt to emerging types of danger without user interaction so that improvements can be made rapidly while serious damage occurred. Various methodologies for peculiarity identification exist in writing, for example, discretizing the persistent space into various measurements, for example, in the reconnaissance framework in [113], for which the researcher has divided the observing region into a grid pattern, where the locations and speeds of moving objects falling in each cell are shown by a Poisson point scale. Another technique is the Gaussian probability test, where the knowledge is celebrated as odd when multiple standard deviations from the mean are identified. For instance, in [114], the creators utilized multivariate Gaussian investigation to distinguish Internet assaults and interruptions through dissecting the measurable properties of the IP traffic caught. In bunching techniques, for example, k-implies grouping, information focuses can be gathered into groups dependent on their separation to the focal point of the bunch. Again at this point, if there is an awareness point beyond the collecting community, these are assumed to be uncertainty. The designers the [115] utilized piece k-implies grouping with nearby neighborhood data to distinguish an adjustment in a picture by ideally figuring the portion loads of the picture highlights, for example, force and surface highlights. Concerning the counterfeit neural organization approach, one execution of such a model is the autoencoder, otherwise called replicator neural organization, which banners irregularities dependent on estimations of the distinction between the test information and the reproduced one. This implies if the blunder among test and remade information surpasses a predetermined limit, at that point, it is considered far away from a sound framework appropriation [116]. A case of such a methodology is given in [117], for which developers used the auto-encoder as high efficiency and low idleness model to discern the characteristics of the use of productivity and the operation of the higher meters. Security protecting information investigation and mining can be very testing assignments since breaking down scrambled information is a wasteful, exorbitant, and non-direct arrangement. Homomorphic encryption is one of the arrangements proposed to empower explanatory activities to be performed on figure messages utilizing different numerical tasks [118, 119]. For example, in [120], the creators utilized Efficient Privacy-protecting Outsourced estimation with Multiple keys (EPOM) homomorphic encryption to encode information before sending it to the cloud. The cloud, at that point, uses the ID3 estimation to conduct data mining on complicated information. The relevant control of a dynamic tree selection to decide the qualities of a lot of tests deliver the best expectations or data benefit. A further technique for optimizing mining for coded cloud information using homomorphic encryption has been proposed [121]. The Cloud Specialist Co-op (CSP) collects and stores encrypted information, while the worker, referred to as the Evaluator, teams up with the CSP to carry out the mining of scrambled information. A digger submits scrambled mining questions to the CSP, which thus defines the internal point between the vectors to determine the recurrence of the mining objects without the CSP and the Evaluator approaching the touch information. However, the encryption algorithm can be computationally intensive and illogical for large datasets [122]. One possible way to deal with safe, private information during the investigation processes is by using the h t-anonymization suggested in [123]. To start with, clients who access the information should be confirmed and approved dependent fair and square of shared outcomes' security. Now at this stage, a breakdown of encrypted and necessary markers is created to be used as an information channel for the data that can be accessed by the authorized client. K-anonymization is then applied to the known segments in the dataset to summarise or remove the significance of the yield dataset. The effect is a k-anonymized list on which the investigation and mining of the authorized open access can be carried out. Even though k-anonymization has all the hallmarks of being a compelling flexible way to deal with security safety of information investigations independently of the specific cycles, its probability for spatial frequencies and simulation efficiency is feasibly not further assessed in the vast information settings. Also, k-anonymization can be difficult if different datasets have the same sensitive characteristics [124]. One methodology that endeavors to tackle this issue are the cosine closeness calculation convention recommended in [125]. The proposed approach takes into consideration bigger datasets adaptability for both twofold and mathematical information types in a periodic proficient way. The thought is to permit information to be shared without uncovering the touchy data to unapproved clients. This should be possible using figuring the scalar item between various vectors of mathematical qualities, for example, computing the edge cosine among both. Getting a result more like one indicates that variables are just like each other. Then again, a significant number of the huge information applications have various leveled structures in nature, and in this manner, require progressive protection safeguarding arrangements. For example, in [126], various leveled cloud and network access control can be executed to reinforce security protection in savvy homes and keen meters. The home regulator, which ensures family close to home information, is associated with a cloud stage through a network organization, which gives protection saving answers for homes through information detachment, total, and combination. The cloud consolidates the entrance control plans for homes and networks in more mind-boggling and more grounded security assurance measures.

10.8.3   Big Data CPS Applications

We are actively presenting a portion of key CPS large-scale information applications in various areas, such as the use of productivity, city officials, and failed projects, along with an open security contextual investigation model. Figure 10.6 demonstrates identifiable CPS technologies and their enormous knowledge age. For instance, the shrewd transport infrastructure will yield tremendous details on the behavior of operators, traveler data, vehicles' areas, traffic lights the executives, mishaps' announcing, mechanized charge figurings, etc. Every last one of the CPS applications creates a lot of information that should be put away, prepared, and investigated to improve administrations and applications' exhibition.

10.9   Smart Grids

Smart lattices comprise a significant part of manageable vitality usage and are getting more famous, particularly with the advances in detecting and sign handling advances. Robotized shrewd choices dependent on the huge number of information and control focus assume a significant function in dealing with the vitality utilization designs, understanding clients' practices, decreasing the need to manufacture power plants, and tending to flexibly vacillations by utilizing inexhaustible assets [127]. The enormous number of implanted force generator sensors and their interchanges with various home sensors and apparatuses are required to create a lot of information shown in Figure 10.4. These serious detecting and control innovations utilized in keen frameworks are regularly restricted to a little district, for example, a city; anyway, they are imagined to be conveyed on a lot bigger scope, for example, the entire nation. This will present a few difficulties, among which data the board, handling, and investigation are the fundamental ones [128]. These enormous information assignments get much more confounded with the expanding number of exchanges that should be prepared for many clients. For example, one brilliant network utility is relied upon to deal with 2,000,000 clients with 22 GB of information every day [129]. That is the reason huge information apparatuses

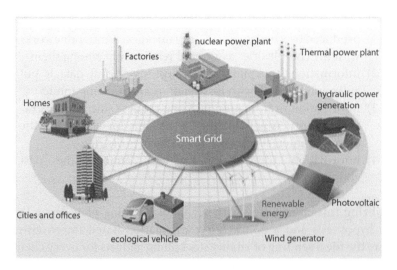

Figure 10.4 Shows CPS smart grid.

from distributed computing [130], mining and examination [131], execution enhancement [132], and others have been devoted for brilliant lattices applications. Additionally, for solid force networks, savvy matrices profoundly rely upon the digital framework. This represents a few difficulties, for example, uncovering the physical activities of savvy matrix frameworks to digital security assaults [133]. Besides, the assortment of clients' vitality utilization data, for example, the sorts of machines they use, the eating/resting designs, etc., can be useful in enhancing savvy matrices' exhibition; anyway, clients' protection can likewise be influenced. In [134], Yassine *et al.* proposed a hypothetical game system to adjust between clients' private data and the gainful employment of information. In [135], major information design for brilliant frameworks dependent on irregular grid hypothesis was proposed to lead a high dimensional investigation, distinguish information relationships, and oversee information and vitality streams among utilities. The proposed design permits enormous scope large information examination as well as can be utilized as an inconsistency identification apparatus to recognize security imperfections in keen lattices. For security dangers that happen in a brief timeframe, a security situational mindfulness procedure was proposed in [136], which utilizes fluffy bunch investigation dependent on game hypothesis and support figuring out how to improve security in keen frameworks. A major information processing design for keen frameworks was proposed in [137] with four fundamental components:

1) information asset where brilliant matrices information is produced by various gadgets, organizations, and frameworks with the complexities associated relationship among them
2) information stockpiling where just significant data is put away and handled with in-stream mode or clump mode
3) information examination utilizing request side administration or burden anticipating for reasons for classifying the complete interest reaction in a particular district
4) information transmission, which connects the past components

Utilizing this engineering with a vitality planning plan dependent on game hypothesis and a nonexclusive calculation-based improvement to acquire the ideal sending of vitality stockpiling gadgets for every client, the outcomes show a critical decrease in all-out expenses of customers over the long haul. In [138], the consolidated worldly encoding, postponed input organizations (DFNs), supply registering (RC) usage, and a multi-layer perceptron (MLP) were utilized to execute powerful assault identification for savvy lattice organizations.

10.10   Military Applications

Big information can likewise be misused to improve military encounters, administrations, and preparation. Constant verification of order and control messages in digital–physical foundations is of high significance for military administrations to guarantee security is shown in Figure 10.5. In [139], the creators built up a novel transmission confirmation conspire to utilize extraordinary computerized marks for quicker mark age and check and bundle misfortune resilience. This can be valuable to effectively and quickly secure military correspondences. In [140], the creators utilized the Markov choice cycle to propose a way to deal with distinguishing and lessen assaults' expense in military tasks to ensure significant data through acquiring assault arrangements. Military satellite correspondences require being tough to guarantee missions' prosperity. This can be accomplished utilizing a network put together security evaluation approach based on conventional danger examination, where an assault can be surveyed as far as both simplicities of assault and effect of assault [141]. Moderating the accompanying five center dangers permits the satellite correspondences to be liberated from frail weaknesses that can be handily misused by

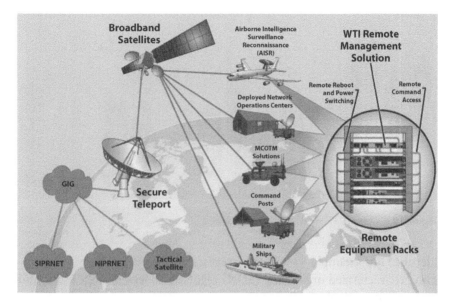

Figure 10.5 Shows CPS military application.

assailants: waveform, RF admittance to foe, unfamiliar presence, physical access, and traffic focus [142].

10.11   City Management

Big data will promote day-to-day activities by using amazing systems and administrations. With such the different sensors being sent cosmopolitan conditions, whether indoor or open-air, from developed mobile phones, smart cards, on-board vehicle detectors, etc., the city is confronted with a lot of data that should be misused to discern identifiable metropolitan distinct [143]. For example, traffic examples can be examined, and courses can be registered to permit individuals to arrive at their objections quicker is shown in Figure 10.6. In [144], the creators proposed to convey street sensors to acquire data on the general traffic, for example, speed and area of individual vehicles. This data is then handled utilizing chart calculations by exploiting enormous information instruments, for example, Giraph, Spark, and Hadoop. This gives continuous wise choices to keen productive transportation. Since remote sensor organizations (WSN) are the principal frameworks for keen urban communities to screen and accumulate data from nature, a few works have zeroed in on broadening the organization's

Figure 10.6 Shows CPS smart city application.

lifetime. For example [145], the creators proposed utilizing programming characterized organizing (SDN) regulator to lessen WSN traffic and improve choice making.

IoT-based general engineering for shrewd urban communities was introduced in , which comprises of four distinct layers:

1) advancements layer comprising of self-arranged and distantly controlled sensors and actuators,
2) middleware layer where information from various sensors are gathered to give setting data,
3) the board layer where diverse information logical apparatuses are utilized to separate data, test theory and reach inferences, and
4) administrations layer comprising of administrations gave by keen urban areas dependent on the past layers, for example, ecological observing, vitality effectiveness in structures, astute transportation frameworks, and so on.

Security frameworks, for instance, the transmission of tactile sensors, are vast knowledge applications from the other city to the board. A CP vision deep learning estimation for the identification of human gestures has been proposed. The platform is developed for the interpretation of twelve types of human exercises with extreme accuracy without the need for any prior knowledge, which makes it useful for security observation purposes. Community identification and appreciation is yet another wellbeing mechanism for a broad application of knowledge.

An impartial person should be derived successfully from sensor information. In, the developers suggested a system that would be able to identify the target area and update the movement data without too much stretch to enhance the discovery.

10.12   Clinical Applications

CPS wellbeing frameworks are predicted to shape the eventual fate of tele-medication in various regions, for example, cardiology, medical procedure, patients' wellbeing observing, which will altogether improve the medical care framework by giving opportune, proficient, and compelling clinical choices for a bunch of wellbeing applications, for example, diabetes the executives, pulse and heart cadence checking, old help, etc. With 774 million associated wellbeing related gadgets, a huge volume of information from little scope organizations, for example, e-wellbeing frameworks or versatile wellbeing frameworks, should be put away, prepared, and investigated to empower opportune mediation and better administration of patients' wellbeing. With e-wellbeing frameworks getting broadly conveyed in emergency clinics and wellbeing focuses, research has been centered around productively sending clinical body territory organizations (MBANs) to diminish obstruction on clinical groups from different gadgets. In MBANs, biomedical sensors are set in the region of the patient's body or even inside her to detect wellbeing related indispensable signs utilizing short-run remote advancements. The gathered information is then multi-bounced to far off stations, so the clinical staff can productively screen patients' physiological conditions and infection movement. For example, in, old patients' wellbeing following application was proposed, where a blended situating calculation takes into consideration 24-hour observing of patients' exercises and sends an alert to clinical staff through SMS, email or phone if there should be an occurrence of an irregular occasion or crisis. Notwithstanding, sending this wellbeing data in an ideal and vitality effective way is of the most extreme significance for e-wellbeing frameworks. In, Structured engineering accomplishes lower memory overhead, lower programming segment load time, and lower occasion proliferation time than other comparable propositions, which are, on the whole, basic prerequisites for vitality proficiency, unwavering quality, and adaptability of e-wellbeing frameworks. The paper proposed region delicate hashing to learn sensor designs for observing the well being states of scattered clients.

10.13   Calamity Events

Applications Network strength and survivability are the most extreme prerequisites for open security organizations. If there should arise an occurrence of a fiasco or crisis occasion, the individuals who are first on the scene are alluded to as specialists on call, and they incorporate law requirements, firemen, clinical faculty, and others (Figure 10.7). A portion of the significant open security prerequisites identifies with the need for specialists on call for trade data (voice and additionally information) in an opportune way. The large information can be utilized to help calamity occasions, for example, by examining huge information. The distant detecting large information can be examined utilizing a versatile half and half parallelism way to deal with decrease the examination execution time. The huge measure of information gathered from past quakes can be utilized to anticipate the future help accessibility regions, which can improve readiness and reaction to such occasion. A fiasco space explicit web index can be built utilizing ample information to comprehend and plan calamity assaults simpler and quicker for specialists.

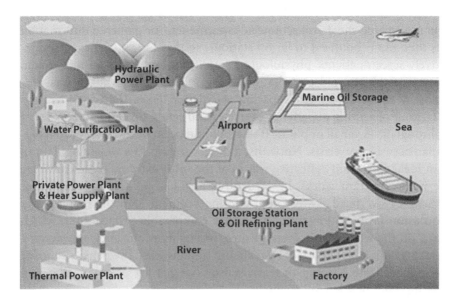

Figure 10.7 Shows CPS environmental application.

10.14   Data Streams Clustering by Sensors

Remote sensor networks are conveyed independent organizations comprised of miniature hubs with sensors, information preparing unit, and remote correspondence segment. Remote sensor networks give solid tasks in different application regions, including ecological checking, wellbeing checking, vehicle global positioning framework, military watch spear, and quake perception. Sensors networks encourage the way toward checking the physical condition and settle on a constant choice about occasions in nature. In such checking applications, programmed occasion identification is a fundamental assignment that targets distinguishing new physical wonders of specific worry to the clients. Specifically, the difference in bunching designs frequently demonstrates something significant is happening. For instance, bunching network occasion streams can assist us with understanding the typical examples, and assault alerts can be raised if the grouping design changes. In an inescapable figuring condition, sensors are frequently dispersed and, as a rule, installed in a few gadgets. Information, perhaps as streams, might be exuded from different sensors, and these streams must be collected, combined, put away, oversaw, and examined for different applications. Rather than endeavoring to stream an enormous measure of information into a focal handling office, we propose to incorporate the outer sources into an organization for portable specialist registering. This organization of specialist handling hubs is an equal PC for design location. Bunching streaming sensors is the assignment of grouping various wellsprings of information streams because of the information similitude. This cycle attempts to remove information about the closeness between information created by various sensors through time. The necessities as a rule introduced for bunching information streams are that the framework must have a smaller portrayal of groups, must deal with information quickly and gradually, and ought to recognize changes in the bunching structure. Calculations intend to discover gatherings of sensors that have comparable conduct through time. In the following segments, after a prologue to the rushing model, a methodology for bunching information streams because of a bio-motivated model is described.

10.15   The Flocking Model

The Flocking model is a learning algorithm of nature that mimics the behavior of a herd of components. In this design, every individual (likely referred to as a fowl) decides on creation preferences without consultation with others. Instead, it works as suggested by a few basic concepts, subject only to flock adjacent individuals and ecological snags. These simple guidelines establish a dynamic worldwide course of action. The basic speeding model was introduced by Craig where only he referred to every human as a "boid." This design consists of three basic control rules that the body needs to follow in each example over time: divergence (leading to stay away from crashing with neighbors); synchronization (leading towards the normal direction and controlling the speed of neighbors); harmony (leading towards the normal situation of neighbors). A Multiple Species Flocking (MSF) method has been built to replicate rushing behavior among a heterogeneous population of substances more precisely. MSF implements a part comparability decision that allows each body to segregate from its neighbors and to aggregate only those like itself. The extension of this pattern allows the herd to filter out heterogeneous multi-species populations into homogeneous segments containing only people of similar species. Different bodies try to escape different bodies that have divergent highlights by an awkward force which, in turn, correlates to the distinction between the bodies and the closeness between the bodies. The advantage of the operating estimation is the algorithm function of the person looking through the device. The algorithm's way of looking through all the instruments encourages the bodies to quickly form the group.

10.16   Calculation Depiction

Blockstream is an algorithm thickness-related data flow clustering analysis based on the Numerous Specimen Flocking Method. The measurement requires experts with distinctive simple features to replicate the action of the operation. Each multifaceted knowledge element is connected to a specialty. In our approach, despite the normal operation rules of the running model, we are mindful of the increase in the running model by talking about its type of user. Consultants can be of three types: simple (trying to represent any point in one unit time), p-representative, and o-representative. The description of the last two categories of users reflects the differentiated issues presented by their width-based bundling calculation DenStream for information streams of the micro-group. In the following method, we inspect efficiently the conceptual frameworks used in this procedure. A micro bundle is an extension of the concept of a center point defined by the grouping method DBS May to store a packed image of the knowledge focuses inspected up to now and to compare it with the thoughts of the possible core micro cluster (p-micro bundle) and anomaly micro bundle (o-micro bundle) of these authors. A center point is an object in which the general load of the focal points is, in any case, an integer μ. Bunching is a lot of center objects with group names. The objective of the micro-bundles depends on the idea of schematic specifications and weights. Subsequently allowing for an incorrect representation of the data guides assigned to the micro-bundle, and therefore for the collection of run-down information on the definition of the collection of knowledge. The above gives less importance to intelligence as a means of timing. The mass w of the micro bundle must be at the end of the target that w ≥ μ, for example, must be above the predefined edge μ, to be perceived as the middle. As controlled entirely, the quantity of knowledge in streaming applications is enormous or maybe unlimited, too large to even think of fitting into the primary memory of the Computer. In this manner, a component to store run-down of information seen so far is fundamental.

10.17   Initialization

To establish a lot of main operators, for instance, a lot of emphases are arbitrarily transmitted to the virtual environment and operates at the same time as a predefined number of accents. Basic specialists move as per the MSF classifier and, compared to birds operators who share comparable item vector highlights, will aggregate and become a herd, while different flying creatures will move away from the group. In our measure, we use the Euclidean separation to gauge the consistency between the two data points A and B and consider A and B to be analogous if their Euclidean distance is equal. $d(A,B) \leq \epsilon$. The Euclidean separation is picked because it is required in the calculation of the run-down measurements, just as in DenStream.

While emphasizing, the conduct (*speed*) of every specialist A with position P_a is affected by all the operators X with position P_x in its neighborhood. The operator's speed is figured by applying the nearby principles of Reynolds and the likeness rule. The comparability rule prompts versatile conduct to the calculation since the operators can leave the gathering they partake for another gathering containing specialists with the higher likeness. Along these lines, during this predefined number of cycles, the focuses join and leave the gatherings shaping various groups. Toward the finish of the cycles, for each made gathering, synopsis insights are registered, and the surge of information is disposed of. As an aftereffect of this underlying stage, we have two sorts of specialists: *p-representative and o-representative* operators.

10.18   Representative Maintenance and Clustering

At the point when another information stream greater part of operators is embedded into the virtual space, at a fixed stream speed, the upkeep of the *p*-and *o-representative* specialists and internet bunching are per-framed for a fixed number of cycles. Various cases can happen (see Figure 10.8).

- A p-representative c_p or an o-representative c_o-experience another representative operator. On the off chance that the separation between them is below ∈, at that point, they register the speed vector by applying the Reynolds' and comparability rule (step 5) and join to frame a swarm (i.e. a, a group) of comparable representative (stage 6).

- A fundamental specialist A meets either a *p-representative* c_p or an *o-representative* c_o in its permeability run. The similitude between An and the representative is figured and, if the new range of c_p (c_o individually) is beneath or equivalent to ∈, An is consumed by $c_p(c_o)$ (stage 9). Note that at this stage, FlockStream doesn't refresh the run-down insights because the accumulation of the essential specialist A to the micro bunch could be dropped if A, during its development on the virtual space, experiences another operator more like it.

- An essential specialist *A* meets another fundamental operator *B*. The similitude between the two specialists is determined, and if $d(A, B) \leq$ ∈, at that point, the speed vector is registered (stage 11), and *A* is gotten together with *B* to shape an *o-representative* (step12).

```
1. for i=1...MaxIterations
2. forevery specialist (all)
3. if (type specialist is (p-representative V o- representative))
4. then {
5.              computeVelocityVector(flockmates, MSF rules);
6.              move Representative And Form Swarm(v̄);}
7. else {
8. if (type Representative is (fundamental ∧ in neighborhood of a comparative multitude) )
9. then operator transitory ingested in the multitude;
10. else {
11.             process Velocity Vector (flockmates, MSF rules);
12.             move Representative And Form Swarm(v̄);}}
13. end forevery
14. end for
```

Figure 10.8 FlockStream Algorithm's pseudo-code.

At the finish of the most extreme number of cycles permitted, for each multitude, the outline measurements of the representative operators it contains are refreshed and, if the weight w of a *p-representative* decrease below $\beta\mu$, where β is a fixed exception ness edge, it is debased to turn into an o-representative. In actuality, if the weight *w* of an *o-representative* becomes above $\beta\mu$, another *p-representative* is made. It is worth taking note of that multitudes of operators speak to bunches; hence the grouping age on request by the client can be fulfilled whenever by essentially demonstrating all the multitudes processed up until now.

10.19   Results

In this section, we are studying the feasibility of FlockStream on the databases generated. The analysis was modified in Java, and all analysis methods

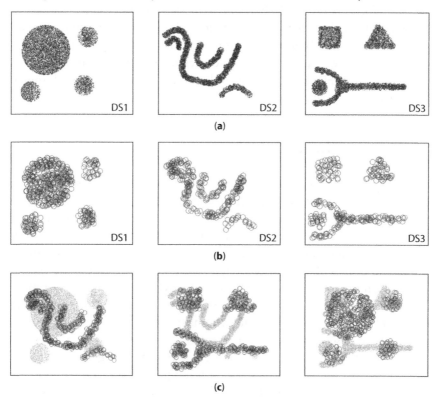

Figure 10.9 (a) Synthetic information sets. (b) Clustering was performed by FlockStream on the manufactured datasets. (c) Clustering performed by FlockStream on the developing information stream EDS.

were conducted on an Intel(R) Core(TM)2 6600 with 2 Gb of memory. The developed databases used, DS1, DS2, and DS3, are shown in Figure 10.9(a). Each of them comprises 10,000 points and is similar to those used to test DenStream. For a fair analysis, the progress of the information stream indicated by the EDS was rendered by obtaining a similar method [10]. Each dataset was haphazardly chosen ten times, resulting in the creation of an interconnection network of an absolute length of 100,000 with a block of 10,000 for each time unit. The limits used by FlockStream in the tests are comparable to those adopted which are starting focus/representatives Na = 1,000, stream velocity v = 1,000, rot factor λ = 0.25, supply = 16, μ = 10, exception limit β = 0.2, and MaxIterations = 1,000. We evaluated the FlockStream calculation for the non-advanced datasets DS1, DS2, and DS3 (2(a)) to verify the ability of the way to deal with the acceptable status of each category. The results are shown in Figure 10.9(b). In this figure, the circles represent the micro bundle defined by the measurement. We could see that FlockStream precisely restores the shape of the group. The results obtained by FlockStream on the creation of the EDS information stream are shown in Figure 10.9(c) on several occasions. In the figure, the emphasis shows the raw data, whereas the circles display the micro bunches. It can be seen that FlockStream efficiently captures the status of each bunch as information streams grow.

10.20   Conclusion

The rising CPS advances commonly advantage the innovative progressions in enormous information preparation and investigation. At the point when joined with man-made consciousness, AI, and neuromorphic processing strategies, CPS can accomplish new projects, management, and opportunities, all of which are supposed to be fully automated with little to no human involvement. This would help shift the concept of the "keen world" where the more intelligent water the executives have, the more clever medical treatment, the more perceptive infrastructure, more astute vitality, and more intelligent food will make an extreme move in our lives. In this paper, an extensive description of CPS presented an extensive array of perspectives, accumulating, entry, reservation, steering, handling, and investigation to help us understand and identify the problems faced by CPS, the proposed new solutions, and the key challenges are yet to be addressed.

With the expanding volume in the gathered huge information from digital–physical frameworks, we need an overall instrument to recognize spatial-fleeting examples in an organization of heterogeneous wellsprings of ongoing information. This paper proposes a new knowledge streaming approximation for concept exploration in emerging identify relevantly. The estimate depends on the perceptual thickness of the model developed together for the Multiple Species Flocking. The technique uses a nearby probabilistic multi-specialist search method that allows users to behave independently from each other and to address it exotically only with immediate neighbors. Decentralization and non-competition make the measurement adaptable to exceptionally enormous databases. Future work will zero in on procedures to naturally screen the advancement of the groups, exploiting from the versatile update of bunches previously actualized in the framework. Moreover, we are setting up the arrangement of the framework in the Rainbow stage to all the more likely evaluate the affectability and focal points of the framework regarding limited assets necessities.

References

1. Amini, A., Saboohi, H., Wah, T.Y., Herawan, T., A Fast Density-Based Clustering Algorithm for Real-Time Internet of Things Stream. *Sci. World J., Hindawi Publishing Corporation*, 5, 326, 2–11, 2014.
2. Stojmenovic, I., Machine-to-Machine Communications With In-Network Data Aggregation, Processing, and Actuation for Large-Scale Cyber-Physical Systems. *Internet Things J., IEEE*, 1, 2, 122–128, 2014.
3. Giordano, A., Spezzano, G., Vinci, A., Rainbow: An Intelligent Platform for Large-Scale Networked Cyber-Physical Systems. *UBICITEC2014*, pp. 70–85, 2014.
4. Eberhart, R.C., Shi, Y., Kennedy, J., *Swarm Intelligence*, The Morgan Kaufmann Series in Artificial Intelligence, USA, 2001.
5. Forestier, A., Pizzuti, C., Spezzano, G., A Single Pass Algorithm for Clustering Evolving Data Streams based on Swarm Intelligence. *Data Min. Knowl. Discovery J., Springer*, 26, 1, 1–26, 2013.
6. Vallim, R.M.M., Filho, J.A.A., de Carvalho, A.C.P.L.F., Gama, J., A Density-Based Clustering Approach for Behavior Change Detection in Data Streams. *Neural Networks (SBRN), 2012 Brazilian Symposium on*, pp. 37–42, 20–25 Oct. 2012.
7. Gama, J., Rodrigues, P.P., Lopes, L.M.B., Clustering Distributed Sensor Data Streams Using Local Processing and Reduced Communication. *Intell. Data Anal.*, 15, 1, 3–28, 2011.
8. Reynolds, C.W., Flocks, herds and schools: A distributed behavioral model. *SIGGRAPH '87: Proceedings of the 14th Annual Conference on Computer Graphics and Interactive Techniques*, ACM, pp. 25–34, 1987.

9. Cui, X. and Potok, T.E., A Distributed Agent Implementation of Multiple Species Flocking Model for Document Partitioning Clustering. *Cooperative Information Agents*, pp. 124–137, 2006.
10. Caom, F., Ester, M., Qian, W., Zhou, A., Density-based Clustering over Evolving Data Stream with noise. *Proceedings of the Sixth SIAM International Conference on Data Mining (SIAM 2006)*, pp. 326–337, 2006.
11. Ester, M., Kriegelm, H.P., Sander, J., Xu, X., A Density-Based Algorithm for Discovering Clusters in Large Spatial Databases with Noise. *Proceedings of the Second ACM SIGKDD International Conference on Knowledge Discovery and Data Mining (KDD'96)*, 1996.
12. Tang, L., Yu, X., Kim, S., Han, J., Hung, C., Peng, W., Trualarm: Trustworthiness analysis of sensor networks in cyber-physical systems, in: *ICDM*, 2010.
13. Tang, L., Gu, Q., Yu, X., Han, J., La Porta, T., Leung, A., Abdelzaher, T., Kaplan, L., Intrumine: Mining intruders in untrustworthy data of cyber-physical systems, in: *Proc. Of SIAM International Conference on Data Mining (SDM)*, 2012.
14. Deshpande, A., Guestrin, C., Madden, S., Hellerstein, J.M., Hong, W., Model-driven data acquisition in sensor networks, in: *VLDB*, 2004.
15. Elnahrawy, E. and Nath, B., Cleaning and querying noisy sensors, in: *WSNA*, 2003.
16. Koushanfar, F., Potkonjak, M., Sangiovanni-Vincentelli, A., On-line fault detection of sensor measurements, in: *IEEE Conference on Sensors*, 2003.
17. Subramaniam, S., Palpanas, T., Papadopoulos, D., Kalogeraki, V., Gunopulos, D., Online outlier detection in sensor data using non-parametric models, in: *VLDB*, 2006.
18. Xiao, X., Peng, W., Hung, C., Lee, W., Using senior ranks for in-network detection of faulty readings in wireless sensor networks, in: *DEWMA*, 2007.
19. Wu, J., Bisio, I., Gniady, C., Hossain, E., Valla, M., Li, H., Context-aware networking and communications: Part 1 [guest editorial]. *IEEE Commun. Mag.*, 52, 6, 14–15, June 2014.
20. Nugroho, A.P., Okayasu, T., Horimoto, M., Arita, D., Hoshi, T., Kurosaki, H., Yasuda, K.-i., Inoue, E., Hirai, Y., Mitsuoka, M., Development of a field environmental monitoring node with over the air update function. *Agric. Inf. Res.*, 25, 3, 86–95, 2016.
21. Tang, L., Cui, B., Li, H., Miao, G., Yang, D., Zhou, X., Effective variation management for pseudo periodical streams, in: *SIGMOD*, 2007.
22. Krishnamachari, B. and Iyengar, S., Distributed Bayesian algorithms for fault-tolerant event region detection in wireless sensor networks. *IEEE Trans. Comput.*, 53, 3, 241–250, 2004.
23. Jeffery, S.R., Alonso, G., Franklin, M.J., Hong, W., Widom, J., Declarative support for sensor data cleaning, in: *ICPC*, 2006.
24. Yu, X., Tang, L., Han, J., Filtering and refinement: A two-stage approach for efficient and effective anomaly detection, in: *ICDM*, 2009.

25. Lin, C., Peng, W., Tseng, Y., Efficient in-network moving object tracking in wireless sensor network. *IEEE Trans. Mob. Comput.*, 5, 8, 1044–1056, 2006.

26. Ni, K., Ramanathan, N., Chehade, M.N.H., Balzano, L., Nair, S., Zahedi, S., Kohler, E., Pottie, G.J., Hansen, M.H., Srivastava, M.B., Sensor network data fault types. *ACM Trans. Sens. Netw.*, 5, 360, 1–29, 2009.

27. Ni, K. and Pottie, G., Bayesian selection of non-faulty sensors, in: *IEEE International Symposium on Information Theory*, 2007.

28. Chorafas, D.N., *Business, Marketing, and Management Principles for IT and Engineering*, Auerbach Publications, Boca Raton, FL, USA, June 22, 2011.

29. Sanchez, L., Bauer, M., Lanza, J., Olsen, R., Girod-Genet, M., A generic context management framework for personal networking environments, in: *Proc. the 2006 Third Annual International Conference on Mobile and Ubiquitous Systems: Networking and Services*, IEEE Computer Society, Los Alamitos, CA, USA, pp. 1–8, 2006.

30. Bellavista, P., Corradi, A., Fanelli, M., Foschini, L., A survey of context data distribution for mobile ubiquitous systems. *ACM Comput. Surv.*, 44, 4, 24:1–24:45, Sep. 2012. [Online]. Available: http://doi.acm.org/10.1145/2333112.2333119.

31. Perera, C., Zaslavsky, A., Christen, P., Georgakopoulos, D., Context-aware computing for the internet of things: A survey. *IEEE Commun. Surv. Tutorials*, 16, 1, 414–454, First 2014.

32. Atzori, L., Iera, A., Morabito, G., The Internet of Things: A survey. *Comput. Netw.*, 54, 15, 2787–2805, Oct. 2010. [Online]. Available: http://dx.doi.org/10.1016/j.comnet.2010.05.010.

33. Swapna, and Raja, R., An Improved Network-Based Spam Detection Framework for Review In online Social Media. *Int. J. Sci. Res. Eng. Manage.* (IJSREM), 03, 09, 748–752, Sep 2019.

34. Zhang, L., Zhang, L., Du, B., Deep learning for remote sensing data: A technical tutorial on the state of the art. *IEEE Geosci. Remote Sens. Mag.*, 4, 2, 22–40, June 2016.

35. Rathore, M.M.U., Paul, A., Ahmad, A., Chen, B.W., Huang, B., Ji, W., Real-time big data analytical architecture for remote sensing application. *IEEE J. Sel. Top. Appl. Earth Obs. Remote Sens.*, 8, 10, 4610–4621, Oct 2015.

36. Wang, L., Zhong, H., Ranjan, R., Zomaya, A., Liu, P., Estimating the statistical characteristics of remote sensing big data in the wavelet transform domain. *IEEE Trans. Emerging Top. Comput.*, 2, 3, 324–337, Sept 2014.

37. Xie, H., Tong, X., Meng, W., Liang, D., Wang, Z., Shi, W., A multilevel stratified spatial sampling approach for the quality assessment of remote-sensing-derived products. *IEEE J. Sel. Top. Appl. Earth Obs. Remote Sens.*, 8, 10, 4699–4713, Oct 2015.

38. Alsheikh, M.A., Niyato, D., Lin, S., Tan, H.P., Han, Z., Mobile big data analytics using deep learning and apache-spark. *IEEE Network*, 30, 3, 22–29, May 2016.

39. Zhang, X., Yi, Z., Yan, Z., Min, G., Wang, W., Elmokashfi, A., Maharjan, S., Zhang, Y., Social computing for mobile big data. *Computer*, 49, 9, 86–90, Sept 2016.

40. Tang, M., Zhu, H., Mao, X., A lightweight social computing approach to emergency management policy selection. *IEEE Trans. Syst. Man Cybern.: Syst.*, 46, 8, 1075–1087, Aug 2016.

41. Parameswaran, M. and Whinston, A.B., Social computing: An overview. *Commun. Assoc. Inf. Syst.*, 19, 762–780, 2007, [Online]. Available: http://aisel.aisnet.org/cais/vol19/iss1/37/.

42. Ning, H., Liu, H., Ma, J., Yang, L.T., Huang, R., Cybermatics: Cyber physical-social thinking hyperspace based science and technology. *Future Gener. Comput. Syst.*, 56, 504–522, March 2016.

43. Kraska, T., Finding the needle in the big data systems haystack. *IEEE Internet Comput.*, 17, 1, 84–86, Jan 2013.

44. DeWitt, D.J. and Stonebraker, M., Mapreduce: A major step backward. Accessed on July 10, 2017. [Online]. Available: http://databasecolumn.vertica.com/database-innovation/mapreduce-a-major-step-backwards/.

45. Wang, D. and Liu, J., Optimizing big data processing performance in the public cloud: opportunities and approaches. *IEEE Network*, 29, 5, 31–35, September 2015.

46. Armbrust, M., Fox, A., Griffith, R., Joseph, A.D., Katz, R., Konwinski, A., Lee, G., Patterson, D., Rabkin, A., Stoica, I., Zaharia, M., A view of cloud computing. *Commun. ACM*, 53, 4, 50–58, Apr. 2010, [Online]. Available: http://doi.acm.org/10.1145/1721654.1721672.

47. Tang, S., Lee, B.S., He, B., Towards economic fairness for big data processing in pay-as-you-go cloud computing, in: *Proc. 2014 IEEE 6th International Conference on Cloud Computing Technology and Science (CloudCom)*, pp. 638–643, Dec 2014.

48. Blanas, S., Patel, J.M., Ercegovac, V., Rao, J., Shekita, E.J., Tian, Y., A comparison of join algorithms for log processing in MapReduce, in: *Proc. the 2010 ACM SIGMOD International Conference on Management of Data, ser. SIGMOD '10*, ACM, New York, NY, USA, pp. 975–986, 2010, [Online]. Available: http://doi.acm.org/10.1145/1807167.1807273.

49. Destounis, A., Paschos, G.S., Koutsopoulos, I., Streaming big data meets backpressure in distributed network computation, in: *Proc. IEEE INFOCOM 2016—The 35th IEEE International Conference on Computer Communications*, pp. 1–9, April 2016.

50. Yang, C. and Chen, J., A scalable data chunk similarity-based compression approach for efficient big sensing data processing on cloud. *IEEE Trans. Knowl. Data Eng.*, 29, 6, 1144–1157, 2016.

51. Lillo-Castellano, J.M., Mora-Jimenez, I., Santiago-Mozos, R., Chavarria-Asso, F., Cano-Gonzalez, A., Garcia-Alberola, A., Rojo-Alvarez, J.L., Symmetrical compression distance for arrhythmia discrimination in cloud-based big-data services. *IEEE J. Biomed. Health Inf.*, 19, 4, 1253–1263, July 2015.

52. Tawalbeh, L.A., Mehmood, R., Benkhlifa, E., Song, H., Mobile cloud computing model and big data analysis for healthcare applications. *IEEE Access*, 4, 6171–6180, 2016.

53. Whaiduzzaman, M., Gani, A., Naveed, A., Pfc: Performance enhancement framework for cloudlet in mobile cloud computing, in: *Proc. 2014 IEEE International Symposium on Robotics and Manufacturing Automation (ROMA)*, pp. 224–229, Dec 2014.

54. Zhang, D., Shou, Y., Xu, J., The modeling of big traffic data processing based on cloud computing, in: *Proc. 2016 12th World Congress on Intelligent Control and Automation (WCICA)*, pp. 2394–2399, June 2016.

55. Yeo, H. and Crawford, C.H., Big data: Cloud computing in genomics applications, in: *Big Data (Big Data), 2015 IEEE International Conference on*, pp. 2904–2906, Oct 2015.

56. Zinno, I., Mossucca, L., Elefante, S., Luca, C.D., Casola, V., Terzo, O., Casu, F., Lanari, R., Cloud computing for earth surface deformation analysis via spaceborne radar imaging: A case study. *IEEE Trans. Cloud Comput.*, 4, 1, 104–118, Jan 2016.

57. Wu, C.Q. and Cao, H., Optimizing the performance of big data workflows in multi-cloud environments under a budget constraint, in: *Proc. 2016 IEEE International Conference on Services Computing (SCC)*, pp. 138–145, June 2016.

58. Pham, L.M., Thana, A., Donsez, D., Zurczak, V., Gibello, P.Y., de Palma, N., An adaptable framework to deploy complex applications onto multi-cloud platforms, in: *Proc. 2015 IEEE International Conference on Computing Communication Technologies—Research, Innovation, and Vision for the Future (RIVF)*, pp. 169–174, Jan 2015.

59. Li, H., Dong, M., Ota, K., Guo, M., Pricing and repurchasing for big data processing in multi-clouds. *IEEE Trans. Emerging Top. Comput.*, 4, 2, 266–277, April 2016.

60. Li, X., Ma, H., Yao, W., Gui, X., Data-driven and feedback-enhanced trust computing pattern for large-scale multi-cloud collaborative services. *IEEE Trans. Serv. Comput.*, 11, 4109, 671–684, 2015.

61. Wang, S., Zhou, A., Hsu, C.H., Xiao, X., Yang, F., Provision of data-intensive services through energy- and QoS-aware virtual machine placement in national cloud data centers. *IEEE Trans. Emerging Top. Comput.*, 4, 2, 290–300, April 2016.

62. Zhang, J., Chen, J., Luo, J., Song, A., Efficient location-aware data placement for data-intensive applications in geo-distributed scientific data centers. *Tsinghua Sci. Technol.*, 21, 5, 471–481, Oct 2016.

63. Xia, Q., Xu, Z., Liang, W., Zomaya, A.Y., Collaboration- and fairness-aware big data management in distributed clouds. *IEEE Trans. Parallel Distrib. Syst.*, 27, 7, 1941–1953, July 2016.

64. Zhao, Y., Huang, Z., Liu, W., Peng, J., Zhang, Q., A combinatorial double auction-based resource allocation mechanism with multiple rounds for

geo-distributed data centers, in: *Proc. 2016 IEEE International Conference on Communications (ICC)*, pp. 1–6, May 2016.

65. Kumar, D., Bezdek, J.C., Palaniswami, M., Rajasegarar, S., Leckie, C., Havens, T.C., A hybrid approach to clustering in big data. *IEEE Trans. Cybern.*, 46, 10, 2372–2385, Oct 2016.

66. Reddy, C.K.K., Chandrudu, K.E.B., Anisha, P.R., Raju, G.V.S., High performance computing cluster system and its future aspects in processing big data, in: *Proc. 2015 International Conference on Computational Intelligence and Communication Networks (CICN)*, pp. 881–885, Dec 2015.

67. Zhao, Y., Yang, L.T., Zhang, R., A tensor-based multiple clustering approach with its applications in automation systems. *IEEE Trans. Ind. Inf.*, 14, 1, 283–291, 2018.

68. Shettar, R. and Purohit, B.V., A MapReduce framework to implement enhanced k-means algorithm, in: *Proc. 2015 International Conference on Applied and Theoretical Computing and Communication Technology (iCATccT)*, pp. 361–363, Oct 2015.

69. Chandrakar, R., Raja, R., Miri, R., Tandan, S.R., Ramya Laxmi, K., Detection and Identification of Animals in Wild Life Sanctuaries using Convolutional Neural Network. *Int. J. Recent Technol. Eng. (IJRTE)*, 8, 5, 181–185, January 2020 in Regular Issue on 30 January 2020.

70. Karimov, J., Ozbayoglu, M., Dogdu, E., k-Means performance improvements with centroid calculation heuristics both for serial and parallel environments, in: *Proc. 2015 IEEE International Congress on Big Data*, pp. 444–451, June 2015.

71. Data Visualization Tips, Accessed on December 17, 2016. [Online] Available: http://www.sthda.com/english/wiki/hierarchical-clustering-essentials-unsupervised-machine-learning.

72. Kabul, I.K., Understanding data-mining clustering methods, SAS Research & Development, India, 2016, May 26. Accessed on December 17, 2016. [Online]. Available: http://blogs.sas.com/content/subconsciousmusings/2016/05/26/data-mining-clustering/.

73. Zhao, Y., Chi, C.H., Ding, C., Wong, R., Zhao, W., Wang, C., Hierarchical clustering using homogeneity as a similarity measure for big data analytics, in: *Proc. 2015 IEEE International Conference on Services Computing (SCC)*, pp. 348–354, June 2015.

74. Xu, T., Chiang, H., Liu, G., Tan, C., Hierarchical K-means Method for Clustering Large-Scale Advanced Metering Infrastructure Data. *IEEE Trans. Power Deliv.*, 32, 2, 609–616, 2017.

75. AlShami, A., Guo, W., Pogrebna, G., Fuzzy partition technique for clustering big urban dataset, in: *Proc. 2016 SAI Computing Conference (SAI)*, pp. 212–216, July 2016.

76. Fu, J., Liu, Y., Zhang, Z., Xiong, F., Big data clustering based on summary statistics, in: *Proc. 2015 First International Conference on Computational Intelligence Theory, Systems and Applications (CCITSA)*, pp. 87–91, Dec 2015.

77. Dutta, S., Ghatak, S., Roy, M., Ghosh, S., Das, A.K., A graph-based clustering technique for tweet summarization, in: *Proc. 2015 4th International Conference on Reliability, Infocom Technologies, and Optimization (ICRITO) (Trends and Future Directions)*, pp. 1–6, Sept 2015.

78. Cao, J. and Li, H., Energy-efficient structuralized clustering for sensor-based cyber-physical systems, in: *Proc. 2009 Symposia and Workshops on Ubiquitous, Autonomic and Trusted Computing*, pp. 234–239, July 2009.

79. Huang, Z., Wang, C., Nayak, A., Stojmenovic, I., Small cluster in cyber-physical systems: Network topology, interdependence, and cascading failures. *IEEE Trans. Parallel Distrib. Syst.*, 26, 8, 2340–2351, Aug 2015.

80. Bali, R.S. and Kumar, N., Secure clustering for efficient data dissemination in vehicular cyber-physical systems. *Future Gener. Comput. Syst.*, 56, 476–492, 2016. [Online]. Available: http://www.sciencedirect.com/science/article/pii/S0167739X15002836.

81. Huo, Y., Dong, W., Qian, J., Jing, T., Coalition game-based secure and effective clustering communication in the vehicular cyber-physical system (vcps). *Sensors*, 17, 3, 475, 2017.

82. Spezzano, G. and Vinci, A., Pattern detection in cyber-physical systems. *Proc. Comput. Sci.*, 52, 1016–1021, 2015. [Online]. Available: http://www.sciencedirect.com/science/article/pii/S1877050915008960.

83. Kang, Y.S., Park, I.H., Rhee, J., Lee, Y.H., Mongodb-based repository design for IoT-generated RFID/sensor big data. *IEEE Sens. J.*, 16, 2, 485–497, Jan 2016.

84. Cattell, R.R., Scalable SQL and NoSQL data stores. *SIGMOD Rec.*, 39, 4, 12–27, May 2011, [Online]. Available: http://doi.acm.org/10.1145/1978915.1978919.

85. Patel, J.M., Operational NoSQL systems: What's new and what's next? *Computer*, 49, 4, 23–30, Apr 2016.

86. Strauch, C., Sites, U.-L.S., Kriha, W., NoSQL databases, Stuttgart Media University, Germany, URL: http://www. Christof-Strauch. de/NoSQL Dbs. pdf (Ħ ŁĦ 07.11. 2012), 2011.

87. Mohan, A., Ebrahimi, M., Lu, S., Kotov, A., A NoSQL data model for scalable big data workflow execution, in: *Proc. 2016 IEEE International Congress on Big Data (BigData Congress)*, pp. 52–59, June 2016.

88. Atat, R., Liu, L., Chen, H., Wu, J., Li, H., Yi, Y., Enabling cyber-physical communication in 5G cellular networks: Challenges, spatial spectrum sensing, and cyber-security. *IET Cyber-Phys. Syst.: Theory Appl.*, 2, 1, 49–54, Apr. 2017.

89. Gai, K., Qiu, M., Zhao, H., Security-aware efficient mass distributed storage approach for cloud systems in big data, in: *Proc. 2016 IEEE 2nd International Conference on Big Data Security on Cloud (BigDataSecurity), IEEE International Conference on High Performance and Smart Computing (HPSC), and IEEE International Conference on Intelligent Data and Security (IDS)*, pp. 140–145, April 2016.

90. Kang, S., Veeravalli, B., Aung, K.M.M., A security-aware data placement mechanism for big data cloud storage systems, in: *Proc. 2016 IEEE 2nd International Conference on Big Data Security on Cloud (BigDataSecurity), IEEE International Conference on High Performance and Smart Computing (HPSC), and IEEE International Conference on Intelligent Data and Security (IDS)*, pp. 327–332, April 2016.

91. Sekar, K. and Padmavathamma, M., Comparative study of encryption algorithm over big data in cloud systems, in: *Proc. 2016 3rd International Conference on Computing for Sustainable Global Development (INDIACom)*, pp. 1571–1574, March 2016.

92. Dorazio, C.J., Choo, K.-K.R., Yang, L.T., Data exfiltration from internet of things devices: iOS devices as case studies. *IEEE Internet Things J.*, 4, 2, 524–535, April 2017.

93. Ni, J., Lin, X., Zhang, K., Yu, Y., Shen, X.S., Secure outsourced data transfer with integrity verification in cloud storage, in: *2016 IEEE/CIC International Conference on Communications in China (ICCC)*, pp. 1–6, July 2016.

94. opened up., Dedupe your data to local or cloud storage Gateway and Filesystem, Backblaze B2, 2016, Accessed on July 1, 2017. [Online]. Available: http://opendedup.org/.

95. Meyer, D.T. and Bolosky, W.J., A study of practical deduplication, in: *9th USENIX Conference on File and Storage Technologies*, pp. 14:1–14:20, Feb. 2011.

96. Yan, Z., Ding, W., Yu, X., Zhu, H., Deng, R.H., Deduplication on encrypted big data in the cloud. *IEEE Trans. Big Data*, 2, 2, 138–150, June 2016.

97. Gahi, Y., Guennoun, M., Mouftah, H.T., Big data analytics: Security and privacy challenges, in: *2016 IEEE Symposium on Computers and Communication (ISCC)*, pp. 952–957, June 2016.

98. Rao, S., Suma, S.N., Sunitha, M., Security solutions for big data analytics in healthcare, in: *Advances in Computing and Communication Engineering (ICACCE), 2015 Second International Conference on*, pp. 510–514, May 2015.

99. Mahmood, T. and Afzal, U., Security analytics: Big data analytics for cybersecurity: A review of trends, techniques, and tools, in: *Information Assurance (NCIA), 2013 2nd National Conference on*, pp. 129–134, Dec 2013.

100. He, D., Chan, S., Zhang, Y., Wu, C., Wang, B., How effective are the prevailing attack-defense models for cybersecurity anyway? *IEEE Intell. Syst.*, 29, 5, 14–21, Sept 2014.

101. Ristic, B., Detecting anomalies from a multitarget tracking output. *IEEE Trans. Aerosp. Electron. Syst.*, 50, 1, 798–803, January 2014.

102. Kumar, S., Jain, A., Prakash Shukla, A., Singh, S., Rani, S., Harshitha, G., AlZain, M.A., Masud, M.A., A Comparative Analysis of Machine Learning Algorithms for Detection of Organic and Nonorganic Cotton Diseases. *Math. Probl. Eng.*, 2021, Article ID 1790171, 18 pages, 2021, https://doi.org/10.1155/2021/1790171.

103. Jia, L., Li, M., Zhang, P., Wu, Y., Zhu, H., Sar image change detection based on multiple kernel k-means clustering with local-neighborhood information. *IEEE Geosci. Remote Sens. Lett.*, 13, 6, 856–860, June 2016.

104. Murphree, J., Machine learning anomaly detection in large systems, in: *2016 IEEE Autotestcon*, pp. 1–9, Sept 2016.

105. Yuan, Y. and Jia, K., A distributed anomaly detection method of operation energy consumption using smart meter data, in: *2015 International Conference on Intelligent Information Hiding and Multimedia Signal Processing (IIH-MSP)*, pp. 310–313, Sept 2015.

106. Plantard, T., Susilo, W., Zhang, Z., Fully homomorphic encryption using hidden ideal lattice. *IEEE Trans. Inf. Forensics Secur.*, 8, 12, 2127–2137, Dec 2013.

107. Kumarage, H., Khalil, I., Alabdulatif, A., Tari, Z., Yi, X., Secure data analytics for cloud-integrated internet of things applications. *IEEE Cloud Comput.*, 3, 2, 46–56, Mar 2016.

108. Li, Y., Jiang, Z.L., Wang, X., Yiu, S.M., Privacy-preserving id3 data mining over encrypted data in outsourced environments with multiple keys, in: *Proc. 2017 IEEE International Conference on Computational Science and Engineering (CSE) and the IEEE International Conference on Embedded and Ubiquitous Computing (EUC)*, vol. 1, pp. 548–555, July 2017.

109. Qiu, S., Wang, B., Li, M., Liu, J., Shi, Y., Toward practical privacy-preserving frequent itemset mining on encrypted cloud data. *IEEE Trans. Cloud Comput.*, 8, 1127, 312–323, 2017.

110. Lu, R., Zhu, H., Liu, X., Liu, J.K., Shao, J., Toward efficient and privacy-preserving computing in the big data era. *IEEE Network*, 28, 4, 46–50, July 2014.

111. Chakravorty, A., Wlodarczyk, T., Rong, C., Privacy-preserving data analytics for smart homes, in: *Proc. 2013 IEEE Security and Privacy Workshops*, pp. 23–27, May 2013.

112. Truta, T.M. and Vinay, B., Privacy protection: p-sensitive k-anonymity property, in: *Proc. 22nd International Conference on Data Engineering Workshops (ICDEW'06)*, pp. 94–94, 2006.

113. Gheit, Z. and Challah, Y., An efficient and privacy-preserving similarity evaluation for big data analytics, in: *Proc. 2015 IEEE/ACM 8th International Conference on Utility and Cloud Computing (UCC)*, pp. 281–289, Dec 2015.

114. Lee, Y.T., Hsiao, W.H., Lin, Y.S., Chou, S.C.T., Privacy-preserving data analytics in the cloud-based smart home with community hierarchy. *IEEE Trans. Consum. Electron.*, 63, 2, 200–207, May 2017.

115. Simmhan, Y., Aman, S., Kumbhare, A., Liu, R., Stevens, S., Zhou, Q., Prasanna, V., Cloud-based software platform for big data analytics in smart grids. *Comput. Sci. Eng.*, 15, 4, 38–47, July 2013.

116. Mo, L., Li, F., Zhu, Y., Huang, A., Human physical activity recognition based on computer vision with a deep learning model, in: *Proc. 2016 IEEE*

International Instrumentation and Measurement Technology Conference Proceedings, pp. 1–6, May 2016.

117. Zitouni, M.S., Dias, J., Al-Mualla, M., Bhaskar, H., Hierarchical crowd detection and representation for big data analytics in visual surveillance, in: *Proc. 2015 IEEE International Conference on Systems, Man, and Cybernetics (SMC)*, pp. 1827–1832, Oct 2015.

118. Kumar Lenka, R., Kumar Rath, A., Tan, Z., Sharma, S., Puthal, D., Simha, N.V.R., Raja, R., Tripathi, S.S., Prasad, M., Building Scalable Cyber-Physical-Social Networking Infrastructure Using IoT and Low Power Sensors. *IEEE Access, Special Section on Cyber-Physical-Social Computing and Networking*, 6, 1, 30162–30173.

119. Ukil, A. and Zivanovic, R., Automated analysis of power systems disturbance records: Smart grid big data perspective, in: *Proc. 2014 IEEE Innovative Smart Grid Technologies—Asia (ISGT ASIA)*, pp. 126–131, May 2014.

120. Yang, J., Zhao, J., Wen, F., Kong, W., Dong, Z., Mining the big data of residential appliances in the smart grid environment, in: *Proc. 2016 IEEE Power and Energy Society General Meeting (PESGM)*, pp. 1–5, July 2016.

121. Liu, L. and Han, Z., Multi-block admm for big data optimization in smart grid, in: *Proc. 2015 International Conference on Computing, Networking, and Communications (ICNC)*, pp. 556–561, Feb 2015.

122. Cui, S., Han, Z., Kar, S., Kim, T.T., Poor, H.V., Tajer, A., Coordinated data-injection attack and detection in the smart grid: A detailed look at enriching detection solutions. *IEEE Signal Process. Mag.*, 29, 5, 106–115, Sept 2012.

123. Yassine, A., Shirehjini, A.A.N., Shirmohammadi, S., Smart meters big data: Game-theoretic model for fair data sharing in deregulated smart grids. *IEEE Access*, 3, 2743–2754, 2015.

124. He, X., Ai, Q., Qiu, R.C., Huang, W., Piao, L., Liu, H., A big data architecture design for smart grids based on random matrix theory. *IEEE Trans. Smart Grid*, 8, 2, 674–686, March 2017.

125. J. Wu, K. Ota, M. Dong, J. Li and H. Wang, Big Data Analysis-Based Security Situational Awareness for Smart Grid. *IEEE Trans. Big Data*, 4, 3, 408–417, 2018.

126. Wang, K., Wang, Y., Hu, X., Sun, Y., Deng, D.J., Vinel, A., Zhang, Y., Wireless big data computing in smart grid. *IEEE Wireless Commun.*, 24, 2, 58–64, April 2017.

127. Hamedani, K., Liu, L., Rachad, A., Wu, J., Yi, Y., Reservoir computing meets smart grids: Attack detection using delayed feedback networks. *IEEE Trans. Ind. Inf.*, 14, 2, 2743–2754, 2017.

128. Yavuz, A.A., An efficient real-time broadcast authentication scheme for command and control messages. *IEEE Trans. Inf. Forensics Secur.*, 9, 10, 1733–1742, Oct 2014.

129. Raja, R., Sinha, T.S., Patra, R.K., Tiwari, S., Physiological Trait Based Biometrical Authentication of Human-Face Using LGXP and ANN Techniques. *Int. J. Inf. Comput. Secur.*, 10, 2/3, 303–320, 2018.

130. Lehto, G.M., Edlund, G., Smigla, T., Afinidad, F., Protection evaluation framework for tactical Satcom architectures, in: *Proc. MILCOM 2013—2013 IEEE Military Communications Conference*, pp. 1008–1013, Nov 2013.

131. Moreno, M.V., Terroso-Saenz, F., Gonzalez-Vidal, A., Valdez-Vela, M., Skarmeta, F., Zamora, M.A., Chang, V., Applicability of big data techniques to smart cities deployments. *IEEE Trans. Ind. Inf.*, 13, 2, 800–809, April 2017.

132. Sahu, A.K., Sharma, S., Tanveer, M., Internet of Things attack detection using hybrid Deep Learning Model. *Comput. Commun.*, 176, 146–154, 2021, https://doi.org/10.1016/j.comcom.2021.05.024.

133. de Oliveira, B.T. and Margi, C.B., Distributed control plane architecture for software-defined wireless sensor networks, in: *Proc. 2016 IEEE International Symposium on Consumer Electronics (ISCE)*, pp. 85–86, Sept 2016.

134. Rawat, N. and Raja, R., Moving Vehicle Detection and Tracking using Modified Mean Shift Method and Kalman Filter and Research. *Int. J. New Technol. Res. (IJNTR)*, 2, 5, 96–100, 2016.

135. Raja, R., Kumar, S., Rashid, Md., Color Object Detection Based Image Retrieval using ROI Segmentation with Multi-Feature Method. *Wirel. Pers. Commun. Springer J.*, 1, 1–24, 2020, https://doi.org/10.1 007/s11277-019-07021-6.

136. Yuce, M.R., Implementation of wireless body area networks for healthcare systems. *Sens. Actuators A: Phys.*, 162, 1, 116–129, 2010, [Online]. Available: http://www.sciencedirect.com/science/article/pii/S0924424710002657.

137. Yan, H., Huo, H., Xu, Y., Gidlund, M., Wireless sensor network based e-health system—Implementation and experimental results. *IEEE Trans. Consum. Electron.*, 56, 4, 2288–2295, November 2010.

138. Martinez, J.F., Familiar, M.S., Corredor, I., Garcia, A.B., Bravo, S., Lopez, L., Composition and deployment of e-health services over wireless sensor networks. *Math. Comput. Modell.*, 53, 3–4, 485–503, 2011, Telecommunications Software Engineering: Emerging Methods, Models, and Tools. [Online]. Available: http://www.sciencedirect.com/science/article/pii/S0895717710001548.

139. Mahmood, Md. R., Raja, R., Gupta, A., Jain, S., Implementation of Multi-Sensor and Multi-Functional Mobile Robot for Image Mosaicking. *SAMRIDDHI: A Journal of Physical Sciences, Engineering and Technology*, 12, Special Issue (3), 189–196, 2020.

140. Dewangan, A.K., Raja, R., Singh, R., Multi-Sensor and Multifunctional Robot with Image Mosaic. *Int. J. Sci. Eng. Technol. Res. (IJSETR).*, 3, 4, 677–680, 2014.

141. Dewangan, A.K., Raja, R., Singh, R., An Implementation of Multi Sensor-Based Mobile Robot With Image Stitching Application. *Int. J. Comput. Sci. Mob. Comput.*, 3, 6, 603–609, 2014.

142. Cui, D., Risk early warning index system in the field of public safety in the big data era, in: *Proc. 2015 Sixth International Conference on Intelligent Systems Design and Engineering Applications (ISDEA)*, pp. 704–707, Aug 2015.

143. Tiwari, L., Raja, R., Awasthi, V., Miri, R., Sinha, G.R., Alkinani, M.H., Polat, K., Detection of lung nodule and cancer using novel Mask-3 FCM

and TWEDLNN algorithms. *Measurement*, 172, 108882, https://doi.org/10.1016/j.measurement.2020.108882, 2021.

144. Zhong, L., Takano, K., Ji, Y., Yamada, S., Big data-based service area estimation for mobile communications during natural disasters, in: *Proc. 2016 30th International Conference on Advanced Information Networking and Applications Workshops (WAINA)*, pp. 687–692, March 2016.

145. Tin, P., Zin, T.T., Toriu, T., Hama, H., An integrated framework for disaster event analysis in big data environments, in: *Proc. 2013 Ninth International Conference on Intelligent Information Hiding and Multimedia Signal Processing*, pp. 255–258, Oct 2013.

146. Ma, Y., Wu, H., Wang, L., Huang, B., Ranjan, R., Zomaya, A., Jie, W., Remote sensing big data computing. *Future Gener. Comput. Syst.*, 51, C, 47–60, Oct. 2015. [Online]. Available: http://dx.doi.org/10.1016/j.future.2014.10.029

11

Developing Decision Making and Risk Mitigation: Using CRISP-Data Mining

Vivek Parganiha[1]*, Soorya Prakash Shukla[2] and Lokesh Kumar Sharma[3]

[1]Department of Computer Science &Engineering, Bhilai Institute of Technology, Durg, India
[2]Department of Electrical Engineering, Bhilai Institute of Technology, Durg, India
[3]ICMR-National Institute of Occupational Health, Department of Health Research, Ministry of Health and Family Welfare, Ahmedabad, India

Abstract

In this chapter, we will examine the usage of CRISP-DM philosophy in an ERP framework, which contains gigantic measures of the Information associated with the actual implementation of the business steps. Such systems get a particular method of tracking activities that leads to a confusing description of business measures in opportunity reports. A few works have been led on ERP frameworks, the greater part of them zeroing in on the improvement of new calculations for the programmed revelation of business measures. We zeroed in on tending to issues like, in what capacity can associations with ERP frameworks apply measure mining for breaking down their business measures to improve them. CRISP-DM had already emerged as that of the agreed standard for the development of data analytics and data Discovery Projects. Productive Data Mining involves three classes of exposure capabilities in a specific incident, sequence and determination. The Data operator uses more than a single testing technique to secure optimum performance. The goal of this article is to upgrade the efficiency usability comprehensibility of data mining processes by updating the CRISP-DM system about its use in ERP cases, defined in terms of specific execution tools and bit-by-bit synchronization. The research confirms that the availability of ERP content improves vital and organizational dynamics. The terms Big Data and Data mining are regularly utilized in a similar setting.

*Corresponding author: vivekparganiha@gmail.com

Rohit Raja, Kapil Kumar Nagwanshi, Sandeep Kumar and K. Ramya Laxmi (eds.) Data Mining and Machine Learning Applications, (281–316) © 2022 Scrivener Publishing LLC

Be that as it may, it is essential to isolate the two terms appropriately. Big Data manages data that can't be handled effectively and inside a sensible time frame utilizing traditional techniques and devices. Data Mining is frequently utilized for a lot of data, yet isn't restricted to Big Data. This is a major test for data science. In this way, for organizations like Get Your Guide, it is critical to deal with a lot of Data appropriately, decipher them effectively, and act as needs are. Cross-Industry Standard Process for Data Mining (CRISP-DM) would be an identical process method that can be used for data analysis to search sets of data for instances, shapes, and connexions. For this, the standard characterizes six unique stages, which must be completed at least multiple times. CRISP-DM has built up itself worldwide and is one of the most now and again utilized investigation models in this condition.

Keywords: Enterprise Resource Management (ERP), Systems, Applications, and Products (SAP), Auditory processing disorder (APD), Clustering, Classification, Cross-Industry Standard Process for Data Mining (CRISP-DM), regression, association analysis

11.1   Introduction

CRISP-DM was imagined in late 1996 by three veterans of the youthful and juvenile Data mining market. CRISP-tells the Data Processing predictable ways of the Cross Industries. Such an information retrieval Period system gives a schematic of the existing pattern of the data gathering undertaking. It contains all the periods of a venture, their errands, and the connections between these undertakings. Interfaces can occur for the said data-mining operation, focusing on the intent, system, and enthusiasm of the developer and, most of all, details. CRISP-DM separates the existence pattern of a Data mining venture into six stages. These six elevated level periods of CRISP-DM are as yet a decent portrayal for the examination cycle.

Data mining can be utilized to consequently decide critical examples and concealed relationships from a lot of Data. Data mining gives experiences and relationships that had in the past gone unrecognized or been overlooked because it had not been viewed as conceivable to investigate them [1]. As a rule, Functional prerequisites and Business rules can't be ported starting with one ERP usage then onto the next because nearby tasks have exceptionally explicit [2] and altered techniques for working that hardware [3]. ERP frameworks execute exceptionally tweaked answers to meet explicit business necessities of undertakings. As each undertaking has distinct and unique Data Mining needs, this is completely absurd to assume static designs to produce national statistical. Data mining specialists are being developed to create different systems to meet global needs that benefit dynamically. Information retrieved mostly from the ERP framework could always be retrieved to identify operational issues, often including—comparative element estimation to manage service requests, user beat, deliberately promoting new items capacity, sales analysis, and so on. ERP can assume a basic part of driving accurate and fast decisions (product perceived usefulness, development expenditure) with accurately defined Information. Each benefit of ERP execution is being measured through both quantitative and subjective contexts, such as acceptable market strategies, enhanced customer service, reduced costs, improved profit margins, faster transaction times, the panel's process flow, and a reduction in the amount of funding the leaders are blundering [4]. Throughout this paper, we addressed how well the CRSIP-Data Mining technique could be modified scheduled the ERP structure Facts of an immense assembly effort, whereby SAP will be the provider of the ERP structure [5].

11.2   Background

Throughout the mid-1990s, as data analysis matured via a small child to a young person, investigators spent a lot of effort to prepare data with truly limited equipment and minimal day-to-day recording speed. It is just frequently that there were one or two 'data analysts' in a specific space, and we were significantly more likely to be named 'prescient modelers' because this kind of demonstration became cutting-edge throughout its day.

Although this '90s progressed, there was a distinctive process that led others to normalize the activities we had studied in a traditional method. Undertakings like this do proceed through, considering so anyone might hear whether there even was a typical methodology given that the issues looked so disparate. Notably, there seemed to be.

The majority of current rivals of operating equipment, SPSS, and Teradata, together with three early-initiated client collaborations, Daimler, NCR, and OHRA brought together a particular SIG (SIG) in 1996 (apparently one of the early-initiated community-oriented projects over the currently available global web) because, over not even one year, they worked out yet how to systematize whatever will always be the CR currently.

The CRISP-DM wasn't the best choice. The SAS Organization, which has been around older than anyone can remember, had its implementation named SEMMA (Sample, Explore, Modify, Model, and Assess), but within just a year or two, some experts put forward the CRISP-DM framework.

11.3   Methodology of CRISP-DM

CRISP (Cross Industry Standard Process for Data Mining) seems to be an information analysis assessment design that illustrates normally recycled methods used by structured data diggers to deal with market speculation [5]. It has acquired insights from the much more significant pre-2000 designs and remains the basis aimed at several further schemes. The CRISP-DM 2.0 Special Interest Group (SIG) is being established for the sole purpose of modifying the CRISP-DM design towards an outlying, more competent representation of the advances made in the corporate sector, although the updated iteration becomes comprehensive [6]. The CRISPED technique is portrayed regarding a progressive cycle model, comprising of sets of errands depicted at four degrees of reflection (from general to explicit): stage, conventional undertaking, particular assignment, and cycle occasion shown in Figure 11.1.

The Orientation Model for CRISP-DM:
Each existing Data Mining Period Model outlines the existing pattern of the Data Mining undertaking. It contains the periods of a venture, their

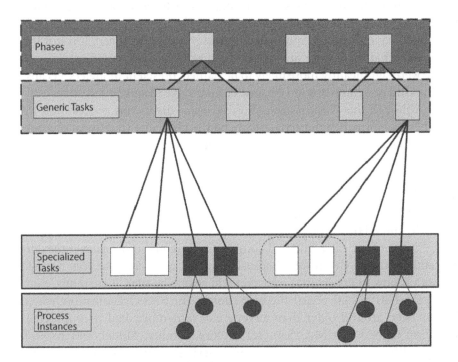

Figure 11.1 Shows CRISP-DM methodology.

particular assignments, and the connections between these undertakings. At this portrayal level, it is absurd to expect to recognize all connections. Interfaces can exist for any information retrieval undertaking, focusing on the intent, context, and enthusiasm of the client and, above all else, on the proof.

The existing pattern of a Data mining venture comprises six stages, which appeared in Figure 11.2. The succession of the stages isn't unbending. Moving to and for between various stages is consistent.

Required. Each stage figures out which stage, or specific assignment of a stage, must be performed straight away. The bolts demonstrate the most significant and continuous conditions between stages. The external hover in Figure 11.2 is a recurrent concept of data analysis activity. Big data did not stop until the response has been transmitted. Activities that have taken place throughout the period and from the sent agreement will cause new, often more active, business questions. Resulting Data mining cycles can benefit from past experiences. In the corresponding segment, we conveniently outline each phase:

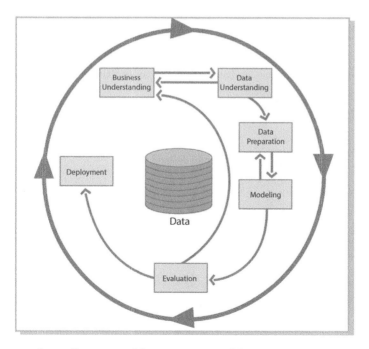

Figure 11.2 Shows all six stages of the CRISP-DM model.

11.4   Stage One—Determine Business Objectives

The initial step is attempting to show signs of improvement thought of what business needs ought to be extricated from Data. The investigator needs to comprehend what the client truly needs from a business point of view. The client frequently has a few contending objectives and limitations that should be appropriately organized. Besides, the business understanding stage is tied in with characterizing the particular goals and prerequisites for Data mining. The consequence of this stage is the definition of the errand and the portrayal of the arranged harsh methodology to accomplish both business and Data mining objectives. This likewise incorporates the underlying choice of apparatuses and strategies.

Figure 11.3 shows the business understating phase of CRISP-DM model. Furthermore, it seems you're going to lay out the organizational achievement criteria that you're going to use to determine if the mission has been successful from a marketing point of view. Expectations of this progression are some significant reports. The stock of assets records all assets accessible for the task. These may incorporate individuals (Data excavators, yet additionally those with master).

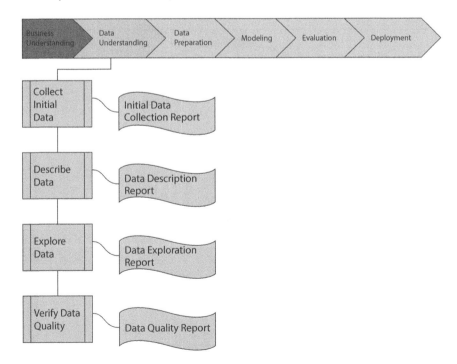

Figure 11.3 Shows business understanding phase of CRISP-DM model.

Data on the business issue, Data supervisors, specialized help, and others), Data, equipment, and programming. Prerequisites, suspicions, and compels are recorded.

Prerequisites, for instance, incorporate a timetable for culmination, legitimate and security commitments, and necessities for adequate completed work. Also, you distinguish causes that could postpone the finish of the undertaking and set up an emergency course of action for every one of them. A significant part is making a typical comprehension of phrasing. You may make a glossary with meanings of business and Data mining terms that apply to your task so everybody engaged with it can have a typical comprehension of those terms. Besides, you set up a money-saving advantage investigation. If the advantages don't fundamentally surpass the costs, stop and rethink this examination and your undertaking. After that, you likewise characterize Data mining achievement rules, which are specialized models important to help the business achievement standards. You attempt to characterize these in quantitative terms (for example, model precision or prescient improvement contrasted with a current strategy).

11.4.1 What Are the Ideal Yields of the Venture?

Set targets—This implies depicting your essential goal from a business viewpoint. There may likewise be other related inquiries that you might want to address. For example, the main goal seems to be to maintain existing users on track by predicting if they are already likely to switch to the contestant. Business development Concerns could be "would the network used affect not just whether users stay or go?" or "Will bring down ATM charges fundamentally decrease the quantity of high-esteem clients who leave?"

Produce venture plan—Then, you'll see the framework for all the achievement of information gathering and core competencies. The agreement should specify the resources to be used throughout the remaining amount of the undertaking, including all the fundamental options of technologies and techniques.

Business achievement measures—Sometimes, you can distribute the parameters that you will use to determine if such an initiative has so far been successful from a business point of view. This should also ideally be clear and measurable, for instance, a decrease of client stir to a specific level, anyway. In some cases, it may be important to have more abstract measures, for example, "give helpful experiences into the connections." If this is the case, then it should be clear who it is that makes the emotional judgment.

11.4.2   Evaluate the Current Circumstance

It, therefore, involves further point-by—Reference details describing almost every resource, restrictions, expectations, and influences that you will have to decide on the Data Analysis Purpose and Action Strategy.

Availability of assets—Inventory of resources that are available to the venture, such as:

- Workers (industry experts, computer analysts, technical assistance, data mining experts)
- The aid of information technology (resolved main product, real, stored, or functional data)
- Identification of properties (appliances stages)
- computing (Data mining equipment, other related computing).

Basic requirements, theoretical framework—Outline all the conditions of the undertaking, for example, the schedule for resolution, the requisite understandability and consistency of the measurement, and any data protection issues, as well as every regulatory matter. Try to make sure users are permitted to use the Data. Pulled away from the worries of the operation. There might be some concerns more about details that can be confirmed throughout data mining, but these may also include vague requirements of the organization involved. Throughout reality, it is especially noteworthy to emphasize the last ones listed in the sense that they influence the reliability of the experiment. Rundown the imperatives on the venture. These might be imperatives on the accessibility of assets, however, they may likewise incorporate innovative requirements, for example, the size of the informational collection that it is common sense to use for demonstrating.

Hazards and Opportunities—List the hazards or opportunities that could delay the plan or make it short. Run down the list of possible actions— which steps would you take if certain hazards or circumstances arise?

Phrasing—Formulate a synopsis of the text specific to the project. And in the most aspect, this could have two sections:

- A checklist of significant trade phrasing that establishes part of every business concept that is available to the company. Creating this flowchart is a useful investment of "data identification" and guidance.
- A definition of the text of Data Mining, outlined with the concepts related to the market problem resorted to.

Expenditures and Benefits—Create a money-saving opportunity analysis for an activity that measures the costs of the endeavor and the potential benefits of the arrangement in the condition of its effectiveness. The whole association should be as clear as might normally be considered. For example, in a work setting, you can use strategic actions.

11.4.3   Realizes Data Mining Goals

The main business specifies the locations in the industry text. The data mining goal specifies company goals on a comprehensive basis. For example, the sector motive may consist of 'Incremental Index Offers to Current Clients.' The data mining objective may consist of 'Anticipate how many devices and consumer transactions have taken into account their transactions in recent years, the details segment (age, income, location, etc.) and the cost of the item.'

Technological breakthrough Models—portrays the anticipated returns of an initiative encouraging the acquisition of company attractions.

Data mining accomplishment models—characterize the criteria for the successful performance of an activity in advanced requirements—for instance, a special degree of sensory precision or identity identification at a particular stage of the "boost" process. As with marketing achievement phases, theoretical Information may be needed in which cases the user or individuals trying to make a sensible choice are involved.

A project of advancement production:
Depict the planned structure for the accomplishment of the Data Mining objectives and the success of the strategic goals in this context. The agreement should specify the methods to be used for the rest of the mission, except the basic specification of the technologies and techniques.

Scope statement—List several processes to be completed throughout the undertaking, including the length of the undertaking, the resources provided, the structured data, the outcomes, and the parameters. Wherever practicable, request and clearly state the focus of the Broad Scale in the Data Mining method, e.g., repetition of the show and evaluation phases. In particular, as part of the risk strategy, it is important to examine the circumstances throughout time schedules and hazards. Mark the implications of such inquiries specifically in the risk plan, possibly with events and strategies where the hazards are illustrated. Select again which assessment technique would remain utilized at the estimation stage? The business strategy is going to be a special collection. Towards the end of each point, you can audit progress and milestones and update the business plan as well. The emphasis of the specific research on these updates should be relevant for the business strategy.

Start of Assessment of Equipment and Procedures—just at the end of the main point, an assessment of the tools and techniques should be attempted. After this, for example, users choose a Data Mining System that supports different strategies in different phases of the process. It is important to track techniques and services right from the start in the method because of the choice of devices and systems which affect the entire project.

11.5   Stage Two—Data Sympathetic

Figure 11.4 shows data understanding phase of CRISP-DM model. As a feature of the Data understanding, an endeavor is made to get a first outline of the accessible Data and their quality. This includes checking whether all the necessary Data (to meet the Data Mining objectives) is accessible, just as building up an arrangement to figure out which Data is required. To begin with, users present the Information that has been gathered, along with its structure, its magnitude, some new substrate outlines that have already been established. Users determine unless the Data you have collected fulfills certain requirements. On the off chance that a portion of the

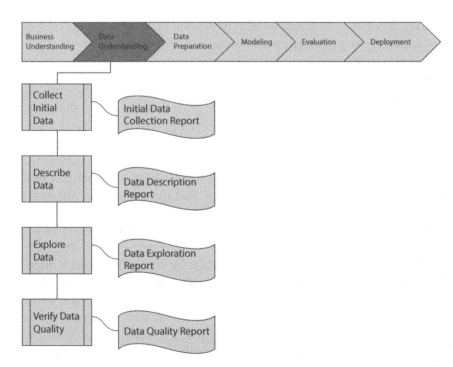

Figure 11.4 Shows data understanding phase of CRISP-DM model.

Data you need is inaccessible, you need to conclude how to address that issue. Choices could be subbing with an elective Data source, narrowing the extent of the undertaking, or assembling new Data. Bringing the Data into the Data mining stage, you'll be utilizing for the task causes it conceivable to affirm you to do as such and that you comprehend the cycle. Throughout this preliminary, you may find programming (or equipment) restrictions you had not envisioned, such as cutoff points on the number of cases, fields, or on the measure of memory you may utilize or powerlessness to peruse the Data arrangements of your sources.

At that point, you investigate the Data utilizing questioning, Data perception, and detailing procedures. This may incorporate discovering the dissemination of key characteristics, basic accumulations, or basic factual examinations. To maintain a strategic distance from potential traps, the Data quality is investigated and assessed. Issues with the nature of the current Data comparable to the assignment characterized in the past stage must be recognized.

- Normal investigations during that point are as follows:
- Is indeed the Information full (spreads out all the cases requisite)?
- Would it be right, or would it cause complications, so if there are mistakes, how natural is it?
- Are there insufficient attributes throughout the dataset?

11.5.1 Portray Data

Inspect the "gross" or "surface" properties of the obtained Information and statement proceeding with the outcomes.

Knowledge portrait document—Identify the Information that has been gathered, as well as its structure, its quantity (the number of proceedings and turfs in the respective table taken as an instance), objects elements, and any new substrate details that consume already remained defined. Evaluate if the Information gathered satisfies the needs.

11.5.2 Investigate Facts

In this fact, you will discuss data mining attributes using questioning, statistical modeling, and disclosure methods. They may include:

- Utilization of main characteristics (e.g., objective consistency of the target task)

- Relations among collections or limited amounts of quality
- Findings of specific collections
- Assets of notable sub-populations
- Simple analysis of the evidence.

Such reviews can directly answer Data Mining priorities. These can also incorporate or improve information description and presentation assessments and feeding into improvements and other steps in the preparation of data required for advanced analysis.

Information investigation report—Explain the devastation of the data processing and its impact on the rest of the tasks like first findings or assumptions. To display data quality, which suggests further evaluation for compelling data subsets, illustrations and graphs may be integrated into this.

11.5.3   Confirm Data Quality

Look at the nature of the Data, tending to questions, for example,

- would be the data correct (distributes all specific points)?
- would it be correct or includes errors and, also, if flaws, so fundamental is it?

Seem to be the Data deficient in quality? If so, who are they openly discussed, where else are they occurring, and even how important are they?

11.5.4   Data Excellence Description

Redesign the results from the data product testing. If quality issues exist, propose potential arrangements. Answers for Data quality issues by and large rely intensely upon both Data and Business Data.

11.6   Stage Three—Data Preparation

In this stage, the Data is ready for further Data mining measures. Data readiness is one of the most significant and frequently tedious parts of Data mining. Indeed, it is assessed that Data planning, as a rule, takes 50–70% of an undertaking's time and exertion. Business choices depend on examination. Yet, on the off chance that the Data is off base or inadequate, your investigation illuminates wrong business choices. Terrible investigation implies helpless business choices.

In this manner, data from various sources is blended and tidied up so that there is no copy, erroneous or inadequate passages (see Figure 11.5). Changes are made, for example, finding sources to make explicit Data amendments, barring a few cases or individual cells (things of Data), or supplanting a few things of Data with default esteems. The deliverable for this undertaking is the Data cleaning report, which records each choice and activity used to clean the Data. This report should cover and allude to every Data quality issue that was distinguished in the confirm Data quality errand in the Data understanding period of the cycle. The subsequent stage is to set up the substance of the Data, which implies that the Data is moved into usable organizations. Users could require certain assets to include, in a great structure, maximum data, or entirely new traits, innovative devices that are formed from at least one already current structure. Methods should be identified other than choices. This includes features (segments) as well as the selection of data in a graph. The guidelines where you can also use for this selection implement the accuracy of the study for your information retrieval goals, the characteristics of the research, and

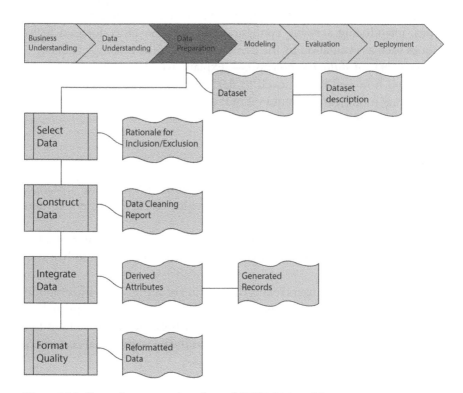

Figure 11.5 Shows data preparation phase of CRISP-DM model.

additional specific considerations, such as large data thresholds and data types. The data system is used for a final instance show that describes the purpose of the subsequent demonstration timespan.

11.6.1   Select Your Data

This will be the stage of the organization in which you select the Data that can be analyzed. The criteria that may use to assess this option include the purpose of data mining information, information quality, and many other future challenges like bandwidth utilization or data types limitations. Make sure that data evaluation includes quality selection (sections) as well as record selection (columns) in the graph.

Justification for concern/exclusion—Describe the facts and intent behind options to be transformed/excluded.

11.6.2   The Data Is Processed

That order involves the quality of the data to the degree specified by the testing procedures selected. It might involve selecting precise data sub-types, introducing sensible configurations, or even more focused techniques such as evaluation by the demonstration of the incomplete data.

Reporting on data pre-processing—Explain which solutions you have made and how you have moved to deal with data production problems. Accept any modifications required in the data for cleansing and its potential effect on the results of the case.

11.6.3   Data Needed to Build

This company involves valuable data preparation activities, for instance, the development or improvement in the quality of current assets, certain characteristics, or the whole records.

Defined Attributes—New features came up with a similar database of at minimum one existing feature that may be used to evaluate another area attribute, for example.

Databases created—users reflect the creation of entirely new Information now. It will also have to log users who won't be buying in the preceding period, for example. None no justification for these details to be found in the rough details, yet it can communicate loudly the way normal customers have made nil purchases for illustrating uses.

11.6.4   Combine Information

There are methods by which Data is compiled into new documents or values from several files, tables, or Information.

Combined data—The merger of tables applies to at least two tables of separate data involving common aspects being consolidated. For example, there might be a table with data on the overall efficiency of stores (for example, floor room, sort of center), a table with a description of deals (for example, incentives, improvements in deal percentages from previous years), and a table with data on the socioeconomics of the area as a whole. Each table includes for each store one record. These tables can be combined into another one-store table with fields from source tables entering each store.

Collections—arrangements refer to operations in which data from different documents and specific tables are gathered in new characteristics. For example, turning over a client's table transactions where each transaction has one record at another table and where there is one report at each client with fields such as purchase amounts, regular purchase sums, percentage of MasterCard requests prepared, percentage of items in progress, etc.

11.7   Stage Four—Modeling

Displaying is the explanatory center of the Data mining measure. This is the place the determination and utilization of demonstrating procedures occur. Before really constructing a model, you ordinarily separate the dataset into train, test, and approval sets. At that point, you construct the models on the train set. Several signifying procedures mark open presumptions approximately the Data, for occurrence, the entire behaviors have constant circulations or not any lost abilities are acceptable. Also, with any demonstrating device, there is frequently an enormous number of boundaries that can be balanced. You need to record any suspicions made and list the boundaries and their picked qualities. The discovered models at that point go through a specialized assessment stage. They are evaluated for precision and over-simplification. The discovered standards are applied to test Data records that were not utilized in the demonstrating.

Figure 11.6 shows the modeling phase of CRISP-DM model. Iterative advances are utilized to move toward step by step the last Model, which just permits negligible upgrades from a Data diagnostic point of view.

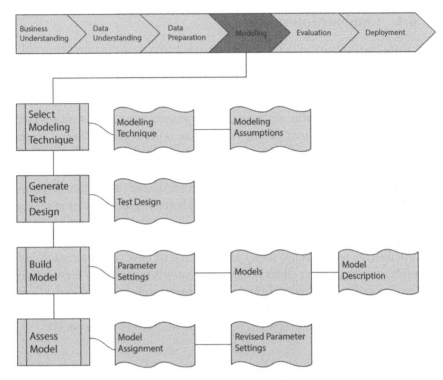

Figure 11.6 Shows modeling phase of CRISP-DM model.

11.7.1   Select Displaying Strategy

Also, as preliminary stages of the show, users will pick a specific demonstration technique that they will be using. It's because you've only selected a technique mostly during the corporate strategy. At this point, you will choose a specific display system, e.g., the tree of selection operating with C5.0 or the cognitive organization age with return propagation. If various approaches are used, perform this assessment separately for each process.

Demonstration Process—Report the actual show technique that will be used.

Showing assumptions—Several presentation techniques state clearly assumptions about either the data, for example, that all attributes require standard commercial activities, that neither lacking values are required, that the category feature should be indicative, and so on. Track any questions raised.

11.7.2   Produce an Investigation Plan

Ever since users produce a product, one must build a strategy or part to evaluate the accuracy and reliability of the scale. For instance, in controlled data mining firms, for example, arrangement, it is entirely assumed that error rates will be used as quality metrics for data mining models. As a result, you usually divide the dataset into the train and test sets, install the Model on the train set, and measure its consistency on the different test sets.

Test strategy—Explain the intended plans for the planning, implementation, and evaluation of the designs. A crucial part of the settlement is determining how and where to isolate the open database in the planning, review, and acceptance of databases.

11.7.3   Fabricate Ideal

She is outing the displaying instrument on the prepared dataset towards making at least a single demonstration.

Boundary settings—With any displaying instrument, there is frequently an enormous number of boundaries alright, it could be done. They were running down the barriers and their preferred attributes, along with the reason for the judgment on frontier variations.

Models—those would be the real models produced by the demonstration system, not the design study.

Concept Portraits—Identify the following models, report on the perception of the models, and document any problems with their consequences.

11.7.4   Evaluation Model

Read and understand the designs as suggested by the Storage space, certain Data Mining Efficiency Expectations, and the desired test schedule. Evaluate the success of the use of demonstration and disclosure techniques; in fact, at that stage, connect market analysts and area experts afterward to speak regarding data mining creates a workplace environment. This undertaking just thinks about models, while the assessment stage likewise considers all different outcomes that were delivered throughout the task.

At this stage, you should rank the models and survey them as indicated by the assessment standards. You should consider the business destinations and business achievement rules as far as possible here. In most Data mining ventures, a solitary strategy is applied more than once, and Data mining results are produced with a few distinct strategies.

Model appraisal—Review the aftereffects of this project, list the appearances of one's produced replicas (e.g.in expressions of precision), and flourishing their excellence corresponding to some alternative.

Changed boundary backgrounds—Permitting to the ideal appraisal, modify boundary sets, and adjust them for the subsequent displaying course. Demonstrate the structural Model and assessment once users completely embrace the discovery of the appropriate system(s). Document all these modifications and reviews.

11.8   Stage Five—Evaluation

The assessment guarantees a definite examination of the made Data models with the assignment and chooses the most appropriate Model (see Figure 11.7 which shows evaluation phase of the CRISP-DM model). The consequences of the past advances are assessed utilizing the business rules built up toward the start of the undertaking. So this stage is tied in with checking whether the Data mining arrangement fulfills the business issue and trying can determine if there would be a market motive behind its lack of a blueprint. One option is to evaluate the system(s) for test applications in such a real program, to decide if it fills in as well in the work environment

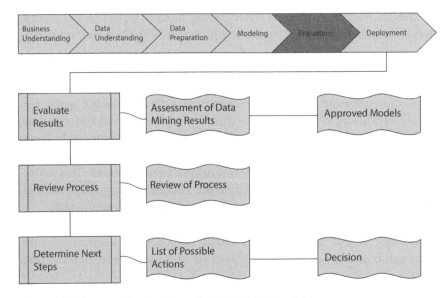

Figure 11.7 Shows evaluation phase of the CRISP-DM model.

as it did in your tests if time and spending limitations grant. Presently you may set aside an effort to survey your cycle. This is a chance to spot gives that you may have neglected furthermore, that may cause you to notice imperfections in the work that you've done while you, despite everything, have the opportunity to address the issue before the organization.

At long last, the Model might be prepared to send, or you may decide that it is smarter to rehash a few stages and attempt to improve it.

11.8.1   Assess Your Outcomes

Previous evaluation measures have handled variables such as accuracy and generalization of the method. Throughout this development, one will determine how often the Model meets your business targets and try to determine if there is any corporate incentive behind its failure of this design. Another other option is to validate the system(s) for application areas in a specific implementation if the time and cost conditions are given. In contrast, the evaluation process involves the review of some of the other data mining algorithms that you could have made. Data mining findings involve models that are associated with the first business objectives and all the various discoveries that are not really associated with the first business objectives but may also reveal additional challenges, details, or indicators for potential disturbances.

Assessment of data mining algorithms—Overview assessment sets out the terms of business achievement steps, along with the current declaration as to whether the project already meets the underlying business objectives.

Authorized Models—After reviewing models for business achievement standards, the models developed that achieve the chosen parameters remain defined versions.

11.8.2   Survey Measure

Now, the subsequent models give off an impression of being agreeable and to fulfill business needs. This is currently necessary if you to carry out something more supervisory review of the Data Mining commitment to determine there is some big issue or mistake which has already been ignored in one aspect other. This audit additionally covers quality confirmation issues—for instance: did we accurately fabricate the Model? Did we utilize just the characteristics that we are permitted to utilize and that are accessible for future investigations?

Audit of a cycle—Illustrate the process analysis or the characteristics of the activities which have been skipped so those that should be repeated.

11.8.3   Decide on the Subsequent Stages

Contingent upon the consequences of the appraisal and the cycle audit, you currently conclude how to proceed. Do you finish this undertaking and proceed onward to sending, start further emphasizes, or set up new Data mining ventures? You ought to likewise assess your outstanding assets and financial plan as this may impact your choices.

Overview of possible activities—Describe the planned additional tasks, as well as the goals beyond and against each substitute.

Alternative—Explain the option about how to proceed, including the reasoning.

11.9   Stage Six—Deployment

Figure 11.8 shows deployment phase of the CRISP-DM model. After Data planning, model structure, and model confirmation, the chose model is utilized in the organization stage. Creating an ideal remains usually not

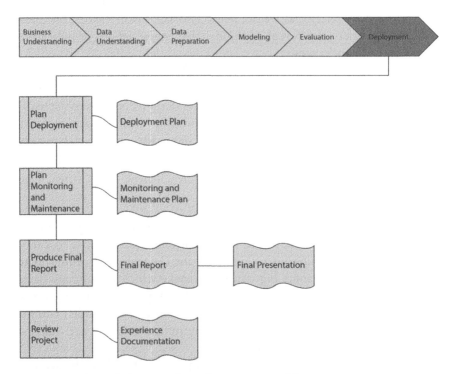

Figure 11.8 Shows deployment phase of CRISP-DM model.

the appearance of the project. Irrespective of whether the objective was to extend the Data on the Data, the Data increased should now be handled and introduced to the client so the client can utilize it with no issues. Contingent upon the prerequisites, this improvement stage can comprise the formation of a straightforward report or the perplexing usage of a repeatable Data mining measure all through the organization. The cautious arrangement of a support methodology assists with evading superfluously large proportions of inaccurate use of data mining results. To monitor the transfer of the Data Mining result(s), the group requires a point-by-point calculation program. The whole structure acknowledges a specific type of organization.

At last, the Data mining group should survey its work. This is the place a blueprint of any work techniques that worked especially well ought to be done, so they are archived to utilize again later on, and any upgrades that may be made to your cycle. It's additionally the spot to archive issues and terrible encounters, with your suggestions for evading comparative issues later on.

11.9.1   Plan Arrangement

At the phase of the agreement, users will consider the findings of the evaluation and settle on a method for submitting them. When an effective strategy for making the related model(s) has been established, this approach is recorded here for later organization. It is necessary to recognize the required assets of the firm mostly during the phase of business comprehension because although delivering is crucial to the implementation of the initiative. That's where the perceptive analysis helps to strengthen the objective function of the market.

Mailing a proposal—Outline the agreement process, discussing essential developments, and how to make them work.

11.9.2   Plan Observing and Support

Observation and assistance are major concerns unless the findings of data mining prove to be of interest to day-to-day activity and its situation. The careful structure of the maintenance approach helps to prevent unnecessarily broad areas of abuse of data mining performance. In screening the structure of the Data Mining Outcome(s), the business requires a thorough control plan. This structure is known to be a special form of organization.

Testing and Maintenance Plan—Review evaluation and management strategies, including key developments and how to execute them.

11.9.3 Produce the Last Report

Towards the end of the plan, users are always going to check the last article. Dependent on the attempting to send a proposal, the whole article could only be a summary of the arrangement and its meetings (if it isn't being reported as a constant flow for now though) or it could be a final and in-depth presentation of the Data Mining result(s).

Final Report—it will be the last recorded study on the Data Mining Contribution. It involves all previous assumptions, summarising, and filtering out all the data.

Final Presentation—A conference will also take place regularly after the company, at which the findings will be reported to the user.

11.9.4 Audit Venture

Review whatever worked with and what turned out to be incorrect, what worked well, and what needs to be changed.

Perception reports—Review the substantial experience acquired during the undertaking. For example, any entanglements you have encountered, deluding methods, or insights into the choice of the most suitable Data Mining approaches in comparative and correlational may be important to this report. In ideal obligations, the record of experience shall also cover any records which have been made up of individual projects in the past duration of the mission.

11.10 Data on ERP Systems

The ERP systems offer an improved degree of association to support focus company activities and are a mixture of the three most important segments—Market Management Techniques, Data Technology, and Clear Business Objectives. Until the previous decade, organizational and specific requirements and not data were the central focus of most ERP use. At the heart of ERP is an all-around distributed data store, which collects data from and flexibly into fragmented applications running at an all-inclusive processing level. Data in big corporations Partnerships are aggregated across a wide variety of functional categories and at times separated by geographical boundaries [10]. Such information areas can help support structural units, but do not attempt to extend to a wide range of operations, speeds, and capabilities (see Figure 11.9 for ERP Framework).

Figure 11.9 Shows coordination of various modules in ERP frameworks.

In such situations, it is time critical to store the dispersed data in a solitary database called a Data Warehouse (DW) before sending it to the Data Mining Movement. The main goal of the ERP system is to integrate and aggregate data and cycles from all useful divisions of the association for easy access and structured work processes. Joining is typically developed through the creation of a single data set shop, which corresponds to numerous product requirements, putting together separate categories of business insights and results.

This main element of data mining in ERP Systems is to manage data in the Company database system for the digitalization of adaptive and measure planning. SAP provides a complete data storage situation that optimizes its most challenging activity in developing a data distribution center—data capture from ERP applications and developing closed-circuit highly customized for business-particular purposes [1, 10]. For our analysis, the liquidity Calculation Data of the financially supported is used to update the CRSIP methodology and to focus on useful data. Fund flow declaration consists of ERP Data from Sales, Deposits, Loans, Transactions, and Collections through subsidiaries and Specific recreation activities.

11.11   Usage of CRISP-DM Methodology

The development of the design is not generally the end of the company. Despite as to whether the purpose and behind the model is to create Data on Data, the data collected must be filtered out again and constructed in such a way that it can be used by the client. The methodology adopted for working capital Data mining is shown in Figure 11.10.

We have utilized instruments accessible in SAP Business Data Warehouse (BIW) to deal with exceptions, missing, conflicting, and copy esteems in the source Data [7]. The regularly looked for an advantageous incentive from this DM Model incorporates forestalling extortion, offering showcasing guidance, looking for productive clients, foreseeing deals and stock, and rectifying Data during mass stacking of the Database, otherwise called the Extract-TransformLoad activity (ETL) [8]. Encouragement for the use of DM originates from the value it brings to the candidates, and it lowers costs almost every time, for example by leaving aside cash if the process is efficient [9].

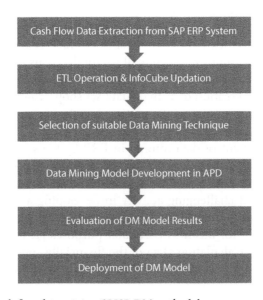

Figure 11.10 Cash flow data mining CRISP-DM methodology.

Two elevated level DM objectives are expectation and depiction. The first attempts to discover examples to anticipate the worth or conduct of some substance later on and the subsequent one attempts to discover designs portraying the qualities or conduct in a structure justifiable to people. These elevated level objectives are sought after through a few DM techniques, for instance, arrangement, relapse, bunching, summarisation, reliance displaying, and change, just as deviation identification [15]. The technique seems to have several computations that can be used to accomplish the goal, but a few calculations are best suited to certain challenging areas than others [20]. The ETL map is generated in the SAP BIW workstation with InfoCube Update shown below. This InfoCube is the DM Model

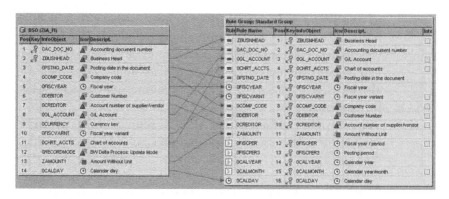

Figure 11.11 InfoCube loading in SAP BIW's ETL mapping.

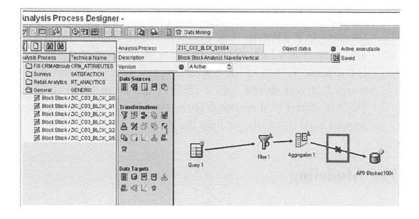

Figure 11.12 DM modeling & visualization of SAP ADP.

Data Hotspot to be developed later in the SAP Analysis Process Designer (APD) work table (see Figures 11.11 and 11.12).

APD is a worktable used to visualize, alter, and submit data from the Company Delivery Center [22, 24]. APD software supports KDD steps where we can integrate and monitor data locations for complex data mining requirements.

Modeling and implementation of mining data:

The specific steps concerning CRISP-DM are set out below.

a. Commercial knowledge

   Following discussions with the Financing Working Board, the data related to accounting, Receipt and Payment Power, G/L Transactions for each date of posting, and the comparison of amounts registered shall be selected. In contrast, it is preferred to construct a processing method to forecast that G/L is likely to reflect those vendors with similar abilities. From that kind of data, we can determine amounts that are supposed to be paid or credited by each vendor on each date of publishing. These data can also be used in the Services and Expenditure Sub-Capacity field.

b. Recognizing of data

   Voluntary Data generated in SAP ECC sources of data are managed in the SAP Business Distribution Center by highly trained data extraction [22]. The extraction process includes source data metadata and is designed to support the delta system, re-crysp-BIW with modified consistency. Quality management issues are resolved in the BIW worktable by limiting the relevant feature performance and the perceived attributes of the DM model.

c. Preparation of data

   Released Source Data reaches the PSA (Persistent Staging Area) level of SAP BIW. in this, developers can change any database and correct any bugs if any. The specificity level of the PSA level is the same as that of the source frameworks. After the data was purged, it was stored into a DSO (Data Store Object). Data in DSO is stored in a respond correctly which can also be used to mount SAP InfoCube or Info Provider.

11.12   Modeling

Bring up the proper Data Mining Model is a complex arrangement but should recognize the confidence and self for the preparation of the evaluation period. With SAP APD equipment, we can construct Mining Simulations using DM Algorithms such as—cluster analysis, Grouping, Association analysis, and multiple regression analysis. The descriptive material used in these DM measurements [10] and the reasons and behind the compilation of a particular measurement is provided below.

11.12.1   Association Rule Mining (ARM) or Association Analysis

It is a The Data Mining method that was designed to assess the relationship between individual circumstances. The purpose of the association review is to explore designs, primarily in the field of commercial steps, and to prepare acceptable guidelines, such as 'If a customer selects item A, the customer purchases items B and C also.' Association Analysis Models are used to differentiate between strategically targeting doors open for different objects. Most of the analysis centers around the standard items and the processing sub-problem, i.e., finding all the constant items, each occurring at more than a base recurrence (min. maintain) between all transactions. Notable successive calculations incorporate Apriori, Eclat, FP-development, and CLUB. For the Cash Flow Data examination, the ARM model isn't discovered reasonably, and henceforth the investigation results are not examined.

11.12.2   Classification Algorithms

Similar methods aim, only with the aid of certain approximation, to classify things into predetermined target audiences. The framework of the agreement model includes the preparation of data sets with known, separable objective classes, which means that the order results are continuously discreet [11]. Grouping targets vary from parallel to multi-class characteristics, and the models that attempt to predict the target class are correct with the aid of illustrative connexions from the data quality. Data grouping is a two-stage method in which the basic stage is the initiation phase in which the classifier measurement manufactures the classifier with the tuple preparation set, and the subsequent stage is the characterization stage in which the model is used for organization, and its execution is broken down by the tuple test set [12]. Option three is a Classification Scheme that generates a tree and a lot of rules, based on a model of different groups, from a given informative set [13]. Records that are open to the development of order techniques are usually partitioned into two different subsets—Training Set and Test Set. The former is used to evaluate the classifier, while the latter is used to calculate the accuracy of the classifier. Also, the precision of the classifier is regulated by the level of the test models that are successfully organized. Choice Tree The results of our evaluation are presented in the next region.

11.12.3   Regression Algorithms

The Projection model suggests the calculation of the statistical data area; this is the objective field in which the data record is based on the established predictions of other data fields with a similar nature. Established estimates of other required fields are termed input data fields or logical data fields. They can be either statistical or unmitigated. The predicted value is not likely to be distinct from any value found in the data used to produce the design [14]. A regression model is rendered and configured based on the informative sets of data records, the target field values of which are known. You may apply the planned model to recognized or unidentified data. The estimates of the knowledge fields are recognized in ambiguous data; however, the approximation of the objective field is not known [15]. A simple instance of cause similar, where the totality of measured mistakes is restricted.

$$w = \sum \frac{x_i y_i}{\sum x_i^2}$$

The most extreme probability model is out(x) = wx, which is utilized for the forecast.

11.12.4   Clustering Algorithms

Grouping in Data mining remains a revelation cycle That packages a large amount of data with the final aim of boosting the intracluster similarity and limiting the clustering resemblance. Unless there is no fixed class, bundling is used to collect items that seem to drop away naturally. For our investigation, bunching calculations are generally discovered appropriate to distinguish important groups for examination. Bunching calculations are mostly of three kinds in particular—Hierarchical, Partition based, and Density-based Methods [16]. The significant calculations under every one of these techniques are examined herein.

a) *Hierarchical Methods*: Such methodology bundles data elements into a group tree. This approach can be frequently alluded to as either amount of starch or obstructive, depending on whether different leveled destruction is arranged in a base-up (pairing) or top-down (splitting) layout [17]. This strategy examines all the clusters that have so far been available at each process of the combination; the clustering strategies that we have gradually analyzed work, for example, by event occurring [18]. At any point, the grouping frameworks a tree with events on the leaves and a root hub that corresponds to the whole database. And first highest, the tree consists of a single root. Occurrences are included on an individual basis, and the tree is updated appropriately at each point. Relevant measurements in the different graduated groupings are:

I.   *Agglomerative Clustering (Bottom-up):* It calculates the difference between the same two categories and handles every circumstance as a variety on its own, at which point it identifies the two closest classes, combines them, and proceeds to do this until only one community is left. Evidence of the convergence of the frameworks of the different graded particular construct—parallel primarily available [19]

II.   *Spider web Algorithm:* It generally thinks about the best host, including another leaf, consolidating the dual top has and parting the greatest host while thinking about wherever to put another case

b) *Partition-based Method:* The bunches are framed to advance a target apportioning basis, for example, a difference work dependent on separation, so the articles inside a group are "comparable," though the objects of various groups are "divergent" regarding the informational collection traits. Given D, an informational index of n articles, and k, the number of groups to frame, an apportioning calculation composes the items into k segments (k ≤n), where each segment speaks to a group [20]. Significant parcel grouping calculations are K-Means and EM (Expectation-Maximization)

c) *Density-based Methods:* This finds bunches with subjective shapes and commonly see groups as thick districts of articles in the Data space that are isolated by areas of a low thickness (speaking to clamor) [21, 22]. DBSCAN develops groups as indicated by a thickness-based network investigation. OPTICS stretches out DBSCAN to create a bunch requesting got from a wide scope of boundary settings. DENCLUE bunches objects are dependent on a lot of thickness dispersion capacities

11.13   Assessment

Only for evaluation of group, instance-based models, designers provide component data input for the planning and research process. The separating norm is that 66% of the information is used to plan and the remainder to test the effects of the model. The bunch model has formed ten groups and used to obtain yield visualization quantization time. Various What-If scenarios were run on these models; the accuracy is discovered to be within the desired range. The required quality characteristics are accepted against known outcomes, and as needs are the option of the model Data boundary as many leaf hubs, stooping standards are balanced to achieve the desired accuracy of the model. Care should be taken to refrain from over-fitting data with the intention that perhaps the design can require variations in data input [24].

11.14   Distribution

The consequences of SAP Data Mining replicas can be gotten to by all the worried in the subsequent manners. Model outcomes can be composed on to a level record and distributed on big business entryways of SAP, for example, at individuals combination layer

ii. Model outcomes are graphically imagined, and wanted outcome outlines are communicated to all partners

iii. Model outcomes in text structure are taken care of go into Enterprise Reports for dynamic at all levels.

11.15   Results and Discussion

The Decision Tree is a classification method that uses the approximation of data variables to predict the assessment of a specific factor. In the SAP Decision Tree Model, we have defined the G/L Accounts as an expected factor [25]. The area DT Pred Val002 in Table V refers to the estimate expected by the DM Model for the G/L Account. Field DT Pred Node002 is the core value in the decision tree, and Field DT Pred Prob002 is the probability of predicting accuracy. Certainly, the 1.0 probability estimate provides a clear accuracy of the predicted outcome, but the findings are exceptionally reliable with such a probability estimate of 0.2, 0.48, 0.78, and so on, as shown in Table 11.1 below.

Table 11.1 Shows cash flow statement source field in SAP System.

Field	Description	SAP data type	Length	Default value
BUKRS	Company code	Char	4	1000
SAKNR	G/L Account	Char	10	No Default Value
BUDAT	Posting Date	Dats	8	No Default Value
BIZ_HEAD	Business Head	Char	10	OPER
WRBTR	Amount in LC	Curr	13	No Default Value
BELNR	Document Number	Char	10	No Default Value
GJAHR	Fiscal Year	Nume	4	2012
LIFNR	Vendor	Char	10	No Default Value
KUNNR	Customer	Char	10	No Default Value
WAERS	Currency	Cuky	5	INR

The boundary used for the Cluster model is—Binning Interval—10; Reference Factor Weight—1.0. In Table 11.2 and Figure 11.13 below, field CL Pred Cluster002 speaks to the expected input data community. Again from Generalized Impact Map in Figure 11.14, Cluster No 6 has a specific number of items and can be used for mysterious data estimations.

For Regression Model, field SC_Score002 represents the predicted score for attribute *amount.*

11.16   Conclusion

In this examination, the CRISP-DM calculation and steps were explored; later, the Data related phases of the CRISP-DM use in a task (Data checking and assessment) were analyzed and clarified by utilizing a model application. In this cycle, the ERP frameworks situated in CRISP-DM

Table 11.2 Shows key figures, dimensions, and characteristics of infocube.

Dimension	Characteristics	Technical name	Data type	Length
Business Head (ZFI_CASH1)	Business Head	ZBUSNHEAD	Char	10
	Accounting Document No	0AC_DOC_NO	Char	10
	Company Code	0COMP_CODE	Char	04
GL Account (ZFI_CASH2)	G/L Account	0GL_ACCOUNT	Char	10
	Chart of Accounts	0CHRT_ACCTS	Char	04
	Posting date in the Document	0PSTING_DATE	Dats	08
Customer (ZFI_CASH3)	Customer Number	0DEBITOR	Char	10
	Account Number of Vendor	0CREDITOR	Char	10
Key Figure	Amount Without Unit	ZAMOUNT1	Char	09

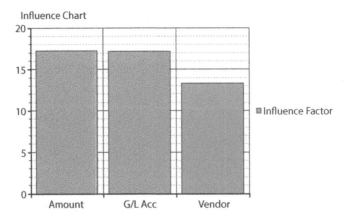

Figure 11.13 Shows overall influence chart of relative dominance in clustering model.

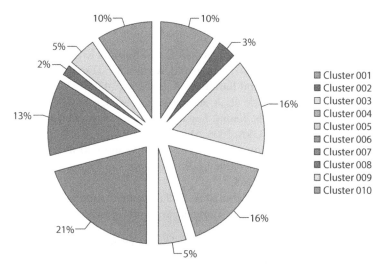

Figure 11.14 Overall influence chart of clustering model.

calculation for Data Mining are broken down and prepared and demonstrated that the ERP framework has restricted abilities concerning research that really can resolve core business concerns, Mutual Knowledge, and Actionable Awareness to respond quickly to advertising requests with appropriate choices at each stage. Company analysts highly rely on analysis and answers to provide them with the Data they need to come to a firm conclusion on income and misfortunes, products and advantages, budgetary execution and business drifts, etc. Individuals should have a far-reaching discussion and disclosure capability that can tap Data from massive amounts of Item advancement, and here CRISP-DM provides an operation that can be obtained to assist these needs. Through Data Mining Techniques, ERP Systems will facilitate the examination of a large amount of data from all sides to assess the existing business situation, to analyze the complexities, and to predict involved in critical consequences of further progress, through certainty if the analysis is carried out. The aftereffect of a Data Mining venture under the CRSIP-DM teaching method isn't simply Designs yet furthermore findings that are considerable in achieving the objectives of the company or that are considerable in giving rise to new inquiries, lines of approach, or effects. There will be various directions for future work and discovery, such as delineating more issue districts in ERP frameworks and illustrative properties with CRSIP-DM by investigating more informational indexes. Along these lines, it is expected that make mindfulness about CRISP-DM, and the effect of this cycle on ventures is required to be perceived.

References

1. Marbán, O., Mariscal, G., Segovia, J., A Data Mining & Knowledge Discovery Process Model, in: *Data Mining and Knowledge Discovery in Real Life Applications*, Ponce, J. and Karahoca, A. (Eds.), pp. 438–453, February 2009.
2. Kurgan, L. and Musilek, P., A survey of Knowledge Discovery and Data Mining process models. *Knowl. Eng Rev.*, 21, 1, 1–24, Cambridge University Press, New York, NY, USA, 2006, March 2006.
3. Azevedo, A. and Santos, M.F., KDD, SEMMA, and CRISP-DM: A parallel overview, in: *Proceedings of the IADIS European Conference on Data Mining 2008*, pp. pp 182–185, 2008.
4. Sastry, S.H. and Prasada Babu, M.S., ERP implementation for Manufacturing Enterprises. *Int. J. Adv. Res. Comput. Sci. Software Eng. (IJARCSSE)*, 3, 4, 18–24, April 2013.
5. Chapman, P., Clinton, J., Kerber, R. *et al.*, *The CRISP-DM User Guide*, 1999. https://s2.smu.edu/~mhd/8331f03/crisp.pdf
6. Chapman, P., Clinton, J., Kerber, R., Khabaza, T., Reinartz, T., Shearer, C., Wirth, R., CRISP-DM 1.0 Step-by-step data mining guide, CRISP-DM consortium: NCR Systems Engineering Copenhagen, USA and Denmark, DaimlerChrysler AG, Germany, SPSS Inc., USA and OHRA Verzekeringen en Bank Groep B.V, The Netherlands, 2000. https://www.kde.cs.uni-kassel.de/wp-content/uploads/lehre/ws2012-13/kdd/files/CRISPWP-0800.pdf
7. Sastry, S.H. and Prasada Babu, M.S., Cluster Analysis of Material Stock Data of Enterprises. *Int. J. Comput. Inf. Syst. (IJCIS)*, 6, 6, 8–19, June 2013.
8. Kamber, H.M., *Introduction to Data Mining*, pp. 429–462, Morgan Kaufman Publishers: an imprint of Elsevier, Waltham, MA, USA, 2006.
9. Rokach, L. and Maimon, O., *Data Mining and Knowledge Discovery Handbook*, pp. 322–350, Springer, USA, 2010.
10. Sastry, S.H. and Prasada Babu, M.S., Performance evaluation of clustering Algorithms. *Int. J. Comput. Sci. Inf. Technol.*, 1, 4, 95–109, 2013.
11. Tan, P.-N., Steinbach, M., Kumar, V., *Introduction to Data Mining*, pp. 330–340, Pearson Addison-Wesley, March 2006. https://www-users.cse.umn.edu/~kumar001/dmbook/index.php
12. Hand, D., Mannila, H., Smyth, P., *Principles of Data Mining*, pp. 292–305, Prentice Hall of India, 2001.
13. Sastry, S.H. and Prasada Babu, M.S., Analysis of Enterprise Material Procurement Leadtime using Techniques of Data Mining. *Int. J. Adv. Res. Comput. Sci. (IJARCS)*, 4, 4, 288–301, April 2013.
14. Sahu, A.K., Sharma, S., Tanveer, M., Internet of Things attack detection using hybrid Deep Learning Model. *Comput. Commun.*, 176, 146–154, 2021. https://doi.org/10.1016/j.comcom.2021.05.024.
15. Dunham, M.H., *Data Mining: Introductory and Advanced Topics*, pp. 135–162, Prentice Hall of India, 2003. http://index-of.co.uk/Data-Mining/Dunham%20-%20Data%20Mining.pdf

16. Shmueli, G., Patel, N.R., Bruce, P.C., *Data Mining for Business Intelligence*, pp. 220–237, John Wiley & Sons, 2007. https://onlinelibrary.wiley.com/doi/abs/10.1111/j.1751-5823.2007.00015_9.x

17. Pyle, D., *Data Preparation for Data Mining*, pp. 100–132, Morgan Kaufmann Publishers, San Francisco, USA, 1999.

18. Boudaillier, E., Interactive Interpretation of Hierarchical Clustering. *Principles of Data Mining and Knowledge Discovery: Proceedings of First European Symposium, PKDD'97*, Trondheim, Norway, June 24–27, 1997, pp. 280–288.

19. Ester, M., Kriegel, H.-P., Sander, J., Xiaowei, X., A Density-Based Algorithm for Discovering Clusters in Large Spatial Databases with Noise, in: *Proc. of 2nd International Conference on Knowledge Discovery and Data Mining (KDD '96)*, AAAI Press, 1996.

20. Fayyad, U., Piatetsky-Shapiro, G., Smyth, P., From Data Mining to Knowledge Discovery in Databases. *AI Mag.*, 17, 37–54, 1996b.

21. Kurgan, L.A. and Musilek, P., A survey of Knowledge Discovery and Data Mining process models. *Knowl. Eng. Rev.*, 21, 1, 1–24, 2006.

22. Sastry, S.H. and Prasada Babu, M.S., Implementing a successful Business Intelligence framework for Enterprises. *J. Global Res. Comput. Sci. (JGRCS)*, 4, 3, 55–59, April 2013.

23. Jain, S., Mahmood, Md. R., Raja, R., Laxmi, K.R., Gupta, A., Multi-Label Classification for Images with Labels for Image Annotation. *SAMRIDDHI: A Journal of Physical Sciences, Engineering and Technology*, 12, Special Issue (3), 183–188, 2020.

24. Grabmeier, J. and Rudolph, A., Data Mining and Knowledge Discovery, in: *Techniques of Clustering Algorithms in Data Mining*, vol. 6, pp. 303–360, Springer, 1996. https://link.springer.com/article/10.1023/A%3A1016308404627

25. Shtub, A., *Enterprise Resource Planning (ERP): The dynamics of operations management*, Kluwer Academic, Boston, 2002.

12

Human–Machine Interaction and Visual Data Mining

Upasana Sinha[1]*, Akanksha Gupta[2]†, Samera Khan[3]‡, Shilpa Rani[4]§
and Swati Jain[5]

[1]J.K. Institute of Engineering, Bilaspur, India
[2]IT Department, GGV Central University, Bilaspur, India
[3]Amity University Chhattisgarh, Raipur, India
[4]CSE Department, NGIT, Hyderabad, India
[5]Govt. J.Y. Chhattisgarh College, Raipur, India

Abstract

Human-Computer Interaction (HCI) brings about colossal measures of information-bearing possibilities for understanding a human client's aims, objectives, and wants. Realizing what clients need and need is a key to shrewd framework help. The hypothesis of psyche idea known from concentrates in creature conduct is embraced and adjusted for an expressive client displaying. Speculations of the brain are theoretical client models speaking to, somewhat, a human client's musings. A hypothesis of the spirit may even uncover unsaid information. Along these lines, client displaying becomes information disclosure going past the human's information and covering explicit space experiences. Speculations of the psyche are incited by mining HCI information. Information mining ends up being an inductive demonstrating. Insightful collaborator frameworks are inductively demonstrating a human client's aims, objectives, and so forth, just as space information is, essentially, learning frameworks. To adapt to the danger of failing to understand the situation, learning frameworks are furnished with the expertise of reflection.

Here we proposed Gesture recognition; Gesture recognition is a developing theme in the present advancements. The fundamental focal point of this is

*Corresponding author: upasana.sihna@gmail.com
†Corresponding author: akanksha.me2011@gmail.com
‡Corresponding author: skhan@rpr.amity.edu
§Corresponding author: shilpachoudhary1987@gmail.com

Rohit Raja, Kapil Kumar Nagwanshi, Sandeep Kumar and K. Ramya Laxmi (eds.) Data Mining and Machine Learning Applications, (317–348) © 2022 Scrivener Publishing LLC

to perceive the human motions utilizing numerical calculations for Human-Computer cooperation. Just a couple of methods of Human-Computer Interaction exist, are: through the console, mouse, contact screens, and so on.

Every one of these gadgets has its restrictions with regards to adjusting more flexible equipment in computers. Motion recognition is one of the basic methods to fabricate easily to use interfaces. Typically motions can be started from any substantial movement or state; however, they normally begin from the face or hand. Signal recognition empowers clients to interface with the gadgets without truly contacting them. This Chapter depicts how hand signals are prepared to play out specific activities like exchanging pages, looking up or down on a page.

Keywords: Human–Computer Interaction, HCI, visual data mining, data mining, data visualization

12.1   Introduction

Human–Computer Interaction (HCI) is situated at the intersection of a variety of functional areas, comprising human brainpower, image recognition, facial recognition, follow-up activity, and so forth.

Of late, there has already been an increasing passion for enhancing many forms of communication between humans and computers. This is believed that to truly achieve effective human–computers shrewd cooperation (HCII), there is a necessity for computer to have the option of communicating properly with the user, such as how human–human communication takes place.

Systems interact with each other, ultimately via discussion, but also through body movement, to underscore a particular feature of debate and discussion and to display emotions. Mostly as an effect, the latest interface developments are progressively moving towards mandatory exchange in data through normal, observable methods of sight, sound, and touch. In a near and personal company, people use these forms of communication all the time and in combination, using one to complement and enhance others. To a large degree, the exchanged data is reflected in this distinctive, integrative architecture. Frequently, interactional collaboration has a focal mass in human interaction, with vision, look, specificity, and automatic signals that frequently contribute significantly, quite as much time adorning characteristics, such as emotion, disposition, attitude, and awareness. However it may be, the sections of the multiple methods and their interaction continue to be calculated and logically interpreted. What is needed is a study of human–computer correspondence that sets up a multi-modal "dialect" and "debate and discussion" scheme, just like the framework that we have established for spoken exchange.

A further important perspective is the development of human-centered information security. The most critical problem here is the way to achieve cohesion between man and machine. The word "Human-Centered" is used to illustrate how, while all available data systems have been designed for human clients, a significant number of them are a long way from possible to understand. What could the logical/design system be doing to make an advancement influence?

Data frameworks are pervasive in all human undertakings, including logical, clinical, military, transportation, and customer. Singular clients use them for picking up, looking for data (counting information mining), doing investigate (counting visual registering), and composing. Different clients (gatherings of clients and gatherings of clients) use them for correspondence and coordinated effort. Furthermore, either single or various ous clients use them for amusement. A data framework comprises of two parts:

Computer (information/information base and data are preparing motor), and people. It is the canny connection between the two that we are tending to. We plan to recognize the significant exploration issues and to discover conceivably productive future examination headings. Moreover, we will talk about how a domain can be made which helps complete such examination.

In numerous significant HCI applications, for example, computer helped to mentor and in learning; it is exceptionally attractive (even obligatory) that the reaction of the computer consider the passionate or intellectual condition of the human client. Feelings are shown via graphic, spoken, and other functional methods. There remains an emergent measure of proof demonstrating the enthusiastic aptitudes stay important for what is designated "knowledge" [1, 2]. Computers today can perceive a lot of what is stated, and somewhat, who said it. Yet, they are totally in obscurity with regards to how things are stated, the full of a feeling channel of data. This is genuine in the discourse, yet also in visual interchanges, notwithstanding the way that outward appearances, stance, and signal impart the absolute most basic data: how individuals feel. Full of feeling correspondence unequivocally think about how feelings can be perceived and communicated during Human–Computer cooperation. Figure 12.1 represents the CRISP and KDD process Flowchart.

Only as norm currently, in the condition that users participate in human-human collaboration and replace one of the humans with a Machine, psychological interaction fails at that stage. Besides, it isn't because individuals quit conveying influence—surely we have all observed

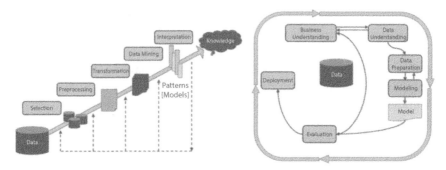

Figure 12.1 Shows the CRISP and KDD process flowchart.

an individual communicating outrage at his machine. The issue emerges because the computer cannot perceive if the human is satisfied, irritated, intrigued, or exhausted. Consider so if this information were ignored by a user and began ranting long once we had winced, we wouldn't recognize that person to be particularly focused. Acknowledgment of emotion is a central aspect of awareness. Operating systems have a clear effect diminished.

Besides, if you embed a computer (as a channel of correspondence) between at least two people, at that point, the emotional transmission capacity might be incredibly diminished. Email might be the most as often as possible utilized method for electronic correspondence, yet regularly the entirety of the enthusiastic data is lost when our considerations are changed over to the Computerized media.

Exploration is accordingly required for better approaches to convey influence through computer intervened situations. Computer interceded correspondence today quite often has less emotional transfer speed than "being there, vis-à-vis". The approach of full of feeling wearable computers, which could help enhance emotional data as seen from the physical condition of the organism, is indeed one ability to alter the concept of interaction.

12.2   Related Researches

The papers in the processes contain specific sections of the advances that support the human–computer interaction. The number of developers is sight researchers of machine that research is associated with a human–computer relation.

The report of Warwick and Gasson [3] describes the suitability of the instant connection between the human cognitive modality and the Machine organization. The developers evaluate the recent circumstance with neuronal assembles and discuss the possible implications of certain embedded technology as a widely useful human-computer interface for what is about to follow.

Human–robot collaboration (HRI) is already extended as of late. Peer-ruling, flexible devices can interpret and obey a user, understand his voice command, and perform an action to support him. A major thing that makes HRI distinctive from the normal HCI is that machines can not only passively bring data out of their situation but can also make good choices and efficiently alter their design. Huang and Weng [4] have implemented an interesting approach in this context. Their paper provides a compelling structure for HRI that incorporates interest and promotes learning. The machine creates a convincing structure via its interactions with the environment and instructors.

Paquin and Cohen also implemented a vision-based gestural guidance design for flexible, interactive levels [5]. The framework regulates the robot's relative motion by using a variety of predetermined static analysis and dynamic handing gestures that are guided by the marshaling code. Images taken by an onboard camera are equipped to obey the hand and the head of the operator. Nickel and Stiefelhagen have adopted a qualitative approach [6]. Given the images provided by the modified audio system image, the highlighting and variance information are integrated into the multi-theories supporting the design to explore the 3D positions of the distinct body parts. Given the movements of the hands, an HMM-based methodology is adopted for the interpretation of object indications.

Mixed Reality (MR) introduces a wide framework for the Human-Computer Association. It is feasible, by computer vision techniques, to render advanced input devices. This device is presented by Tosas and Li [7]. They depict a virtual qwerty keyboard application that reflects the thinking of the virtual user interface. Image follow-up and comprehension of the client's hand and wrist activity allows the recognition of keystrokes on the virtual touch screen. An application customized to render a proposal for a realistic MR workspace is implemented [8]. An expanded human reality graphic organizer for the position of objects is implemented [9]. A 3D pointing interface capable of performing 3D recognition of a bearing pointing arm is proposed [10]. Also, Licsar and Sziranyi are suggesting a system for the identification of hand gestures [11].

A hand-in-hand evaluation methodology is investigated [12]. They present an investigation of the classification plan for use in a more general approach to the different leveled image recognition. The new down-measuring of computers and tactile devices allows people to wear such devices like clothes. A few of the main fields of wearable finding analysis is smartly supporting people regularly. Authors in [13] suggest a body-connected system to collect visual and audio data relevant to the quality of service. This material provides function efficiently for the recording/examination of human activities and can be used in a wide variety of applications, such as computerized journals or organization inquiries. Some other interactive system has been developed [14].

The 3D head in a visual progression was viewed as necessary for intense outer appearance/emotion analysis, facial recognition, and model-based coding. The paper by Dornaika and Ahlberg [15] introduces a system for continuous head and facial movements using deformable 3D models. A comparative framework has been developed [16]. They are likely to use their ongoing global positioning system to view valid external appearances. Lee and Kim are suggesting a pose invariant approach to face recognition [17]. A 3D head-to-head assessment approach is proposed [18]. They introduce another strategy for the finding of the existing head using the projective invariance of the evaporating point. Du and Lin present a multi-see face image configuration using a factorization model [19]. The performance of the proposed method can be extended to a few HCI regions, such as free face recognition or face movement in a simple difference.

The creation of an interpretation of information would be another trend in the human–computer association. The state of the surrounding knowledge is sensitive to the involvement of individuals and responsive to their needs. Nature will be prepared to welcome us back home, to make a decision about our state of mind, and to change our condition to represent it. Such a realm is still a vision, but it is one that evokes an emotional reaction in the minds of researchers across the globe and is the focus of a few major industrial activities. One such operation is implemented [20]. They utilize discourse recognition and computer vision to demonstrate the modern age of applications in a private situation. A significant part of such a system is the localization module. The prospective use of this system is suggested by Okatani and Takuichi [21]. Another critical feature of the relevant, wise system is the analysis of the typical tasks carried out by the customer. Ma and Lin respond to this question [22].

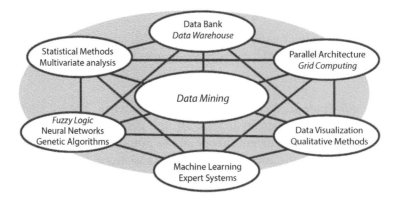

Figure 12.2 Shows data mining process.

12.2.1 Data Mining

Information Mining is characterized as the way toward working with information; it is a cycle that makes information helpful and mines data from it to arrive at intelligent, strong resolutions utilizing different techniques as indicated below. Data for the framework that can be taken from the Swedish disease register can be utilized for the pilot study. Data mining processes is shown in Figure 12.2.

12.2.2 Data Visualization

Information perceptions make it simpler for the individual to comprehend what the investigation of the information has derived. Under the area of discernment, the term representation is alluded to as the development of visual picture in the psyche targeting shaping a psychological model of the information that is being examined. Elementary representations incorporate pixel-based representations, chart-based perception, and mathematical-based perceptions. In this framework separated from these worldly perceptions, volumetric picture perception is a kind of information representation that is likewise utilized. For the representation of transient information, there are numerous procedures, for example, divider charts, plain portrayal, star portrayal, winding portrayal, concentric circles method, lifesaver strategy, etc. Temporal portrayals are done at each phase of the information-digging measure so that for future reference, they are available. In the situation of Volumetric Image Viewing strategies, we have a couple of standard methods, for example, multiplanar reconstruction (MPR), surface delivery (SR), and volume delivery (VR).

12.2.3   Visual Learning

In this part, we depict various parts of the visual structure that permit us to screen and steer the ML calculation. Figure 12.3 represents the Visual Analytics Flowchart.

a) *Affirmation inclination:* Cognitive science shows that there is a propensity to look for new data in a manner that confirms the current theory and to nonsensically maintain a strategic distance from data and translations, which repudiate earlier convictions [23].

b) *No free lunch:* From the hypothesis, we realize that there is no generally acceptable inquiry/learning configuration (English *et al.*, 2000). Transforming one boundary may improve the exhibition for certain issues; however, it normally lessens it for other people. Human information is needed to indicate great boundaries and to control the AI calculation in the privileged direction. For the model, the choice can be locally ideal, yet the client comprehends that incapacitating pieces of the speculation port end well by the by.

c) *Qualities and shortcomings:* The most significant quality of the human client is his capacity to comprehend the current issue. In this way, he can frequently choose when to perform coordinated inquiry (enhancement) and how to restrict the hunt space. Besides, given the perception, he is regularly ready to separate data from boisterous or fragmented

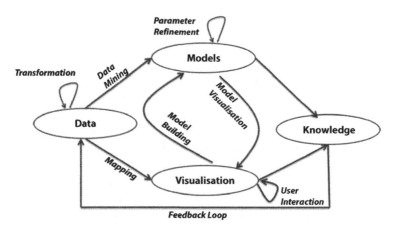

Figure 12.3 Shows visual analytics flowchart.

information. The client can offer importance to the high-lights recognized in the data. The machine then again has numerous capacities the client lacks: its work is reasonable, quick, and vigorous. It can perform enormous hunts, and we realize that heuristic pursuit calculations can perform very well in huge and unstructured inquiry spaces [24].

d) *No Labels:* Flow highlights can be fluffy for different reasons. Regularly, their limits are not sharp. Bigger highlights (for example, vortices)are made out of littler structures that can highlight themselves. When investigating recreation information, it isn't pre-figured out which information ranges are significant. Simply after the architect has increased comprehension of the circumstance, we acquire names for the information (e.g., 'excessively hot').

e) *Client Requirements:* The three focal prerequisites are control, strength, and understandability. Control empowers the designer to define what he thinks about intriguing and to guide the AI cycle the correct way. Strength is the heartlessness toward little blunders or deviations from suspicions. The third necessity is understandability. This implies a direct perception of results and their literary portrayal to encourage revealing.

12.3   Visual Genes

We call the littlest thing, which conveys data a quality. In the current setting, we consider a solitary one-dimensional fluffy choice a quality. That is a tuple of the structure (fuzzyin, fullmin, fullmax, fuzzymax, ai), where the first four qualities define a fluffy choice and ai the pertinent trait. Point-by-point data about determinations is obvious in little dissipate plot symbols. These symbols go about as switch catches to permit the deactivation of all determinations in a single property sees. For more specific connections, the client can amplify these dissipate plots to alter, move, include, or eliminate choices. In the first steps of information investigation, one of the most significant undertakings is to find the information ascribes which apply to the current issue. In contrast, if an immense set of instances are available, algorithm calculations could develop more easily when only substantial attributes are considered. Subsequently, we expand the UI by a basic shading-based sign portraying which credits are normal in the genetic supply. For each quality, we process recurrence esteem and coordinate this data as the foundation shading into the presentation of theories. For instance, the significant ascribes a0and a1 are incessant in the genetic supply and get hazier shading than the others.

12.4   Visual Hypotheses

Speculation is a fluffy rationale mix of choices. Every theory is pictured as an even edge of intuitive quality perspectives. Disjunctively joined perspectives (statements) are put one next to the other without isolating space. Conditions themselves are set in discrete edges. A combination of conditions shapes speculation. The client speculation is demonstrated by a little symbol on the left and further featured by an alternate foundation shading. Along these lines, the theories in a populace can be seen and thought about. To determine novel qualities, determinations from connected perspectives can be moved to the client theory. To analyze the contextual characteristics of a material hypothesis, the user should demonstrate a corresponding fuzzy option in the related 3D delivery, where fuzzy participation values can be integrated into the transfer work, e.g. as scheduling of the degree of the option of murkiness or highlighting.

12.5   Visual Strength and Conditioning

The goal is to find hypotheses that contribute to outlines that are relative in real objects and versatile in the selection of resources. These ideas should be as simple as it could be predicted. Throughout this way, we need initiatives that promote consistency, multi-layered existence, and differentiation to define the fitness of analysis. Constructing the amounts of these factors provides an overview of what to look for at the intensity training phase. Higher motivation attributes can lead to an elevated performance in one or more of the three segments, including proximity, human consciousness, and uncertainty. As these are important results, these three elements occur as modified shades of green in the fitness counter to one side of each prediction. For example, the advancement in fitness somewhere between the context of (2) and (3) is due to lower complexities (most limited modest green bar), while the differentiation between the range of (3) and (4) is due to better matching between the high points [26].

12.6   Visual Optimization

A vital shortcoming of streamlining calculations which do not have the help from foundation information is the way that they frequently can't segregate among nearby and worldwide optima. Accordingly, they are inclined to stall out at neighborhood optima, where the fitness of a theory is moderately high yet a long way from a worldwide ideal. The inquiry of whether a nearby ideal is significant or not in the current setting can't be replied to by the machine. Then again, regardless of whether including the nearby neighborhood just, a broad inquiry regularly can't be performed by the human client. Thus, we add an advance catch to every proviso with the end goal that the client can choose when and where to look. We have actualized a straightforward hillclimbing administrator who plays out a sloping climb towards the nearby ideal: The operator passes each restriction part of each option and sets the fitness for all shifts. Of all possible changes, it's the one with the highest enhancement that is recognized. This would be done for decreasing progress dimensions again until the greatest point drops below the defined edge of the user. Consider, for example, a one-dimensional, highly nonlinear decision S = (smin, smax) contained in theory. For a given advance δs, the fitness of the theory changes when Sis replaced by S1 = (smin − δs, smax), S2 = (smin +δs, smax), S3 = (smin, smax − δs) or S4 = (smin, smax +δs).

12.7   The Vis 09 Model

This model depends on a manufactured informational collection containing a well discernable component ('Vis09') which is identified with different ascribes in the information. Over a 3D space, we define ten scalars ascribes. Voxels outside the element have characteristic irregular qualities in the [25, 27] interval. The information esteems inside the element are picked with the end goal that the element is describable by two distinct theories. The first theory includes a choice on ascribes a0 and a1. The subsequent theory is defined among credits a2, a3, a4, a5, a6 and a7, which must be joined in a specific way. The 'Vis' portion of the element can be chosen by brushing the a2 vs. a3 scatterplot related to a6 vs. a7. The '09' section can be chosen by brushing the a4 vs. a5 scatterplot related to a6 vs. a7. Neither a2 versus a3 nor a6 versus a7 alone outcome in helpful speculation. In this manner, the 'Vis09' highlight is of the structure ((a2∧a3)∨(a4∧a5)) ∧(a6∧a7). Such a component is practically difficult to find for the human client, even though it is still fairly basic from the perspective of the machine. The engineered informational collection contains a third component defined in ascribes a8, a9 which is effortlessly found and chosen intelligently. It has been master-minded to contain the area of the 'Vis09' highlight. The client has figured out that ascribes a8 and a9 might depict a component of intrigue. This is typically where one characteristic generally portrays what a designer is searching for (for example, low weight is generally identified with vorti-ces). The subsequent component isn't exceptionally sharp, however.

12.8   Graphic Monitoring and Contact With Human–Computer

A key fundamental of the visual examination approach is the recognition that mechanical arrangements are inadequate to manage the complexi-ties of data and the requirement for novel arrangements. Human exam-iners must use data innovation to accomplish knowledge and imaginative answers for new and advancing issues described by gigantic and complex information. In characterizing visual examination as a study of diagnostic thinking encouraged by intuitive representation innovations, the origina-tors of visual investigation set equivalent accentuation on propelling our comprehension of human psychological cycles and on the plan, usage, and assessment of models and calculations for handling (e.g., AI), showing and connecting with data.

From this point of view, visual examination and HCI share a lot of shared opinions. Both accept the Human–Computer framework as an important unit of examination as they try to comprehend the unpredict-ability and assorted variety of clients' capacities and exercises in innovative settings. On account of visual investigation, the center is all the more tuned to human perceptual, psychological, and synergistic capacities as they identify with the dynamic, intuitive visual portrayals of data with regards to scientific methodologies and techniques in the objective space. Visual investigation places specific accentuation on intellectual undertakings, and explicitly errands that are poorly characterized, e.g., "Toto distinguish the normal and find the unforeseen" [28]. The accentuation on complex cog-nizance, theory development, and assessment in outwardly rich settings requires visual examination scientists to coordinate their methodology and techniques with advancing speculations of psychological mastery, innova-tiveness, design recognition, and visual thinking from intellectual science.

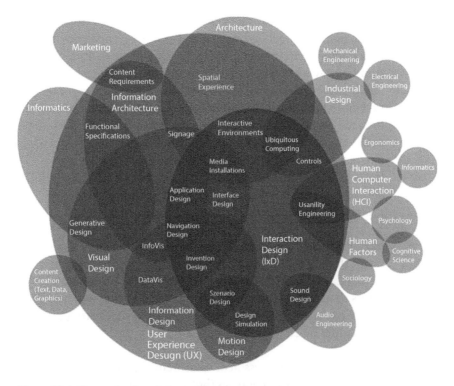

Figure 12.4 Shows visual analytics and human–interaction.

In making the change to visual investigation work, customary HCI strategies, for example, convention examination, intellectual errand investigation, and action hypothesis must be adjusted to reveal insight into the utilization of complex visual presentations in scientific cycles. The study of visual examination is uncommon in that it was made in discourse with a specific way to deal with tackling complex issues, the utilization of intuitive and in some cases Mixed activity Human–Computer representation situations. This exchange among science and application makes limitations just as open doors for both. For understanding and propelling human collaboration with representation frameworks, difficulties to HCI may be shown in [29] Figure 12.4:

a) *Graphical legitimacy.* Analysts must address complex perceptual conditions and errands. This necessity takes out by far most of the current research center examinations in recognition and comprehension.

b) *Frameworks are thinking.* Exploration groups must expand the sociology model of the portrayal of human capacities in characteristic circumstances to seeing how human/innovation frameworks will play out their undertakings.

c) *Situational requirements.* Specialists must expand their comprehension of human execution in novel circumstances, under time tension, and so forth. to empower "satisficing" execution of the human administrator under those conditions.

d) *Singular contrasts.* Exploration must address execution contrasts inside a populace of clients, e.g., social contrasts, levels, and sorts of ability (particularly the remarkable attributes of profoundly talented people, "Thinking styles", and so on.).

e) *Solid forecast.* A study of cooperation must move past interface-plan rules to give explicit expectations of execution. Although evaluative concept analysis has its position, numerical and computational models, the autonomous limits of which can be modified and tested for the user and the usage environment, provide more analytical strength and should be emphasized.

Observationally approved assessment measurements could assist with figuring out what impacts singular contrasts (both intrinsic and obtained through involvement in intuitive perception) in perceptual and intellectual capacities may have on the capacity to pick up understanding through connection with the various visual portrayal of data. Throughout the analysis for all these predictive models, our investigation in the Personal Equation of Interaction (PEI) takes a closer look at potential measures of conceptual performance, including Trevarthan's Two Visual Systems Hypothesis from Intellectual Neuroscience; Pylyshyn's FINST Hypothesis of Spatial Consideration; and normally known quantitative figures, such as Rotter's Locus of Control.

Similar research in research examines the social and organizational usage of automatic awareness structures. This approach is defined by the HCI Convention on Subjective Research on social psychological concepts and methods to Resolve Human–Mechanical Frameworks. Usually consider a "couple-examination" method, with a professional visual investigation device client (a supposed "VA Expert" or VAE) operating with a theme master to conduct a practical arrangement using real facts. Our pair-examination work looks at the airplane security investigation with the Boeing Company. As a team with these examiners, we recognized a few investigative issues to test the productivity of systematic visual devices. Our technique depended on utilizing our systematic visual specialists, who worked together intimately with Boeing wellbeing investigators to tackle a certifiable issue. This nearby cooperation dodged one of the impediments for innovative progress, in particular, the expenses in time and exertion for a specialist wellbeing examiner to gain proficiency with another product application and another way to deal with imagining and collaborating with security information. Video of diagnostic cooperation could then be examined utilizing Grounded Theory and Joint Activity Theory draws near.

Of equivalent significance for visual examination are the social and authoritative parts of innovation recognition. Our work with genuine perception applications exhibits scientific fitness is regularly conveyed across hierarchical, social, and social settings. Mechanical help for these cycles must be adjusted to their disseminated nature. The focal point of consideration here extends from the human–mechanical frameworks accentuation of pair investigation to socio-specialized frameworks that incorporate a further examination of social and social collaborations. A few difficulties, some of them notable to HCI professionals, are to be tended to here; among them: protection from mechanical advancements, psychological inclinations strengthened by social structures, and the impact of social contrasts on an understanding of visual portrayals.

Mechanical progress systems to bring visual examination into associations and decrease opposition must be additionally improved. What seems to work best is to initially comprehend hierarchical culture and objectives, at that point assemble client commitment in the creating and testing of models, trailed by the engaged utilization of existing and model visual examination apparatuses and methods to important expository issues and practical informational indexes. Recognizing lead trend-setters in the association whose systematic inquiries are not at present being tended to by accessible advances can create research partners and backers for hierarchical contribution. This has been the procedure of utilization situated visual examination designers, for example, those in the Charlotte Visualization Center at the University of North Carolina. Its WireVis application centers around helping master wire-extortion investigators distinguish designs in wire-move information that may show misrepresentation. In the improvement of these interfaces, visual investigation researchers work intimately with both master experts and innovation designers to address important issues with real clients and genuine information.

As we have seen, the visual investigation has aspiring objectives: to help complex individual expository discernment and social and social conveyed comprehension with balanced and one-to-numerous HCI, and to help these complex intellectual cycles under the strain of time, overpowering information, and restricted assets. Inquest for these objectives, psychological science specialists, analyze individual intellectual and perceptual processes and the intuitive visual pictures that encourage them, and cooperation and representation architects make collective interfaces that take into consideration simpler sharing and investigation of data between contributing gatherings. Computational visual examination analysts create numerical and computational devices for Mixed activity frameworks, in which the computer can start certain undertakings or cycles in the quest for an objective or produced theories. Establishing the whole cycle is progressing client tests and client contribution being developed cycles.

If fruitful, the innovation of visual investigation will test and approve the logical discoveries. On the off chance that the frameworks it makes can show quality improvement of psychological handling that can be offered as a powerful influence for certifiable issues, we can affirm the estimation of the science. Investigation of the utilization of VA frameworks will create new logical inquiries concerning the idea of intellectual preparing in innovative situations that can be tended to through research facility experimentation. Through this multidisciplinary, translational exploration approach [30], visual investigation tries to manufacture more prescient psychological models, science-mindful collaboration and perception plan techniques, and centered interdisciplinary programming improvement measures [31].

The last test that visual examination faces are maybe the hardest to conquer. In an attempt to re-visit our failure condition, we could see that the inclination towards the unpredictable nature of this situation would involve data and invention inventors and designers to know not only the requirements of the task and the circumstances of the user but also the impact of the new appearance and interaction on the cognitive, emotional and analytical cycles. We agree that this ability could ideally be done through a diverse consortium of HCI experts and condition monitoring practitioners. A virtual range of effects and seminars can be hosted at IEEE Visweek, the International Conference on Systems Sciences in Hawaii, and the annual VAC Consortium. Vibrant expenditure by HCI experts and practitioners on these and number of incidents would be fundamental to this essential and critical means of coping with the creation of data and communications to resolve the issues of the community and its structures [32].

12.9 Mining HCI Information Using Inductive Deduction Viewpoint

As opposed to before approaches that are far and wide (see Figure 12.1, wherein the CRISP-like model on the right, the "model" hub is brought forth, as it is absent in the first figure [33], the creators stress the viewpoints showed by the (four gatherings of) hazier boxes. Most importantly, information is not seen as a solid item inside the cycle idea yet as a rising succession. Second, while in the Fayyad cycle [34], the example idea shows up from no place, the wording of shaping theories is seen as a focal issue—the choice of a rationale and the plan of reasonable spaces of speculations, both conceivably subject to amendment after some time. Third, the inductive displaying methodology examined in some more detail all through this section is distinguishing proof by identification. HCI information mining approach with an accentuation on parts of inductive displaying is shown in Figure 12.5 [35].

Included sensible thinking may effectively get befuddling—less to a computer or a rationale program [36], yet to an individual. Inside the advanced game contextual analysis [37], the age of a solitary ordered group of legitimate recipes has been adequate. ID by list functions admirably for recognizing even somewhat treacherous human player expectations. Business applications, as in [38], are more unpredictable and may require unforeseeable updates of the wording being used, i.e., the dynamic age of spaces of speculations on request [39].

In Figure 12.6, the hazier boxes with white engravings mean customary ideas of recursion-hypothetical inductive derivation. The different boxes reflect formalizations of this current section's center ways to deal with HCI information mining by methods for ID by the specification. The ideas got from the current part's commonsense examinations structure a formerly

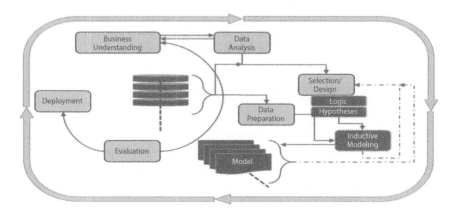

Figure 12.5 HCI information mining approach with an accentuation on parts of inductive displaying.

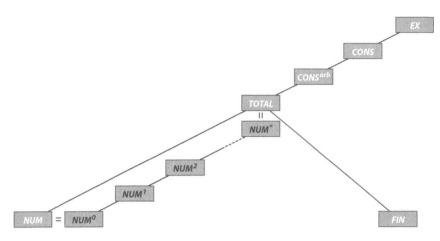

Figure 12.6 Reflections of basic inductive learning ideas thought about and related; climbing lines mean the correct set consideration of the lower learning idea in the upper one. All through the rest of the aspect of this part, the creators limit themselves to just rudimentary ideas.

obscure endless progression between the recently known ideas NUM and TOTAL.

Learning coherent speculations is a lot like learning recursive capacities. Both have limited portrayals yet decide a typically unbounded measure of realities—the hypotheses of a hypothesis and the estimations of a capacity, separately. In the two cases, the arrangements of realities are recursively enumerable however normally undecidable. The profound transaction of rationale and recursion hypothesis is surely known for very nearly a century and gives a firm premise of original outcomes [40]. Inductively learning a recursive capacity implies, in some sense, mining the capacity's chart, which is introduced in developing pieces after some time, a cycle fundamentally the same as mining HCI information.

12.10   Visual Data Mining Methodology

The information expert regularly specifies first a few boundaries to confine the pursuit space; information mining is then performed naturally by a calculation, and finally the examples found by the programmed information mining calculation are introduced to the information examiner on the screen. For information mining to be successful, it is essential to remember the human for the information investigation cycle and consolidate the flexibility, imagination, and general information on the human with the huge stockpiling limit and the computational intensity of the present computers. Since there is a gigantic measure of examples produced by a programmed information mining calculation in literary structure, it is practically unimaginable for the human to decipher and assess the example in detail and concentrate fascinating information and general qualities. Visual information mining targets incorporating the human in the information mining measure and applying human perceptual capacities to the examination of huge datasets accessible in the present computer frameworks. Implementing knowledge into an informative, visual framework also promotes new perspectives, encouraging the creation and acceptance of new assumptions to the limits of better problem solving and growing more knowledge in the sector [41].

Visual information investigation, for the most part, follows a three-advance cycle: Overview first, zoom and filter, and afterward subtleties on-request (which has been known as the Information Seeking Mantra [42]. To start with, the information examiner needs to get an outline of the information. In the diagram, the information examiner identifies fascinating examples or gatherings with regards to the information and spotlights on at least one of them. For investigating the examples, the information investigator needs to bore down and access the subtleties of the information. Perception innovation might be utilized for each of the three stages of the information investigation measure. Representation methods help demonstrate a diagram of the information, permitting the information expert to distinguish fascinating subsets. In this progression, it is essential to keep the review perception while zeroing in on the subset utilizing another representation method. The alternative is always to rotate the design description to empty in the fascinating subsections. It could be achieved by contributing a higher degree of the display to fascinating subsections while reducing monitor use for unremarkable content. Also, to examine interesting subtypes, the data analyst requires a drill-down capability to track knowledge perspectives. Notice that depiction invention not just provides the basic vision processes for each of the three levels but also links the gaps between the means. Visual data mining can be seen as an aging index of speculation; data expectations allow the data analyst to collect insight into evidence and develop new concepts. The verification of the theories should likewise be possible through information perception. However, it may likewise be cultivated via programmed procedures from insights, design recognition, or AI. Subsequently, visual information mining, for the most part, permits quicker information investigation and regularly gives better outcomes, particularly in situations where programmed information mining calculations come up short. What's more, visual information investigation strategies give a lot of further extent of client fulfillment and confidence in the findings of the investigation. This reality prompts an appeal for visual investigation procedures and makes them basic related to programmed investigation techniques. Visual information mining depends on a programmed part, the information mining calculation, and an intelligent part, the perception method. There are three basic ways to deal with incorporate the human in the information investigation cycle to acknowledge various types of visual information mining approaches:

a) *Preceding Visualization (PV):* Data is envisioned in some visual structure before running an information mining calculation. By cooperating with the crude information, the information examiner has full power over the examination in the inquiry space. Intriguing examples are found by investigating the information.

b) *Subsequent Visualization (SV):* A programmed information mining calculation plays out the information mining task by extricating designs from a given dataset. These examples are envisioned to make them interpretable for the information examiner. The resulting perceptions empower the information investigator to indicate inputs. In light of the perception, the information investigator might need to re-visitation of the information mining calculation and utilize distinctive info boundaries to get better outcomes.

c) *Tightly Integrated Visualization (TIV):* An programmed information mining calculation plays out an examination of the information yet doesn't deliver the final results. A perception strategy is utilized to introduce the transitional consequences of the information investigation measure. The mix of some programmed information mining calculations and representation procedures empowers specified client criticism for the following information mining run. At that point, the information expert identifies fascinating examples with regards to the perception of the transitional outcomes dependent on his area information. The inspiration for this methodology is to accomplish the autonomy of the information mining calculations from the application. A given programmed information mining calculation can be helpful in one space however may have downsides in some other area. Since there is no programmed information mining algorithm(with one boundary setting) appropriate for all application spaces, firmly incorporated perception prompts a superior comprehension of the information and the separated patterns.

In expansion to the immediate inclusion of the human, the primary points of interest of visual information investigation over-programmed information mining procedures are the following:

Visual information investigation can undoubtedly manage exceptionally nonhomogeneous and loud data. Visual information investigation is instinctive and requires no comprehension of complex numerical or measurable calculations or boundaries. Perception can give a subjective diagram of the information, permitting information marvels to be disconnected for additional quantitative examination. Visual information mining procedures have been demonstrated to be of high incentive in exploratory information investigation and have a high potential for investigating huge information bases [43].

Visual information investigation is particularly valuable when little is thought about the information, and the investigation objectives are unclear

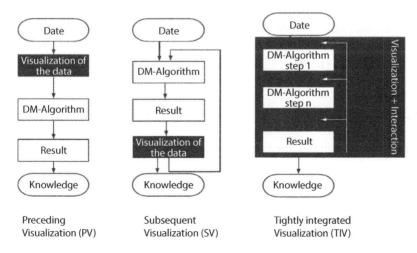

Figure 12.7 Shows human involvement in different data mining approaches.

and it is represented in Figure 12.7. Since the information examiner is straightforwardly engaged with the investigation cycle, moving and modifying the investigation objectives is consequently done if necessary. In the following segments, we show that the combination of the human in the information mining measure and applying human perceptual capacities to the examination of huge datasets can assist with giving more compelling outcomes insignificant information mining application spaces, for example, in the digging for affiliation rules, grouping, classification, and text recovery.

12.11   Machine Learning Algorithms for Hand Gesture Recognition

Image recognition is a tool used to recognize and analyze human non-verbal activity and to communicate with either the user in the very same way. This works to develop a plinth seen between the computer and the user to talk to each other. Image recognition becomes effective in relieving data that cannot be carried on by discussion or writing. Transmissions are the best way to convey that which is significant. This Chapter involves the use of a system that requires a vision-based hand motion recognition application with a high rate of position within an exceptional structure, which can work in a continuous Human–Computer Interaction framework without having any of the impediments (gloves, uniform foundation, and so on.) on the client condition. The framework can be characterized by utilizing a flowchart that contains three fundamental advances, they are Learning, Detection, Recognition [44].

12.12   Learning

It includes two angles, for example,

- *Training dataset:* This is the dataset that comprises of various kinds of hand motions that are utilized to prepare the framework dependent on which the framework plays out the activities.
- *Feature Extraction:* It includes deciding the centroid that isolates the picture into equal parts at its mathematical Center.

12.13   Detection

This progression includes:

- *Capture scene:* Captures the pictures through a web camera, which is utilized as a contribution to the framework that is assembled.
- *Pre-processing:* Images that are caught through the webcam are contrasted with the dataset with perceiving the substantial hand developments that are expected to play out the necessary activities.
- *Hand Detection:* The prerequisites for hand identification include the information picture from the webcam. The picture ought to be gotten with a speed of 20 edges for each second. Separation ought to likewise be kept up between the hand and the camera. The rough separation that ought to be between the hand the camera is around 30 to 100 cm. The video input is put away edge by outline into a framework in the wake of pre-processing.

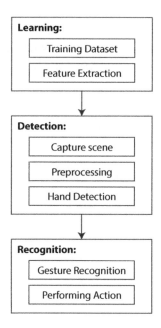

Figure 12.8 Flowchart of gesture recognition.

12.14   Recognition

This progression includes:

- *Gesture Recognition:* The quantity of fingers present in the hand motion is dictated by utilizing imperfection focuses present in the signal. The resultant motion got is taken care of through a 3Dimensional Convolutional Neural Network sequentially to perceive the current signal is represented in Figure 12.8.
- *Performing activity:* The perceived motion is utilized as a contribution to play out the activities required by the client. These activities incorporate zooming in, zooming out, and swiping the page left or right.

12.15   Proposed Methodology for Hand Gesture Recognition

A hand signal recognition framework was created to catch the hand motions being performed by the client and to control a computer framework dependent on the approaching data. A considerable lot of the current frameworks in writing have executed signal recognition utilizing just spatial demonstrating, i.e., recognition of a solitary motion and not fleeting displaying for example recognition of movement of signals. Likewise, the

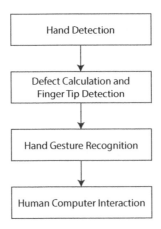

Figure 12.9 Block diagram of Gesture Recognition framework.

current frameworks have not been actualized continuously, they utilize a pre caught picture as a contribution to signal recognition. To resolve these existing challenges, further innovation has indeed been developed that aims to design a vision-based hand expression showed system with a high correct position rate accompanying an influencing skills that can function in a consistent HCI environment without having any of the referenced extreme regulations (gloves, standardized platform, etc.) on the client's situation shown in Figure 12.9.

The plan is made out of a human–computer association framework which uses hand motions as a contribution for correspondence.

The framework is partitioned into four subsystems:

a) *Identification of Hand:* This module distinguishes the hand signal by catching a picture through the web camera.

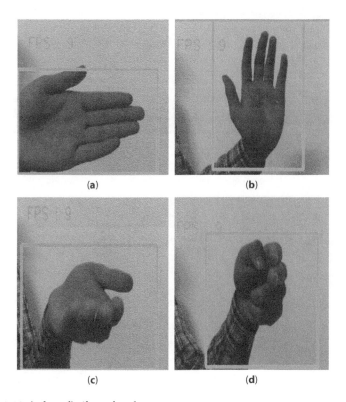

(a) **(b)**

(c) **(d)**

Figure 12.10 (a, b, c, d): Shows hand gestures.

b) *Fingertip Detection and Defect Calculation:* A limit box is drawn around the hand for which the fingertips are recognized and the foundation space around it is killed.

c) *Motion Recognition:* The picture is contrasted with the dataset all together with remembering it and play out the activities required.

d) *Human–Computer Interaction:* PyAutoGUI is utilized to interface with the PDF and play out the necessary activity shown in Figure 12.10.

Algorithm Used:

Figure 12.11 Zoom-in gesture recognized.

Figure 12.12 Zoom-out gesture recognized.

Figure 12.13 Towards right movement gesture recognized.

    a)   A calculation called Haar Cascade is utilized.
    b)   Haar Cascade is an AI object location calculation.
    c)   It is utilized to distinguish the items in a picture or a video. and draws a limit around the recognized article.

12.16   Result

We can locate the accompanying figures as the yield, that perceives the signals caught from the web camera as zoom-in, zoom-out, and moving towards the right. The productivity of the model is around 80% since the model expects time to get prepared with the dataset and results are shown in Figures 12.11, 12.12 and 12.13.

12.17   Conclusion

In this chapter, we examined the human–computer association which is an especially wide zone which includes components from differing zones, for example, brain research, ergonomics, building, man-made consciousness, information bases, and so forth. This procedure speaks to a depiction of the cutting edge in human computer cooperation with an accentuation on keen Interaction through computer vision, man-made consciousness, and example recognition strategy. We hope that, quite far from now on, the research system may have made significant strides in the study of human–computer cooperation, and that new standard will be raised that will lead to common interaction between humans, machines, and the environment.

We likewise examine the significance of gesture recognition that lies in building a proficient human–machine connection. This paper depicts how the usage of the framework is done depends on the pictures caught, and how they are deciphered as signals by the computer to perform activities like exchanging the pages, looking up or down the page. The framework is manufactured utilizing OpenCV and TensorFlow item indicator.

References

1. Salovey, P. and Mayer, J., Emotional intelligence. *Imagin. Cogn. Pers.*, 9, 185–211, 1990.
2. Rawat, N. and Raja, R., Moving Vehicle Detection and Tracking using Modified Mean Shift Method and Kalman Filter and Research. *Int. J. New Technol. Res. (IJNTR)*, 2, 5, 96–100, 2016.
3. Warwick, K. and Gasson, M., Practical interface experiments with implant technology, in: *International Workshop on Human–Computer Interaction, Lecture Notes in Computer Science*, vol. 3058, Springer, pp. 6–16, 2004.
4. Huang, X. and Weng, J., Motivational system for human-robot interaction, in: *International Workshop on Human-Computer Interaction, Lecture Notes in Computer Science*, vol. 3058, Springer, pp. 17–27, 2004.
5. Paquin, V. and Cohen, P., A vision-based gestural guidance interface for mobile robotic platforms, in: *International Workshop on Human–Computer Interaction, Lecture Notes in Computer Science*, vol. 3058, Springer, pp. 38–46, 2004.
6. Nickel, K. and Stiefelhagen, R., Real-time person tracking and pointing gesture recognition for human–robot interaction, in: *International Workshop on Human–Computer Interaction, Lecture Notes in Computer Science*, vol. 3058, Springer, pp. 28–37, 2004.
7. Tosas, M. and Li, B., Virtual touch screen for mixed reality, in: *International Workshop on Human–Computer Interaction, Lecture Notes in Computer Science*, vol. 3058, Springer, pp. 47–57, 2004.
8. Gheorghe, L., Ban, Y., Uehara, K., Exploring interactions specific to mixed reality 3D modeling systems, in: *International Workshop on Human–Computer Interaction, Lecture Notes in Computer Science*, vol. 3058, Springer, pp. 113–123, 200.
9. Siegl, H., Schweighofer, G., Pinz, A., An AR human–computer interface for object localization in a cognitive vision framework, in: *International Workshop on Human–Computer Interaction, Lecture Notes in Computer Science*, vol. 3058, Springer, pp. 167–177, 2004.
10. Hosoya, E., Sato, H., Kitabata, M., Harada, I., Nojima, H., Onozawa, A., Arm-pointer: 3D pointing interface for real-world interaction, in: *International*

Workshop on Human–Computer Interaction, Lecture Notes in Computer Science, vol. 3058, Springer, pp. 70–80, 2004.

11. Kumar, S., Jain, A., Shukla, A.P., Singh, S., Rani, S., A Comparative Analysis of Machine Learning Algorithms for Detection of Organic and Non-Organic Cotton Diseases, in: *Mathematical Problems in Engineering, Special Issue— Deep Transfer Learning Models for Complex Multimedia Applications*.

12. Stenger, B., Thayananthan, A., Torr, P., Cipolla, R., Hand pose estimation using hierarchical detection, in: *International Workshop on Human–Computer Interaction, Lecture Notes in Computer Science*, vol. 3058, Springer, pp. 102–112, 2004.

13. Yamazoe, H., Utsumi, A., Tetsutani, N., Yachida, M., A novel wearable system for capturing user view images, in: *International Workshop on Human–Computer Interaction, Lecture Notes in Computer Science*, vol. 3058, Springer, pp. 156–166, 2004.

14. Tsukizawa, S., Sumi, K., Matsuyama, T., 3D digitization of a hand-held object with a wearable vision sensor, in: *International Workshop on Human–Computer Interaction, Lecture Notes in Computer Science*, vol. 3058, Springer, pp. 124–134, 2004.

15. Dornaika, F. and Ahlberg, J., Model-based head and facial motion tracking, in: *International Workshop on Human-Computer Interaction, Lecture Notes in Computer Science*, vol. 3058, Springer, pp. 211–221, 2004.

16. Sun, Y., Sebe, N., Lew, M., Gevers, T., Authentic emotion detection in real-time video, in: *International Workshop on Human–Computer Interaction, Lecture Notes in Computer Science*, vol. 3058, Springer, pp. 92–101, 2004.

17. Lee, H.S. and Kim, D., Pose invariant face recognition using linear pose transformation in feature space, in: *International Workshop on Human–Computer Interaction, Lecture Notes in Computer Science*, vol. 3058, Springer, pp. 200–210, 2004.

18. Wang, J.G., Sung, E., Venkateswarlu, R., EM enhancement of 3D head pose estimated by perspective invariance, in: *International Workshop on Human–Computer Interaction, Lecture Notes in Computer Science*, vol. 3058, Springer, pp. 178–188, 2004.

19. Du, Y. and Lin, X., Multi-view face image synthesis using factorization model, in: *International Workshop on Human–Computer Interaction, Lecture Notes in Computer Science*, vol. 3058, Springer, pp. 189–199, 2004.

20. Kleindienst, J., Macek, T., Seredi, L., Sedivy, J., Djinn: Interaction framework for home environment using speech and vision, in: *International Workshop on Human–Computer Interaction, Lecture Notes in Computer Science*, vol. 3058, Springer, pp. 145–155, 2004.

21. Okatani, I. and Takuichi, N., Location-based information support system using multiple cameras and LED light sources with the compact battery-less information terminal (CoBIT), in: *International Workshop on Human–Computer Interaction, Lecture Notes in Computer Science*, vol. 3058, Springer, pp. 135–144, 2004.

22. Kumar, K.R. and Raja, R., Broadcasting the Transaction System by Using Blockchain Technology. pp. 2115–21, Design Engineering, India, June 2021, http://thedesignengineering .com/ index.php/DE/article/view/1912.

23. Jeng., A selected history of expectation bias in physics. *Am. J. Phys.*, 74, 578–583, 2006.

24. Shukla, S. and Raja, R., Digital Image Fusion using Adaptive Neuro-Fuzzy Inference System. *Int. J. New Technol. Res. (IJNTR)*, 2, 5, 101–104, 2016.

25. Ankerst, M., *Visual Data Mining*. Ph.D. thesis, Faculty of Mathematics and Computer Science, University of Munich, Germany, 2000.

26. Asimov, D., The grand tour: a tool for viewing multidimensional data. *SIAM J. Sci. Stat. Comput.*, 6, 1, 128–143, 1985.

27. Wirth, R. and Hipp, J., CRISP-DM. Towards a standard process model for data mining, in: *Proceedings of the 4th International Conference on the Practical Applications of Knowledge Discovery and Data Mining*, pp. 29–39, 2000.

28. Fayyad, U., Piatetsky-Shapiro, G., Smyth, P., The KDD process for extracting useful knowledge from volumes of data. *Commun. ACM*, 39, 27–34, 1996.

29. Schmidt, B., *Theory of Mind Player Modeling* [Bachelor Thesis], University of Applied Sciences, Erfurt, Germany, 2014.

30. Jantke, K.P., Schmidt, B., Schnappauf, R., Next-generation learner modeling by the theory of mind model induction, in: *Proceedings of the 8th International Conference on Computer Supported Education (CSEDU 2016)*, Rome, Italy, 21–23 April 2016, SCITEPRESS, Sétubal, pp. 499–506.

31. Raja, R., Kumar, S., Rashid, Md., Color Object Detection Based Image Retrieval using ROI Segmentation with Multi-Feature Method. *Wirel. Pers. Commun. Springer J.*, 1–24, 2020, https://link.springer.com/article/10.1007/s11277-019-07021-6, https://doi.org/10.1 007/s11277-019-07021-6.

32. Arnold, O., Drefahl, S., Fujima, J., Jantke, K.P., Vogler, C., Dynamic identification by enumeration for co-operative knowledge discovery. *IADIS Int. J. Comput. Sci. Inf. Syst.*, 12, 65–85, 2017.

33. Jantke, K.P. and Beick, H.R., Combining postulates of naturalness in inductive inference, in: *EIK*, vol. 17, pp. 465–484, 1981.

34. Gödel, K., Über formal unentscheidbare Sätze der "Principia Mathematica" und verwandter Systeme. *Mon. Math. Phys.*, 38, 173–198, 1931.

35. Tiwari, L., Raja, R., Awasthi, V., Miri, R., Sinha, G.R., Alkinani, M.H., Polat, K., Detection of lung nodule and cancer using novel Mask-3 FCM and TWEDLNN algorithms. *Measurement*, 172, 1–14, 2021, 108882, https://doi.org/10.1016/j.measurement.2020.108882.

36. Panwar, M. and Mehra, P.S., Hand Gesture Recognition for Human–Computer Interaction. *International Conference on Image Information Processing*, India, 2011.

37. Sahu, A.K., Sharma, S., Tanveer, M., Internet of Things attack detection using hybrid Deep Learning Model. *Comput. Commun.*, 176, 146–154, 2021, https://doi.org/10.1016/j.comcom.2021.05.024.

38. Sarkar, A.R., Sanyal, G., Majumder, S., Hand Gesture Recognition Systems: A Survey. *Int. J. Comput. Appl.*, 71, 15, 26–37, May 2013.

39. Manjunath, A.E., Vijaya Kumar, B.P., Rajesh, H., Comparative Study of Hand Gesture Recognition Algorithms. *Int. J. Res. Comput. Commun. Technol.*, 3, 4, 25–37, April-2014.

40. Dnyanada, R., Jadhav, L., M.R., Lobo, J., Navigation of PowerPoint Using Hand Gestures. *Int. J. Sci. Res. (IJSR)*, 4, 833–837, 2015.

41. Patra, R.K., Raja, R., Sinha, T.S., Mahmood, Md R., Image Registration and Rectification using Background Subtraction method for Information security to justify Cloning Mechanism using High-End Computing Techniques. *3rd International Conference on Computational Intelligence and Informatics (ICCII-2018)*, held during 28–29 Dec 2018.

42. Xu, P. and Department of Electrical and Computer Engineering, University of Minnesota, A Real-time Hand Gesture Recognition and Human-Computer Interaction System, Research Paper, Xie Pu, University of Minnesota, USA, April 2017.

43. Suganya, P., Sathya, R., Vijayalakshmi, K., Detection, and Recognition of Gestures To Control The System Applications by Neural Networks. *Int. J. Pure Appl. Math.*, 118, 399–405, 2018.

44. Chandrakar, R., Raja, R., Miri, R., Tandan, S.R.K., Laxmi, R., Detection and Identification of Animals in Wild Life Sancturies using Convolutional Neural Network. *Int. J. Recent Technol. Eng. (IJRTE)* that will publish at, 8, 5, 181–185, January 2020 in Regular Issue on 30/12/2020.

13

MSDTrA: A Boosting Based-Transfer Learning Approach for Class Imbalanced Skin Lesion Dataset for Melanoma Detection

Lokesh Singh*, Rekh Ram Janghel and Satya Prakash Sahu

Department of Information Technology, National Institute of Technology, Raipur, India

Abstract

Pigmented skin lesion datasets comprise a higher percentage of benign lesion than the malignant lesions which lead to the class skewness issue in the dataset. Classifiers trained for analyzing the automated dermatoscopic pigmented lesions often suffer from data scarcity. Transfer learning permits to leverage the knowledge from the source domain to train a classifier towards the target domain when the data is rare. Importing knowledge from multiple or several sources towards increasing the chance of searching a source closer to a target may alleviate the negative transfer. A framework is proposed in this work to transfer knowledge from multiple different sources utilizing AdaBoost, TrAdaBoost and MultiSource Dynamic TrAdaBoost (MSDTrA), for melanoma detection. The effectiveness of the proposed framework is evaluated on four benchmark skin lesion datasets namely, PH2, ISIC16, ISIC17, and HAM1000 which demonstrate promising performance by alleviating negative-transfer by increasing multiple different sources.

Keywords: Dermoscopic, classification, melanoma, class imbalance, boosting, sampling

13.1 Introduction

One of the most lethal types of skin cancer called malignant melanoma is responsible for the wide majority of skin cancer deaths. Cancer is an

---

Corresponding author: lsingh.phd2017.it@nitrr.ac.in

Rohit Raja, Kapil Kumar Nagwanshi, Sandeep Kumar and K. Ramya Laxmi (eds.) Data Mining and Machine Learning Applications, (349–364) © 2022 Scrivener Publishing LLC

ailment of the rampant growth of abnormal cells, which are the rudimentary blocks of the body [1, 2]. The body persistently develops novice cells for rapid growth, exchange tattered tissues and repair injuries. Moreover, cells multiply themselves and die in an orderly fashion. But sometimes the process of cells gets disturbed, neither they grow nor die in an orderly fashion. Due to which the body's lymph fluid becomes abnormal and as a result, tumor arises. A tumor might be benign or malignant. A benign tumor is not cancerous while malignant is, as it spread themselves in other parts of the body via lymph fluid [3]. Melanoma occurs over those parts of the body which are exposed to the sun, but sometimes very rarely it appears anywhere in the body which are not at all exposed to the sun like inside the mouth, eyes, nervous system, etc. [4, 5]. From the latest reports, the melanoma deaths have cross over 20,000 early in Europe. Nevertheless, if we diagnosed early to melanoma, it becomes the most treatable type of cancer in the world [6]. In skin lesion detection, benign lesions are found in majority while malignant lesions are rare in the dataset [7], which makes the melanoma detection challenging with skewed class distribution. In account of size of data and skewness in class distribution datasets are categorized in four sections as shown in Figure 13.1. The skin lesion datasets used in this experimentation are small in size and imbalanced as well thus, falls under the category of 'absolute rarity'.

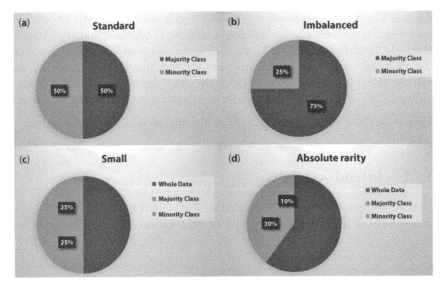

Figure 13.1 Different types of datasets: (a) standard (balanced), (b) unbalanced, (c) small-size, and (d) absolute-rare.

A. *Standard Dataset:* This includes the adequate number of data within each class in a balanced manner i.e., each class contains an almost equal amount of data.

B. *Imbalanced Dataset:* This includes an adequate number of data of one class called majority class and other class with fewer data in it generally known as a minority class.

C. *Small Dataset:* This type of dataset includes the exiguous data in both the classes but is balanced.

D. *Rare Dataset:* This type of dataset contains the exiguous data in an unbalanced manner i.e., classes containing data having large differences in the amount of data.

Transfer learning (TL) [8, 9] is a family of algorithms that employs the conventional machine learning approaches with an assumption of identical distribution. Learning algorithms are moved from one domain (S) to another domain (T) to exploit and transfer insightful information. When the training data points are small, the information leveraged improvise the target domain's learning. Transferring knowledge from one domain (S) to another domain (T) depends on the way they are connected. The stronger the association is, the greater the usability of the previous information. On the contrary, brute-force transfer in the case of poor relationships might lead to performance degradation of classifiers that negates transfer.

A general assumption of conventional machine learning approach is that training and testing dataset have similar probability distribution. Under such a presumption where a dataset is of dissimilar distribution, training data is needed to be acquired towards learning new classifiers [10]. A classifier when trained in such circumstances, it may overfit the new data which leads to poor generalization. Utilizing the knowledge from the same domain would be more effective towards regularizing the learning. Towards relaxing the similar distribution presumption of the conventional machine learning methods, transfer learning presents a family of approaches [11]. The knowledge transferred helps to improve learning in the target domain with rarity in training samples [12]. TrAdaBoost is gaining popularity for boosting by re-sampling amidst the work conducted in this area and is related to our work [13, 14]. The ability of knowledge transfers from source domain to target domain in general depends on how they relate. Earlier information will be more usable with strong relationships. Alternatively, transferring brute-force with weak relationships might deteriorate the learner's performance and thus is termed as negative transfer [15].

In this framework, we utilized an enhanced transfer boosting approach Multisource Dynamic TrAdaBoost [16, 17] for leveraging transfer learning which considers the balance among source and target skin lesion datasets. It resolves the problem of multiclass classification using transfer learning with the same distribution of data and class unbalance amidst negative and positive instances in the source and target domain of datasets. The negative transfer problem is avoided by the approach in the datasets by transferring knowledge from multiple sources using a boosting-based framework. The approach is designed on the basis of conventional TrAdaBoost that evaluates the importance of every datapoint considered, as per the availability of number of source and target skin lesion datasets. The key contribution of proposed framework is as follows:

- A boosting-based TL framework is proposed towards transferring knowledge from multiple different sources utilizing AdaBoost, TrAdaBoost and **MultiSource Dynamic TrA**daBoost (MSDTrA), for melanoma detection.
- The designed approach overcomes the challenging issues encountered during melanoma classification and trains a robust learning method with skewed dataset and scarce lesion training set.
- It improves the poor generalization ability and prevents the classifier from being overfitted with inadequate skin lesion training data.
- It avoids negative-transfer from skin lesion datasets by transferring knowledge from multiple sources using a boosting-based framework.
- It removes the biasing to the majority class and improves the prediction performance of the framework by leveraging knowledge of transfer learning from multiple sources.
- The designed framework is evaluated on seven skin lesion datasets namely, ISIC2016, ISIC2017, PH2 and HAM10000 demonstrate promising performance by alleviating negative-transfer by increasing multiple different sources.

The remaining of the work is structured as follows: *Section 13.2*, represents the literature based on TL methods in brief, the proposed framework is elaborately discussed in *Section 13.3*. *Section 13.4* describes the measures for evaluating the effectiveness of framework. Experimental evaluations are represented in *Section 13.5* while the work is concluded by *Section 13.6*.

13.2   Literature Survey

This section discusses the work conducted leveraging transfer learning to overcome the challenges confronted in datasets with skewed class distributions. One such framework is designed by Liu *et al.* [18], with the scarce training data towards improving the classification accuracy utilizing ensemble transfer learning framework. They first, proposed a weighted-resampling method TrResampling [19], where in each iteration TrAdaBoost algorithm is used to resample the data in the source domain and adjusts the weights for the source and the target domain.

Al-Stouhi *et al.* [20], tackle the problems of small dataset with imbalance in class distribution by proposing an instance transfer method with an update mechanism dependent on label, to gradually compensate for the imbalances and the issue of lack of samples. The method creates a balance with transfer learning [21] and significantly improves the classification results. This learning is known as 'Absolute Rarity' and is very effective in case of real-world problems. Zhang *et al.* [22], provided a framework which effectively builds a robust classifier that functions well in case of class imbalance. It takes the benefit of auxiliary-data using TL methods and develops a classifier that tackles with the class imbalance and gives considerable results in case of less training instances in a specific domain. This method simultaneously augments the training data and creates a balance with the unbalanced datasets. A label-dependent update mechanism is used in a novel boosting-based instance TL. Zhang *et al.* [13], designed an instance TL method based on multisource dynamic TrAdaBoost, considering the fact that the sample data from one domain (S) to another domain (T) have similar distribution. Knowledge is collected from different sources to avoid negative transfer. Promising classification results are achieved by the proposed algorithm using multiple source domains for leveraging transfer.

Torralba *et al.* [23] proposed a boosting-based multiclass classification framework which elects weak learners shared between distinct learners. They leveraged the instance based and parameter-based knowledge, transferred from different multiple sources towards boosting an individual target learner. They considered comparable amount of training instances for each task as well.

Our work overcomes the challenging issues confronted in melanoma classification as benign and malignant. The designed framework effectively deals with data scarcity and negative transfer utilizing multiple sources.

13.3 Methods and Material

Dataset

In this experiment, four benchmark skin lesion datasets namely, ISIC2016, ISIC2017, PH2, and HAM10000 are used as the source and target datasets which are available publicly. To solve the data imbalance problem for both the training and testing dataset we perform multiple augmentation operations to the images. Images were normalized, and flipped vertically and horizontally, changed the brightness, towards improving the accuracy by a significant margin [24]. Figure 13.2 shows sample images of the source and target skin lesion datasets [25]. Data augmentation process increases the size of the dataset by keeping semantic meaning of the images thus helps in reducing overfitting, the summarized detail of four target datasets is discussed in Table 13.1.

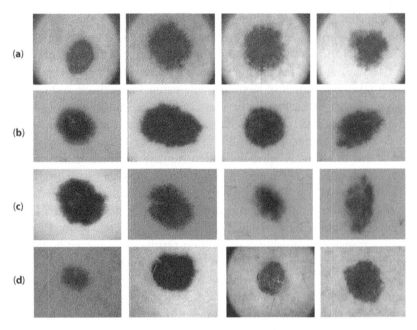

Figure 13.2 Sample skin lesion images from public dataset (a) PH2, (b) ISIC2016, (c) ISIC2017, and (d) HAM10000.

Table 13.1 Summarized detail of source and target datasets.

Datasets	Category	Number of images	No. of classes	Index
PH2 [26]	Multiclass	200	03	A
ISIC 2016 [27]	Binary	1,279	02	B
ISIC 2017 [28]	Multiclass	2,750	03	C
HAM10000 [29]	Multiclass	10,015	07	D

13.3.1 Proposed Methodology: Multi Source Dynamic TrAdaBoost Algorithm

The framework first utilizes TrAdaBoost with the single positive target training instance, towards utilizing the knowledge from several sources. By discarding the first half of the ensemble, TrAdaBoost degrades the performance. Due to this issue samples of source domain converge before they applied for transfer learning. In addition, relying of TrAdaBoost on single-source makes it vulnerable towards negative transfer thus, considering the co-relation among several target and source domains, we utilized 'Multisource TrAdaBoost' (MSTrA) [15] transfer learning method for the uneven class distribution. Ensuring that the transferred knowledge is co-related with the target domain, it neglects the impact of another source domain. We thus resolved the issue incorporated in TrAdaBoost by integrating Dynamic TrAdaBoost (DTrAdaBoost) with a dynamic-cost. However, DtrAdaBoost causes convergence of source samples prior employed for transfer learning. To overcome the aforementioned drawbacks, we then utilized multisource dynamic TrAdaBoost algorithm (MSDTrA). The method reduces the convergence-rate of weight of source instances on the basis of weak-correlation towards target domain. The MSDTrA at every step, trains the classifiers by selecting the ensemble learning of TrAdaBoost based on combining the samples of source and target. Weighted Majority Algorithm is utilized towards adjusting the source sample's weights by reducing the weight of mis-classified source samples and keeping the present weights of correctly classified source samples. The method greatly decreases the cost of memory of unwanted data in the source domain using multiple source domains. The problem of negative transfer has been addressed by utilizing several multiple sources (skin lesion datasets) which increases the chance of importing the information from a source to the target. MSDTrA permits the training instances of source domain for participating in the learning process in every iteration, and assigns distinct weights to distinct training samples of source domain. Higher weight is assigned to the source training instance towards improving the target task learning. In general, the MSDTrA takes the benefit of significant knowledge obtained from all source domains which enhances the learning impact of target tasks. We utilized n source domains $S_1, S_2, \ldots S_n$, n source tasks, $T_{a1}, T_{a2}, \ldots, T_{an}$ and n source training set as $D_{a1}, D_{a2}, \ldots, D_{an}$, the designed framework aims to leverage the knowledge from transfer learning towards improvising the effectiveness of learning of target learner function as: $\hat{f} \; b : X \to Y$. The MSDTrA algorithm is more elaborately explained in pseudo code discussed in Algorithm 1 and the designed framework is depicted in Figure 13.3.

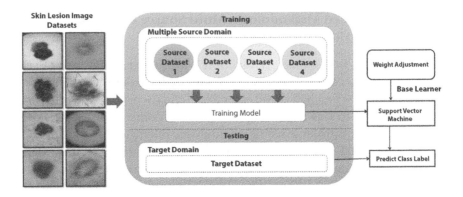

Figure 13.3 Illustration of proposed framework.

Algorithm 1: Multi Source Dynamic TrAdaBoost Algorithm

Input:

      N Source training set $(Ds_1, ..., Ds_k, ..., Ds_N)$

      Where Ds_k is the $k - th$ source training set, a target training set D_T, the maximum number of iterations M.

Procedure:

Step 1: Set $\propto_s = 1/(1 + \dfrac{\sqrt{2 l n n_s}}{M})$ where $n_s = \displaystyle\sum_{k=1}^{N} n_{s_k}$ denotes the total number of training samples on N source domains, n_{s_k} is the number of training samples on the $k - th$ source domain.

Step 2: Initialize a weight vector $(w^{s_1}, ..., w^{s_k}, ..., w^{s_N}, w)$ where $w^{s_k} = (w_1^{s_k}, w_2^{s_k}, ..., w_{n_{s_k}}^{s_k})$ and $(w_1, ..., w_j, ..., w_{n_T})$ are the weight vectors of samples on $k - th$ source and target domains respectively Where, w = Combines D_{s_k} and D_T to constitute a training set $D_k = (D_{s_k}, D_T)$.

Step 3: For $t: 1 \rightarrow M$

Step 4: Normalize the weight vectors $(w^{s_1}, ..., w^{s_k}, ..., w^{s_N}, w)$ and (w^{s_k}, w).

Step 5: For each training set D_k, call a traditional classifier training phase to obtain a weak Classifier h_t^k.

Step 6: Calculate error of h_t^k on D_T according to $\varepsilon_t^k = \displaystyle\sum_{i'=1}^{n_T} |w_{i'}| |w y_{i'} - h_t^k(x_{i'})|$

and update the weight of h_t^k based on $w_t^k = \dfrac{e^{1-\varepsilon_t^k}}{e^{\varepsilon_t^k}}$. Thus, we can

obtain a candidate classifier $h_t = \displaystyle\sum_k \dfrac{w_t^k}{\sum_k w_t^k} h_t^k$ at the $t - th$ itera-

tion. The error of h_t on D_t is $\varepsilon_t = \displaystyle\sum_{i'=1}^{n_T} |w_{i'}| |y_{i'} - h_t(x_{i'})|$.

Step 7: Set $\alpha_t = \dfrac{\varepsilon_t}{1-\varepsilon_t}$ where $0 \le \varepsilon_t \le \dfrac{1}{2}$.

Step 8: Update the weight vector according to the following rules:

$$w_{i(t+1)}^{sk} = w_{it}^{sk} \alpha_S^{|h_t(x_i^{sk}) - y_{it}^{sk}|},$$

$$w_{i'(t+1)} = \begin{cases} w_{i't}\alpha_t^{1-\varepsilon_t}, & 0 < \varepsilon_t \le \dfrac{1}{2} \\[2ex] w_{i't}, & \varepsilon_t = 0 \end{cases}$$

Step 9: If $t < M$, return to Step 5, otherwise turn to Step 9.

Step 10: The final strong classifier is $f(x) = sign(\Sigma_t(1 - \alpha_t)h_t(x))$.

Output:

   Classifier for the target domain $f\colon X \to Y$.

13.4   Experimental Results

Experimentations are conducted towards evaluating the effectiveness of the framework designed for detection melanoma using four benchmark skin lesion datasets namely, PH2, ISIC16, ISIC17, and HAM10000 datasets. Without losing the generalization, we considered small amount of training instances of a target skin lesion datasets while large amount of training instances of source skin lesion datasets.

13.5   Libraries Used

Following is the major open-source tools and libraries are used in conducting the experimentation. Below are the discussed libraries.

- keras library (www.keras.io)
- tensorflow library (https://www.tensorflow.org/)
- pandas library (https://pandas.pydata.org/)
- scikit-learn library (http://scikit-learn.org/)
- matplotlib library (https://matplotlib.org/)

13.6   Comparing Algorithms Based on Decision Boundaries

Figure 13.3 demonstrates the procedure of separating the samples by the algorithms. Squares represent negative instances; cross indicates positive

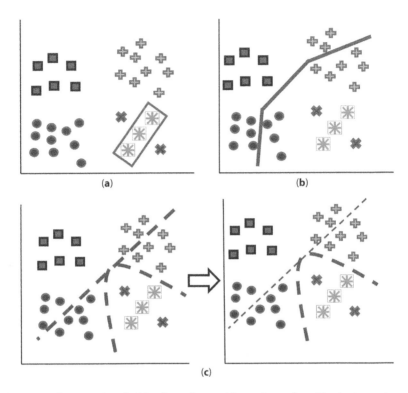

Figure 13.4 Representing decision boundary amid negative and positive instances in the target domain computed by (a) AdaBoost, (b) TrAdaBoost and (c) MSDTrA. Orange colored stars and crosses demonstrate positive instances of the target, dashed lines show candidate- decision boundary while solid line represents learned boundary.

instances belong to single source. Circles shows positive instances belong to another source. Orange colored stars (*) and crosses (+) are positive training and testing observations in the target domain correspondingly. Figure 13.4(a) represents overfitting of target data with poor generalization by the AdaBoost. Figure 13.4(b) demonstrates the decision boundaries achieved by TrAdaBoost when two sources are employed jointly. Figure 13.4(c) represents improved decision boundaries obtained by MSDTrA where every source separately combined with the target.

13.7   Evaluating Results

The performance of MSDTrA is evaluated on four pigmented lesion datasets. The datasets employed comprise of small amount of training observations with respect to target data and abundant training instances corresponding to source datasets. We conducted a fair comparison of employed methods namely AdaBoost, TrAdaBoost with the MSDTrA to test its generalized characteristics. Liner Support Vector Machine is used as a base learner towards developing a weak learner for every experimentation. The performance of methods is evaluated using the receiver operating curve (ROC) and area under the ROC curve (AUCROC). Since the number of positive samples for training was very limited, image augmentation was performed using different transformations to increase the number of images. We varied the source domains from A-D towards investigating the learner's performance corresponding to the domain's variability.

The amount of positive instances considered for one data source is 5,000, while the negative instances of both the domains are drawn at random from the augmented dataset. The amount of negative training instances in the target dataset is set to 20% of the source domain dataset. Similarly, the amount of negative test instances in the target dataset is set to 500. For every target domain, the learner's performance is assessed over the six random combinations of source domains categories. With given source and target domain, the performance of learner is achieved by taking the average over fifty trials of experimentations while the overall learner's performance is average on four target sets.

Figure 13.5 represents visual illustration of comparison of AdaBoost, TrAdaBoost, and MSDTrA based on AUCROC with distinct amount of positive target training instances as 1, 5, 15, 50 and source domain $N = 1, 2, 3, 5$. Figure 13.5(a) considers $N = 3$ and demonstrates the behavior of methods as the number of positive training instances increases. Since AdaBoost doesn't perform knowledge transfer from the source, its performance is dependent on number of positive training instances. TrAdaBoost integrates the three sources into one and improvised the performance utilizing TL mechanism. By transferring knowledge from multiple single domains, MultiSource Dynamic TrAdaBoost demonstrates significant improvement in classification accuracy, even with small training sample. TrAdaBoost integrates the three sources into one, improves on AdaBoost because of transfer learning mechanism. MSDTrA shows significant improvements in accuracy even with small amount of positive training instances by incorporating knowledge transfer from multiple single domains.

Figure 13.5(b) considers $N = 1$, which demonstrate that TrAdaBoost reduces to AdaBoost and thus, showing similar performances. While TrAdaBoost outperforms MultiSource Dynamic TrAdaBoost (MSDTrA) when the number of positive training instances is less and performs poor with large number of positive training instances. Figure 13.5(c) considers number of positive training instances = 1, and proves that with increase in source domain, AUCROC of MultiSource Dynamic TrAdaBoost increases

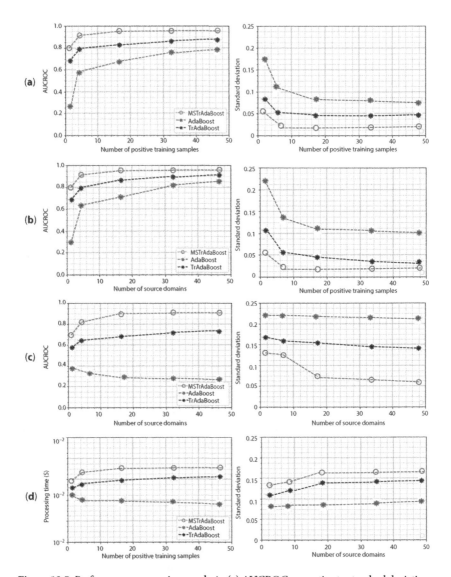

Figure 13.5 Performance comparison analysis. (a) AUCROC respective to standard deviation against amount of positive training instances with N = 3 sources. (b) AUCROC respective to standard deviation against amount of positive training instances with . (c) AUCROC respective to standard deviation against amount of positive training instances with N = 1. (d) Execution time against amount of positive training instances with N = 2 (upper), and N = 1 (lower).

with respect to decrease in standard deviations. This indicates an enhance performance in terms of consistency and accuracy. Figure 13.5(d) plots the average training-time with respect to experimentation conducted against number of positive training instances and *N* of entire methods.

13.8   Conclusion

The relationship among source and target domain affects the impact of transfer learning. Instead of improving the process of learning, leveraging the brute-force poorly from the source with respect to the target might degrade the performance of a classifier. We reduced the negative-transfer by importing of knowledge from multiple different sources for increasing the chance of searching a source corresponding to the target. In this work, MultiSource Dynamic TrAdaBoost (MSDTrA) an instance transfer-learning approach is designed for the classification of imbalanced class distribution in pigmented skin lesion datasets towards melanoma detection. The proposed framework integrates the knowledge obtained from different source domains and resolves the problem of multiclass classification using transfer learning with the same distribution of data and class unbalance among negative and positive instances of datasets. The proposed method averts the effect of negative-transfer and skewed class distribution in skin lesion datasets by incorporating multiple sources. The experimental results and theoretical analysis illustrate that the proposed method provides promising performance of classification than the several conventional methods.

References

1. Mendonca, T., Ferreira, P.M., Marques, J.S., Marcal, A.R.S., Rozeira, J., PH^2–A dermoscopic image database for research and benchmarking, in: *Conference proceedings: Annual International Conference of the IEEE Engineering in Medicine and Biology Society*, vol. 2013, pp. 5437–40, 2013.
2. Hosny, K.M., Kassem, M.A., Fouad, M.M., Classification of Skin Lesions into Seven Classes Using Transfer Learning with AlexNet. *J. Digit. Imaging*, 33, 5, 1325–1334, 2020.
3. Li, Y. and Shen, L., Skin lesion analysis towards melanoma detection using deep learning network. *Sensors*, 18, 2, 556, 2018.
4. Amelard, R., Glaister, J., Wong, A., Clausi, D.A., High-Level Intuitive Features (HLIFs) for intuitive skin lesion description. *IEEE Trans. Biomed. Eng.*, 62, 3, 820–831, 2015.
5. Noar, S.M., Leas, E., Althouse, B.M., Dredze, M., Kelley, D., Ayers, J.W., Can a selfie promote public engagement with skin cancer? *Preventive Med.*, 111, November, 280–283, 2018.
6. A.C. Society, *Colorectal cancer facts & figures 2014–2016*, American Cancer Society, Atlanta, Georgia, 2014.

7. Al-Stouhi, S., *Learning with an insufficient supply of data via knowledge transfer and sharing*. Wayne State University. ProQuest Dissertations and Thesis, p. 1–148, 2013, [Online]. https://manchester.idm.oclc.org/

8. Pan, S.J., Transfer learning, in: *Data Classification: Algorithms and Applications*, pp. 537–570, 2014.

9. Singh, L., Janghel, R.R., Sahu, S.P., TrCSVM: A novel approach for the classification of melanoma skin cancer using transfer learning. *Data Technol. Appl.*, 55, 1, 1–18, 2020.

10. Bang, S.H., Ak, R., Narayanan, A., Lee, Y.T., Cho, H., A survey on knowledge transfer for manufacturing data analytics. *Comput. Ind.*, 104, 116–130, 2019.

11. Yuan, Z., Bao, D., Chen, Z., Liu, M., Integrated Transfer Learning Algorithm Using Multi-source TrAdaBoost for Unbalanced Samples Classification, in: *International Conference on Computing Intelligence and Information System, (CIIS)*, pp. 188–195, 2017.

12. Yuhu, C., Ge, C.A.O., Xuesong, W., Jie, P.A.N., Weighted Multi-source TrAdaBoost *. 22, 3, 505–10, 2013.

13. Zhang, Q., Li, H., Zhang, Y., Li, M., Instance Transfer Learning with Multisource Dynamic TrAdaBoost Qian. *Sci. World J.*, 10, 1–8, 2014.

14. Liu, X., Wang, G., Cai, Z., Zhang, H., A multiboosting based transfer learning algorithm. *J. Adv. Comput. Intell. Intell. Inform.*, 19, 3, 381–388, 2015.

15. Yao, Y. and Doretto, G., Boosting for transfer learning with multiple sources, in: *Proceedings of the IEEE Computer Society Conference on Computer Vision and Pattern Recognition*, pp. 1855–1862, 2010.

16. Eaton, E. and Desjardins, M., Set-based boosting for instance-level transfer, in: *IEEE International Conference on Data Mining (ICDM)*, pp. 422–428, 2009.

17. Wenyuan Dai, Y.Y., Yang, Q., Xue, G.-R., Boosting for Transfer Learning, in: *Proceedings of the 24th International Conference on Machine Learning*, pp. 193–200, 2007.

18. Liu, X., Liu, Z., Wang, G., Cai, Z., Zhang, H., Ensemble Transfer Learning Algorithm. *IEEE Access*, 6, 2389–2396, 2017.

19. Liu, X., Liu, Z., Wang, G., Cai, Z., Zhang, H., A weighted-resampling based transfer learning algorithm. *Proceedings of the International Joint Conference on Neural Networks*, May, vol. 2017, pp. 185–190, 2017.

20. Al-Stouhi, S. and Reddy, C.K., Transfer learning for class imbalance problems with inadequate data. *Knowl. Inf. Syst.*, 48, 1, 201–228, 2016.

21. Weiss, K., Khoshgoftaar, T.M., Wang, D., A survey of transfer learning. *J. Big Data*, 3, 1–40, 2016.

22. Zhang, X., Zhuang, Y., Wang, W., Pedrycz, W., Transfer boosting with synthetic instances for class imbalanced object recognition. *IEEE Trans. Cybern.*, 48, 1, 357–370, 2018.

23. Torralba, K., Murphy, P., Freeman, W.T., Sharing visual features for multiclass and multiview object detection. *IEEE Trans. Pattern Anal. Mach. Intell.*, 29, 5, 854–869, 2007.

24. Pham, T.-C., Luong, C.-M. Visani, M., Hoang, V.-D., Deep CNN and data augmentation for skin lesion classification. In Asian Conference on Intelligent Information and Database Systems, Springer, Cham, pp. 573–582, 2018.
25. Tschandl, P., Rosendahl, C., Kittler, H., The HAM10000 dataset, a large collection of multi-source dermatoscopic images of common pigmented skin lesions. Scientific data, 5, 1, 1–9, 2018.
26. Teresa Mendonca, J.R., Ferreira, P.M., Marcal, A.R.S., Barata, C., Marques, J.S., Rocha, J., PH2: A Public Database for the Analysis of Dermoscopic Images, in: *Dermoscopy Image Analysis*, pp. 419–439, April 2015.
27. Gutman, D., Codella, N.C.F., Celebi, E., Helba, B., Marchetti, M., Mishra, N., Skin Lesion Analysis toward Melanoma Detection: A Challenge at the International Symposium on Biomedical Imaging (ISBI) 2016, hosted by the International Skin Imaging Collaboration (ISIC). In [Online]. Available: https://arxiv.org/abs/1605.01397.
28. Noel, K.L., Codella, C.F., Gutman, D.M., Celebi, E., Helba, B., Marchetti, M.A., Dusza, S.W., Kalloo, A., Nabin Mishra, A.H., Kittler, H., Skin lesion analysis toward melanoma detection: A challenge at the 2017 International Symposium on Biomedical Imaging (ISBI), hosted by the International Skin Imaging Collaboration (ISIC). *Proceedings—International Symposium on Biomedical Imaging*, 2018-April, pp. 168–172, 2018.
29. Tschandl, P., Rosendahl, C., Kittler, H., Data descriptor: The HAM10000 dataset, a large collection of multi-source dermatoscopic images of common pigmented skin lesions. *Sci. Data*, 5, 1–9, 2018.

14

New Algorithms and Technologies for Data Mining

Padma Bonde[1], Latika Pinjarkar[2]*, Korhan Cengiz[3], Aditi Shukla[4]
and Maguluri Sudeep Joel[5]

[1]CSE, SSTC, Bhilai, India
[2]Shri Shankaracharya Technical Campus SSGI Bhilai, India
[3]Department of Electrical-Electronics Engineering, Edirne, Turkey
[4]Guru Ghasidas Vishwavidyala (A Central University) Bilaspur CG, Bhilai, India
[5]Sreyas Institute of Engineering and Technology, Hyderabad, India

Abstract

Information mining alludes to the disclosure and extraction of examples and information from enormous informational collections of organized and unstructured information. Information mining procedures have been around for a long time, notwithstanding continuous development with ML (Machine Learning). Computer performance, including computational computing, has made knowledge mining techniques easier to update with extensive information collections and business-driven undertakings. Developing ubiquity of information mining in the business investigation and showcasing is likewise because of the expansion of Big Data and Cloud Computing. Massive circulated information bases and strategies for similar preparation of information, for example, MapReduce, make immense volumes of information reasonable and valuable for organizations and the scholarly world. Thus, the expense of putting away and overseeing information is decreased by cloud specialist organizations (CSPs) which compromise a paymore only by way of costs arise ideal towards getting to interconnected workers, stockpiling limits (plate drives), GPUs (Graphics Processing Unit), and disseminated data sets. Thus, organizations can store, measure, and break down more information showing signs of improvement in business experiences.

Without anyone else, cutting-edge information mining strategies are groundbreaking in numerous classes of assignments. Some of them are inconsistency discovery, grouping, characterization, affiliation rule learning, relapse, and rundown. Every

*Corresponding author: latikabhorkar@gmail.com

Rohit Raja, Kapil Kumar Nagwanshi, Sandeep Kumar and K. Ramya Laxmi (eds.) Data Mining and Machine Learning Applications, (365–396) © 2022 Scrivener Publishing LLC

one of these errands assumes a critical part in whatever setting one may consider. For instance, abnormality discovery procedures assist organizations with securing against network interruption and information penetrate. In essence, regression models become effective in predicting market trends, sales, and charges. Bunching methods are among the most significant value in collecting enormous amounts of information on reliable objects that provide examples, situations both within and between them, despite prior knowledge on any legislation that administers beliefs. Because these models reflect, knowledge mining can position knowledge in the management of organizations and systems overall.

Data mining is now one of the real systems in data science with an emerging mechanical impact in the last several years. Without any probability, the data mining research would pursue and sometimes even improve over its upcoming years. All through this research, developers' scribbling their vision of changes to come from data mining. Starting with the unique sense of "data mining," we focus on issues which — as we would like to think — would also establish learnings in data mining.

Keywords: Future patterns, knowledge discovery, data mining, learning algorithm

14.1   Introduction

Throughout the 21st century, entities are used to a massive extent in the regular community in numerous developments. Every single day, entities use big data analytics and this data is in multiple areas. It could be as records, maybe visual setups, a recording, maybe a document (fluctuating cluster) while the data is presented in the different sorts such that the best available moves can be developed. Not only to analyze this evidence but also to make a good selection and follow relevant information. The user wants the relevant data, it should be retrieved from the data source and decided on a good alternative. Such a method is called data mining or Knowledge Hub or simply KDD (Knowledge Discovery Process). There is also a tremendous amount of knowledge, but we are merely prepared to give it valuable records/knowledge for market dynamics. It takes a massive amount of data to generate data. It may be different setups, such as sound/video, numbers, text, statistics, hypertext designs. Again for the exploitation of data, the retrieval of data is, in essence, inadequate, it involves a device for the scheduled analysis of data, the retrieval of the pit of data discarded, & the distribution of samples in original information [1].

Through vast quantities of data collected in papers, data sets, and various databases, it is essential to promote flexible tools for analyzing and recognizing specific data and analyzing useful information that could gain rapidly. The best response to all the above is 'Data Mining.' Data analysis is the processing of confidential, knowledgeable data from broad predetermined standards; this is an incredible innovation with an incredible community to enable organizations with the procurement of its most valuable data in their database server [2–4].

Data mining arrangements anticipate future patterns and activities, inspire organizations to implement constructive information-driven decisions. The mechanized, upcoming studies provided by data mining have pushed past reviews of various examinations, offering the proposed devices a specific option of incredibly expressive networks. Information mining techniques will resolve investigations that were usually too time-consuming to evaluate. We prepare sets of data for the discovery of secret instances, also for the detection of observant data, specialists can neglect the fact that it is beyond their expectations [5].

Data mining, known as Knowledge Discovery in Databases (KDD), is a non-trivial retrieval of evidence, previously unrecognized and essential data from data sources. It is a way of defining the embedded data/instance of the vaults.

AI & measurable calculation are two regular information mining calculations. The first is to utilize computerized reasoning innovation to naturally locate the necessary examples and boundaries in preparing and learning many example sets. The second is to utilize discriminant and likelihood examination, grouping, and relationship investigation to do tasks. Various calculations have diverse relating objectives and zones. These calculations can be free and they can be joined with one another for their utilization. Counterfeit neural organization strategy in AI calculation has a broad scope of uses, has a decent capacity to manage information, and self-sorting out learning capacity, yet can precisely distinguish, which is helpful for the grouping of issue information handling. Displaying can be utilized to work. Models are more assorted and various needs can be met. From the general perspective, the model of this strategy has higher exactness, better power, and more grounded elucidating capacity. It need not bother with the help of specialists for application, yet additionally has a few weaknesses. It is essential to prepare information. Additional time is spent, information is not insightful to comprehend, and there are constraints of versatility and receptiveness. AI is an approach to improve execution consequently by utilizing gathered information. The forerunner of the AI technique is the measurable learning and improvement hypothesis. It was brought into the world with the development of the PC. Up to now, numerous calculations have been proposed for various controls and various issues. The delegate calculations incorporate

Bayesian assessment, choice tree, and neural organization, uphold vector machine, k neighbor strategy, etc. It is an effective method to take care of information mining issues. Information mining is an interdisciplinary, application-situated idea. On the off chance that there is a lot of information gathering in enterprises and fields, for example, media communications, money, retail, and logical exploration, there are issues and needs of information mining [6, 7].

14.2   Machine Learning Algorithms

There will be countless estimates that can appear difficult as the details of the facts and figures are being spread around, and you are just supposed to know what they are doing where they are heading [8].

- First, is a set of rules related to knowledgeability?
- The second is sets of rules through their comparison in design or ability (such as collecting equivalent organisms).

Calculations Grouped by Learning Style
There are several other contexts in which a measurement could illustrate a problem that depends on its relationship to an activity or situation or something that we want to call data information. It is indeed prominent in AI and human-made thinking research articles to understand the teaching strategies that the estimation will take.

There are only a few simple cognitive processes or educational models that computation can have, and we are starting to discover them here with a few occurrences of measurements and issues the ways they fit.

One such quality laboratory or process of organizing Evaluated based is beneficial because it allows us to evaluate the roles of information examination and design prevention steps and choose a better-suited issue to produce the highest probable result [9].

14.3   Supervised Learning

Data information is called the production of data with a label or effect, e.g. spam/non-spam or an inventory value instantly. A framework is designed through some planning period in which it would be necessary to make assumptions and is modified when certain assumptions are not accurate. The security support continues until the deliverables meet

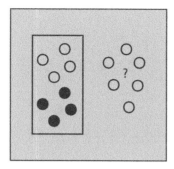

Figure 14.1 Shows supervised learning algorithm.

a desirable level of precision in the planning details shown in Figure 14.1 [10].

14.4   Unsupervised Learning

Data is not labeled and has no established result. The framework is designed by assuming the frameworks that are currently in the data sets. This may be to delete the essential advice. It may be by a statistical loop that the amount is systematically minimized, or it could be that the data is ordered by proximity shown in Figure 14.2 [11].

14.5   Semi-Supervised Learning

Data information seems to be a combination of identified and unprocessed versions. There seems to be an optimal forecasting problem, but the system

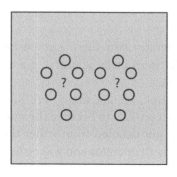

Figure 14.2 Shows unsupervised learning algorithm.

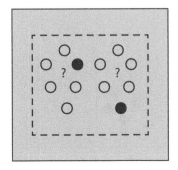

Figure 14.3 Shows semi-supervised learning algorithm.

must acquire expertise in composing the data and the objectives shown in Figure 14.3.

Review of Machine Learning Algorithms
While munching information towards appearance corporate choices, this is best commonly utilizing managed besides unaided knowledge strategies. An emotionally debated issue is semi-managed learning strategies in regions, such as picture order where massive datasets with not many named models [12].

Algorithm Grouped By Similarity
Measurements are being routinely collected based on their ability (how they qualify). Design, tree-based methods, and computational organization-motivated strategies.

It is a valuable technique used to collect, but it is not perfect. Also, some algorithms might easily match such various groups, such as learning image segmentation, which is both a simulated neuronal process and a case-based technique. In contrast, some categories have a similar structure that defines the problem and the category of measurements, such as regression and grouping [13].

Developers may operate with these circumstances through posting computations multiple times or by identifying a number that is qualitatively the "right" contest.

Throughout this section, we list many well-known Data frameworks compiled in the way we consider to become the most evolutionarily adaptive. The description is not detailed from either the activities or the estimates, but we believe it is an operator and will be helpful to think about the state of the property.

14.6   Regression Algorithms

Regression is concerned with demonstrating the link among both variables that are recursively developed using a quantity of the error in the method's assumptions shown in Figure 14.4.

Multivariate approaches are a solid performer of observations and have been suggested that pre-selected for realistic AI. It can also be misleading in recognizing that we can use regression to relate to the particular complaint and evaluation category. Relapse is a loop [14].

14.7   Case-Based Algorithms

Occasion-based supervised learning remains a matter of preference for circumstances or instances of preparation of knowledge deemed essential or essential to the design shown in Figure 14.5.

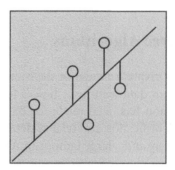

Figure 14.4 Shows regression learning algorithm.

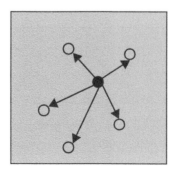

Figure 14.5 Shows instance-bases learning algorithm.

Those approaches periodically build necessary data for developed models and correlate additional knowledge with existing data are using a degree of similarity to find the best solution and make a prediction. Such example-based tactics are collectively known challengers physically carry all the strategies of prominence and memory-based practice. Zero is used for the portrayal of remote instances and the calculation of similarity used across incidents [15].

14.8   Regularization Algorithms

Enhancement to the following strategic approach (usually relapse strategies) that persecutes designs that rely solely on their complexity, favoring simpler designs that are also effectively summed up [16]. Recorded regularisation algorithms independently here, counting the fact that they are popular, ground-breaking, and essential modifications introduced to advanced methodologies in the most component shown in Figure 14.6.

14.9   Decision Tree Algorithms

Choice tree techniques create a model of decisions made in an accurate evaluation of the relevant data features. Choices fork in the decision tree until an expected decision has been made for data records [17]. Choice trees are planned for identification and relapse details. Choice trees are fast and accurate continuously and a large famous in AI shown in Figure 14.7.

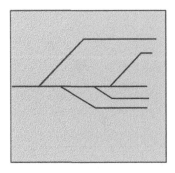

Figure 14.6 Shows regularization algorithm.

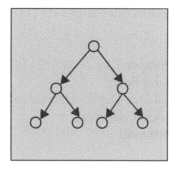

Figure 14.7 Shows decision-tree algorithm.

The most famous choice tree calculations are:

- CART(Classification and Regression Tree)
- ID3(Iterative Dichotomiser 3)
- C4.5 & C5.0
- CHAID(Chi-squared Automatic Interaction Detection)
- Decision Stump
- M5
- Conditional Decision Trees.

14.10   Bayesian Algorithms

Bayesian techniques explicitly apply Bayes' Theorem for issues, such as characterization and relapse shown in Figure 14.8.

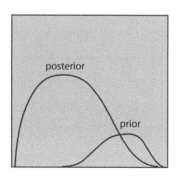

Figure 14.8 Shows bayesian algorithm.

The most famous Bayesian calculations are [18]:

- Naive Bayes
- Gaussian Naive Bayes
- Multinomial Naive Bayes
- AODE(Averaged One-Dependence Estimators)
- BBN(Bayesian Belief Network)
- BN(Bayesian Network).

14.11   Clustering Algorithms

Bunching, related to recurrence, shows the category of issues and the category of technologies.

Bunching algorithms are generally composed of display methods, e.g. centroid-based and hierarchical. All technologies are concerned overusing the relevant data's characteristic structures to recognize the relevant data through the most intense accessed treasury collections shown in Figure 14.9.

The most mainstream bunching calculations are [19]:

- k-Means
- k-Medians
- EM (Expectation–Maximization)
- Hierarchical Clustering.

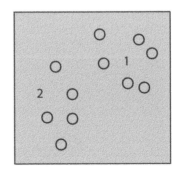

Figure 14.9 Shows clustering algorithm.

14.12   Association Rule Learning Algorithms

Association decides on different precepts for learning strategies that best illustrate the linkages among information factors [20]. Such recommendations can consider a meaningful and money-related beneficial relationship in massive, multifaceted databases that an organization can assault shown in Figure 14.10.

The most mainstream affiliation rule learning calculations are:

- Apriori calculation
- Eclat calculation.

14.13   Artificial Neural Network Algorithms

Counterfeit neural network models are concepts that stimulate the system and extra investment of natural neural organizations [21]. They are

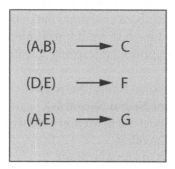

Figure 14.10 Shows association rule learning algorithm.

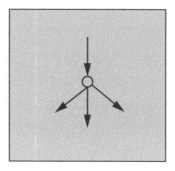

Figure 14.11 Shows artificial neural network algorithm.

responsible for coordinating examples that are usually used for remission and clustering problems but are a massive site-field that includes so many computations and variations for all types of problems (Figure 14.11).

The most famous counterfeit neural organization calculations are:

- Perceptron
- MLP(Multilayer Perceptrons)
- Back-Propagation
- Stochastic Gradient Descent
- Hopfield Network
- RBFN(Radial Basis Function Network).

14.14 Deep Learning Algorithms

Profound Learning Methods [22] are mostly a cutting-edge improvement to the Artificial Neural Networks that misuses plentiful respectable calculations. They are seriously concerned about constructing a bit larger and much more mind-boggling cognitive organizations. As noted above, methods are mainly concerned about enormous datasets of named simple information, for example, picture, text, sound, and video shown in Figure 14.12.

The most mainstream profound learning calculations are [23]:

- CNN(Convolutional Neural Network)
- RNNs(Recurrent Neural Networks)
- LSTMs(Long Short-Term Memory Networks)
- Stacked Auto-Encoders
- DBM(Deep Boltzmann Machine)
- DBN(Deep Belief Networks).

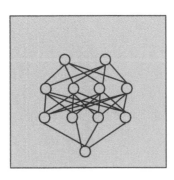

Figure 14.12 Shows deep learning algorithm.

14.15   Dimensionality Reduction Algorithms

Besides clustering methods, computational complexity reduces the search for and misappropriation of the intuitive design of the data, but for this circumstance in a solo manner or asks to summarize or illustrate information using fewer data [24]. This may be of value to visualize under-representation or disaggregate data that could then be used in controlled learning theory. A considerable lot of these techniques can be adjusted for use in arrangement and relapse shown in Figure 14.13.

- PCA (Principal Component Analysis)
- PCR (Principal Component Regression)
- PLSR (Partial Least Squares Regression)
- Sammon Mapping
- MDS (Multidimensional Scaling)
- Projection Pursuit
- LDA (Linear Discriminant Analysis)
- MDA (Mixture Discriminant Analysis)
- QDA (Quadratic Discriminant Analysis)
- FDA (Flexible Discriminant Analysis).

14.16   Ensemble Algorithms

Gathering techniques are designs made up of several more delicate designs that are easily ready and able and whose objectives are united here and there to make a particular prediction. Much effort is being put into helpless learners to participate and how they can be consolidated [25]. This seems

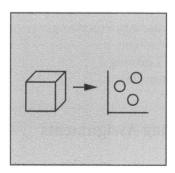

Figure 14.13 Shows dimensionality reduction algorithm.

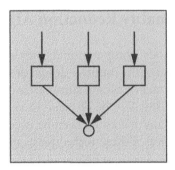

Figure 14.14 Shows ensemble algorithm.

to be an amazingly wonderful category of methodologies, and it is standard shown in Figure 14.14.

- Enhancement
- Bootstrapped clustering
- AdaBoost
- conventional system
- layered Generalization
- GBM (Gradient Boosting Machine)
- GBRT (Gradient Boosted Trees of Regression)
- Random Forests.

14.17   Other Machine Learning Algorithms

- Feature selection algorithms
- Algorithm precision assessment
- Performance measures
- Optimization calculations
- Computational intelligence
- CV(Computer Vision)
- NLP(Natural Language Processing)
- Recommender Systems
- Reinforcement Learning
- Graphical Models [26].

14.18   Data Mining Assignments

Data mining aims to identify permissible innovative, feasibly useful, and acceptable links and instances in available systems [27]. Data mining tasks can be shown either as predictive or descriptive. The Predictive Model predicts the estimation of information using realized results from different information, while the Descriptive Model recognizes examples or links in information. Compared to the perceptive model, an illuminating model is used to examine the inspected properties, not to predict new properties. Prescient model information Mining initiatives include the investigation of order, forecasting, relapse, and timing. The Descriptive Errand includes clustering, summaries, association rules, and sequence examination (Figure 14.15).

Among all the predictive analytics, identification is expected to be the strongest-perceived of all data mining is approaching. There are three main features in sorting undertakings.

- The learning process is handled
- The element required is a straight shot
- The design constructed can assign additional knowledge to one with several well-defined groups.

For example, provided groups of patients linked to clinical treatment reactions, the form of care to which each patient is expected to respond are recognized [28]. Unlike the model of characterization, the motive behind the analysis model is to determine the potential outcome related to present behavior. Its output can be a clear cut or a unique identifier. For example, given the prediction models of the Mastercard transactions, the likelihood that a specific transaction is wrong can be expected.

Another Analytical Model known as Factual Regression is a Controlled Learning Technique, which involves analyzing the dependency of specific performance characteristics on the approximation of various acronyms in a similar circumstance and developing a model capable of predicting these characteristics in new situations. For example, in the sense of the

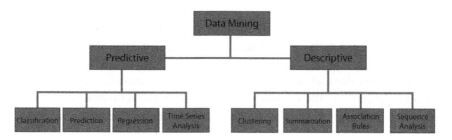

Figure 14.15 Information mining assignments and models.

Mastercard Exchange Information Index, a method that can predict the likelihood of deception for new services can be created. Prediction programs including at least one previous-subordinate feature are referred to as time-arrangement issues.

Time arrangement investigation typically involves numerical forecasting outcomes, such as the potential cost of individual stocks [29].

The second data mining approach is known as the Descriptive Technique. Expressive knowledge mining is usually used to create recurrence, cross-organization, and linkages. The enlightenment technique can be characterized by discovering interesting knowledge-related normalities, revealing examples, and discovering fascinating subgroups concerning the central part of the information [30]. In preparation, considers [31] used Descriptive to assess the effect of the section on individual elements. Rundown maps details in subsets of associated basic images [32]. Essential metrics, e.g. Mean, Standard Deviation, Variance, Mode, and Median, may be used as a Summary approach.

In Clustering, much knowledge is divided into many groups to gather items with comparative attributes. Bunching is best used to discover the gatherings of objects that are comparative. For example, provided an informative set of clients, subgroups of clients with similar purchase activity can be identified. Affiliations or Relation Analysis are used to find similarities between attributes and objects, e.g., the presence of one example implies another example. For example, how often one thing is identified with another in terms of circumstances and logical outcomes. This is regular in establishing a form of objective relation between the different related factors of the model. These relationships may be the relationship between ascribes within a similar information thing like ('Out of the customers who bought milk, 64% also bought bread') or the relationship between different information things like ('very time a particular stock drops 5%, it triggers a resultant 13% in another stock somewhere in the range of 2 and a month and a half later'). Affiliation Rules are a well-known form of business bin checking, as all possible blends of conceivably fascinating item groupings can be investigated [33].

Consequently, the study of relations between items over an unknown timeframe is regularly referred to as a sequence analysis [34]. Succession Analysis is used to classify consecutive examples of knowledge. Examples in the dataset depend on the timing of the events, and they are like affiliation information. The relationship depends on the schedule and Market Basket inquiry. The goods are to be purchased simultaneously for Sequence Analysis.

14.19   Data Mining Models

There exist various approaches to sort out and investigate information. How to deal with select relies much upon our motivation and the type of information (organized versus unstructured). However, we can wind up with a specific setup of information that may be beneficial for one errand, however not very great for another. Subsequently, to make information usable, one ought to know about hypothetical models and approaches utilized in information mining and acknowledge possible compromises and traps in every one of them.

14.20   Non-Parametric & Parametric Models

The viewpoint on the data processing paradigm is whether or not it has borders. As far as limits are concerned, we get a judgment between parametric and non-parametric models. In the main type of models, we choose the ability that, in our opinion, is ideally suited to the planning details. For example, we can choose the straightforward capacity of the structure $F(X) = q0 + q1\ x1 + q2\ x2 + q. + qp\ xp$, in which x's are the outlines of the details (e.g., house size, floor, different rooms), and q's are the ambiguous limits of the model. These limits may be conceived of as amounts that specify the contribution of various gatherings (e.g., house size, floor size, number of rooms) to calculate capacity Y (e.g., house cost). The task of a functional form is then to explore limits Q using certain measurable methods, such as straight relapse or measured relapse.

The fundamentally best position of estimation methods is that they contain an ability for connexions between peaks in our knowledge. This allows parametric models an incredible heuristic, deriving, and anticipatory system. At the same time, whatever it might be, parametric models have a few entanglements. If the capacity we have chosen is overly simplistic, it may fail to explain the intricate details' designs adequately. This problem, known as under-fitting, is continuously used in direct capacity with non-direct details. Again, suppose our ability is overly intricate (e.g., with polynomials). In that case, it may end up in overfitting, a situation in which our model responds to the disturbance of knowledge instead of the actual examples and is not generally applicable to new products shown in Figure 14.16.

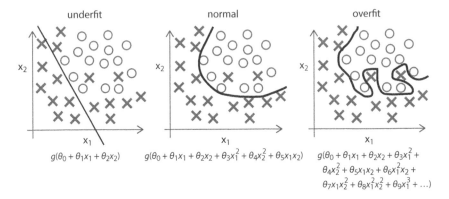

Figure 14.16 Descriptions of under-fit, standard, and over-fit versions.

Non-parametric systems are exempt from all these concerns because they are not suspicious of the primitive sense of capability. In this manner, non-parametric models are appropriate for the management of unorganized data. Also, because non-parametric systems do not reduce the issue by evaluating a few limits, they require extensive databases to obtain an accurate assessment of power.

14.21   Flexible vs. Restrictive Methods

Data mining and ML designs can also differ in terms of versatility. As a rule, solution methods, such as direct relapse, are known to be deeply infeasible on the basis that they require ordered information and genuine reactions (Y) to function. However, this very aspect makes them ideal for deduction – the discovery of similarities among features (e.g., how the percentage of local crime impacts household costs). In the same way, prohibitive prototypes are subject to interpretation and simple. Even so, this definition is not valid for able to adapt models (e.g., non-parametric models). Since adaptable models do not doubt the form of ability that regulates cognition, they are minor subject to interpretation. In specific environments, however, the lack of usability is not an issue. For, e.g., when our solitary intrigue is a forecast of stock costs, we should not, in any way, worry about both the usability of the design.

14.22   Unsupervised vs. Supervised Learning

These days, we receive a ton of nearly administered and solo Machine Learning. New neural organizations dependent on these ideas remain to gain ground in picture &discourse acknowledgment or self-ruling driving consistently. A characteristic inquiry, however, is the contrast between unaided and directed learning draws near? The principle distinction is in the type of information utilized and strategies to investigate it. In a managed getting the hang of setting, we utilize marked information that comprises highlights/factors and ward factors (Y or reaction). This information is then taken care of to the learning calculation that looks for designs and a capacity that controls connections among autonomous and subordinate factors. The restored potential could then be related to the anticipation of high expectations. We are also watching a vector of highlights in unaided learning (e.g., house size, floor). That being said, the differentiation with active learning

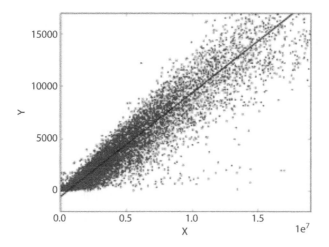

Figure 14.17a Shows supervised learning.

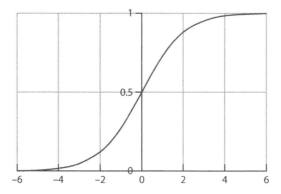

Figure 14.17b Shows sigmoid function.

does not have any associated outcomes (Y). In this case, we cannot have any significant bearing on a straight relapse model since there is no reaction esteems to anticipate. Along these lines, in a solo setting, we are working visually impaired in some sense shown in Figures 14.17a and 14.17b.

14.23   Data Mining Methods

In this segment, we will portray specialized subtleties of a few information mining techniques. Our decision fell on direct relapse, grouping, and bunching strategies. Such strategies are amongst the best known in knowledge mining as they cover a wide range of activities involving assumption and anticipation. In comparison, such techniques thoroughly highlight the critical outlines of the data mining models mentioned above. For example, straight relapse and order (strategic relapse) are parametric, administered, and restrictive techniques, whereas clustering (k-implies) has a position with a subsection of non-parametrical methods unaided strategies [35].

Linear Machine Learning Regression
Simple regression is a technique for seeking a specific capability that intelligently resembles the relation between some of the objectives of the knowledge and the hierarchical parameter. It finds an enhanced capacity to speak to and clarify information. Contemporary advances in handling force and calculation techniques permit utilizing direct relapse in the mix with ML calculations to deliver snappy and effective capacity streamlining. In this segment, we will portray an execution of the direct relapse with slope plummet to create an algorithmic fitting of information to straight capacity.

Logistic Regression Classification
The command is a period of judgment on the class/categorization to whom the object has its location. Analysis methods using AI calculations have different applications varying from marketing emails to diagnostic techniques and suggested structures. Relating to specific regression, we are working on a grouping problem with a designated collection of preparations that integrates a few examples. However, expectations in the knowledge index map do not reflect a numerical reward, as it necessarily implies, but rather a simple reduction in value (e.g., class). For example, patients' clinical data may reflect on groups of patients: those with heart disease and those with a deadly illness. The activity to measure the order is to acquire the expertise to predict better what kind of illness (dangerous or amiable) a patient has. If there are only two groups, the problem is known as a dual

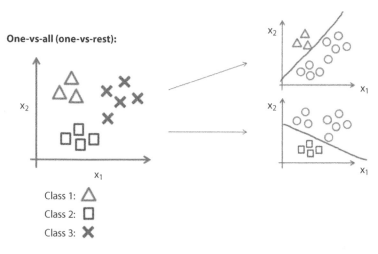

Figure 14.18 Shows one-versus all or multi-class classification.

classification. Alternatively, a multi-class structure may be used when we have more groups of knowledge.

Proactive regression is one of the most well-known mechanisms of classification in health sciences and ML. Proactive regression focuses on the perceptron ability with a remarkable property: it maps every actual number to the (0,1) range. Therefore, it can be helpful to determine the probability (somewhere between the range of 0 and 1) that perception falls within a particular class. For example, a theoretical calculation. Six would mean a 60% likelihood that a patient's malignant growth would be at risk if we defined the disease as 0 and harmful malignancy as 1. These properties make sigmoid ability useful for simultaneous depiction, but the multi-class structure is also imaginable shown in Figure 14.18.

Clustering Methods

As we have seen, grouping is an unaided strategy that is helpful when the information is not marked or if there is no reaction esteems (y) [36]. Bunching perceptions of an informational index include apportioning them into unmistakable gatherings, so perceptions inside each gathering are very like one another, while perceptions in the various gatherings share less for all intents and purpose. To delineate this technique, we should take a model from advertising. Accept that we have a significant volume of information about customers. This information may include middle family salary, occupation, good ways from the closest metropolitan territory, etc. This data might then be utilized for the market division. Our errand is to recognize different gatherings of clients without the earlier information on shared characteristics that may exist among them. Such division might be then utilized for fitting advertising efforts that target explicit bunches of shoppers.

There are various grouping strategies to do this; however, the most well-known are k-mean bunching calculation and progressive bunching. This segment will portray the k-implies strategy, an exceptionally productive calculation covering a broad scope of utilization cases. In the k-implies bunching, we need to parcel perceptions into a pre-indicated number of groups. Even though setting various groups before bunching is viewed as a constraint of the k-implies calculation, it is a highly incredible procedure. In our grouping issue, we are given a preparation set of xi,...,x(m) shoppers with particular highlights xj. Highlights are vectors of factors that depict different properties of customers, for example, middle pay, age, sexual orientation, etc. The standard is that every perception (customer) ought to have a place with precisely one group and no perceptions ought to have a place with more than one bunch shown in Figure 18.19.

The concept behind the k-implies bundling is that a decent crew is the one for which even the internal bundle variation or the internal bundle of squares (WCSS) (difference) is insignificant. Buyers in a common category should interact more with each other for all purposes and purposes than with buyers from separate classes. Our involvement is to restrict WCSS computationally to all pre-indicated classes to achieve this design. This task shall be done in the corresponding state.

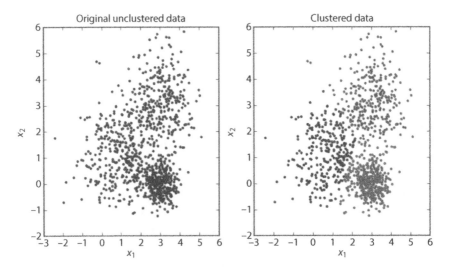

Figure 18.19 Shows illustration of clustering process.

14.24   Proposed Algorithm

14.24.1   Organization Formation Procedure

Initially, an unfocused and weighted organization with a related solitary section is worked for each class. In the existing system, Gl describes the fundamental class l $\in$ {1,2, ..., L}. There would be an interface between an individual's vertexes, on the off possibility that they are not necessarily a predetermined edge between both the element vectors of the Euclidean separation (ED). Even the relation should have been at odds with the heaviness of the component divergence. Therefore, the intensity border between some of the centers is conveyed as an equation.

$$a_{ij} = a_{ji} = \begin{cases} 1 & if \left\| x_i - x_j \right\| = 0 \\ \left(\dfrac{1}{\left\| x_i - x_j \right\|} \right)^{\alpha} & if \ 0 < \left\| x_i - x_j \right\| \leq \varepsilon \\ 0 & if \left\| x_i - x_j \right\| > \varepsilon \end{cases} \tag{14.1}$$

In the built organization, all the hubs are inward associated under the rule of a contiguous grid. There is a d feature in any significant developments in the situation, and there should be a dimensional information package. The second feature of the I-th tuple properties referred to the knowledge object type mark. The motive behind AI is to plan from x to y, and this preparation is called a classification algorithm. Note that each class needs to have an organization association part, so the selection of boundaries of ε must mirror the circumstance. After the progression, we effectively develop our organization, which is additionally communicated in formula (14.2).

$$G_l^{(i)}, \forall l \in \{1,2,\dots\dots L\}, \forall i \in \{1,2,\dots\dots u\} \tag{14.2}$$

In the next span of the depiction cycle, the whole of the is first of the organizations will be addressed, analyzed, outlined in the subsequent parts.

Network Entropy Computing [37]
The Network Control Theories for the plan of distributed control method, the whole structure made up of various subsystems, each of which was

decided by a particular regulator. For example, one possible implementation subsystem and communication between the regulatory diagrams, use the issue to schedule the regulator, conduct some regulation or limit control costs, and simultaneously consider these connectivity models. Organizational entropy is the entropy of a stochastic system connected to the constituent network [34, 36]. In this manner, we set out the definition of the stochastic system in formula (14.3).

$$P_{ij} = \frac{a_{ij} v_j}{\lambda v_i} \tag{14.3}$$

With this severe technique, we can ascertain the organization utilizing the stochastic cycle of the extent of p_{ij} dynamic entropy portrays the change $i \to j$. Furthermore, it is the fixed dispersion of $\pi = \pi p$. Combined optimizing of the presentation of the distributed data mining system are preparing an analyzed web-based learning measurement and drawing out its usual incentive. The best-suited combination arrangement could get online content grouping problem gives total data on characteristics and their classification ability is added to the accuracy and expense of the data. We describe the regret of the contrast between the absolute expected return best-expressed order scheme is given maximum information classification ability of accuracy and the expected absolute returns of each participant using the measurement. We render H(p) a complex abundance. Point by point of enrolment shall be defined as:

$$H(p) = \Sigma_i \pi_i H_i, \text{ where } H_i = -\Sigma_j p_{ij} \log p_{ij} \tag{14.4}$$

14.25   The Regret of Learning Phase

Throughout this segment, we define the lament as the exhibition proportion of the learning measure used by learners [38]. Simple to understand, it is a sorrow that has been decreased due to the mysterious structure elements. Researchers sincerely apologize for the student's learning estimation has characterized the best for us. The article work for the stage is characterized as:

$$R(T) = \sum_{t=1}^{T} \pi_{k(x_t)} x(t) - E\left[\sum_{t=1}^{T} (I(y_t^i = y_t) - d_{k(x_t)}) \right] \tag{14.5}$$

The information collected in the transmitted handling of many disseminated heterogeneous students with the precision of the grouping capability is ambiguous. Throughout this context, counting and service costs find it irrational to assume learners use the centralized information mining innovation to access the entire collected data. Will regulate first get acquainted with a classification algorithm for each view case using the labels. Most confident about the perceptions of each unidentifiable information classifier and then use the focus to create extra named information planning. By determining the various perspective on a similar data index, it is possible to find a correlation between specific types of information from a predetermined context. Some other linked specialized committee device is designed from the classification of the object. The portrait is shown in Figure 14.20.

The Validation & Decision Procedure

At last, we will characterize the fluffy classifier C that chooses what class the information thing has a place with. The plan to clarify the organization's property to manage irregular changes, so the information thing does not have a place with a specific class will not influence the separate organization.

Consequently, the task order is the significance of class. The SVN calculation is a "delicate" grouping strategy in which the articles are allocated to the bunches with a level of conviction. In this way, an item can have more than one bunch with various degrees of conviction. It attempts to discover the component focuses in each bunch, named the group's focal point,

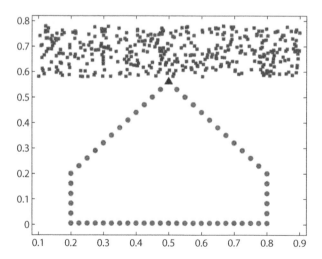

Figure 14.20 The description of the learning phase.

ascertaining each item's enrolment in the bunch. The numerical articulation appears as follows.

$$C(i,l) = \frac{\delta_l^{(i)}}{\sum_{k \in L} \delta_k^{(i)}}, \text{ where } \delta_l^{(i)} = \frac{H(G_l^{(i)})}{H(G_l)} \tag{14.6}$$

Experimental Discussion and Simulation
To check the viability and possibility of our proposed technique, we lead mathematical and exploratory reenactment in this segment. Right off the bat, we present the test condition. Later, we present three reproductions to outline the productivity of the significant proposed level order technique when applied in genuine and counterfeit informational collections and contrast its outcomes and conventional order strategies.

Condition of the Experiment
The state of reenactment shall be set out in the corresponding conditions. Four physical devices (MacBook Pro) with 4 TB hard rings and 6 GB of RAM and a rehabilitation program are implemented on Windows Win7 level. The databases we have adopted change a lot. The following datasets are simply models: (1) Seeds Data Set; (2) UCI database; (3) Iris Information Index; (4) Cornell University database; (5) Harvard College database [38].

Reenactment of Harvard Datasets
The Harvard database contains three classes (*Iris setosa, Iris versicolour, Iris virginica*) and 150 times, where each class refers to a kind of plant. Figure 14.21 indicates our result, and we should conclude that our methodology is hearty. The different results are shown in Figures 14.22–14.24.

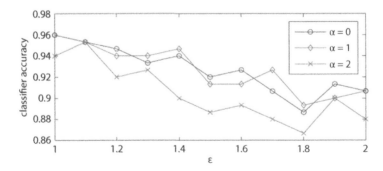

Figure 14.21 Harvard database result.

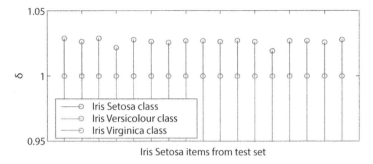

Figure 14.22 Sub-part result of *Iris setosa*.

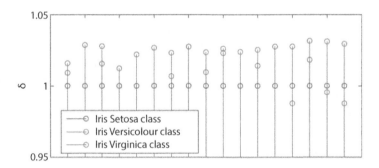

Figure 14.23 Sub-part result of iris versicolour.

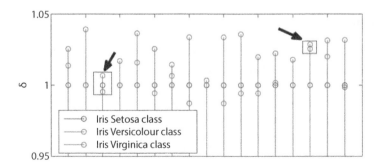

Figure 14.24 Sub-part result of *Iris virginica*.

14.26   Conclusion

Many enormous data technologies are also being built and discussed in the software engineering network, requiring online sorting and an example of recognition of enormous data pools obtained from component organizations, picture and video structures, online conversation phases, medical offices, and so on. However, as a complicated NP problem, data mining processes are facing many challenges. In this part of the progression.

Information mining models and strategies depicted in this paper permit information researchers to play out a wide cluster of errands, including surmising, forecast, and investigating. Direct relapse is impressive in the expectation of patterns and induction of connections between highlights. In its turn, a strategic relapse might be utilized in the programmed grouping of practices, cycles, and items, which makes it helpful in the business examination and inconsistency recognition. At last, grouping permits to make bits of knowledge about unlabeled information and derive concealed connections that may drive compelling business choices and critical decisions.

Throughout this Chapter, we propose an innovative explanation analysis and data order method for mining techniques and the release of information. We are receiving the organization to change the standard technologies. The outcome shows the viability of our work and we intend to accomplish more test investigation and numerical exploration and quickly checked on the different information mining patterns and applications from its initiation to the future. This audit puts the center around the hot and promising zones of information mining. Even though not many territories are named here in this paper, they are typically overlooked. This paper gives another view of a specialist concerning the utilization of information mining in colonial government assistance.

References

1. *Introduction to Data Mining and Knowledge Discovery*, Third Edition, Two Crows Corporation, Potomac, MD, U.S.A, 1999.
2. Larose, D.T., *Discovering Knowledge in Data: An Introduction to Data Mining*, John Wiley & Sons Inc., Hoboken, New Jersey, 2005.
3. Dunham, M.H. and Sridhar, S., *Data Mining: Introductory and Advanced Topics*, 1st Edition, Pearson Education, New Delhi, 2006.
4. Chapman, P., Clinton, J., Kerber, R., Khabaza, T., Reinartz, T., Shearer, C., Wirth, R., SPSS, *CRISP-DM 1.0: Step-by-step data mining guide, NCR Systems Engineering Copenhagen (USA and Denmark), DaimlerChrysler AG*

(Germany), SPSS Inc. (USA) and OHRA Verzekeringenen Bank Group B.V (The Netherlands), SPSS, USA, 2000.

5. Pathak, S., Raja, R., Sharma, V., Ramya Laxmi, K., A Framework of ICT Implementation on Higher Educational Institution with Data Mining Approach. *Eur. J. Eng. Res. Sci.*, 5, 2506–8016, 2019.

6. Camargo, A., Papadopoulou, D., Spyropoulou, Z., Vlachonasios, K., Doonan, J.H., Gay, A.P., Objective definition of rosette shape variation using a combined computer vision and data mining approach. *PLoS One*, 9, 5, e96889, 2014.

7. Samei, B., Li, H., Keshtkar, F., Rus, V., Graesser, A.C., Context-based speech act classification in intelligent tutoring systems, in: *Intelligent Tutoring Systems*, pp. 236–241, Springer International Publishing, Honolulu, HI, USA, 2014.

8. Samei, B., Li, H., Keshtkar, F., Rus, V., Graesser, A.C., Context-based speech act classification in intelligent tutoring systems, in: *Intelligent Tutoring Systems*, pp. 236–241, Springer International Publishing, Honolulu, HI, USA, 2014.

9. Valsamidis, S., Kazanidis, I., Kontogiannis, S., Karakos, A., A Proposed Methodology for E-Business Intelligence Measurement Using Data Mining Techniques, in: *Proceedings of the 18th Panhellenic Conference on Informatics*, ACM, pp. 1–6, 2014.

10. Shukla, D.P., Patel, S.B., Sen, A.K., A literature review in health informatics using data mining techniques. *Int. J. Software Hardware Res. Eng. J.*, 2, 1–8, 2014.

11. Berry, M.J. and Linoff, G., *Data mining techniques: For marketing, sales, and customer support*, John Wiley & Sons Inc., The Hague, Netherlands, 1997.

12. Vaughan, L. and Chen, Y., Data mining from web search queries: A comparison of google trends and Baidu index. *J. Assoc. Inf. Sci. Technol.*, 66, 1, 13–22, 2015.

13. Sonawane, N. and Nandwalkar, B., Time-Efficient Sentinel Data Mining using GPU. *Int. J. Eng. Res. Technol.*, ESRSA Publications, 4, 02, pp. 10–17, February 2015.

14. Barrera, L.E., Montes-Servín, A.B., Ramírez-Tirado, L.A., Salinas-Parra, F., Bañales-Méndez, J.L., Sandoval-Ríos, M., Arrieta, Ó., Cytokine profile determined by data-mining analysis set into clusters of non-small-cell lung cancer patients according to prognosis. *Ann. Oncol.*, 26, 2, 428–435, 2015.

15. Kao, J.-H., Chen, H.-I., Lai, F., Hsu, L.-M., Liaw, H.-T., Decision Tree Approach to Predict Lung Cancer the Data Mining Technology, in: *Ubiquitous Computing Application and Wireless Sensor*, pp. 273–282, Springer Netherlands, 2015.

16. Tiwari, L., Raja, R., Awasthi, V., Miri, R., Sinha, G.R., Alkinani, M.H., Polat, K., Detection of lung nodule and cancer using novel Mask-3 FCM and TWEDLNN algorithms. *Measurement*, 172, 19–38, 2021, 108882.

17. Moeyersoms, J., de Fortuny, E.J., Dejaeger, K., Baesens, B., Martens, D., Comprehensible software fault and effort prediction: A data mining approach. *J. Syst. Software*, 100, 80–90, 2015.

18. Fujimoto, M., Higuchi, T., Hosomi, K., Takada, M., Manchikanti, L., Pampati, V., Benyamin, R.M. *et al.*, Association between Statin Use and Cancer: Data Mining of a Spontaneous Reporting Database and a Claims Database. *Int. J. Med. Sci.*, 12, 3, 223–233, 2015.

19. Maucec, M., Singh, A.P., Bhattacharya, S., Yarus, J.M., Fulton, D.D., Orth, J.M., Multivariate Analysis and Data Mining of Well-Stimulation Data by Use of Classification-and-Regression Tree with Enhanced Interpretation and Prediction Capabilities. *SPE Economics & Management Preprint*, 2015.

20. Rohit Kumar, K. and Raja, R., Broadcasting the Transaction System by Using Blockchain Technology, in: *Design Engineering*, pp. 2115–21, June 2021. http://thedesignengineering .com/index.php/DE/article/view/1912.

21. Li, Y., Yang, Q., Lai, S., Li, B., A New Speculative Execution Algorithm Based on C4. 5 Decision Tree for Hadoop, in: *Intelligent Computation in Big Data E.*

22. Sathyadevan, S. and Nair, R.R., Comparative Analysis of Decision Tree Algorithms: ID3, C4. 5 and Random Forest, in: *Computational Intelligence in Data Mining*, vol. 1, pp. 549–562, Springer, India, 2015.

23. Zhang, S.J., Zheng, X.S., Wang, Q., Fan, Y.W., Ma, X.D., Hao, X.O., New satellite image associative classification algorithm based on Gabor texture, in: *Remote Sensing and Smart City*, vol. 64, p. 257, 2015.

24. Hussain, F. and Jeong, J., Efficient Deep Neural Network for Digital Image Compression Employing Rectified Linear Neurons. *J. Sens.*, 2016, 10–25, 2015.

25. Sahu, A.K., Sharma, S., Tanveer, M., Internet of Things attack detection using hybrid Deep Learning Model. *Comput. Commun.*, 176, 146–154, 2021, https://doi.org/10.1016/j.comcom.2021.05.024.

26. Gong, M., Su, L., Jia, M., Chen, W., Fuzzy clustering with a modified MRF energy function for change detection in synthetic aperture radar images. *IEEE Trans. Fuzzy Syst.*, 22, 1, 98–109, 2014.

27. Wang, F., Xiong, Y., Weng, Z., Neural Network Modeling of Submarine Shell, in: *Vibration Engineering and Technology of Machinery*, pp. 1055–1064, Springer International Publishing, India, 2015.

28. Wang, H. and Wang, J., An effective image representation method using kernel classification, in: *Tools with Artificial Intelligence (ICTAI), 2014 IEEE 26th International Conference on*, November 2014, pp. 853–858.

29. Chen, P., Fu, X., Teng, S., Lin, S., Lu, J., Research on Micro-blog Sentiment Polarity Classification Based on SVM, in: *Human-Centered Computing*, pp. 392–404, Springer International Publishing, 2015.

30. Dellepiane, U. and Palagi, L., Using SVM to combine global heuristics for the Standard Quadratic Problem. *Eur. J. Oper. Res.*, 241, 3, 596–605, 2015.

31. Sumit, S., High-performance EEG signal classification using classifiability and the Twin SVM. *Appl. Soft Comput.*, 30, 305–318, 2015.

32. Zhang, T., Wu, S., Dong, J., Wei, J., Wang, K., Tang, H., Yang, X., Li, H., Quantitative and classification analysis of slag samples by laser-induced breakdown spectroscopy (LIBS) coupled with support vector machine (SVM) and partial least square (PLS) methods. *J. Anal. At. Spectrom.*, 1, 1–5, 2015.

33. Ghougassian, P.G. and Manousiouthakis, V., Minimum entropy generation for isothermal endothermic/exothermic reactor networks. *AIChE J.*, 61, 1, 103–117, 2015.

34. Bindzus, N., Cargnoni, F., Gatti, C., Richter, B., Jensen, T.R., Takata, M., Iversen, B.B., Mapping the complete bonding network in KBH 4 using the combined power of powder diffraction and maximum entropy method. *Comput. Theor. Chem.*, 1053, 245–253, 2015.

35. D.C. Frost and S.F. Bryant, Probe Packet Discovery of Entropy Value Causing Specific Paths to be Taken Through a Network. U.S. Patent 20,150,003,255, 2015) January 1.

36. Wright, P., Parker, M.C., Lord, A., Minimum- and Maximum-Entropy Routing and Spectrum Assignment for Flexgrid Elastic Optical Networking [Invited]. *J. Opt. Commun. Networking*, 7, 1, A66–A72, 2015.

37. Yu, D. and Deng, L., Computational Network, in: *Automatic Speech Recognition*, pp. 267–298, Springer, London, 2015.

38. Pathak, S., Bhatt, P., Raja, R., Sharma, V., Weka VS Rapid Miner: Models Comparison in Higher Education with these Two Tools of Data. *SAMRIDDHI*, 12, Special Issue 3, pp. 85–88, 2020.

15

Classification of EEG Signals for Detection of Epileptic Seizure Using Restricted Boltzmann Machine Classifier

Sudesh Kumar, Rekh Ram Janghel* and Satya Prakash Sahu

National Institute of Technology, Raipur, India

Abstract

Epilepsy is a disease that is an electrophysiological disorder related to the brain and is characterized by various types of recurrent seizures. Electroencephalogram (EEG) is a test that is developed by various neurologists to capture the electrical signals that occur in the brain and is widely used for the Analysis and detection of epileptic seizures. As we know that it is tough to identify the various types of electrical activities by visual inspection; thus, it opens up the vast research in the field of biomedical engineering to develop a system and various algorithms for the identification of these activities and changes in the human brain. Therefore an automated seizure detection system is needed for the classification of epileptic seizures. We handled the EEG dataset of CHB-MIT (scalp EEG) to discover if our model could outflank the best in class proposed models. We have proposed a methodology based on the Restricted Boltzmann Machine (RBM) neural network model, which is used to perform classification over the EEG signals among binary classes, namely a healthy (non-seizure) and non-healthy (seizure) classes. The analysis is performed on an open accessible CHB-MIT data set. The model performance is assessed based on various performance metrices like accuracy, specificity and sensitivity. The test results accomplished in terms of accuracy, sensitivity, and specificity are 99.20%, 98.94%, and 98.89%, individually. The results outperformed the existing methods.

*Corresponding author: rrjanghel.it@nitrr.ac.in

Rohit Raja, Kapil Kumar Nagwanshi, Sandeep Kumar and K. Ramya Laxmi (eds.) Data Mining and Machine Learning Applications, (397–422) © 2022 Scrivener Publishing LLC

Keywords: Deep learning, restricted boltzmann machine, epilepsy, classification, electroencephalogram, seizure detection, contrastive divergence, Gibbs sampling

15.1 Introduction

Epilepsy is a common disorder which affects more than 40 million people worldwide, and affecting mostly people coming from developing countries like China, the U.S.A, India, etc. The research study of the World Health Organization shows that more than 2 million people are affected with epilepsy. Also, their study shows that at least 40% of the cases occur during childhood or adolescence [1]. Most of the people whose age is more than 65 years are also affected by the onset seizure of this disease. Study shows that the people who are affected by this disease are likely to die at an early age when compared with the normal people who do not have this disease. Hence, researchers have found that the study of epilepsy is a field that needs to be researched in biomedical studies.

Epilepsy is a disorder that occurs in the human brain, and it is characterized by various seizures which can affect various aged persons because it is a disease that normally occurs in any person. Recurrent convulsions occur effectively over a time period in the human brain when the seizure occurs. The episodes may vary as long as 1 s to as long as one year over a time period. Many think that epilepsy and the disorder that occurs due to seizures are the same, but this is not true as both are considered to be two different things [2]. One of the most important things, if one has to detect an epileptic seizure in the human brain, is that they have to be kept under constant monitoring, which usually requires a patient to take in-admission in the hospital. This is considered to be the most expensive thing, and it might take many days to detect the epileptic seizure in the human brain. The disadvantage is that when the patient is being screened for the seizure from the EEG records across the many days can become quite an unusual task. So, in these types of situations automated seizure detection system can become quite useful [3].

In addition to the modern-day seizure detection systems, early warning seizure systems have also become quite useful these modern days. Research studies show that there is growing awareness that this system has become a powerful tool in the detection of seizures in the brain [4]. Many researchers have proposed various types of machine learning and deep learning algorithms to elaborate the study of epilepsy in order to design such algorithms which can detect the epileptic seizure with high-performance metrics like accuracy, etc. [5]. Researchers have categorized the brain signals in five different waveforms, which can be seen in Table 15.1. The beta and the gamma waveforms are the waveforms in which an epileptic seizure is more likely to be found. Our study shows that the algorithm which we have proposed is quite unique as it is the first algorithm which is designed using Restricted Boltzmann Machine algorithms, which is a novel deep learning algorithm [6].

Our Chapter is set up in the accompanying manner. The literature review work that has been done in the past for epilepsy classification has been

Table 15.1 Different waveforms present in the brain.

Waveform	Range (Hz)	Preferred locality	Symptoms
Delta waveform	<4	Visually in grown-ups, back in kids, high amplitude waves	Grown-up slow wave rest has been found during some constant consideration tasks
Theta waveform	4–7	Found in areas not identified with the in hand task	Higher in little youngsters, laziness in grown-ups and teenagers
Alpha waveform	8–15	Posterior regions of the brain, the two sides higher in amplitude on the dominant model	Loose/reflecting, shutting the eyes, related with restraint control, inhibitory action in various areas across the brain
Beta Waveform	16–31	The two sides, balanced appropriation, most obvious visually, low amplitude waves	Dynamic thinking, center, high ready, anxious
Gamma waveform	>32	Part of your cerebrum that receives and processes sensory data from the whole body (Somatosensory cortex)	Shows during cross-modular sensory handling, appeared during short term memory coordinating of recognized items

portrayed in Section 15.2. Section 15.3, depicts the proposed methodology, description of dataset, normalization and preprocessing of the dataset where all the training and testing evaluations that has been applied for epilepsy identification. All the experimental arrangements for training and testing data have been discussed in Section 15.4. Experimental results and discussion of the proposed work for epileptic seizure classification have been done in Sections 15.5 and 15.6. Section 15.7 represents the conclusion of work.

15.2   Related Work

Electroencephalogram (EEG) is a sort of procedure that examines or recognizes movement in cerebrum signals [7]. Artificial Neural Networks (ANNs) were first developed several decades ago by researchers attempting to develop the learning process of the human brain. Artificial Neural Networks (ANNs) are typically composed of interconnected "units" which denote the modeled neurons. Nigam and Graupe represented a novel approach for the classification of epileptic seizures from EEG signals in 2004 [8]. Kannathal *et al.* [9] compared different entropy estimators when applied to EEG data, and it has been proven that EEG data using ANFIS classifier have achieved an accuracy of up to 90%. Guo *et al.* [10] put forward a technique that uses Relative Wavelet Energy (RWE) for the Analysis of EEG signals which are then classified using ANNs; this method has achieved an accuracy of 95.20%. Homan *et al.* [11] proposed an Epileptic Seizure Prediction system based on Recurrent Neural Networks. Guler *et al.* [12] proposed an EEG signal classification system based on Recurrent Neural Networks using Lyapunov exponents, which have achieved an accuracy of up to 97.38%.

In 2017, Talathi [13] proposed an Epileptic Seizure classification method dependent on deep RNNs, which have accomplished an accuracy of up to 99%. Taking into account this paper, the author does right off the normalization of CHB-MIT dataset. This classification is useful for the medical procedure choice of epilepsy patients. The CHB-MIT Children's Hospital Boston database [14] is used for feature extraction and characterization utilizing the DBNs models. They contrast on the aligned heartbeat. The performance is evaluated using specificity and sensitivity metrics Nowadays, when millions of data come into the clinical area for better accuracy, they use deep learning algorithms. Further, Pereira *et al.* [15] have done automatic segmentation of brain tumors with the help of the convolutional neural network. Acharya *et al.* [16] in 2017 proposed an application that detection automated infraction using EEG signal that given 92.50% accuracy. Acharya *et al.* have done a deep Convolutional neural network in EEG signals for detection of coronary artery disease and get an accuracy of 94.95%.

In 2018, Troung *et al.* [17] separated the features utilizing Short Term Fourier Transform (STFT) method, and four distinct features are extracted; and for performing classification, ConvNets classifier is utilized for the seizure detection and his proposed strategy accomplished an sensitivity of 81.2% while in year 2019 Ozcan *et al.* [18] extracted the statistical features and utilized convolutional neural network classifier for epilepsy classification and got a sensitivity of 87.01%. Numerous scientists have been focusing on the ConvNets classifier because of the more number of layers associated with this classifier, and in 2018, Zhou *et al.* [19] have extracted the features with time-domain signals utilized this classifier and recorded an accuracy if of 97.5%. Other than Convolutional neural network, researchers have likewise utilized recurrent neural networks (RNNs), DBNs, and auto-encoder in classifying epilepsy.

In 2018, Tsiouris *et al.* [20] utilized RNNs by extraction of features numerous methodologies have been proposed by various researchers. However a couple of researchers have accomplished the ideal outcome for the detecting and classifying an epileptic seizure.

The hybridization concept also plays a crucial role in detecting epileptic seizures as many researchers have proposed many deep learning hybrid algorithms. In 2019, Frieselbern *et al.* [22] proposed a hybrid algorithm that uses CNN and GRU (Gated Recurrent Unit) on time-domain signals and achieved a sensitivity of 89% and accuracy of 75.6%, while in 2019, Hisham *et al.* [23] achieved an accuracy of 99.6% by using CNN and LSTM (Long Short Term Memory) on extracting the features based on wavelet coefficients. In 2019, Xiaoyan *et al.* [24] have used CNN and LSTM and achieved an accuracy of 93.4%, sensitivity of 91.66%, and specificity of 86.13%. In 2019, Weixia *et al.* [25] have proposed his methodology and achieved an accuracy of 99%, and proved that his methodology outperformed all the existing methodology which was used in epilepsy seizure detection. In this paper, we have proposed a new type of deep learning algorithm called Restricted Boltzmann Machine, which is the first classifier used for the detection of an epileptic seizure.

15.3   Material and Methods

15.3.1   Dataset Description

The informational index used to assess the presence of our patient explicit locator comprises consistent Scalp EEG chronicles from 23 pediatric patients (age <18) experiencing medicine withdrawal for epilepsy medical procedure assessment at the Boston Children's Hospital. The EEG was inspected at 256 Hz and recorded utilizing a 23-channel, 10–20 bipolar montage. As indicated by the 10–20 bipolar montage, EEG cathodes can be seen on the scalp as appeared in the physionet.org dataset. Generally, this 23 understanding informational index contained 844 h of persistently recorded EEG and 198 seizures [26].

Table 15.2 shown above describes the CHB-MIT dataset in which 23 pediatric patients of different age has been used for the study of epilepsy detection. The data shown above describe the age of the patient, the number of channels that were used for the recording of the seizure, the number of seizures that were detected during the various periods, and last but not least, the total time of the seizure (ictal) during the study of the particular patient.

Table 15.2 CHB-MIT patient wise description.

Patient identifier number	Patient age	Patient sex	Number of channels	Number of seizures	Total seizure time (Minutes:Seconds)
1	11	Female	23	8	7:10
2	11	Male	23	4	2:50
3	14	Female	23	8	5:40
4	22	Male	23	5	4:00
5	7	Female	23	5	9:00
6	1.5	Female	21	11	2:00
7	14.5	Female	21	4	5:10
8	3.5	Male	23	6	15:10
9	10	Female	21	5	4:00
10	3	Male	21	8	6:50
11	12	Female	23	4	13:20
12	2	Female	23	26	14:50
13	3	Female	18	13	8:10

(Continued)

Table 15.2 CHB-MIT patient wise description. (*Continued*)

Patient identifier number	Patient age	Patient sex	Number of channels	Number of seizures	Total seizure time (Minutes:Seconds)
14	9	Male	23	9	2:30
15	16	Female	22	21	27:20
16	7	Female	23	9	1:20
17	12	Female	23	4	4:40
18	18	Female	23	7	4:50
19	19	Female	23	4	3:40
20	6	Female	23	9	3:30
21	13	Female	23	5	3:10
22	9	Female	23	4	3:10
23	6	Female	21	8	6:40

On the other hand, we can set up the dataset while utilizing the subset of three classes as we have arranged the dataset utilizing ictal and inter-ictal classes. Also, we can prepare the dataset using ictal and pre-ictal classes. Table 15.3 shows the ictal, pre-ictal, and inter-ictal seizure data, which we have prepared for our methodology, but in order to detect epilepsy, we need to take only ictal and inter-ictal data [40].

15.3.2   Proposed Methodology

Figure 15.1 addresses the flow chart of our proposed methodology. The total working of the proposed conspired is partitioned into three sections. The raw EEG signal is gotten to from CHB-MIT database and is available online on physionet.org. First section deals with the normalization methodology over the raw EEG signals. After generating the normalized data, the forwarded into preprocess the data, which is done using PCA (Program Component Analysis). After the preprocessing, the data is split among two different sets i.e. training set and testing set where data is trained using 3-Layer of Restricted Boltzmann Machine, but before applying the RBM algorithm, we have used Contrastive Divergence and Gibbs Sampling to achieve better results. At third section these parameters are passed as

Table 15.3 Ictal (Seizure), Inter-ictal (Normal), and Pre-ictal (Partial Seizure) subdivision.

S. no.	Class	Time	Patients	Seizure records	Total segments
1	Seizure	8 s	23	198	1,200
2	Normal	8 s	23	240	1,200
3	Partial Seizure	8 s	23	248	1,200

input to the classifier which is chosen as Softmax to perform classification between a Non-seizure and Seizure signals.

15.3.3 Normalization

In this proposed technique, our dataset is having a few variables of big variance and some small variance. So essentially, standardization is utilized when information are considered as an random variable; normalizing implies changing to normal distribution. We apply z-score standardization as preprocessing the dataset. Normalization is applied for information preprocessing for learning mechanism. The principle objective of normalization is to enhance the values of numeric sections in the dataset without misjudging differences in the ranges of values [27]. Usually utilized or required just when features have various ranges. Standardization is a more extreme change. The equation which we have utilized for normalizing our dataset is represented as:

$$Z = (x - \mu)/\sigma \tag{15.1}$$

where Z z-score, x is the random variable, μ is referred as mean, and σ represents standard deviation.

15.3.4 Preprocessing Using PCA

The benefit of utilizing Principal Component Analysis (PCA) is that it can extract the valuable data which is required from the EEG dataset and to de-correlate the factors dependent on the extracted data. Perhaps the main properties of PCA is that the Principal Components (PCs) acquired are essentially the linear combinations of the original variables and the weight vector, which is additionally the eigenvector that fulfills the property of

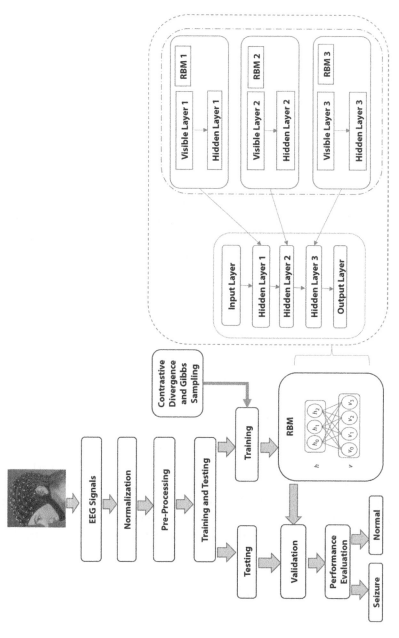

Figure 15.1 Represents the flow chart of proposed methodology using three layers of RBM.

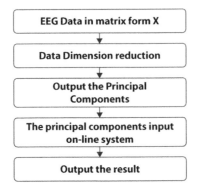

Figure 15.2 Flow diagram of PCA algorithm used in our proposed methodology.

principal of least squares [28]. In this research work, we have utilized X as the input information matrix, whereas k is the number of variables that is 2,048, and t is the total observations i.e. 3,200. Allow us to consider the situation of ordinary PCA, which is discussed underneath:

1. Suppose we have k original variables: s1, s2, ..., Sk.
2. We need to produce k new variables: t1, t2, ..., tk.

$$t1 = a11s1 + a11s2 + \cdots + a1ksk$$

$$t2 = a21s1 + a21s2 + \cdots + a2ksk$$

$$tk = ak1s1 + ak2s2 + \cdots + akksk$$

such that: sk's are uncorrelated (orthogonal)
s1 explains as much as possible of original variance in the data set
s2 explains as much as possible of the remaining variance etc.

By applying the above algorithm, PCA transforms the multivariate data into a new configuration dataset that is easier to interpret.

Figure 15.2 shows how our input data is transformed while applying the PCA algorithm for dimensionality reduction.

15.3.5   Restricted Boltzmann Machine (RBM)

RBM is an undirected variant that assumes an important role in Deep Belief Networks (DBNs). It characterizes a bunch of rules in the method, which is useful in dimensionality decrease, pattern recognition, regression,

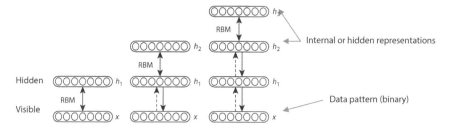

Figure 15.3 Simple architecture of 3-Layer RBM.

and collaborative filtering [29]. Rather than utilizing deterministic dispersion, RBM utilizes stochastic units of probability distribution represented in Section 15.3.1. RBM utilizes two different biases which make it not the same as auto-encoders:

1. The hidden bias which helps in to reproduce the activation on the forward pass.
2. The visible bias which helps in to reproduce the activation on the backward pass.

RBM is an external model that represents a two-layered network which is visible and hidden layer. Figure 15.3 shows the architecture of RBM, where each circle represents the neuron-like unit where calculation takes place. One of the most important features of RBM is that there is no communication between the internal layers which is there as a restriction in RBM model. Each node in this model performs stochastic decisions on whether to send that to the input or not. Low level features are taken by the visible layer for the data to be learned.

15.3.6   Stochastic Binary Units (Bernoulli Variables)

Stochastic Binary Units or we simply say Bernoulli variables are the units that have a state of 0s and 1s. The probability of turning on is determined by the weighted input from the other inputs (plus a bias) [30]. Let us suppose s be the stochastic unit variable, b be the bias, and w be the weights used, then the formula is given by:

$$p(s_i = 1) = \frac{1}{1 + \exp\left(-b_i - \sum_j s_j w_{ji}\right)}$$

The above formula is used to calculate the probability distribution when the input is in a state 0 or 1. Stochastic binary units utilize similar conditions which are used by logistic units, however they represent the output of the logistic as generating a spike in a brief timeframe.

Working Principle of RBM
As we all know that low level feature is being taken by the RBM in order to learn the data. Restricted Boltzmann Machine is a deep learning model that comprises of two layers, the first layer to a hidden layer and the second layer to be a hidden layer. Suppose x is the input layer at a particular node, and w is the weights that are fed into each input layer, and b is the bias used. Now to produce the node's output, we use the formula given below:

Output a = Activation f ((weight w * input X) + biasb)

where 'a' represents the output, and this proceeds for all other layers which are available in the network. In the instance of numerous hidden layers, the weights are changed until that layer is able to approximate the input from the previous layer [31]. Proper initial value of weights to later training and performing classification is one of the benefits of a Restricted Boltzmann machine (RBM).

In our proposed methodology, we have made an algorithm in which three layers of RBM are used, which is shown in Figure 15.1. Each output of the RBM layer becomes an input to the succeeding input layer of RBM, which are shown in the form of a hidden layer in the proposed methodology. The input layer is in which all the initial calculation of the weights is done and are fed into the hidden layer, and from there, new weights are calculated, and this process continues until all the hidden layers update their weights likewise in backpropagation network. Finally, the output is fetched from the last layer, which is present in the restricted Boltzmann machine network [32].

15.3.7 Training

The training of RBM is different than another neural network as this neural network works on the stochastic gradient descent method. There are two types of methods that are involved in training the data via restricted Boltzmann machine.

15.3.7.1   Gibbs Sampling

Gibbs Sampling is a Markov Chain Monte Carlo (MCMC) method used to get the observations in sequential from the multivariate probability distribution of information. It can also be used to approximate the joint probability distribution. Gibbs sampling generates the samples which are related to Markov Chains which are similar to the other samples which are generated.

Algorithm 15.1 described below shows how the Gibbs Sampling works on our proposed methodology. Gibbs Sampling is preferred for our methodology as it helps us to make accurate results while performing the training further [33].

Algorithm 15.1 Gibbs Sampling

Begin Gibbs-Sampler(y,Φ, P (0) (y), z)
// y—Sampling of the set of variables
// Φ—Number of factors which defines PΦ
// P $_{(0)}$ (y)—Distribution of the initial state
//z—Time steps calculation

....
....

1. Sample $y_{(0)}$ from $P_{(0)}(y)$
2. **for** z=1, ..., z
3. $y_{(z)} \neg y_{(z-1)}$
4. **for** each yi y
5. Sample $yi_{(z)}$ from $P\Phi_{(yi \,|\, y\text{-}i}$)
6. // Change yi in $y_{(z)}$
7. **return**$y_{(0)}$, ..., $y_{(T)}$

15.3.7.2   Contrastive Divergence (CD)

Contrastive Uniqueness is a Monte Carlo Markov Chain (MCMC) gradient descent learning method especially appropriate for learning products of experts (PoE) and energy-based model parameters. A general algorithm for contrastive divergence is described below, which is used in our proposed methodology [34]. Although contrastive divergence algorithm is very tricky to solve, it provide better results than any other convergence algorithm, which is better for our proposed methodology. Algorithm 15.2 describes how the CD algorithm works on our dataset, which is used in our proposed methodology.

Algorithm 15.2 Contrastive Divergence

---

1. Set the visible units to a training vector;
2. For k ← 1 to a maximum of iterations, do
3. For s ← 1 to the size of training, data do
4.   Update in parallel each hidden units using Eq. 2;
5.   Update in parallel each visible unit using Eq.3; to get "reconstruction"
6.   Update all hidden units again in Eq. 2;
7.   Update weight and biases with Eqs. 4–6;
8.   Select another training vector;
9.   End
10. End

15.4   Experimental Framework

In this research work, we have employed different ratios for training and testing data split as 90–19, 80–20, and 70–30 Additionally, we make a ten-fold cross validation approach.Firstly, the signals are divided into ten equal parts. Then to perform the signals in the training phase, nine parts are used. For the testing phase, one-tenth of the part is used which is used for validation of our proposed algorithm. This methodology was sustained up to 10 times by changing the testing and training dataset. It fills in as a convolutional backpropagation where batch is 11. Evaluation of the gradient of loss function contrary to the weights in backpropagation is employed during training phase. It results feedback for error signals in backward direction to the network. In training phase, it helps in updating the weights of the network. Batch size is utilized for getting various signals for training updations. Gibbs Sampling is performed during training stage, which is utilized to get the observation sequentially for the multivariate probability distribution of information. A Contrastive divergence an algorithm which is useful in giving better results while in the training phase of the algorithm. The whole dataset is tuned with multiple training and testing parameters so that results can be improved during the calculation of the various measures.

Table 15.4 Performance evaluation measures.

Performance measures	Mathematical representation	Depiction
Accuracy	$\dfrac{T_P + T_N}{T_P + T_N + F_P + F_N}$	It can be represented as the ration of the accurately marked labels to the entire dataset. It is the most common performance representation.
Sensitivity/ Recall	$\dfrac{T_P}{T_P + F_N} \times 100$	Sensitivity is depicted as the division of the accurately positive labeled by methodology to every data which represents individuals who have seizures truly.
Specificity	$\dfrac{T_N}{T_N + F_P} \times 100$	Specificity measures how effectively a classifier measures the negative labels
Precision	$\dfrac{T_P}{F_P + F_P} \times 100$	It is a class agreement between the data labels and the positive labels the classifier gives
f1-score	$\dfrac{2*(Recall * Precision)}{Recall + Precision}$	Metric which uses both precision and recall. It is calculated as the average of the precision and recall (harmonic mean)

The software which is utilized for this methodology is Anaconda version 2019.10, in which python 3.6 is used as our programming language on Windows 8.1. Libraries like keras, tensorflow have been included for accomplishing better results. An 8-GB RAM Lenovo ThinkStation P330 is used as a hardware. To reduce the time operational ability, this workstation which requires 2 min for each epochs to run while contrasting it and the ordinary system, may requires 8 min for each epoch to execute. The entire methodology has been operated over 200 epochs to accomplish better performance result while contrasting to already proposed methodology. Different parameters have been tuned to get the best results; a representation of different performance metrics is represented in Table 15.4 [39]. The best outcome is resulted by setting the parameters as batch size 11, the size proportion as 80–20, and learning rate as 0.01, which gives us the higher results measures when contrasted with tuning other parameters of the model.

15.5   Experimental Results and Discussion

15.5.1   Performance Measurement Criteria

Following are the various performance measures which have been calculated:

15.5.2   Experimental Results

In order to achieve the best results for the detection of an epileptic seizure, we used various tuning parameters like learning rate, size ratio, batch size,

Table 15.5 Performance metric when learning rate is set to 0.001.

Batch size	Size ratio	Sensitivity	F1-score	Accuracy	Specificity	Precision
2	90–10	95.23	94.87	94.87	95.25	94.97
4	90–10	94.97	94.81	94.81	95.21	94.23
6	90–10	95.23	94.92	94.92	95.67	95.01
8	90–10	95.21	94.91	94.91	95.61	94.90
10	90–10	95.14	94.67	94.67	95.21	94.28
11	90–10	92.23	92.87	92.87	93.25	93.97
2	80–20	91.19	92.12	92.12	92.12	92.09
4	80–20	92.97	92.81	92.81	93.21	92.23
6	80–20	93.23	92.92	92.92	92.67	93.01
8	80–20	93.21	93.91	92.91	93.61	92.90
10	80–20	92.14	93.67	93.67	92.21	92.28
11	**80–20**	**96.34**	**95.47**	**95.47**	**95.28**	**95.12**
2	70–30	95.12	94.47	94.47	94.12	93.16
4	70–30	95.23	94.92	94.92	95.01	95.01
6	70–30	92.34	90.69	90.69	91.23	91.98
8	70–30	92.56	90.94	90.94	91.35	92.01
10	70–30	92.45	90.91	90.91	91.30	91.98
11	70–30	93.21	91.21	91.21	92.27	92.30

etc. Various performance measures have been calculated, which are shown in the tables below.

Table 15.5 represents the various performance measures which is calculated with different tuning parameters but one of the parameter is kept constant which is the learning rate used. The best results are achieved with the tuning parameters when batch size was kept as 11, the training testing size ratio set as 80–20 and learning rate was fixed as 0.001. More results have been calculated with the learning rate of 0.01 and 0.1, which are shown in Tables 15.6 and 15.7, respectively. The best results among all

Table 15.6 Performance metric when learning rate is set to 0.01.

Batch size	Size ratio	Sensitivity	F1 score	Accuracy	Specificity	Precision
2	90–10	95.12	94.47	94.47	94.12	93.16
4	90–10	95.23	94.92	94.92	95.01	95.01
6	90–10	92.34	90.69	90.69	91.23	91.98
8	90–10	92.56	90.94	90.94	91.35	92.01
10	90–10	92.45	90.91	90.91	91.30	91.98
11	90–10	93.21	91.21	91.21	92.27	92.30
2	80–20	94.56	94.36	94.36	94.56	94.78
4	80–20	95.97	95.81	95.81	95.21	94.23
6	80–20	96.23	96.92	96.92	95.67	96.01
8	80–20	97.21	97.91	97.91	96.61	96.90
10	80–20	98.14	98.67	98.67	98.21	97.28
11	**80–20**	**98.94**	**99.20**	**99.20**	**98.89**	**98.86**
2	70–30	95.12	94.47	94.47	94.12	93.16
4	70–30	95.23	94.92	94.92	95.01	95.01
6	70–30	92.34	90.69	90.69	91.23	91.98
8	70–30	92.56	90.94	90.94	91.35	92.01
10	70–30	92.45	90.91	90.91	91.30	91.98
11	70–30	93.21	91.21	91.21	92.27	92.30

Table 15.7 Performance metrics when learning rate is set to 0.1.

Batch size	Size ratio	Sensitivity	F1 score	Accuracy	Specificity	Precision
2	90–10	93.23	92.87	92.87	92.25	92.97
4	90–10	92.97	92.81	92.81	92.21	92.23
6	90–10	92.23	92.92	92.92	92.67	92.01
8	90–10	92.21	92.91	92.91	92.61	92.90
10	90–10	93.14	93.67	92.67	93.21	93.28
11	90–10	92.23	92.87	92.87	93.25	93.97
2	80–20	92.21	92.45	92.45	92.89	92.19
4	80–20	92.97	92.81	92.81	93.21	92.23
6	**80–20**	**93.27**	**92.92**	**92.92**	**92.67**	**93.01**
8	80–20	93.21	93.91	92.91	93.61	92.90
10	80–20	92.14	93.67	93.67	92.21	92.28
11	80–20	91.34	91.47	91.47	91.28	91.12
2	70–30	91.12	91.47	91.47	91.12	91.16
4	70–30	91.23	91.92	91.92	91.01	91.01
6	70–30	92.34	90.69	90.69	91.23	91.98
8	70–30	92.56	90.94	90.94	91.35	92.01
10	70–30	92.45	90.91	90.91	91.30	91.98
11	70–30	93.21	91.21	91.21	92.27	92.30

the three learning rate is achieved with the learning rate of 0.01 which is shown in Table 15.6.

15.6 Discussion

Restricted Boltzmann Machine is a methodology that is valuable in dimensionality reduction, regression, pattern classification, topic demonstration and collaborative filtering. Various researchers have extracted a large number of features from the EEG signals in the time domain and frequency domain in order to detect or predict epileptic seizures. Table 15.8 shows the various

Table 15.8 Comparative analysis of already proposed methodologies.

Authors	Features	Classifier used	Performance metric
Thodoroff *et al.* [35]	Discrete wavelet transform coefficients	RCNN	Sens: 85%
Yusuf Khan *et al.* [36]	Discrete wavelet transform coefficient	ConvNets	Sens: 87.8%
Truong *et al.* [17]	Short Term Fourier Transform	ConvNets	Sens: 81.2%
Yoo, Ji-Hyun [26]	Frequency Domain Signals	RCNN	Sens: 90%
Rajamanickam *et al.* [37]	Discrete wavelet transform coefficients	ConvNets	Sens: 86.29%
Zhou *et al.* [19]	Time Domain Signals	ConvNets	Accu: 97.5%
Ozcan *et al.* [18]	Spectral power, Statistical moments	ConvNets	Sens: 87.01%
Xinghua *et al.* [21]	Time Domain Signals	Bi-LSTM	Sens: 88.80% Spec: 88.60%
Frieselbern *et al.* [22]	Time Domain Signals	CNN-GRU	Sens: 89% Accu: 75.6%
Xiaoyan *et al.* [24]	Time Domain Signals	CNN-LSTM	Acc: 93.4% Sens: 91.88% Spec: 86.13%
Wei Xia *et al.* [25]	Discrete wavelet transform coefficients	CNN-LSTM	Acc: 98.60% Spec: 98.54%, Sens: 84%
Choi *et al.* [38]	Short Term Fourier Transform	CNN-GRU	Sens: 89.4%
Proposed Method	**Time Domain Signals**	**Restricted Boltzmann Machine**	Acc: 99.20% Spec: 98.89%, Sens: 98.94%

existing methods which have been proposed before this work. In 2018, Troung *et al.* [17] used the CNN classifier to achieve the sensitivity of 81.2% using Short Term Fourier Transform for the feature extraction. Various researchers have also proposed their methodology; in 2017, Khan *et al.* [36]

proposed his technique dependent on wavelet transform coefficients and a ConvNet classifier that accomplished a sensitivity of 87.8%. In 2019, Xingua *et al.* [21] used a new classifier known as Bi-LSTM. They achieved 88.80 and 88.60% of sensitivity and specificity, while in the same year, Xiaoyan *et al.* [24] have used a hybrid method which used CNN and LSTM on the time domain signals and achieved an accuracy of 93%, sensitivity of 91.88% and specificity of 86.13%. But in 2018, Zhou *et al.* [19] forwarded his mechanism, which utilizes a ConvNet classifier and accomplished an accuracy of 97.5%, outperforming all the state-of-art methods. The methodology which is used by our paper uses Restricted Boltzmann Machine, which is the first algorithm used on the CHB-MIT dataset. The results achieved by our methodology that has an accuracy of 99.20%, a sensitivity of 98.94%, and a specificity of 98.89%, outperformed all the state-of-the-art methods which have been performed for epilepsy seizure detection. Figure 15.4 shows the comparison of the accuracy of the three learning rates by using 80–20 as the size ratio. Figure 15.5 shows the comparison of the sensitivity of the three learning rates by using 80–20 as the size ratio. Figure 15.6 shows the comparison of specificity of the three learning rates by using 80–20 as the size ratio.

As the characteristics of seizure may vary over time, the algorithm for seizure detection is necessary. One of the great advantage for an expert to predict the seizure is through minimum feature extraction, which allows faster update so that the patients can benefit from the seizure prediction algorithm rather than detecting a seizure which requires a large amount of time. The methodology that we have proposed can be improved

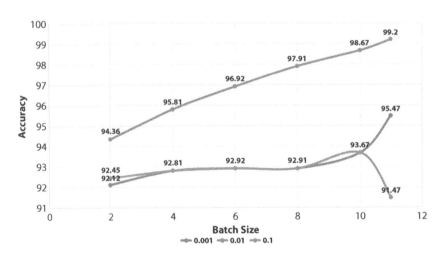

Figure 15.4 Performance Metric Comparison (Accuracy) by using 80–20 as size ratio with learning rate 0.001, 0.01, and 0.1 used in our proposed methodology.

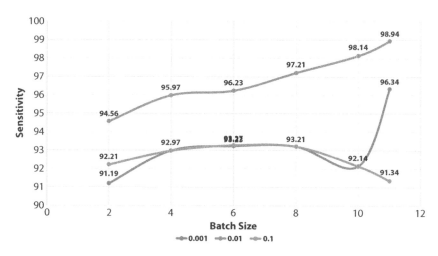

Figure 15.5 Performance Metric Comparison (Sensitivity) by using 80–20 as size ratio with learning rate 0.001, 0.01, and 0.1 used in our proposed methodology.

further by taking the huge amount of EEG data related to the time domain and frequency domain which contains epileptic seizures. This epileptic seizure can have distribution over time as one seizure can be as long as one year or 1 h. Figure 15.7 describes the details of the seizure which occurs at each hour for all the subjects combined for the CHB-MIT dataset. From the graph, we can see that the lowest number of seizures occurs around 9 p.m. while the highest number of seizures occurs around 7 a.m. in the morning.

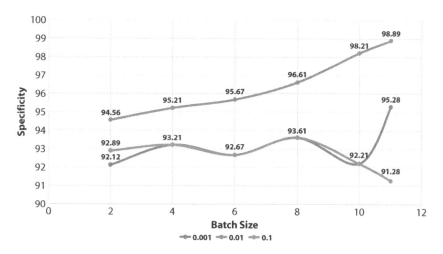

Figure 15.6 Performance Metric Comparison (Specificity) by using 80–20 as size ratio with learning rate 0.001, 0.01, and 0.1 used in our proposed methodology.

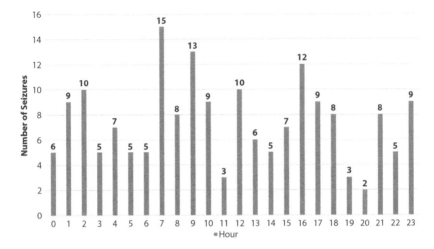

Figure 15.7 The seizure occurs during each hour for all the pediatric patients of CHB-MIT.

15.7 Conclusion

In this research work, we have dealt with the Restricted Boltzmann machine neural network architecture for spontaneous seizure detection utilizing EEG signals. Thinking about the best in class strategy, this model has an ability that learns better and done viably separates among seizure and normal EEG. We have played out all ratios of training and testing dataset and saw that when our model is getting the training dataset of lower extents, at that point it gives us lower accuracy when contrasted to the training dataset of higher ratios. The primary reason for lower accuracy is the lesser proportion of the training dataset. During learning phase, it naturally takes feature extraction and selection in this way; it needs more numbers for data for learning. We have performed binary class classification in our proposed system, and it acquired an average accuracy of 99.20%, specificity of 98.89%, and sensitivity of 98.94%, the proposed model has been inspected on an open accessible CHB-MIT EEG dataset and contrasted with various baseline methodologies. The outcomes decide the effectiveness and primacy of the proposed model in recognizing epileptic seizures. One more benefit of the proposed model is that it doesn't need any feature extraction and selection mechanism. The performance of the proposed methodology can be enhanced by giving more amounts of data.

References

1. Satapathy, S.K., Dehuri, S., Jagadev, A.K., EEG signal classification using PSO trained RBF neural network for epilepsy identification. *Inform. Med. Unlocked*, 6, June 2016, 1–11, 2017.

2. Satapathy, S.K., Dehuri, S., Jagadev, A.K., ABC optimized RBF network for classification of EEG signal for epileptic seizure identification. *Egypt. Inform. J.*, 18, 1, 55–66, 2017.

3. Kerr, M.P., The impact of epilepsy on patients' lives. *Acta Neurol. Scand.*, 126, S194, 1–9, 2012.

4. Zhou, W. and Gotman, J., Removal of EMG and ECG artifacts from EEC based on wavelet transform and ICA. *Annu. Int. Conf. IEEE Eng. Med. Biol.— Proc.*, vol. 26 I, pp. 392–395, 2004.

5. Alickovic, E., Kevin, J., Subasi, A., Performance evaluation of empirical mode decomposition, discrete wavelet transform, and wavelet packed decomposition for automated epileptic seizure detection and prediction. *Biomed. Signal Process. Control*, 39, 94–102, 2018.

6. Kannathal, N., Min, L.C., Acharya, U.R., Sadasivan, P.K., Erratum: Entropies for detection of epilepsy in EEG. *Comput. Methods Programs Biomed.*, 80, 187–194, 2005, *Comput. Methods Programs Biomed.*, 81, 2, 193, 2006.

7. Tessy, E., Shanir P.P.M. and Manafuddin S., "Time domain analysis of epileptic EEG for seizure detection", in: *2016 International Conference on Next Generation Intelligent Systems (ICNGIS)*, pp. 1–4, 2016.

8. Nigam, V.P. and Graupe, D., A neural-network-based detection of epilepsy. *Neurol. Res.*, 26, 1, 55–60, 2004.

9. Kannathal, N., Choo, M.L., Acharya, U.R., Sadasivan, P.K., Entropies for detection of epilepsy in EEG. *Comput. Methods Programs Biomed.*, 80, 3, 187–194, 2005.

10. Guo, L., Rivero, D., Seoane, J.A., Pazos, A., 18.Classification of EEG signals using relative wavelet energy and artificial neural networks, in: *Proceedings of the First ACM/SIGEVO Summit on Genetic and Evolutionary Computation*, pp. 177–184, 2009.

11. Petrosian, A. *et al.*, Recurrent neural network-based prediction of epileptic seizures in intra-and extracranial EEG. *Neurocomputing*, 30, 1–4, 201–218, 2000.

12. Güler, N.F., Übeyli, E.D., Güler, I., Recurrent neural networks employing Lyapunov exponents for EEG signals classification. *Expert Syst. Appl.*, 29, 3, 506–514, 2005.

13. Vidyaratne, L., Glandon, A., Alam, M. and Iftekharuddin, K.M., Deep recurrent neural network for seizure detection, in: *2016 International Joint Conference on Neural Networks (IJCNN)*, pp. 1202–1207, 2016.

14. Acharya, U.R., Fujita, H., Lih, O.S., Adam, M., Tan, J.H., Chua, C.K., Automated detection of coronary artery disease using different durations of ECG segments with convolutional neural network. *Knowledge-Based Syst.*, 132, 62–71, 2017.

15. Pereira, S., Pinto, A., Alves, V., Silva, C.A., Brain tumor segmentation using convolutional neural networks in MRI images. *IEEE Trans. Med. Imaging*, 35, 5, 1240–1251, 2016.

16. Acharya, U.R., Fujita, H., Lih, O.S., Hagiwara, Y., Tan, J.H., Adam, M., Automated detection of arrhythmias using different intervals of tachycardia ECG segments with convolutional neural network. *Inf. Sci. (NY)*, 405, 81–90, 2017.

17. Truong, N.D. *et al.*, Convolutional neural networks for seizure prediction using intracranial and scalp electroencephalogram. *Neural Networks*, 105, 104–111, 2018.

18. Ozcan, A.R. and Erturk, S., Seizure Prediction in Scalp EEG Using 3D Convolutional Neural Networks with an Image-Based Approach. *IEEE Trans. Neural Syst. Rehabil. Eng.*, 27, 11, 2284–2293, 2019.

19. Zhou, M. *et al.*, Epileptic seizure detection based on EEG signals and CNN. *Front. Neuroinf.*, 12, 95, 2018.

20. Tsiouris, K.M. *et al.*, A Long Short-Term Memory deep learning network for the prediction of epileptic seizures using EEG signals. *Comput. Biol. Med.*, 99, 24–37, 2018.

21. Yao, X., Cheng, Q., Zhang, G.-Q., Automated Classification of Seizures against Nonseizures: A Deep Learning Approach. *arXiv preprint arXiv:1906.02745*, 2019.

22. Freisleben, B., A Convolutional Gated Recurrent Neural Network for Epileptic Seizure Prediction. *How AI Impacts Urban Living and Public Health: 17th International Conference, ICOST 2019*, New York City, NY, USA, October 14–16, 2019, Proceedings. Vol. 11862, Springer Nature, 2019.

23. Daoud, H. and Bayoumi, M., Efficient Epileptic Seizure Prediction based on Deep Learning. *IEEE Trans. Biomed. Circuits Syst.*, 13, 5, 804–813, 2019.

24. Wei, X. *et al.*, Early prediction of epileptic seizures using a long-term recurrent convolutional network. *J. Neurosci. Methods*, 327, 108395, 2019.

25. Liang, W. *et al.*, Scalp EEG epileptogenic zone recognition and localization based on long-term recurrent convolutional network. *Neurocomputing*, 396, 569–576, 2019.

26. Yoo, J.-H., Epileptic Seizure Detection for Multi-channel EEG with Recurrent Convolutional Neural Networks. *J. IKEEE*, 22, 4, 1175–1179, 2018.

27. Meng, L., Tan, A., Member, S., Wunsch, D.C., Adaptive Scaling of Cluster Boundaries for Large-Scale Social Media Data Clustering. *IEEE Trans. Neural Netw. Learn. Syst.*, 27, 12, 2656–2669, 2016.

28. Alickovic, E., Kevin, J., Subasi, A., Performance evaluation of empirical mode decomposition, discrete wavelet transform, and wavelet packed

decomposition for automated epileptic seizure detection and prediction. *Biomed. Signal Process. Control*, 39, 94–102, 2018.

29. Lu, N. *et al.*, A deep learning scheme for motor imagery classification based on restricted Boltzmann machines. *IEEE Trans. Neural Syst. Rehabil. Eng.*, 25, 6, 566–576, 2016.

30. Raja, R., Kumar, S., Rashid, Md., Color Object Detection Based Image Retrieval using ROI Segmentation with Multi-Feature Method. *Wireless Pers. Commun. Springer J.*, 112, 1, 1–24, 2020, https://doi.org/10.1007/s11277-019-07021-6.

31. Tiwari, L., Raja, R., Awasthi, V., Miri, R., Sinha, G.R., Alkinani, M.H., Polat, K., Detection of lung nodule and cancer using novel Mask-3 FCM and TWEDLNN algorithms. *Measurement*, 172, 108882–108900, 2021, https://doi.org/10.1016/j.measurement.2020.108882.

32. Eslami, S.M.A. *et al.*, The shape Boltzmann machine: A strong model of object shape. *Int. J. Comput. Vision*, 107, 2, 155–176, 2014.

33. Cueto, M.A., Morton, J., Sturmfels, B., Geometry of the restricted Boltzmann machine, in: *Algebraic Methods in Statistics and Probability*, vol. 516, pp. 135–153, 2010.

34. Salakhutdinov, R. and Hinton, G.E., Deep Boltzmann machines. *Artificial Intelligence and Statistics*, 2009.

35. Williams, C.K.I. and Agakov, F.V., *An analysis of contrastive divergence learning in gaussian Boltzmann machines*, Institute for Adaptive and Neural Computation, UK, 2002.

36. Thodoroff, P., Pineau, J., Lim, A., Learning robust features using deep learning for automatic seizure detection. *Machine learning for healthcare conference*, 2016.

37. Raja, R., Sinha, T.S., Dubey, R.P., Orientation Calculation of human Face Using Symbolic techniques and ANFIS. *Int. J. Eng. Future Technol.*, 7, 7, 37–50, 2016.

38. Yuvaraj, R. *et al.*, A deep Learning Scheme for Automatic Seizure Detection from Long-Term Scalp EEG. *2018 52nd Asilomar Conference on Signals, Systems, and Computers*, IEEE, 2018.

39. Choi, G. *et al.*, A Novel Multi-scale 3D CNN with Deep Neural Network for Epileptic Seizure Detection. *2019 IEEE International Conference on Consumer Electronics (ICCE)*, IEEE, 2019.

40. Vishwakarma, S.K., Sharma, P.C., Raja, R., Roy, V., Tomar, S., An Effective Cascaded Approach For EEG Artifacts Elimination. *Int. J. Pharm. Res.*, 12, 4, 4822–4828.

16

An Enhanced Security of Women and Children Using Machine Learning and Data Mining Techniques

Nanda R. Wagh* and Sanjay R. Sutar

Information Technology, Dr. Babasaheb Ambedakar Technological University, Lonere, India

Abstract

This chapter studies the security framework for women and children, which permits prompt reactions in any provocation in broad daylight puts and proposed work. Women everywhere all over the world are confronting untrustworthy physical badgering and Children can't be left unattended at a get-together or outside the home. Our undertaking tackles both issues. A convenient gadget that will have a weight switch. When an attacker is going to assault the women/kid or when they detect any frailty from a more interesting, he/she would then be able to squeeze the gadget by pressing or packing it. In a split second, the weight sensor detects this weight, and a customary SMS, with the casualty's area, will be sent to their folks/gatekeepers PDA numbers put away in the gadget while buying it, trailed by a call. On the off chance that the call is unanswered for a delayed time, a call will be diverted to the police, and a similar message will be sent. The principle highlight of our framework is less reaction time will be required for helping the person in question.

Keywords: Child security, women security, security framework, artificial intelligence

*Corresponding author: nrwagh17@gmail.com

Rohit Raja, Kapil Kumar Nagwanshi, Sandeep Kumar and K. Ramya Laxmi (eds.) *Data Mining and Machine Learning Applications*, (423–446) © 2022 Scrivener Publishing LLC

16.1   Introduction

Since the most recent couple of decades, the status of women in India has been experiencing part of changes. To remain part of quick life, women likewise work a ton to endure and bolster their family. They work at better places like BPOs; call focuses, IT firms, and thus numerous spots like it. Yet, even the present women are as confronting numerous social difficulties in India and are frequently casualties of rough violations. Thomson Reuters had said that as per the worldwide survey, India is indeed the fourth greatest visibly terrible nation in the world and perhaps the most troubling nation for women among these 20 rising nations. Step by step, the attacks on women are increasing, and often the females are not prepared to take their flexible and toggle up to the police; this system would allow women in that kind of situations to learn about offenses and, additionally, to send their particular area to the police to close their heads. The Delhi Nirbhaya incident that brought the whole nation in motion was the strongest catalyst for this initiative. This was extremely important that the women needed a shift. Females are battling against men in every viewpoint of the community in the present predicament. Females are contributing 50% to the development of the nation. In either case, women are afraid to get these sorts of female harassment incidents to extend point by point. It also is necessary to ensure the wellbeing of women. Its mission is based around for a safety system that is structured primarily aim of providing women and children with real policing or wellbeing so that they can never feel helpless in the face of these anxiety issues [2–4].

16.2   Related Work

16.2.1   WoSApp

WoSApp [1] furnishes women with a dependable method to put a crisis call to the police. The client can, without much of a stretch, trigger the calling capacity by a straightforward cycle emergency signal screen. The framework helps women at the hour of emergency. This application additionally guarantees the inquiry concerning the client's area and whom to contact. The client should shake her telephone, and a crisis message with her GPS organizes and preselected crisis contact will be sent to the police.

16.2.2   Abhaya

This System utilizes GPS for distinguishing the area of the individual in a tough situation. The framework contains modules that incorporate area following and enlistment of clients and their crisis contact list. It improves mostly in the live follow-up of the region of the accident using GPS across several of the engaged contacts that receive an alert from both the core device. As the root gadget area quickly changes, the GPS recognizes the specific area. The client must tap on the crisis button then the current precise area will be sent to the closest police headquarters and loved one's part [3].

16.2.3   Women Empowerment

Different existing applications are explicit just for crisis call when they might be in danger, a few applications contain total assets for survivors of aggressive behavior at home, just as an approach to get help when you need it [10]. In any case, this Application will give data about aggressive behavior at home counteraction laws, wellbeing tips for women. To utilize the versatile Application, the client needs to enroll. All data of the client is paired in the cloud information base. The GPS framework on the advanced mobile phone of the client will find an accurate situation of the person in question. The GPS arrangement of portable will find a definite situation of the person in question. The Emergency Call System helps the casualty sends messages to the police and relatives that content area and time with this versatile Application makes an impression on pre-chosen contacts when the force catch of the telephone is pushed twice. The message contains the client's GPS area and is conveyed at regular intervals with refreshed directions [11].

16.2.4   Nirbhaya

This portable Application communicates something specific with the client's GPS directions to a rundown of crisis contacts when a catch on the application screen is contacted. The directions are refreshed and hit with each 300 m change in the area. Furthermore, it is complimentary and open-source, permitting upgrades and customizations to be made effectively for fast replication of the Application in different wards [15].

16.2.5   Glympse

This application is possible for the client to share areas utilizing GPS following continuously with loved ones. This Application needn't bother with any signup and needn't bother with any contact to oversee [17, 22, 25].

16.2.6   Fightback

This application is created by the Mahindra group. In prior days, this Application was not complimentary; the client needs to make up for this Application. This Application makes an impression on your companion or contacts that "Client is in a tough situation" utilizing Email, GPS, SMS, and GPRS. This application chips away at portable, which upholds Android Java Programming. The Application will likewise send SMS of area and Map [21].

16.2.7   Versatile-Based

Women Safety Application Many portable based application have been created for women' security like VithU application, Stun firearm application, Fightback application, and so on. These are the crisis application produced for women's security [14, 18, 19, 23].

16.2.8   RFID

GSM granted younger students a security framework. This framework expects to give complete security to younger students. Range and Obstacle recognition and mishap identified sensors are embedded on the front surface of the transport to evade impact with another vehicle on the road. Every understudy is labeled with an exceptional code. Two counters were utilized at the passageway and leave the area of the transport. Remote correspondence innovation (IEEE 802.4.15) is utilized to illuminate the status regarding the transport to the school staff and head [24].

16.2.9   Self-Preservation Framework for Women With Area Following and SMS Alarming Through GSM Network

This framework contains a stunning instrument to deliver non-deadly electric stun in crisis circumstances to stop the aggressor when the trigger key on the band is pressed [26].

16.2.10   Safe: A Women Security Framework

This framework comprises three principal segments, specifically an android application, a fundamental gadget, and a compact camera. Together these gadgets will fill in as a powerful security framework primary gadget which comprises of Raspberry Pi incorporated GPS shield alongside physically work pepper splash. Android application can be utilized in two potential manners by which it will either utilize a telephone GPS framework, or it will utilize GPS arrangement of fundamental gadget to catch location [28].

16.2.11   Intelligent Safety System For Women Security

In this paper, they portray at whatever point we feel perilous, she will press the catch of gadget, that occasion will be perceived by the LPC2148 regulator. At that point regulator will produce a control signal for the GPS framework; it will impart control sign through MAX 232 to the GPS module. GPS will get enacted, so it will follow the specific area of the person in question and send this data back ARM regulator through the MAX 232 interface [30].

16.2.12   A Mobile-Based Women Safety Application

In the proposed framework, with the press of one catch, individuals can alarm chosen contacts that the individual is in harm's way and offer the area. The individual wellbeing application requires the name and number of the individual who is to be reached during the crisis. Clients can include numerous individuals in the crisis contacts list. These are the individuals who will get notices or SMS if there should arise an occurrence of an emergency [29].

16.2.13   Self-Salvation—The Women's Security Module

If any individual needs to endeavor, women, then squeezing a catch will send ready messages to the guardians or companions' telephone numbers and the closest police headquarters. The strategy for security is through GPRS; we can follow the women/vehicle position. By sending SMS "TRACK" to the current telephone number, we can get the pic [32].

16.3   Issue and Solution

16.3.1   Inspiration

The strongest influence for that kind of system has been the case of Hyderabad as well as the case of Delhi Nirbhaya, which sets the whole nation into action. Something else which persuaded us is that the women going to obscure spots don't know about Red Alert Areas. On the off chance that they know about Red ready zones, at that point, they can be set up with preventive measures. The women's wellbeing application will furnish an alert with a warning and crisis help. Such ace applications can be utilized any place. This venture proposes another model for females' security openly puts which expects to give the 100% safe condition. Each lady must not hesitate to travel to any place by giving her the warning identified with the red ready region and giving the crisis board enacted at whatever point she will move to the red ready zone by thusly giving her the wellbeing at each progression [5–9].

16.3.2   Issue Statement and Choice of Solution

Women in homes, on roads, openly ships, or in workplaces are not generally protected. There have been numerous instances of lewd behavior toward little children to mature age women. We live in such a general public that it is important to be ready for our security from all perspectives. The decision of making a versatile application is to accomplish the issue articulation because of the way that a cell phone is typically conveyed by an individual, so than a different equipment gadget that could be lost [12–13].

Starting here, the accompanying pipeline was received to construct an answer:

- Collection of data
- Preprocessing of data
- Simulation
- Assessment
- Forecast.

16.4   Selection of Data

A significant proportion of the quality of and access used for misconduct examinations include loads and loads of nitty-gritty instances, with quantities varying about 100,000 to 100,000,000 records, as they are mainly generated by the surrounding police department, that includes a good mechanized system for processing, organizing, and discharging this important information around a defined area [16, 20, 27].

For both the structural portion, a formula was used that selects the appropriate range and longitude restrictions depending on the number of times of the edge and the separation of the graph. As in Figure 16.1, the first dataset was represented.

We provided details on a temporal calculation between 2002 to 2019. Obtaining them by month, it was feasible to verify that not every year had a relevant or useful proportion of information, such that the method could select only data between both the focused set, as can be imagined in Figure 16.2 [31, 33–35].

If useful geographical and situational knowledge was selected at the next level, designers created the heat maps.

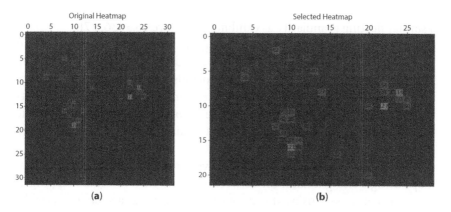

Figure 16.1 Option of boundary space measurements for the Delhi database. (a) will be the first database with all information, whereas (b) is the database with some of the most valuable information.

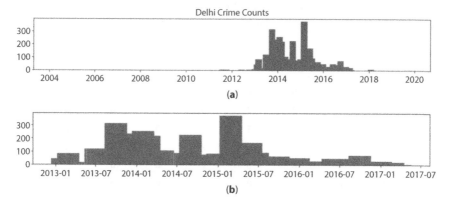

Figure 16.2 Selection of boundary for worldwide calculation of the Delhi dataset. (a) will be the first database for all records operating between 2002 and 2019, whereas (b) displays details chosen between 2013 and 2017.

16.5   Pre-Preparation Data

Throughout the pre-preparing phase of data, developers have defined the spatial and worldly variability of our collected data to construct heat maps. The scale of the 32 by 32 matrix was regularly used in this study. Such attributes tend to be powerful for just a little database but, as described earlier, two-fold directions required further space between cells because they only needed one event on that location and day-to-day complexity was used, even with lots of lacking quality between days, on the premises that with the data support development used below, we achieved several excellent results and after added each one of those examples that fell in a similar organize on a similar fleeting granularity as exhibited in Figure 16.3 [36, 37].

Throughout the context of developing the heat maps, we certainly had a lot of lacking day-to-day maps that could talk too hard while piling them into some kind of progression of details for the ConvLSTM design. One approach may be to consider null-esteemed heat maps for these situations even though we formerly had an enormous amount of negligible networks doing this method would start adding to show regularization to nonexistent.

The technique is used only to fill this void to reassemble the absent heat maps using a straight addition between first and next thermal mapping of the information sets using the all-out missing time as a separate variable. With that same knowledge growth method, this was feasible to increase the database from 586 double guides to 1,546 regular maps.

Since dynamically rendering the required heat maps, the surface estimate was discretionarily chosen to turn them into simultaneous guides (Figure 16.4) as we reported that the model would work with dangerous and quasi-unsafe hotspot forecasts.

0	0	0	2	0	0	0	0
0	0	0	0	0	0	0	0
0	0	0	1	0	0	1	0
0	0	0	0	2	0	0	0
0	0	0	0	2	0	0	0
0	0	4	0	0	0	0	0
0	1	0	0	0	0	0	0
0	0	0	0	0	0	0	0

Figure 16.3 Shows heatmap.

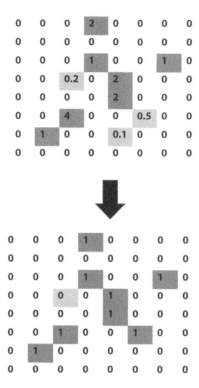

Figure 16.4 Example of transformation from a heatmap into a double guide utilizing a 0.5 limit.

16.5.1   Simulation

Planning and goal sets were created by collecting 16 day-by-day significantly vary manuals and using the preceding as a goal for 576 fictional categories. It is essential and necessary to say that the inaccurate graphs that have been produced have been missed once they've been selected as a goal so they do not transform into an actual situation.

And for training and testing sets separating, the option amount based on the related temporal details during 2013 and 2017, where even the experiment before the actual practically 50% of 2016 was chosen to plan the model and the corresponding term to accept it.

16.5.2   Assessment

No matter how we handle the structure problem, we can't allow a flexible edge like 0.5 and consider all the values across this line to be regarded as

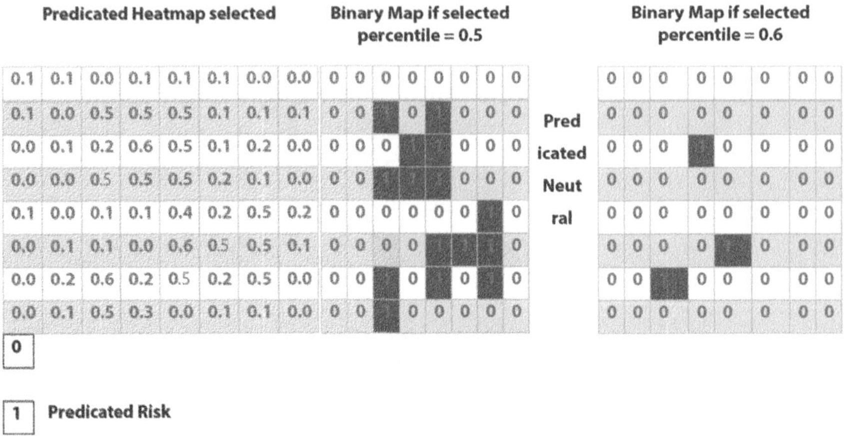

Predicated Heatmap selected   **Binary Map if selected percentile = 0.5**   **Binary Map if selected percentile = 0.6**

0.1	0.1	0.0	0.1	0.1	0.1	0.0	0.0
0.1	0.0	0.5	0.5	0.5	0.1	0.1	0.1
0.0	0.1	0.2	0.6	0.5	0.1	0.2	0.0
0.0	0.0	0.5	0.5	0.5	0.2	0.1	0.0
0.1	0.0	0.1	0.1	0.4	0.2	0.5	0.2
0.0	0.1	0.1	0.0	0.6	0.5	0.5	0.1
0.0	0.2	0.6	0.2	0.5	0.2	0.5	0.0
0.0	0.1	0.5	0.3	0.0	0.1	0.1	0.0

Pred icated Neut ral

0

1 Predicated Risk

Figure 16.5 Binary anticipated guides utilizing various percentiles to characterize unsafe zones.

hazards and all below impartial cores. We're effective in predicting places that have greater probabilities of even an incident happening and don't necessarily know that misconduct is going to be happening. Besides that, designers prepared big, scanty networks so it's normal that all the standards will turn to empty is shown in Figure 16.5 [38].

After selecting the percentile respect and turning over basic outcomes into some kind of two-fold guideline, we calculate the performance against both the real tutorial. To not hit the forecasting too harshly against both the failed results that could clear the way for a shift in the system such that we wind up with a completely overrated estimate, we offer some value for

Table 16.1 Labels for every forecast.

Label	Predicated	True
Correct	01	01
Neutral	00	00
False Positive Neighbor	01	00 with true neighbor 01
False Negative Neighbor	00	01 with predicted 01
False Positive	01	0.0
False Negative	00	1.0

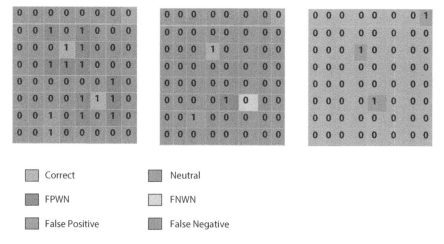

	Correct		Neutral
	FPWN		FNWN
	False Positive		False Negative

Figure 16.6 Label forecast by characterized percentile edge.

the predicted cellular in the adjacent hotspot zones as we haven't missed to such an amount (see Figure 16.6).

Rather than the four characterization names, we have six:

The accompanying table speaks to the marks for every arrangement:

Given this table, we check every one of those names for each anticipated cell as found in Figure 16.17 [39].

For the model above we have the accompanying outcomes relying upon the chose percentile esteem:

The less the percentile level, the larger the proportion of cells we label as dangerous and the higher is the accuracy of our design, but is it feasible?

Table 16.2 Predictions mean various percentiles limits.

Label	p = 0.5	p = 0.6
Correct	02	01
Neutral	48	59
False Positive Neighbor	11	1.0
False Negative Neighbor	00	1.0
False Positive	02	1.0
False Negative	01	1.0

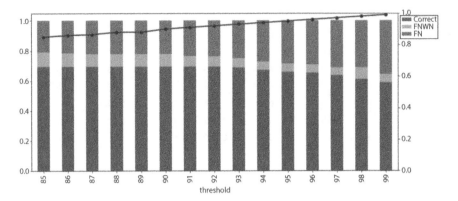

Figure 16.7 Model evaluation against different category levels. It is feasible to remember that the greater the percentile permissible limit, the higher the efficiency (dark line) but the more false-positive will get.

We ought to identify the perfect balance among hazard characterization and design accuracy to get the best end-customer satisfaction.

Along those same sections, between each of these names, are one of the most important ones to take a look at? Noah at that. AI states in the article that Right, False Negative Neighbor, and False Negative should be considered during the evaluation of the model. The aim is to determine the equilibrium among False Negative Vs. Right + False Negative Neighbor Rate and Accuracy.

Figure 16.7 shows the percentile models based which varies from the 85th to the 99th limit. The larger the quality, the more false negative (fn we have despite the growing accuracy of the design. This occurs on the basis that we consider further impartial cells (True Negatives) to be right. These cells are exceptionally imperative to reliable identification because we need to monitor the user in a sheltered area while refraining from displaying such a vast number of spots as hazardous, although most not quite as dangerous.

16.5.3   Forecast

There are some suggested principles for Noah *et al.* to allow the forecast in such a way that people have a clear understanding of the yielding made. The best approach is usually to display the cells called dangerous with one highlighting and at the same time silencing the others while the next direction is to characterize a list of limit values for each phone.

So the general rule for model expectations is as follows:

- Foresee a lone instance or a group as a whole.
- Transform basic attributes to distinct ones using the surface list described.

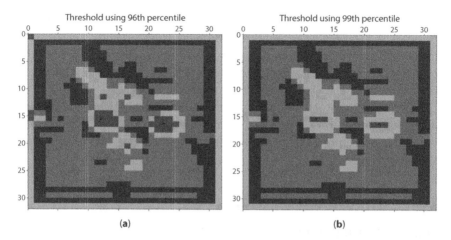

Figure 16.8 Heatmaps assumptions using several edges. (a) uses the 96th percentile while (b) uses the 99th percentile.

Figure 16.8 displays two versions using the 96th and 99th edges as dangerous values covered in red. Unique features are produced using specific threshold options such as the 91st, 75th, and 25th percentile.

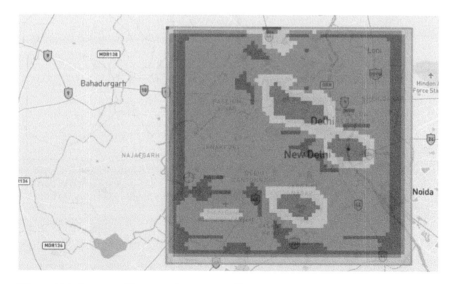

Figure 16.9 Large-goal heatmap from over Delhi region. The rose-colored region of risk is regarded by the estimate. The Darker Dab refers to the corruption that occurred in that area on a particular timeline.

The surrounding's effect of the shock absorption on the Convolutional Network is regarded as an important problem to the system. Zero insulation might not be the most optimal way of handling extremes, specifically on tiny images like heat maps, and it should be ignored when it comes to making because they barely translate to the actual world.

Another solution to increasing the maximize objective is to use the asymmetric injection method and expand the number of the heatmap providing an even more optimized target because the last user is added as shown in Figure 16.9.

16.6   Application Development

16.6.1   Methodology

When the females are signed in and she goes to an obscure area, the current criminal dataset checks whether the current area matches its dataset

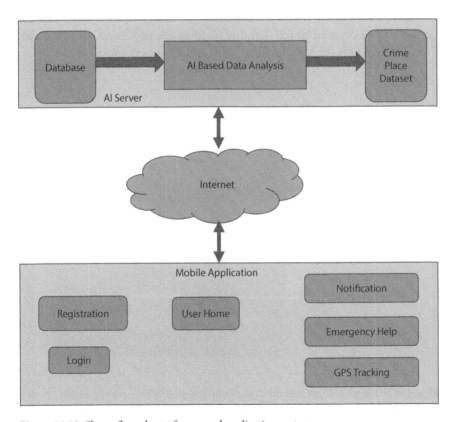

Figure 16.10 Shows flow chart of proposed application system.

or not, and on the off chance that it is coordinated, it informs her that the region is wrongdoing inclined zone. At the point when she gets to know wrongdoing inclined territory, she would have an elective. Possibly she would abstain from going there or she would need to be set up with well-being measures, here Proposed Application can end up being useful for her. On the off chance that she goes to the wrongdoing inclined region and she associates any sort with the threat from outsiders at that point, she is furnished with the assistance button in the application. After squeezing the assistance button, a message will be created. The created message comprises of the scope and longitude of her present area just as a slogan of "I am in a tough situation. Please Help" will likewise be sent. The produced message will be sent to the enlisted crisis contacts shown in Figure 16.10.

16.6.2   AI Model

Artificial Intelligence is a simulation of inductive logic designed by machines, in specific computer servers. It depends on the thought of building machines fit for intuition, acting, and learning like people. SVM calculation is a piece of AI and Artificial Intelligence. Characterization is given in Support Vector Machine Algorithm. Here in this paper SVM calculation encourages our application to recognize the wrongdoing related spots. This calculation causes the framework to produce an alarm to the client after the recognizable proof of the specific recorded wrongdoing place.

16.6.3   Innovations Used The Proposed Application Has Utilized After Technologies

- HTML for Front End creating.
- JAVA for Client and Server-side.
- MySQL for Back End and Processing.
- Visual Studio for Server-side handling.
- Android SDK to construct an Application upheld by Android.

16.7   Use Case For The Application

16.7.1   Application Icon

The figure below outlines the overall perspective on symbols of different android applications. Our application has been named as Proposed Application (Safetyapp for Women: a non-Magnanimous Shield) shown in Figure 16.11.

Figure 16.11 Shows icon of application.

16.7.2   Enlistment Form

An enrollment structure is a rundown of fields that a client will include information into and submit it to a worker. To give security administration,

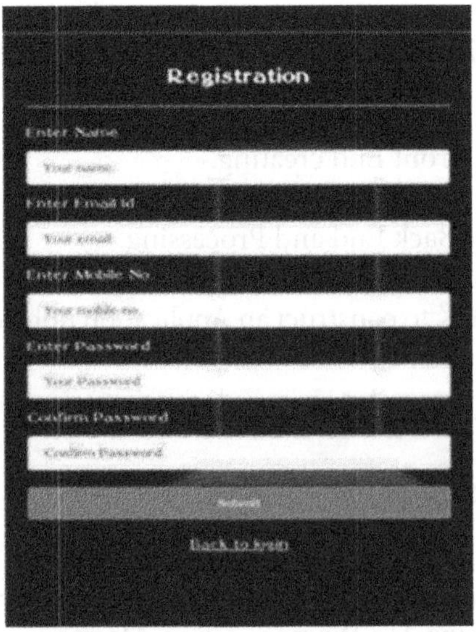

Figure 16.12 Shows form of registration.

the worker requires a portion of the fundamental subtleties of the client. The client needs to fill the necessary subtleties and tap on the Submit button. From that point onward, the client will be heading off to the Login page and continue with their email ID and secret key for venturing into the application. The Emergency contact is spared in the Registration structure which is named "Enter Mobile no." shown in Figure 16.12.

16.7.3   Login Form

When the application is installed, the login page will be shown. For login, enrollment is required so tap on New client alternative shown in Figure 16.13.

16.7.4   Misconduct Place Detector

When the client enters where she will be going, results would be that either the spot is exceptionally wrongdoing inclined or not as indicated by the dataset. Her area will be accessible on the guide and the close by wrongdoing zones will be featured by Google map pin, portrayed as following shown in Figure 16.14:

Figure 16.13 Shows login page.

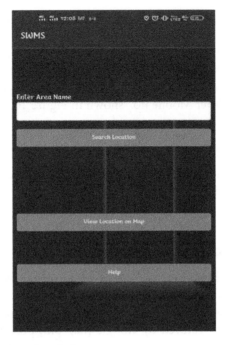

Figure 16.14 Misconduct place finder.

- Green shows the user's current area
- Red shows the horror inclined zone
- Orange shows the moderate wrongdoing inclined zone
- Yellow shows the low wrongdoing zone.

Figure 16.15 portrays the wrongdoing zones of that specific zone contingent on the current area of the client.

16.7.5   Help Button

Below picture portrays the screen capture of the message that the client will send after clicking HELP BUTTON shown in Figures 16.16 and 16.17.

Beneath picture portrays the screen capture of the message that the registered contact will get.

The picture beneath portrays the screen capture where the client area will be followed, from the collector's message shown in Figure 16.18.

Figure 16.15 Location recognized on map.

Figure 16.16 Show message sent by user.

Figure 16.17 Shows received message to enrolled contact.

Figure 16.18 Location of client.

16.8 Conclusion

Multiple measures have been adopted out there using deep learning models to classify corruption using heat maps. This future prospectus to assist by suggesting the approach that best matched the resources that we had for this study, and at the same time assessing what and why usually negotiated did not perform. This versatile application is useful for women. Utilizing PROPOSED APPLICATION can lessen the cases occurring in the public arena. With the assistance of this application, women will get cautions about the obscure spots. With the goal that she will be prepared as of now for any circumstance. The application can be additionally utilized for Machine Learning that can be applied to screen the sound created by encompassing and characterize the word, make examinations, and consequently distinguish the degree of danger.

References

1. Chand, D., Nayak, S., Bhat, K.S., Parikh, S., Singh, Y., Kamath, A., A Mobile Application for Women's Safety: WoSApp. *IEEE Region Conference*, Macao, 2015.
2. Punjabi, S., Chaure, S., Ravale, U., Reddy, D., Smart Intelligent System for Women and Child Security. *IEEE 9th Annual Information Technology, Electronics and Mobile Communication Conference*, Vancouver, BC, pp. 451–454, 2018.
3. Yarabothu, Y. and Thota, B., Abhaya: An Android App For The Safety Of Women. *IEEE 12th India International Conference, Electronics, Energy, Environment, Communication, Computer Control*, Jamia Millia Islamia, New Delhi, India, December 2015.
4. Mahajan, M., Reddy, K., Rajput, M., Design and implementation of a rescue system for the safety of women. *International Conference on Wireless Communications, Signal Processing and Networking*, Chennai, India, pp. 1955–1959, 2016.
5. Harikiran, G.C., Menasinkai, K., Shirol, S., Smart Security solution for women based on Internet of Things(IoT). *International Conference on Electrical, Electronics and Optimization Techniques*, Chennai, India, pp. 3551–3554, 2016.
6. Sharma, K. and More, A., Android Application for women security system. *Int. J. Adv. Res. Comput. Eng. Technol.*, 5, 3, 725–729, March 2016.
7. Sharma, K. and More, A., Advance Woman Security System based on Android. *Int. J. Innov. Res. Sci. Technol.*, 2, 12, 478–488, May 2016.
8. Paradkar, A. and Sharma, D., All in one Intelligent Safety System for Women Security. *Int. J. Comput. Appl.*, 130, 11, 33–40, November 2015.

9. Mahmud, S.R., Maowa, J., Wibowo, F.W., Women Empowerment: One Stop Solution for Women. *2nd International Conferences on Information Technology, Information Systems and Electrical Engineering*, Yogyakarta, pp. 485–489, 2017.

10. Bankar, S.A., Basatwar, K., Divekar, P., Sinha, P., Gupta, H., Foot Device for Women Security. *2nd International Conference on Intelligent Computing and Control System*, pp. 345–347, 2018.

11. Pathak, S., Raja, R., Sharma, V., Ramya Laxmi, K., A Framework Of ICT Implementation On Higher Educational Institution With Data Mining Approach. *Eur. J. Eng. Res. Sci.*, 4, 5, 2019.

12. Pressman, R.S., *Software Engineering: A Practitioner's Approach*, Seventh Edition, pp. 1–888, McGraw-Hill International edition, New Delhi, 2010.

13. Abdul Kalam, A.P.J. and Rajan, Y.S., *India 2020—A Vision for the New Millennium*, Penguin Books India Pvt Limited, 11 Community Centre Panchasheel Park New Delhi 110017 India, Published by Penguin Books, 2002.

14. http://www.un.org/womenwatch/confer/beijing/reports, Report of the Fourth World Conference on Women, New York, United Nations, 1995 (A/CONF.177/20/Rev.1)

15. http://www.nirbhaya.mobi, Nirbhaya: Be Fearless

16. https://www.guardly.com, Android App developed by Guardly Corp. "GUARDLY".

17. https://www.glympse.com, Android app developed by Glympse Corp. "GLYMPSE- SHARE GPS LOCATION"

18. http://apps/who/int/iris/bitstream/10665/85239/1/9789241564625_eng.pdf,World Health Organization, Global and Regional estimates of violence against women.

19. http://timesofindia.indiatimes.com/topic/mobile-apps-for-women's-safety

20. https://play.google.com/store/apps/details?id=com.startv.gumrah, VithU: V Gumrah Initiative on the Google Play Store, Google Play Store, Mountain View, California, United States, 2017.

21. http://www.fightbackmobile.com/welcome, Android app developed by Canvas M Technologies named "FIGHTBACK", Google Play Store, Mountain View, California, United States, 2021.

22. Chougula, B., Naik, A., Monu, M., Patil, P., Das, P., Smart Girl Security System. *Int. J. Appl. Innov. Eng. Manage. (IJAIEM)*, 3, 4, 281–284, April 2014.

23. Bhilare, P., Mohite, A., Kamble, D., Makode, S., Kahane, R., Women Employee Security System using GPS And GSM Based Vehicle Tracking. *Int. J. Res. Emerg. Sci. Technol.*, 2, 1, 65–71, Jan-2015.

24. Vidyasagar, K., Balaji, G., Narendra Reddy, K., RFID-GSM imparted School children Security System. *Commun. Appl. Electron. (CAE)*, 4 Foundation of Computer Science FCS, New York, USA, 2, 2, 17–21, 2015.

25. Al-Suwaidi, G.B. and Zemerly, M.J., Locating friends and family using mobile phones with a global positioning system (GPS). *IEEE/ACS International Conference on Computer Systems and Applications*, 2009.

26. Vijaylashmi, B., Renuka, S., Pooja Chennur, S., Self Defence System for Women With Location Tracking and SMS Alerting Through GSM Network. *Patil Int. J. Res. Eng. Technol.(IJRET)*, 57–60, 04, 05.

27. Monisha, D.G., Monisha, M., Pavithra, G., Subhashini, R., Women Safety Device And Application-Femme. *Indian J. Sci. Technol.*, 9, 10, 1–6, March 2016.

28. Lokesh, S. and Gadgil, A., Safe: A Women Security System, in: *Electronic and Telecommunication*, Savitribai Phule Pune University, Pune, Maharastra, India-411052, 112, 2020.

29. Anandjatti, M., Alisha, R.M., Vijayalakshmi, P., Sinha, S., Design and Development of An IoT Based Wearable Device for the Safety and Security of Women and Girk Children. *IEEE International Conference on Recent Trends in Electronics Information Communication Technology*, India, May 20–21, 2016.

30. Raja, R., Kumar, S., Rashid, Md., Color Object Detection Based Image Retrieval using ROI Segmentation with Multi-Feature Method. *Wirel. Pers. Commun. Springer J.*, 112, 1–24, 2020.

31. Mandapati1, S., Pamidi, S., Ambati, S., A Mobile Based Women Safety Application. *IOSR J. Comput. Eng.*, 17, 29–34, 2015.

32. Nagaraju, J. and Sadanandam, V., Self Salvation—The Women's Security Module. *Int. J. Innov. Res. Electron. Commun.*, 3, 13–19, January 2016.

33. Holm, N. and Plynning, E., *Spatio-temporal prediction of residential burglaries using convolutional LSTM neural networks*, KTH ROYAL INSTITUTE OF TECHNOLOGY, SCHOOL OF ARCHITECTURE AND THE BUILT ENVIRONMENT, Sweden, 2018.

34. Schlegel, U., Universität Konstanz Department of Computer Science Master Thesis, Universität Konstanz, Konstanz, Baden-Württemberg, Germany, 2018.

35. Stalidis, P., Semertzidis, T., Daras, P., *Examining Deep Learning Architectures for Crime Classification and Prediction*, Cornell University, New York, pp. 1–12, 2018, Retrieved from http://arxiv.org/abs/1812.00602.

36. Wang, B., Zhang, D., Zhang, D., Brantingham, P.J., Bertozzi, A.L., *Deep Learning for Real-Time Crime Forecasting*, pp. 33–36, Springer Nature, Switzerland, 2017, Retrieved from http://arxiv.org/abs/1707.03340.

37. Zhang, J., Zheng, Y., Qi, D., Deep Spatio-temporal residual networks for city-wide crowd flow prediction. *31st AAAI Conference on Artificial Intelligence, AAAI 2017*, pp. 1655–1661, 2017.

38. Jain, S., Mahmood, Md. R., Raja, R., Laxmi, K.R., Gupta, A., Multi-Label Classification for Images with Labels for Image Annotation. *SAMRIDDHI: A J. Phys. Sciences, Eng. Technol.*, 12, Special Issue (3), 183–188, 2020.

39. Mahmood, Md. R., Raja, R., Gupta, A., Jain, S., Implementation of Multi Sensor and Multi-Functional Mobile Robot for Image Mosaicking. *SAMRIDDHI: A Journal of Physical Sciences, Engineering and Technology*, 12, Special Issue (3), 189–196, 2020.

17

Conclusion and Future Direction in Data Mining and Machine Learning

Santosh R. Durugkar[1], Rohit Raja[2], Kapil Kumar Nagwanshi[3]* and Ramakant Chandrakar[4]

[1]*Amity University Rajasthan, Jaipur, India*
[2]*IT Department, GGV Bilaspur Central University, Bilaspur, India*
[3]*ASET, Amity University Rajasthan, Jaipur, India*
[4]*CV Raman University, Bilaspur, India*

Abstract

Data becomes a new currency for the world. Due to COVID-19, a significantly fewer number of flights are running, and hence the scientists cannot forecast the weather accurately. The data capturing also goes low because of this smaller number of flights. Data mining techniques play a vital role in collecting data for prediction and forecasting using different machine learning techniques. Recommender systems are available at all emerging places like agriculture, admission, matchmaking, traveling, share market, housing loan, parenting, nutrition, and consultation. Cybersecurity and forensics are also very challenging domains to fight with cybercrimes. Only data can save an entity from cyber-attacks. This chapter concludes with the future direction in data mining and machine learning techniques dealing with some related issues.

Keywords: KDD, stream mining, ANN, machine learning, deep learning, object recognition, object instance segmentation, R-CNN

---

*Corresponding author: dr.kapil@ieee.org

Rohit Raja, Kapil Kumar Nagwanshi, Sandeep Kumar and K. Ramya Laxmi (eds.) Data Mining and Machine Learning Applications, (447–460) © 2022 Scrivener Publishing LLC

17.1   Introduction

This book gives a brief introduction to tools, techniques, algorithms, and methods used in data mining. We hope readers will get a closer look at every aspect of data mining. In chapter 1, the authors have given a brief introduction to basic concepts of data mining such as KDD—knowledge discovery in databases, introduction to classification, and clustering. In this chapter, the authors have discussed clustering algorithms like k-means, nearest neighbor, etc. Authors have given an in-depth introduction to tools one can use in data mining, i.e., Python, KNIME, and RapidMiner. The authors have given a step-by-step guide to the installation of KNIME and other tools of data mining which will surely help the researchers, students to develop numerous applications. Applications of data mining like the healthcare industry, marketing, scientific applications, etc., are nicely discussed in this chapter. KDD—knowledge discovery in the database process with its different phases like data cleaning, data integration, data selection and transformation, representation are discussed. The authors have also given a comparative discussion of classification and clustering.

In Chapter 2—Classification and Mining behavioral of data, authors have discussed the use of data mining in businesses. Nowadays, businesses are using CRM frameworks to identify purchasing habits, customer retention rate, business growth, etc. With this intent to improve businesses, the authors have discussed various complex practices in this chapter also focused on categorizing the clients such as customers, an organization purchasing the products, people inside the organization, etc. Hence, according to such categorization of users, authors have suggested applying different practices to get better results.

A popular application of data mining in recommender systems to consider user's interests and provides suggestions accordingly. Chapter 3 focused on recommender systems, content-based suggestions to the users, etc. The authors have discussed hybrid recommender systems, collaborative filtering that can be used in developing recommender systems. The authors have identified various problems, issues in implementing recommender systems in terms of demographic, utility, etc.

There are various types of data mining, and one is discussed in this chapter is *stream mining*. Nowadays, everyone deals with big data, and analyzing this large volume of data is a critical task. Stream mining addresses the major issue of data analysis when it is not possible to store the incoming stream on the local systems/storage. Chapter 4 focuses on the various issues on analyzing the incoming streams, summarizing the streams, etc.

The authors have given a brief introduction to some of the tools such as Java, Python, and R programming languages.

Data mining tools, techniques, and clustering analysis is discussed in Chapter 5. Different challenges and areas for research of data mining are also discussed in this chapter. Today's era is of big data where data analysis is the emerging trend using data mining. The authors have elaborated and discussed the data mining life cycle with different phases and given an in-depth introduction to clustering and its analysis.

Chapter 6 is dedicated to the data mining implementation process. In this chapter, various applications of data mining such as banking, retail, clinical bioinformatics, etc., are discussed. Different procedures to implement the data mining applications are explained by the authors. Chapter 7 gives an introduction to predictive analytics in IT service management. Authors have compared different machine learning techniques used in various applications. In this chapter, the authors have presented predictive analytics in IT service management. Predictive analysis is the current need of businesses where identifying customer retention is very important for business growth. Similar to this application, the authors have discussed different uses of predictive analysis in businesses. Chapter 8 is dedicated to the modified cross-sell model for a telecom service provider using data mining techniques. In this chapter, the authors have studied and compared different service providers from the telecom industry. Customers are usually shifts from one service provider to another, and the same thing is discussed in this chapter with the help of a modified cross-sell model for the telecom service providers. In addition to this model, the authors have also discussed a logistic regression algorithm to model the given problem scenario.

An interesting Chapter 9 is dedicated to inductive learning with the help of a decision tree and rule induction learning. The authors have given an introduction to different algorithms like ID3, C4.5, and CART. An interesting concept, i.e., rules extraction system along with its strengths, is discussed in the chapter. A decision tree that helps in decision-making processes is also explained in this chapter. Authors have also introduced fuzzy learning and its basics to develop a fuzzy choice tree with multidimensional databases.

Data mining is used in many applications, and one of the applications is cyber-physical systems, a recent research trend of data mining. Actually, due to the 'n' users size of the database is tremendously increased. Providing security to this data is a crucial task, and the same is discussed in Chapter 10. Authors have discussed the use of different gadgets, sensors used in information technology. Different challenges and solutions to the same are discussed in this chapter. Chapter 11 is dedicated to the CRISP-DM method from the ERP framework. ERP with the cloud is explained with CRISP-DM philosophy. The authors have discussed data mining processes and their use in such applications to optimize performance. CRISP-DM is a cross-industry standard process for data mining, and its uses like finding the specific instances, connections, searching sets of specific data are discussed in Chapter 11.

Human–computer interaction—(HCI), which studies the interaction of humans with machines, is presented in Chapter 12. Authors have discussed visual data mining—an idea to identify visuals of the end-users is important, e.g., gesture recognition. It is an attempt to make systems intelligible so that machines can understand the visuals of the users and work accordingly. Motion recognition by the machine and working accordingly is also discussed in the chapter. Authors have explained few examples like how a machine recognizes the hand signals of the user and executes tasks like turning the pages, looking up, etc. A Very nice introduction is given to HCI, along with its different approaches are discussed in this chapter.

Medical image analysis with the AdaBoost algorithm is discussed in Chapter 13. The authors have discussed different advantages of medical image analysis. The authors have discussed supervised learning to generate classification algorithms. In this chapter, the authors have tried to resolve the imbalanced data distribution using the sampling technique.

A focus on new algorithms and technologies is given in Chapter 14 Authors have given an introduction to machine learning, MapReduce, Graphics Processing Unit (GPU), etc. Pattern matching, knowledge discovery in the database are also discussed by the authors to explain the use of data mining in various applications. In Chapter 15, the authors have discussed *EEG signal classification using Restricted Boltzmann Machine Classifier*. In this chapter, the authors have considered an "Epilepsy" disease which is a disorder related to the brain. To evaluate the performance of the model, authors have analyzed the EEG database of CHB-MIT. In-depth analysis is carried out by the authors to achieve a high level of accuracy, sensitivity, and specificity.

A good application of machine learning for the safety of women and children is discussed in Chapter 16. Authors have studied crime cases gathered from the national crime record bureau. Authors have designed a system using GPS, GSM and other sensory devices which collects data and stores it for analysis purpose. Supervised and unsupervised learning with examples to prove algorithmic efficiency are discussed in this chapter. Authors have also proved how the system is cost-effective and beneficial to the end-users, i.e., women and children.

This last chapter, 17, gives a summarized representation of various methods, algorithms, techniques, and applications of data mining. We hope this will surely help the readers to study and understand the concepts discussed in this book. To improvise, we are requesting the readers to give your valuable feedback, suggestions.

17.2   Machine Learning

Machine learning seeks to build computer systems that will increasingly learn and develop. Machine learning has had a huge impact on AI's recent success. One of the first occasions the word "computer learning" was stated in 1959 when a machine-learning software was qualified to play machine-learning checks. There are many ways to explain what machine learning is. One of the most frequently cited descriptions is Mitchell: "It is said that a computer program learns from experience E with some tasks T and measure P, when the performance in T tasks, measured by P, improves with E experience". An algorithm should be trained for better performance in a selected measured task(s) about a performance metric. As data is used to perform algorithms, they "gain" from the method. In the subsequent executions, the algorithms work well. Depending on the nature of the query, a machine learning algorithm can be built in three ways: supervised learning, unattended learning, and strengthened learning. An algorithm with a dataset of input–output examples is educated in supervised learning. The algorithm learns to map inputs by observing data patterns to specify outputs. For example, classification and regression exercises may be used with supervised learning. The dataset consists of input examples without their goal production in unregulated learning. Unattended learning algorithms may be used by analyzing their trends to calculate the similarities or variations between the inputs. Uncontrolled learning tasks include cluster analysis, for example. An algorithm does not have a finite training dataset in reinforcement learning but must extract data by sensing and interacting with its environment. Any acts are recompensed, and some are disciplined. Thus, the algorithm strengthens the behavior that results in rewards and prevents actions that lead to sanctions [1, 17].

17.2.1   Neural Network

The neural organization is an AI calculation that is utilized for regulated learning undertakings. Neural organizations begin in the 1950s. Initially, the motivation of NNs was the natural investigation of the cerebrum and its billions of neurons which measure and convey data in an exceptionally intricate organization [2, 3].

17.2.2   Deep Learning

Customary AI techniques battle to proceed as the dimensionality of the info information increments. For instance, in picture classification, input pictures may contain a large number of pixel esteems. This issue is known as the scourge of dimensionality. To defeat this issue, conventional strategies require manual element designing of crude information to diminish the info measurement. Notwithstanding, by and by, designing these highlights from a mass of information is hard without specific space aptitude [4, 5]. This is the place where profound learning steps in. Profound learning settles the scourge of dimensionality by learning various leveled portrayals of the information with complex models of different layers. This is accomplished with portrayal learning. In portrayal learning, no element designing is utilized. All things considered, a model learns without anyone else, which highlights of the mass of information are significant for the errand. At the point when a profound learning model is prepared, the model learns conceptual portrayals of the information by noticing the information designs. The first layers of a profound learning model learn more straightforward highlights of the information, though the last layers learn more specific highlights of the information [6, 7]. Why has profound learning gotten well known? Profound learning models require impressive measures of information for preparing. These days, during the period of large information, progressively more information is being produced. This is one explanation behind the change. The more there information is, the better it is for model speculation. Profound learning models are likewise a lot more prominent in size than customary AI models. The more prominent size builds their demonstrating limit and empowers them to tackle complex issues yet expands their computational weight. In light of the computational weight, utilization of profound learning was outlandish previously. This has changed. Contrasted with the calculation limit in the 1990s, the calculation limit of advanced illustrations handling units is over multiple times quicker. Notwithstanding the calculation improvement, the advances and programming utilized for profound learning have gained incredible ground. Hypothetical Foundation 7 The vast majority of profound learning, like AI, by and large, is performed utilizing administered learning. Profound learning models have been concentrated to beat conventional AI techniques in the various assignment. A portion of these errands incorporates discourse acknowledgment, object acknowledgment, and article identification. Practically speaking, profound learning is quite often performed utilizing profound neural organizations. In the following segment, we give foundation to neural organizations [8, 9].

17.2.3   Three Activities for Object Recognition

- Classification of the image: Predict the entity form or class of an image.
- Input: a single entity image, such as a snapshot.
- Output: A mark of class (e.g., one or more integers that are mapped to class labels).
- Object Position: Locate items in a picture and show their location using a boundary box.
- Embedding: a picture of one or more items, for example, a frame.
- Output: Output boxes one or two (e.g., defined by a point, width, and height).
- Object detection: Find in a picture the presence of bounding objects and the groups or groups of objects found.
- Input: an image of one or more objects, for example, a photograph [9, 11].
- Output: One or more bounding boxes and a class mark for each bounding box, e.g., specified by point, width, and height.

Another extension of this breakdown of computer vision activities is object segmentation, or "object instance segmentation," where instances of known artifacts are indicated by highlighting the object's pixels rather than a rough boundary box [12, 13].

From this interruption, we can see that object detection applies to a set of complex computer vision activities in Figure 17.1.

It is not news that deep learning has become a genuine advantage in AI, particularly in the PC vision [13, 14]. As deep-seated learning models have squashed most conventional image characterization models, profound learning models are still actually best in class in the area of object exploration. Because you already have a great instinct on what challenges are and how you tackle them, we will outline how the deep learning method has progressed over the last few years.

OverFeat

OverFeat was distributed in 2013 as one of the key developments in the usage of deep learning for entity recognition. They suggested a multi-scale calculation of the sliding window Convolutional Neural Organizations (CNNs) [15].

R-CNN

Quickly after OverFeat, areas of CNN or R-CNN from Girshick *et al.* were spread at UC Berkeley that virtually partially enhanced for the task

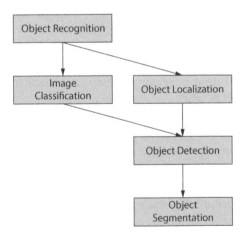

Figure 17.1 Object instance segmentation.

of particle identification. They recommended a method of three phases: extract future papers using a District Proposal Technique (the most mainstream one being Particular Pursuit). Collect highlighting from every CNN region [16].

Recognize All SVMs Locals

Although it obtained tremendous success, the planning had several challenges. To make it, you had originally to make suggestions for the planning dataset, use the CNN highlight collection (usually taking over 200 GB for the Pascal 2012 dataset) and then train the Supervised learning on the last ride [10, 18].

Fast R-CNN

This methodology immediately advanced into a cleaner profound learning one, when after a year Ross Girshick (presently at Microsoft Exploration) distributed Quick R-CNN. Like R-CNN, it utilized Particular Inquiry to create object recommendations, yet as opposed to separating every one of them freely and utilizing SVM classifiers, it applied the CNN on the total picture and afterward utilized both Area of Interest (return for capital invested) Pooling on the component map with the last feedforward organization for grouping and relapse [19].

Not exclusively was this methodology quicker, yet having the return for capital invested Pooling layer and the completely associated layers permitted the model to start to finish differentiable and simpler to prepare. The greatest disadvantage was that the model depended on Specific Inquiry (or some other district proposition calculation), which turned into the bottleneck when utilizing it for surmising [20, 21].

YOLO

You just look once, not long after that: Constant Object Recognition (YOLO) paper circulated by Joseph Redmon was produced together (with Girshick showing up as one of the co-creators). YOLO has suggested a central neural organization method that has both unbelievable results and high tempo, with the first step being continuous article recognition [22].

Challenges

- Report observations are commonly seen in the fields of observation, protection, investigation of the crime scene, mechanized vehicle frameworks. Due to this kind of delicate situation, it is of extreme importance that indicators function with incredible pace and, in general, offer excellent accuracy. Any of the challenges in distinguishing objects are as follows: - • • Identification on multiple scales: Probably the most well-known challenge is that the object recognized on one stage might be found on a smaller/greater scale [23].

- It is therefore essential for the extractor portion to summarize the highlights which can be used on any scale. Highlight Pyramidal Organizations are used with this FPN, which helps to remove the highlights from each scale (small, medium, and huge). The overwhelming majority of article identifiers use these sort of highlight extractors.

- Preparation for different image objectives: A further argument for non-exclusive Recognition of objects is to plan the picture calculated for each detail. Many heads of the regressor and classifier are entirely linked layers. But it is absurd to resize at runtime.

- The network built for one reason cannot deliver great results for the other. Fully progressive organizations are the solution to the crisis. Instead of FC Layers, the FCN meets the groundbreaking 1×1 head and classifier layers.

- Pace/precision: The speed aspect is perhaps the most significant test that many people search for in the industry. It is necessary to transport these significant item identifiers to a modest inserted gadget which can change both the pace and accuracy pieces.

- Open research, therefore, proceeds to grow an organization that is increasingly as quick as YOLOv3 and that has comparable precision to the different best locators in class, like Veil RCNN.

- Social Unevenness: Class comfortability allows the enterprise arbitrarily to learn more simple details and affects accuracy. A portion of the over-sample and under-sample blends are performed in datasets to provide an equal proportion of positive (object) and negative (background) tests for this issue.

- Free anchor identification: the majority of single-shot founders rely on their set anchor sizes. This renders it incredibly challenging to summarize a certain form of learning. We will have to finalize pre-prepared engineering with multiple databases for a particular report.
- The Anchor Free Methodologies are being extensively studied to resolve this problem. CornerNet, ExtremeNet, Fully Convolutional One Stage, CenterNet are both documents pursuing anchored free ideology [24].

17.3   Conclusion

In this chapter, the literature survey made so far related to the work that has been briefly discussed. It has found that in the last 50 years, research in Determination of Object has been intensively carried out worldwide in the field of Computer Vision and Servallence as well as in the engineering field through Video frame. The technological progress in the past 50 years can be summarized by the following changes.

- From template-matching approach to knowledge-based approach
- From distance-based to likelihood-based methods
- From maximum likelihood to Deep Learning
- From no commercial biometrical applications to commercial biometrical applications

It has also found from the literature that knowledge-based models are still playing a vital role in any Object Detection and Recognition research work. Still, there is a scope for RBF-FDLNN, using some CSKM algorithms and tools that have been carried out in the present work.

References

1. Balaji, S.R. and Karthikeyan, S., A survey on moving object tracking using image processing, in: *2017 11th International Conference on Intelligent Systems and Control (ISCO)*, IEEE, pp. 469–474, 2017.
2. Hardware, R.B., Kamble, S.D., Thakur, N.V., Kakde, S., A review on moving object detection and tracking methods in video. *Int. J. Pure Appl. Math.*, 118, 16, 511–526, 2018.

3. Keivani, A., Tapamo, J.-R., Ghayoor, F., Motion-based moving object detection and tracking using automatic K-means, in: *2017 IEEE AFRICAN*, pp. 32–37, IEEE, 2017.

4. Raja, R., Kumar, S., Rashid, Md., Color Object Detection Based Image Retrieval using ROI Segmentation with Multi-Feature Method. *Wirel. Pers. Commun. Springer J.*, 1–24, https://doi.org/10.1 007/s11277-019-07021-6.

5. Mitrokhin, A., Fermüller, C., Parameshwara, C., Aloimonos, Y., Event-based moving object detection and tracking, in: *2018 IEEE/RSJ International Conference on Intelligent Robots and Systems (IROS)*, IEEE, pp. 1–9, 2018.

6. Rashidan, M.A., Mustafah, Y.M., Shafie, A.A., Zainuddin, N.A., Aziz, N.N.A., Azman, A.W., Moving object detection and classification using Neuro-Fuzzy approach. *Int. J. Multimedia Ubiquitous Eng.*, 11, 4, 253–266, 2016.

7. Raja, R., Sinha, T.S., Patra, R.K., Tiwari, S., Physiological Trait Based Biometrical Authentication of Human-Face Using LGXP and ANN Techniques. *Int. J. Inf. Comput. Secur.*, 10, 2/3, 303–320, 2018.

8. Shin, B.-S., Mou, X., Mou, W., Wang, H., Vision-based navigation of an unmanned surface vehicle with object detection and tracking abilities. *Mach. Vis. Appl.*, 29, 1, 95–112, 2018.

9. Ye, Y., Fu, L., Li, B., Object detection and tracking using multi-layer laser for autonomous urban driving, in: *2016 IEEE 19th International Conference on Intelligent Transportation Systems (ITSC)*, IEEE, pp. 259–264, 2016.

10. Yoon, Y., Kim, C., Lee, J., Yi, K., Interaction-Aware Probabilistic Trajectory Prediction of Cut-In Vehicles Using Gaussian Process for Proactive Control of Autonomous Vehicles. *IEEE Access*, 9, 63440–63455, 2021, doi: 10.1109/ ACCESS.2021.3075677.

11. Fernández-Sanjurjo, M., Bosquet, B., Mucientes, M., Brea, V.M., Real-time visual detection and tracking system for traffic monitoring. *Eng. Appl. Artif. Intell.*, 85, 410–420, 2019.

12. López-Sastre, R.J., Herranz-Perdiguero, C., Guerrero-Gómez-Olmedo, R., Oñoro-Rubio, D., Maldonado-Bascón, S., Boosting multi-vehicle tracking with a joint object detection and viewpoint estimation sensor. *Sensors*, 19, 19, 4062, 2019.

13. Raja, R., Sinha, T.S., Dubey, R.P., Recognition of human-face from side-view using progressive switching pattern and soft-computing technique. *Assoc. Adv. Modell. Simul. Tech. Enterp. Adv. B*, 58, 1, 14–34, 2015.

14. Appathurai, A., Sundarasekar, R., Raja, C., Alex, E.J., Palagan, C.A., Nithya, A., An Efficient Optimal Neural Network-Based Moving Vehicle Detection in Traffic Video Surveillance System. *Circuits Syst. Signal Process.*, 39, 2, 734–756, 2020.

15. Raja, R., Patra, R.K., Sinha, T.S., Extraction of Features from Dummy face for improving Biometrical Authentication of Human. *Int. J. Lumin. Appl.*, 7, 3–4, Article 259, 507–512, 2017.

16. Hu, L., Li, Z., Xu, H., Fang, B., An Improved Vehicle Detection and Tracking Model, in: *International Symposium for Intelligent Transportation and Smart City*, Springer, Singapore, pp. 84–93, 2019.

17. Dimililer, K., Ever, Y.K., Mustafa, S.M., Vehicle Detection and Tracking Using Machine Learning Techniques, in: *10th International Conference on Theory and Application of Soft Computing, Computing with Words and Perceptions - ICSCCW-2019*, pp. 373–381, Springer International Publishing, Cham, 2020.

18. Raja, R., Sinha, T.S., Dubey, R.P., Orientation Calculation of human Face Using Symbolic techniques and ANFIS. Published *Int. J. Eng. Future Technol.*, 7, 7, 37–50, 2016.

19. Smitha, J.A. and Rajkumar, N., Optimal feed-forward neural network-based automatic moving vehicle detection system in traffic surveillance system. *Multimed. Tools Appl.*, 1–20, 2020.

20. Mao, Q.-C., Sun, H.-M., Zuo, L.-Q., Jia, R.-S., Finding every car: A traffic surveillance multi-scale vehicle object detection method. *Appl. Intell.*, 2020.

21. Mhalla, A., Chateau, T., Gazzah, S., Amara, N.E.B., An embedded computer-vision system for multi-object detection in traffic surveillance. *IEEE Trans. Intell. Transp. Syst.*, 20, 11, 4006–4018, 2018.

22. Hadi, R.A., George, L.E., Mohammed, M.J., A computationally economic novel approach for real-time moving multi-vehicle detection and tracking toward efficient traffic surveillance. *Arab. J. Sci. Eng.*, 42, 2, 817–831, 2017.

23. Wang, Y., Ban, X., Wang, H., Wu, D., Wang, H., Yang, S., Liu, S., Lai, J., Detection and classification of moving vehicle from video using multiple Spatio-temporal features. *IEEE Access*, 7, 80287–80299, 2019.

24. Tiwari, L., Raja, R., Awasthi, V., Miri, R., Sinha, M., Alkinani, Polat, K., Detection of lung nodule and cancer using novel Mask-3 FCM and TWEDLNN algorithms. *Measurement*, 172, 2021, 108882, https://doi.org/10.1016/j.measurement.2020.108882.

Index

Printed and bound by CPI Group (UK) Ltd, Croydon, CR0 4YY

27/10/2024

14580177-0004